Honda Foreman & Rubicon ATVs Owners Workshop Manual

by Alan Ahlstrand
and John H Haynes
Member of the Guild of Motoring Writers

Models covered:

TRX400FW (Foreman 400), 1995 through 2003
TRX450S/FM, TRX450ES/FE (Foreman 450), 1998 through 2004
TRX500FA/FGA (Foreman Rubicon 500), 2001 through 2007

(2465 - 2P1)

ABCDE
FGHIJ
KLMN

Haynes Publishing
Sparkford Nr Yoovil
Somerset BA22 7JJ England

Haynes North America, Inc
861 Lawrence Drive
Newbury Park
California 91320 USA

Acknowledgments

Our thanks to Craig Adams, Owner of Calcoast Motorsports of Ventura, California, for providing the TRX450 machine used in the production of this manual. Thanks also to Dave Giordano, of G. P. Sports, Campbell, California for providing the TRX450 used for the cover photograph. Wiring diagrams produced exclusively for Haynes North America, Inc. by Valley Forge Technical Information Services.

©-Haynes North America, Inc. 2002, 2006
With permission from J.H. Haynes & Co. Ltd.

A book in the Haynes Owners Workshop Manual Series

Printed in the U.S.A.

All rights reserved. No part of this book may be reproduced or transmitted in any form or by any means, electronic or mechanical, including photocopying, recording or by any information storage or retrieval system, without permission in writing from the copyright holder.

ISBN-13: 978-1-56392-656-3
ISBN-10: 1-56392-656-3

Library of Congress Control Number: 2006938238

We take great pride in the accuracy of information given in this manual, but vehicle manufacturers make alterations and design changes during the production run of a particular vehicle of which they do not inform us. No liability can be accepted by the authors or publishers for loss, damage or injury caused by any errors in, or omissions from, the information given.

06-208

Contents

Honda Foreman 450 (2002 450ES model)

About this manual

Its purpose

The purpose of this manual is to help you get the best value from your vehicle. It can do so in several ways. It can help you decide what work must be done, even if you choose to have it done by a dealer service department or a repair shop; it provides information and procedures for routine maintenance and servicing; and it offers diagnostic and repair procedures to follow when trouble occurs.

We hope you use the manual to tackle the work yourself. For many simpler jobs, doing it yourself may be quicker than arranging an appointment to get the vehicle into a shop and making the trips to leave it and pick it up. More importantly, a lot of money can be saved by avoiding the expense the shop must pass on to you to cover its labor and overhead costs. An added benefit is the sense of satisfaction and accomplishment that you feel after doing the job yourself.

Using the manual

The manual is divided into Chapters. Each Chapter is divided into numbered Sections, which are headed in bold type between horizontal lines. Each Section consists of consecutively numbered paragraphs.

At the beginning of each numbered Section you will be referred to any illustrations which apply to the procedures in that Section. The reference numbers used in illustration captions pinpoint the pertinent Section and the Step within that Section. That is, illustration 3.2 means the illustration refers to Section 3 and Step (or paragraph) 2 within that Section.

Procedures, once described in the text, are not normally repeated. When it's necessary to refer to another Chapter, the reference will be given as Chapter and Section number. Cross references given without use of the word "Chapter" apply to Sections and/or paragraphs in the same Chapter. For example, "see Section 8" means in the same Chapter.

References to the left or right side of the vehicle assume you are sitting on the seat, facing forward.

All-terrain vehicle manufacturers continually make changes to specifications and recommendations, and these, when notified, are incorporated into our manuals at the earliest opportunity.

Even though we have prepared this manual with extreme care, neither the publisher nor the author can accept responsibility for any errors in, or omissions from, the information given.

NOTE

A **Note** provides information necessary to properly complete a procedure or information which will make the procedure easier to understand.

CAUTION

A **Caution** provides a special procedure or special steps which must be taken while completing the procedure where the Caution is found. Not heeding a Caution can result in damage to the assembly being worked on.

WARNING

A **Warning** provides a special procedure or special steps which must be taken while completing the procedure where the Warning is found. Not heeding a Warning can result in personal injury.

Introduction to the Honda Foreman and Rubicon

The TRX400, 450 and 500 (Foreman 400 and 450; Foreman Rubicon 500) series are highly successful and popular utility all-terrain vehicles.

The engine on all models is a single with overhead valves. Foreman models are air cooled; Rubicon models are liquid cooled.

Power transmission from the engine to the driveshaft is accomplished by a centrifugal primary clutch and multi-plate secondary clutch on Foreman models. On Rubicon models, power transmission is by a swash-plate automatic transmission unit mounted in the crankcase and a gear-type sub-transmission, which allows the rider to select high, low and reverse ranges. On Foreman ES models, gear shifting is accomplished by an electric control, rather than the foot pedal used on other Foreman models. A similar electronic control is used on Rubicon models, together with a manual lever for selecting the range.

Shaft final drive is used at the front and rear of all models covered

in this manual. On 2002 and later 450 models, 2WD and 4WD modes can be selected.

Fuel is delivered to the cylinder by a single constant velocity carburetor.

The front suspension uses upper and lower control arms on each side of the vehicle, with a coil spring-shock absorber unit attached to each upper control arm.

The rear suspension on all models uses two shock absorbers with coil springs.

The front brakes on all 2004 and earlier models use a sealed drum brake at each wheel. All models use a single rear drum brake, mounted on the axle shaft inboard of the wheels. All three brake units are sealed to keep out water and dirt. 2005 and later models use a single-piston disc brake at each front wheel.

Identification numbers

The frame serial number is stamped into the front of the frame and printed on a label affixed to the frame. The engine number is stamped into the right side of the crankcase. Both of these numbers should be recorded and kept in a safe place so they can be furnished to law enforcement officials in the event of a theft.

The frame serial number, engine serial number and carburetor identification number should also be kept in a handy place (such as with your driver's license) so they are always available when purchasing or ordering parts for your machine.

The models covered by this manual are as follows:
TRX400 (Foreman 400), 1995 through 2003
TRX450 (Foreman 450), 1998 through 2004
TRX500 (Foreman Rubicon), 2001 through 2007

Identifying model years

The procedures in this manual identify the vehicles by model year. The model year is included in a decal on the frame, but in case the decal is missing or obscured, the following table identifies the initial frame number of each model year.

400 models

Year	Initial frame number
1995	
A models	478TE200*SA000001
AN models	478TE203*SA000001
1996	
A models	478TE200*TA100001
AN models	478TE203*TA100001
1997	
A models	478TE200*VA000001
AN models	478TE203*VA000001
1998	
A, AN models	478TE200*WA300001
AC models	478TE203*WA000001
1999	478TE200*XA400001
2000	478TE200*Y4100001
2001	478TE200*14200001
2002	Not available
2003	Not available

450 models

Year	Initial frame number
1998	
450ES models	478TE224*WA000001
450S models	478TE220*WA000001
1999	
450ES models	478TE224*X4000001
450S models	478TE220*X4000001
2000	
450ES models	478TE224*Y4100001
450S models	478TE220*Y4100001
2001	
450ES models	478TE224*14200001
450S models	478TE220*14200001
2002	
450ES models	478TE224*24300001
450S models	478TE220*24300001
2003	
450ES models	478TE224*34400001
450S models	478TE220*34400001
2004	
450ES models	478TE224*44500001
450S models	478TE220*44500001

500 models

Year	Initial frame number
2001	478TE260*14000001
2002	478TE260*24100001
2003	478TE260*34200001
2004	
FA models	478TE260*44300001
GA models	478TE264*44300001
2005	
FA models	478TE260*54400001
GA models	478TE264*54400001
2006	
FA models	478TE260*64500001
GA models	478TE264*64500001
2007	Not available

The frame serial number is located at the front of the frame

The engine serial number is located on the right side of the crankcase behind the cylinder

Buying parts

Once you have found all the identification numbers, record them for reference when buying parts. Since the manufacturers change specifications, parts and vendors (companies that manufacture various components on the machine), providing the ID numbers is the only way to be reasonably sure that you are buying the correct parts.

Whenever possible, take the worn part to the dealer so direct comparison with the new component can be made. Along the trail from the manufacturer to the parts shelf, there are numerous places that the part can end up with the wrong number or be listed incorrectly.

The two places to purchase new parts for your vehicle - the accessory store and the franchised dealer - differ in the type of parts they carry. While dealers can obtain virtually every part for your vehicle, the accessory dealer is usually limited to normal high wear items such as shock absorbers, tune-up parts, various engine gaskets, cables, chains, brake parts, etc. Rarely will an accessory outlet have major suspension components, cylinders, transmission gears, or cases.

Used parts can be obtained for roughly half the price of new ones, but you can't always be sure of what you're getting. Once again, take your worn part to the wrecking yard (breaker) for direct comparison.

Whether buying new, used or rebuilt parts, the best course is to deal directly with someone who specializes in parts for your particular make.

General specifications

400 models

Wheelbase	1240 mm (48.8 inches)
Overall length	1944 mm (76.5 inches)
Overall width	1156 mm (45.5 inches)
Overall height	
1995 and 1996 models	1080 mm (42.5 inches)
1997 and later models	1094 mm (43.1 inches)
Seat height	785 mm (30.9 inches)
Ground clearance	186 mm (7.3 inches)
Dry weight	
1995 and 1996 models	249.5 kg (551 lbs)
1997 and later models	251 kg (553 lbs)

450 models

Wheelbase	
1998 through 2001 models	1271 mm (50.0 inches)
2002 and later models	1274 mm (50.2 inches)
Overall length	
1998 through 2001 models	1961 mm (76.5 inches)
2002 and later models	1963 mm (77.3 inches)
Overall height	1144 mm (45.0 inches)
Seat height	
1998 through 2001 models	860 mm (33.9 inches)
2002 and later models	854 mm (33.6 inches)
Ground clearance	
1998 through 2001 models	192 mm (7.0 inches)
2002 and later models	196 mm (7.7 inches)
Dry weight	
1998 through 2001 models	
Foot shift	260 kg (573 lbs)
Electric shift	266 kg (586 lbs)
2002 and later models	
Foot shift	274 kg (604 lbs)
Electric shift	280 kg (617 lbs)

General specifications (continued)

500 models

Wheelbase	
2001 through 2004 models	1287 mm (50.7 inches)
2005 and later models	1286 mm (50.6 inches)
Overall length	
2001 through 2004 models	2072 mm (81.6 inches)
2005 and later models	2108 mm (83.0 inches)
Overall height	
2001 through 2003 models	1194 mm (47.0 inches)
2004 models	1198 mm (47.2 inches)
2005 and later models	1179 mm (46.4 inches)
Seat height	
2001 through 2004 models	862 mm (33.93 inches)
2005 and later models	861 mm (33.89 inches)
Ground clearance	
2001 through 2004 models	198 mm (7.8 inches)
2005 and later models	190 mm (7.5 inches)
Dry weight	
2001 through 2003 models	273 kg (602 lbs)
2004 models	271 kg (597 lbs)
2005 and later models	273 kg (602 lbs)

Maintenance techniques, tools and working facilities

Basic maintenance techniques

There are a number of techniques involved in maintenance and repair that will be referred to throughout this manual. Application of these techniques will enable the amateur mechanic to be more efficient, better organized and capable of performing the various tasks properly, which will ensure that the repair job is thorough and complete.

Fastening systems

Fasteners, basically, are nuts, bolts and screws used to hold two or more parts together. There are a few things to keep in mind when working with fasteners. Almost all of them use a locking device of some type (either a lock washer, locknut, locking tab or thread adhesive). All threaded fasteners should be clean, straight, have undamaged threads and undamaged corners on the hex head where the wrench fits. Develop the habit of replacing all damaged nuts and bolts with new ones.

Rusted nuts and bolts should be treated with a penetrating oil to ease removal and prevent breakage. Some mechanics use turpentine in a spout type oil can, which works quite well. After applying the rust penetrant, let it "work" for a few minutes before trying to loosen the nut or bolt. Badly rusted fasteners may have to be chiseled off or removed with a special nut breaker, available at tool stores.

If a bolt or stud breaks off in an assembly, it can be drilled out and removed with a special tool called an E-Z out (or screw extractor). Most dealer service departments and vehicle repair shops can perform this task, as well as others (such as the repair of threaded holes that have been stripped out).

Flat washers and lock washers, when removed from an assembly, should always be replaced exactly as removed. Replace any damaged washers with new ones. Always use a flat washer between a lock washer and any soft metal surface (such as aluminum), thin sheet metal or plastic. Special locknuts can only be used once or twice before they lose their locking ability and must be replaced.

Tightening sequences and procedures

When threaded fasteners are tightened, they are often tightened to a specific torque value (torque is basically a twisting force). Over-tightening the fastener can weaken it and cause it to break, while under-tightening can cause it to eventually come loose. Each bolt, depending on the material it's made of, the diameter of its shank and the material it is threaded into, has a specific torque value, which is noted in the Specifications. Be sure to follow the torque recommendations closely.

Fasteners laid out in a pattern (i.e. cylinder head bolts, engine case bolts, etc.) must be loosened or tightened in a sequence to avoid warping the component. Initially, the bolts/nuts should go on finger tight only. Next, they should be tightened one full turn each, in a criss-cross or diagonal pattern. After each one has been tightened one full turn, return to the first one tightened and tighten them all one half turn, following the same pattern. Finally, tighten each of them one quarter turn at a time until each fastener has been tightened to the proper torque. To loosen and remove the fasteners the procedure would be reversed.

Disassembly sequence

Component disassembly should be done with care and purpose to help ensure that the parts go back together properly during reassembly. Always keep track of the sequence in which parts are removed. Take note of special characteristics or marks on parts that can be installed more than one way (such as a grooved thrust washer on a shaft). It's a good idea to lay the disassembled parts out on a clean surface in the order that they were removed. It may also be helpful to make sketches or take instant photos of components before removal.

When removing fasteners from a component, keep track of their locations. Sometimes threading a bolt back in a part, or putting the washers and nut back on a stud, can prevent mixups later. If nuts and bolts can't be returned to their original locations, they should be kept in a compartmented box or a series of small boxes. A cupcake or muffin tin is ideal for this purpose, since each cavity can hold the bolts and nuts from a particular area (i.e. engine case bolts, valve cover bolts,

Spark plug gap adjusting tool

Feeler gauge set

Control cable pressure luber

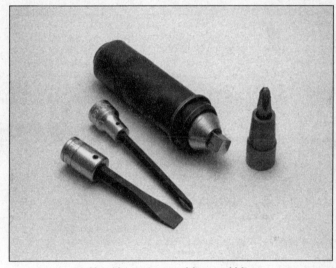

Hand impact screwdriver and bits

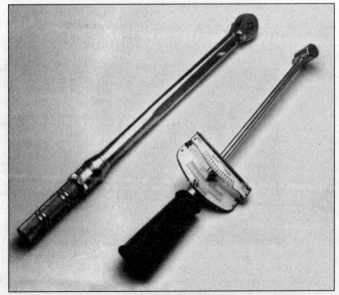

Torque wrenches (left - click type; right, beam type)

engine mount bolts, etc.). A pan of this type is especially helpful when working on assemblies with very small parts (such as the carburetors and the valve train). The cavities can be marked with paint or tape to identify the contents.

Whenever wiring looms, harnesses or connectors are separated, it's a good idea to identify the two halves with numbered pieces of masking tape so they can be easily reconnected.

Gasket sealing surfaces

Throughout any vehicle, gaskets are used to seal the mating surfaces between components and keep lubricants, fluids, vacuum or pressure contained in an assembly.

Many times these gaskets are coated with a liquid or paste type gasket sealing compound before assembly. Age, heat and pressure can sometimes cause the two parts to stick together so tightly that they are very difficult to separate. In most cases, the part can be loosened by striking it with a soft-faced hammer near the mating surfaces. A regular hammer can be used if a block of wood is placed between the hammer and the part. Do not hammer on cast parts or parts that could be easily damaged. With any particularly stubborn part, always recheck to make sure that every fastener has been removed.

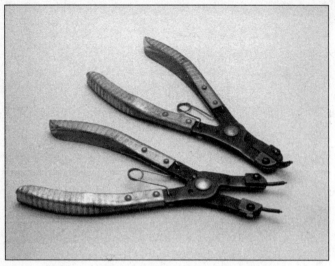

Snap-ring pliers (top - external; bottom - internal)

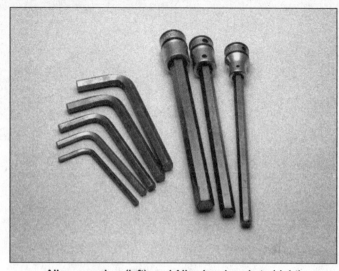

Allen wrenches (left), and Allen head sockets (right)

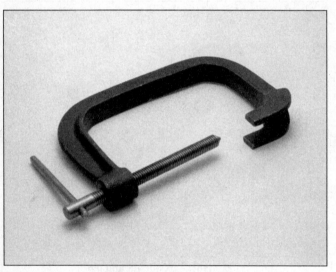

Valve spring compressor

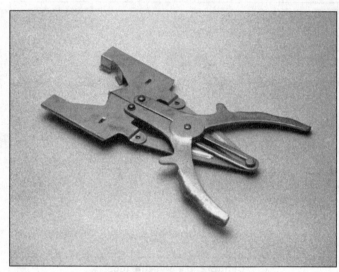

Piston ring removal/installation tool

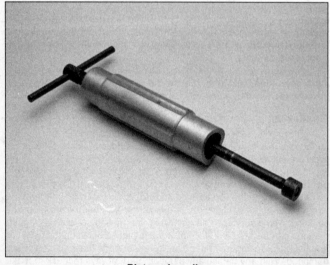

Piston pin puller

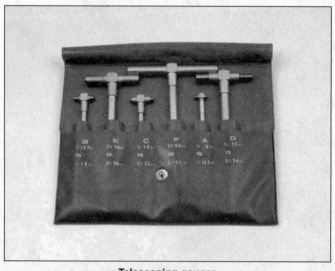

Telescoping gauges

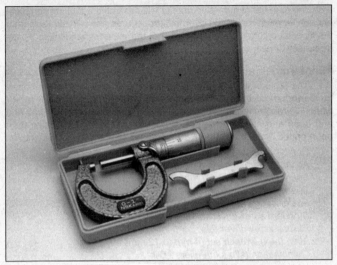

0-to-1 inch micrometer

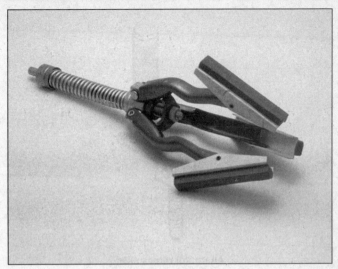

Cylinder surfacing hone

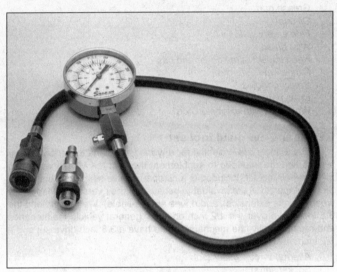

Cylinder compression gauge

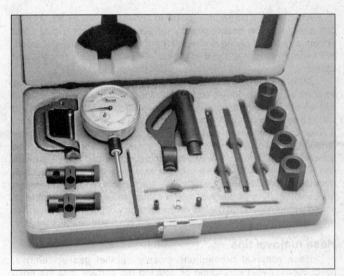

Dial indicator set

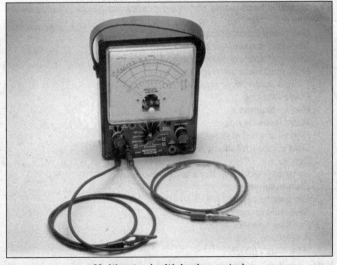

Multimeter (volt/ohm/ammeter)

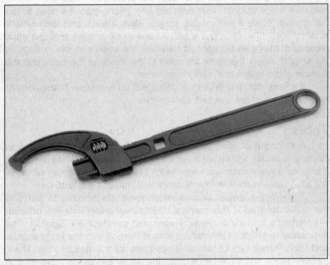

Adjustable spanner

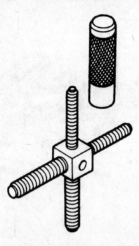

Alternator rotor puller

Avoid using a screwdriver or bar to pry apart components, as they can easily mar the gasket sealing surfaces of the parts (which must remain smooth). If prying is absolutely necessary, use a piece of wood, but keep in mind that extra clean-up will be necessary if the wood splinters.

After the parts are separated, the old gasket must be carefully scraped off and the gasket surfaces cleaned. Stubborn gasket material can be soaked with a gasket remover (available in aerosol cans) to soften it so it can be easily scraped off. A scraper can be fashioned from a piece of copper tubing by flattening and sharpening one end. Copper is recommended because it is usually softer than the surfaces to be scraped, which reduces the chance of gouging the part. Some gaskets can be removed with a wire brush, but regardless of the method used, the mating surfaces must be left clean and smooth. If for some reason the gasket surface is gouged, then a gasket sealer thick enough to fill scratches will have to be used during reassembly of the components. For most applications, a non-drying (or semi-drying) gasket sealer is best.

Hose removal tips

Hose removal precautions closely parallel gasket removal precautions. Avoid scratching or gouging the surface that the hose mates against or the connection may leak. Because of various chemical reactions, the rubber in hoses can bond itself to the metal spigot that the hose fits over. To remove a hose, first loosen the hose clamps that secure it to the spigot. Then, with slip joint pliers, grab the hose at the clamp and rotate it around the spigot. Work it back and forth until it is completely free, then pull it off (silicone or other lubricants will ease removal if they can be applied between the hose and the outside of the spigot). Apply the same lubricant to the inside of the hose and the outside of the spigot to simplify installation.

If a hose clamp is broken or damaged, do not reuse it. Also, do not reuse hoses that are cracked, split or torn.

Tools

A selection of good tools is a basic requirement for anyone who plans to maintain and repair a vehicle. For the owner who has few tools, if any, the initial investment might seem high, but when compared to the spiraling costs of routine maintenance and repair, it is a wise one.

To help the owner decide which tools are needed to perform the tasks detailed in this manual, the following tool lists are offered: Maintenance and minor repair, Repair and overhaul and Special. The newcomer to practical mechanics should start off with the Maintenance and minor repair tool kit, which is adequate for the simpler jobs. Then, as confidence and experience grow, the owner can tackle more difficult tasks, buying additional tools as they are needed. Eventually the basic kit will be built into the Repair and overhaul tool set. Over a period of

time, the experienced do-it-yourselfer will assemble a tool set complete enough for most repair and overhaul procedures and will add tools from the Special category when it is felt that the expense is justified by the frequency of use.

Maintenance and minor repair tool kit

The tools in this list should be considered the minimum required for performance of routine maintenance, servicing and minor repair work. We recommend the purchase of combination wrenches (box end and open end combined in one wrench); while more expensive than open-ended ones, they offer the advantages of both types of wrench.

Combination wrench set (6 mm to 22 mm)
Adjustable wrench - 8 in
Spark plug socket (with rubber insert)
Spark plug gap adjusting tool
Feeler gauge set
Standard screwdriver (5/16 in x 6 in)
Phillips screwdriver (No. 2 x 6 in)
Allen (hex) wrench set (4 mm to 12 mm)
Combination (slip-joint) pliers - 6 in
Hacksaw and assortment of blades
Tire pressure gauge
Control cable pressure luber
Grease gun
Oil can
Fine emery cloth
Wire brush
Hand impact screwdriver and bits
Funnel (medium size)
Safety goggles
Drain pan
Work light with extension cord

Repair and overhaul tool set

These tools are essential for anyone who plans to perform major repairs and are intended to supplement those in the Maintenance and minor repair tool kit. Included is a comprehensive set of sockets which, though expensive, are invaluable because of their versatility (especially when various extensions and drives are available). We recommend the 3/8 inch drive over the 1/2 inch drive for general vehicle maintenance and repair (ideally, the mechanic would have a 3/8 inch drive set and a 1/2 inch drive set).

Alternator rotor puller tool
Socket set(s)
Reversible ratchet
Extension - 6 in
Universal joint
Torque wrench (same size drive as sockets)
Ball peen hammer - 8 oz
Soft-faced hammer (plastic/rubber)
Standard screwdriver (1/4 in x 6 in)
Standard screwdriver (stubby - 5/16 in)
Phillips screwdriver (No. 3 x 8 in)
Phillips screwdriver (stubby - No. 2)
Pliers - locking
Pliers - lineman's
Pliers - needle nose
Pliers - snap-ring (internal and external)
Cold chisel - 1/2 in
Scriber
Scraper (made from flattened copper tubing)
Center punch
Pin punches (1/16, 1/8, 3/16 in)
Steel rule/straightedge - 12 in
Pin-type spanner wrench
A selection of files
Wire brush (large)

Note: *Another tool which is often useful is an electric drill with a chuck capacity of 3/8 inch (and a set of good quality drill bits).*

Special tools

The tools in this list include those which are not used regularly, are expensive to buy, or which need to be used in accordance with their manufacturer's instructions. Unless these tools will be used frequently, it is not very economical to purchase many of them. A consideration would be to split the cost and use between yourself and a friend or friends (i.e. members of an ATV club).

This list primarily contains tools and instruments widely available to the public, as well as some special tools produced by the vehicle manufacturer for distribution to dealer service departments. As a result, references to the manufacturer's special tools are occasionally included in the text of this manual. Generally, an alternative method of doing the job without the special tool is offered. However, sometimes there is no alternative to their use. Where this is the case, and the tool can't be purchased or borrowed, the work should be turned over to the dealer service department or a vehicle repair shop.

> *Valve spring compressor*
> *Piston ring removal and installation tool*
> *Piston pin puller*
> *Telescoping gauges*
> *Micrometer(s) and/or dial/Vernier calipers*
> *Cylinder surfacing hone*
> *Cylinder compression gauge*
> *Dial indicator set*
> *Multimeter*
> *Adjustable spanner*
> *Manometer or vacuum gauge set*
> *Small air compressor with blow gun and tire chuck*

Buying tools

For the do-it-yourselfer who is just starting to get involved in vehicle maintenance and repair, there are a number of options available when purchasing tools. If maintenance and minor repair is the extent of the work to be done, the purchase of individual tools is satisfactory. If, on the other hand, extensive work is planned, it would be a good idea to purchase a modest tool set from one of the large retail chain stores. A set can usually be bought at a substantial savings over the individual tool prices (and they often come with a tool box). As additional tools are needed, add-on sets, individual tools and a larger tool box can be purchased to expand the tool selection. Building a tool set gradually allows the cost of the tools to be spread over a longer period of time and gives the mechanic the freedom to choose only those tools that will actually be used.

Tool stores and vehicle dealers will often be the only source of some of the special tools that are needed, but regardless of where tools are bought, try to avoid cheap ones (especially when buying screwdrivers and sockets) because they won't last very long. There are plenty of tools around at reasonable prices, but always aim to purchase items which meet the relevant national safety standards. The expense involved in replacing cheap tools will eventually be greater than the initial cost of quality tools.

It is obviously not possible to cover the subject of tools fully here. For those who wish to learn more about tools and their use, there is a book entitled *Motorcycle Workshop Practice Manual* (Book no. 1454) available from the publishers of this manual. It also provides an introduction to basic workshop practice which will be of interest to a home mechanic working on any type of vehicle.

Care and maintenance of tools

Good tools are expensive, so it makes sense to treat them with respect. Keep them clean and in usable condition and store them properly when not in use. Always wipe off any dirt, grease or metal chips before putting them away. Never leave tools lying around in the work area.

Some tools, such as screwdrivers, pliers, wrenches and sockets, can be hung on a panel mounted on the garage or workshop wall, while others should be kept in a tool box or tray. Measuring instruments, gauges, meters, etc. must be carefully stored where they can't be damaged by weather or impact from other tools.

When tools are used with care and stored properly, they will last a very long time. Even with the best of care, tools will wear out if used frequently. When a tool is damaged or worn out, replace it; subsequent jobs will be safer and more enjoyable if you do.

Working facilities

Not to be overlooked when discussing tools is the workshop. If anything more than routine maintenance is to be carried out, some sort of suitable work area is essential.

It is understood, and appreciated, that many home mechanics do not have a good workshop or garage available and end up removing an engine or doing major repairs outside (it is recommended, however, that the overhaul or repair be completed under the cover of a roof).

A clean, flat workbench or table of comfortable working height is an absolute necessity. The workbench should be equipped with a vise that has a jaw opening of at least four inches.

As mentioned previously, some clean, dry storage space is also required for tools, as well as the lubricants, fluids, cleaning solvents, etc. which soon become necessary.

Sometimes waste oil and fluids, drained from the engine or cooling system during normal maintenance or repairs, present a disposal problem. To avoid pouring them on the ground or into a sewage system, simply pour the used fluids into large containers, seal them with caps and take them to an authorized disposal site or service station. Plastic jugs are ideal for this purpose.

Always keep a supply of old newspapers and clean rags available. Old towels are excellent for mopping up spills. Many mechanics use rolls of paper towels for most work because they are readily available and disposable. To help keep the area under the vehicle clean, a large cardboard box can be cut open and flattened to protect the garage or shop floor.

Whenever working over a painted surface (such as the fuel tank) cover it with an old blanket or bedspread to protect the finish.

Safety first

Professional mechanics are trained in safe working procedures. However enthusiastic you may be about getting on with the job at hand, take the time to ensure that your safety is not put at risk. A moment's lack of attention can result in an accident, as can failure to observe simple precautions.

There will always be new ways of having accidents, and the following is not a comprehensive list of all dangers; it is intended rather to make you aware of the risks and to encourage a safe approach to all work you carry out on your bike.

Essential DOs and DON'Ts

DON'T start the engine without first ascertaining that the transmission is in neutral.

DON'T attempt to drain oil until you are sure it has cooled sufficiently to avoid scalding you.

DON'T grasp any part of the engine or exhaust system without first ascertaining that it is cool enough not to burn you.

DON'T allow brake fluid to contact the machine's paint work or plastic components.

DON'T siphon toxic liquids such as fuel, hydraulic fluid or antifreeze by mouth, or allow them to remain on your skin.

DON'T inhale dust - it may be injurious to health (see *Asbestos* heading).

DON'T allow any spilled oil or grease to remain on the floor - wipe it up right away, before someone slips on it.

DON'T use ill fitting wrenches or other tools which may slip and cause injury.

DON'T attempt to lift a heavy component which may be beyond your capability - get assistance.

DON'T rush to finish a job or take unverified short cuts.

DON'T allow children or animals in or around an unattended vehicle.

DON'T inflate a tire to a pressure above the recommended maximum. Apart from over stressing the carcase and wheel rim, in extreme cases the tire may blow off forcibly. ATV tires, which are designed to operate at very low air pressures, may rupture if overinflated.

DO ensure that the machine is supported securely at all times. This is especially important when the machine is blocked up to aid wheel or suspension removal.

DO take care when attempting to loosen a stubborn nut or bolt. It is generally better to pull on a wrench, rather than push, so that if you slip, you fall away from the machine rather than onto it.

DO wear eye protection when using power tools such as drill, sander, bench grinder etc.

DO use a barrier cream on your hands prior to undertaking dirty jobs - it will protect your skin from infection as well as making the dirt easier to remove afterwards; but make sure your hands aren't left slippery. Note that long-term contact with used engine oil can be a health hazard.

DO keep loose clothing (cuffs, ties etc. and long hair) well out of the way of moving mechanical parts.

DO remove rings, wristwatch etc., before working on the vehicle- especially the electrical system.

DO keep your work area tidy - it is only too easy to fall over articles left lying around.

DO exercise caution when compressing springs for removal or installation. Ensure that the tension is applied and released in a controlled manner, using suitable tools which preclude the possibility of the spring escaping violently.

DO ensure that any lifting tackle used has a safe working load rating adequate for the job.

DO get someone to check periodically that all is well, when working alone on the vehicle.

DO carry out work in a logical sequence and check that everything is correctly assembled and tightened afterwards.

DO remember that your vehicle's safety affects that of yourself and others. If in doubt on any point, get professional advice.

IF, in spite of following these precautions, you are unfortunate enough to injure yourself, seek medical attention as soon as possible.

Asbestos

Certain friction, insulating, sealing and other products - such as brake pads, clutch linings, gaskets, etc. - may contain asbestos. *Extreme care must be taken to avoid inhalation of dust from such products since it is hazardous to health*. If in doubt, assume that they *do* contain asbestos.

Fire

Remember at all times that gasoline (petrol) is highly flammable. Never smoke or have any kind of naked flame around, when working on the vehicle. But the risk does not end there - a spark caused by an electrical short-circuit, by two metal surfaces contacting each other, by careless use of tools, or even by static electricity built up in your body under certain conditions, can ignite gasoline (petrol) vapor, which in a confined space is highly explosive. Never use gasoline (petrol) as a cleaning solvent. Use an approved safety solvent.

Always disconnect the battery ground (earth) terminal before working on any part of the fuel or electrical system, and never risk spilling fuel on to a hot engine or exhaust.

It is recommended that a fire extinguisher of a type suitable for fuel and electrical fires is kept handy in the garage or workplace at all times. Never try to extinguish a fuel or electrical fire with water.

Fumes

Certain fumes are highly toxic and can quickly cause unconsciousness and even death if inhaled to any extent. Gasoline (petrol) vapor comes into this category, as do the vapors from certain solvents such as trichloroethylene. Any draining or pouring of such volatile fluids should be done in a well ventilated area.

When using cleaning fluids and solvents, read the instructions carefully. Never use materials from unmarked containers - they may give off poisonous vapors.

Never run the engine of a motor vehicle in an enclosed space such as a garage. Exhaust fumes contain carbon monoxide which is extremely poisonous; if you need to run the engine, always do so in the open air or at least have the rear of the vehicle outside the workplace.

The battery

Never cause a spark, or allow a bare light bulb near the vehicle's battery. It will normally be giving off a certain amount of hydrogen gas, which is highly explosive.

Always disconnect the battery ground (earth) terminal before working on the fuel or electrical systems (except where noted).

Do not charge the battery at an excessive rate or the battery may burst.

Take care when cleaning or carrying the battery. The acid electrolyte, even when diluted, is very corrosive and should not be allowed to contact the eyes or skin. Always wear rubber gloves and goggles or a face shield. If you ever need to prepare electrolyte yourself, always add the acid slowly to the water; never add the water to the acid.

Electricity

When using an electric power tool, inspection light etc., always ensure that the appliance is correctly connected to its plug and that, where necessary, it is properly grounded (earthed). Do not use such appliances in damp conditions and, again, beware of creating a spark or applying excessive heat in the vicinity of fuel or fuel vapor. Also ensure that the appliances meet national safety standards.

A severe electric shock can result from touching certain parts of the electrical system, such as the spark plug wires (HT leads), when the engine is running or being cranked, particularly if components are damp or the insulation is defective. Where an electronic ignition system is used, the secondary (HT) voltage is much higher and could prove fatal.

ATV chemicals and lubricants

A number of chemicals and lubricants are available for use in vehicle maintenance and repair. They include a wide variety of products ranging from cleaning solvents and degreasers to lubricants and protective sprays for rubber, plastic and vinyl.

Contact point/spark plug cleaner is a solvent used to clean oily film and dirt from points, grime from electrical connectors and oil deposits from spark plugs. It is oil free and leaves no residue. It can also be used to remove gum and varnish from carburetor jets and other orifices.

Carburetor cleaner is similar to contact point/spark plug cleaner but it usually has a stronger solvent and may leave a slight oily residue. It is not recommended for cleaning electrical components or connections.

Brake system cleaner is used to remove grease or brake fluid from brake system components (where clean surfaces are absolutely necessary and petroleum-based solvents cannot be used); it also leaves no residue.

Silicone-based lubricants are used to protect rubber parts such as hoses and grommets, and are used as lubricants for hinges and locks.

Multi-purpose grease is an all purpose lubricant used wherever grease is more practical than a liquid lubricant such as oil. Some multi-purpose grease is colored white and specially formulated to be more resistant to water than ordinary grease.

Gear oil (sometimes called gear lube) is a specially designed oil used in transmissions and final drive units, as well as other areas where high friction, high temperature lubrication is required. It is available in a number of viscosities (weights) for various applications.

Motor oil, of course, is the lubricant specially formulated for use in the engine. It normally contains a wide variety of additives to prevent corrosion and reduce foaming and wear. Motor oil comes in various weights (viscosity ratings) of from 5 to 80. The recommended weight of the oil depends on the seasonal temperature and the demands on the engine. Light oil is used in cold climates and under light load conditions; heavy oil is used in hot climates and where high loads are encountered. Multi-viscosity oils are designed to have characteristics of both light and heavy oils and are available in a number of weights from 5W-20 to 20W-50. On these machines, the same oil supply is shared by the engine and transmission.

Gas (petrol) additives perform several functions, depending on their chemical makeup. They usually contain solvents that help dissolve gum and varnish that build up on carburetor and intake parts. They also serve to break down carbon deposits that form on the inside surfaces of the combustion chambers. Some additives contain upper cylinder lubricants for valves and piston rings.

Brake fluid is a specially formulated hydraulic fluid that can withstand the heat and pressure encountered in brake systems. Care must be taken that this fluid does not come in contact with painted surfaces or plastics. An opened container should always be resealed to prevent contamination by water or dirt.

Chain lubricants are formulated especially for use on the final drive chains of vehicles so equipped (all models covered in this manual are equipped with shaft drive). A good chain lube should adhere well and have good penetrating qualities to be effective as a lubricant inside the chain and on the side plates, pins and rollers. Most chain lubes are either the foaming type or quick drying type and are usually marketed as sprays.

Degreasers are heavy duty solvents used to remove grease and grime that may accumulate on engine and frame components. They can be sprayed or brushed on and, depending on the type, are rinsed with either water or solvent.

Solvents are used alone or in combination with degreasers to clean parts and assemblies during repair and overhaul. The home mechanic should use only solvents that are non-flammable and that do not produce irritating fumes.

Gasket sealing compounds may be used in conjunction with gaskets, to improve their sealing capabilities, or alone, to seal metal-to-metal joints. Many gasket sealers can withstand extreme heat, some are impervious to gasoline and lubricants, while others are capable of filling and sealing large cavities. Depending on the intended use, gasket sealers either dry hard or stay relatively soft and pliable. They are usually applied by hand, with a brush, or are sprayed on the gasket sealing surfaces.

Thread cement is an adhesive locking compound that prevents threaded fasteners from loosening because of vibration. It is available in a variety of types for different applications.

Moisture dispersants are usually sprays that can be used to dry out electrical components such as the fuse block and wiring connectors. Some types can also be used as treatment for rubber and as a lubricant for hinges, cables and locks.

Waxes and polishes are used to help protect painted and plated surfaces from the weather. Different types of paint may require the use of different types of wax polish. Some polishes utilize a chemical or abrasive cleaner to help remove the top layer of oxidized (dull) paint on older vehicles. In recent years, many non-wax polishes (that contain a wide variety of chemicals such as polymers and silicones) have been introduced. These non-wax polishes are usually easier to apply and last longer than conventional waxes and polishes.

Conversion factors

Length (distance)

Inches (in)	X	25.4	= Millimeters (mm)	X	0.0394 = Inches (in)
Feet (ft)	X	0.305	= Meters (m)	X	3.281 = Feet (ft)
Miles	X	1.609	= Kilometers (km)	X	0.621 = Miles

Volume (capacity)

Cubic inches (cu in; in^3)	X	16.387	= Cubic centimeters (cc; cm^3)	X	0.061 = Cubic inches (cu in; in^3)
Imperial pints (Imp pt)	X	0.568	= Liters (l)	X	1.76 = Imperial pints (Imp pt)
Imperial quarts (Imp qt)	X	1.137	= Liters (l)	X	0.88 = Imperial quarts (Imp qt)
Imperial quarts (Imp qt)	X	1.201	= US quarts (US qt)	X	0.833 = Imperial quarts (Imp qt)
US quarts (US qt)	X	0.946	= Liters (l)	X	1.057 = US quarts (US qt)
Imperial gallons (Imp gal)	X	4.546	= Liters (l)	X	0.22 = Imperial gallons (Imp gal)
Imperial gallons (Imp gal)	X	1.201	= US gallons (US gal)	X	0.833 = Imperial gallons (Imp gal)
US gallons (US gal)	X	3.785	= Liters (l)	X	0.264 = US gallons (US gal)

Mass (weight)

Ounces (oz)	X	28.35	= Grams (g)	X	0.035 = Ounces (oz)
Pounds (lb)	X	0.454	= Kilograms (kg)	X	2.205 = Pounds (lb)

Force

Ounces-force (ozf; oz)	X	0.278	= Newtons (N)	X	3.6 = Ounces-force (ozf; oz)
Pounds-force (lbf; lb)	X	4.448	= Newtons (N)	X	0.225 = Pounds-force (lbf; lb)
Newtons (N)	X	0.1	= Kilograms-force (kgf; kg)	X	9.81 = Newtons (N)

Pressure

Pounds-force per square inch (psi; lbf/in^2; lb/in^2)	X	0.070	= Kilograms-force per square centimeter (kgf/cm^2; kg/cm^2)	X	14.223 = Pounds-force per square inch (psi; lbf/in^2; lb/in^2)
Pounds-force per square inch (psi; lbf/in^2; lb/in^2)	X	0.068	= Atmospheres (atm)	X	14.696 = Pounds-force per square inch (psi; lbf/in^2; lb/in^2)
Pounds-force per square inch (psi; lbf/in^2; lb/in^2)	X	0.069	= Bars	X	14.5 = Pounds-force per square inch (psi; lbf/in^2; lb/in^2)
Pounds-force per square inch (psi; lbf/in^2; lb/in^2)	X	6.895	= Kilopascals (kPa)	X	0.145 = Pounds-force per square inch (psi; lbf/in^2; lb/in^2)
Kilopascals (kPa)	X	0.01	= Kilograms-force per square centimeter (kgf/cm^2; kg/cm^2)	X	98.1 = Kilopascals (kPa)

Torque (moment of force)

Pounds-force inches (lbf in; lb in)	X	1.152	= Kilograms-force centimeter (kgf cm; kg cm)	X	0.868 = Pounds-force inches (lbf in; lb in)
Pounds-force inches (lbf in; lb in)	X	0.113	= Newton meters (Nm)	X	8.85 = Pounds-force inches (lbf in; lb in)
Pounds-force inches (lbf in; lb in)	X	0.083	= Pounds-force feet (lbf ft; lb ft)	X	12 = Pounds-force inches (lbf in; lb in)
Pounds-force feet (lbf ft; lb ft)	X	0.138	= Kilograms-force meters (kgf m; kg m)	X	7.233 = Pounds-force feet (lbf ft; lb ft)
Pounds-force feet (lbf ft; lb ft)	X	1.356	= Newton meters (Nm)	X	0.738 = Pounds-force feet (lbf ft; lb ft)
Newton meters (Nm)	X	0.102	= Kilograms-force meters (kgf m; kg m)	X	9.804 = Newton meters (Nm)

Vacuum

Inches mercury (in. Hg)	X	3.377	= Kilopascals (kPa)	X	0.2961 = Inches mercury
Inches mercury (in. Hg)	X	25.4	= Millimeters mercury (mm Hg)	X	0.0394 = Inches mercury

Power

Horsepower (hp)	X	745.7	= Watts (W)	X	0.0013 = Horsepower (hp)

Velocity (speed)

Miles per hour (miles/hr; mph)	X	1.609	= Kilometers per hour (km/hr; kph)	X	0.621 = Miles per hour (miles/hr; mph)

Fuel consumption*

Miles per gallon, Imperial (mpg)	X	0.354	= Kilometers per liter (km/l)	X	2.825 = Miles per gallon, Imperial (mpg)
Miles per gallon, US (mpg)	X	0.425	= Kilometers per liter (km/l)	X	2.352 = Miles per gallon, US (mpg)

Temperature

Degrees Fahrenheit = (°C x 1.8) + 32   Degrees Celsius (Degrees Centigrade; °C) = (°F - 32) x 0.56

*It is common practice to convert from miles per gallon (mpg) to liters/100 kilometers (l/100km), where mpg (Imperial) x l/100 km = 282 and mpg (US) x l/100 km = 235

Troubleshooting

Contents

Engine doesn't start or is difficult to start

1 Starter motor does not rotate

1 Engine kill switch Off.
2 Fuse blown. Check fuse (Chapter 8).
3 Battery voltage low. Check and recharge battery (Chapter 8).
4 Starter motor defective. Make sure the wiring to the starter is secure. Test starter relay (Chapter 8). If the relay is good, then the fault is in the wiring or motor.
5 Starter relay faulty. Check it according to the procedure in Chapter 8.
6 Starter switch not contacting. The contacts could be wet, corroded or dirty. Disassemble and clean the switch (Chapter 8).
7 Wiring open or shorted. Check all wiring connections and harnesses to make sure that they are dry, tight and not corroded. Also check for broken or frayed wires that can cause a short to ground (see wiring diagram, Chapter 8).
8 Ignition (main) switch defective. Check the switch according to the procedure in Chapter 8. Replace the switch with a new one if it is defective.
9 Engine kill switch defective. Check for wet, dirty or corroded contacts. Clean or replace the switch as necessary (Chapter 8).

2 Starter motor rotates but engine does not turn over

1 Starter motor clutch defective. Inspect and repair or replace (Chapter 8).
2 Damaged starter reduction gears. Inspect and replace the damaged parts (Chapter 8).

3 Starter works but engine won't turn over (seized)

Seized engine caused by one or more internally damaged components. Failure due to wear, abuse or lack of lubrication. Damage can include seized valves, valve lifters, camshaft, piston, crankshaft, connecting rod bearings, or transmission gears or bearings. Refer to Chapter 2 for engine disassembly.

4 No fuel flow

1 No fuel in tank.
2 Tank cap air vent obstructed. Usually caused by dirt or water. Remove it and clean the cap vent hole.
3 Clogged strainer in fuel tap or inside fuel tank. Remove and clean the strainer(s) (Chapter 1).
4 Fuel line clogged. Pull the fuel line loose and carefully blow through it.
5 Inlet needle valve clogged. A very bad batch of fuel with an unusual additive may have been used, or some other foreign material has entered the tank. Many times after a machine has been stored for many months without running, the fuel turns to a varnish-like liquid and forms deposits on the inlet needle valve and jets. The carburetor should be removed and overhauled if draining the float chamber doesn't solve the problem.

5 Engine flooded

1 Float level too high. Check as described in Chapter 3 and replace the float if necessary.
2 Inlet needle valve worn or stuck open. A piece of dirt, rust or other debris can cause the inlet needle to seat improperly, causing excess fuel to be admitted to the float bowl. In this case, the float chamber should be cleaned and the needle and seat inspected. If the needle and seat are worn, then the leaking will persist and the parts should be replaced with new ones (Chapter 3).
3 Starting technique incorrect. Under normal circumstances (i.e., if all the carburetor functions are sound) the machine should start with little or no throttle. When the engine is cold, the choke should be operated and the engine started without opening the throttle. When the engine is at operating temperature, only a very slight amount of throttle should be necessary. If the engine is flooded, turn the fuel tap off and hold the throttle open while cranking the engine. This will allow additional air to reach the cylinder. Remember to turn the fuel tap back on after the engine starts.

6 No spark or weak spark

1 Ignition switch Off.
2 Engine kill switch turned to the Off position.
3 Battery voltage low. Check and recharge battery as necessary (Chapter 8).
4 Spark plug dirty, defective or worn out. Locate reason for fouled plug using spark plug condition chart and follow the plug maintenance procedures in Chapter 1.
5 Spark plug cap or secondary (HT) wiring faulty. Check condition. Replace either or both components if cracks or deterioration are evident (Chapter 4).
6 Spark plug cap not making good contact. Make sure that the plug cap fits snugly over the plug end.
7 Ignition control module defective. Check the unit, referring to Chapter 4 for details.
8 Ignition signal generator defective. Check the unit, referring to Chapter 4 for details.
9 Ignition coil defective. Check the coil, referring to Chapter 4.
10 Ignition or kill switch shorted. This is usually caused by water, corrosion, damage or excessive wear. The kill switch can be disassembled and cleaned with electrical contact cleaner. If cleaning does not help, replace the switches (Chapter 8).
11 Wiring shorted or broken between:
a) *Ignition switch and engine kill switch (or blown fuse)*
b) *Ignition control unit and engine kill switch*
c) *Ignition control unit and ignition coil*
d) *Ignition coil and plug*
e) *Ignition control unit and ignition signal generator*
Make sure that all wiring connections are clean, dry and tight. Look for chafed and broken wires (Chapters 4 and 8).

7 Compression low

1 Spark plug loose. Remove the plug and inspect the threads. Reinstall and tighten to the specified torque (Chapter 1).
2 Cylinder head not sufficiently tightened down. If the cylinder head is suspected of being loose, then there's a chance that the gasket or head is damaged if the problem has persisted for any length of time. The head nuts and bolts should be tightened to the proper torque in the correct sequence (Chapter 2).
3 Improper valve clearance. This means that the valve is not closing completely and compression pressure is leaking past the valve. Check and adjust the valve clearances (Chapter 1).
4 Cylinder and/or piston worn. Excessive wear will cause compression pressure to leak past the rings. This is usually accompanied by worn rings as well. A top end overhaul is necessary (Chapter 2).
5 Piston rings worn, weak, broken, or sticking. Broken or sticking piston rings usually indicate a lubrication or carburetion problem that causes excess carbon deposits or seizures to form on the pistons and rings. Top end overhaul is necessary (Chapter 2).
6 Piston ring-to-groove clearance excessive. This is caused by excessive wear of the piston ring lands. Piston replacement is necessary (Chapter 2).

7 Cylinder head gasket damaged. If the head is allowed to become loose, or if excessive carbon build-up on a piston crown and combustion chamber causes extremely high compression, the head gasket may leak. Retorquing the head is not always sufficient to restore the seal, so gasket replacement is necessary (Chapter 2).
8 Cylinder head warped. This is caused by overheating or improperly tightened head nuts and bolts. Machine shop resurfacing or head replacement is necessary (Chapter 2).
9 Valve spring broken or weak. Caused by component failure or wear; the spring(s) must be replaced (Chapter 2).
10 Valve not seating properly. This is caused by a bent valve (from over-revving or improper valve adjustment), burned valve or seat (improper carburetion) or an accumulation of carbon deposits on the seat (from carburetion or lubrication problems). The valves must be cleaned and/or replaced and the seats serviced if possible (Chapter 2).

8 Stalls after starting

1 Improper choke action. Make sure the choke cable is getting a full stroke and staying in the out position.
2 Ignition malfunction. See Chapter 4.
3 Carburetor malfunction. See Chapter 3.
4 Fuel contaminated. The fuel can be contaminated with either dirt or water, or can change chemically if the machine is allowed to sit for several months or more. Drain the tank and float bowl and refill with fresh fuel (Chapter 3).
5 Intake air leak. Check for loose carburetor-to-intake joint connections or loose carburetor top (Chapter 3).
6 Engine idle speed incorrect. Turn throttle stop screw until the engine idles at the specified rpm (Chapter 1).

9 Rough idle

1 Ignition malfunction. See Chapter 4.
2 Idle speed incorrect. See Chapter 1.
3 Carburetor malfunction. See Chapter 3.
4 Idle fuel/air mixture incorrect. See Chapter 3.
5 Fuel contaminated. The fuel can be contaminated with either dirt or water, or can change chemically if the machine is allowed to sit for several months or more. Drain the tank and float bowls (Chapter 3).
6 Intake air leak. Check for loose carburetor-to-intake joint connections, loose or missing vacuum gauge access port cap or hose, or loose carburetor top (Chapter 3).
7 Air cleaner clogged. Service or replace air cleaner element (Chapter 1).

Poor running at low speed

10 Spark weak

1 Battery voltage low. Check and recharge battery (Chapter 8).
2 Spark plug fouled, defective or worn out. Refer to Chapter 1 for spark plug maintenance.
3 Spark plug cap or secondary (HT) wiring defective. Refer to Chapters 1 and 4 for details on the ignition system.
4 Spark plug cap not making contact.
5 Incorrect spark plug. Wrong type, heat range or cap configuration. Check and install correct plug listed in Chapter 1. A cold plug or one with a recessed firing electrode will not operate at low speeds without fouling.
6 Ignition control module defective. See Chapter 4.
7 Pulse generator defective. See Chapter 4.
8 Ignition coil defective. See Chapter 4.

11 Fuel/air mixture incorrect

1 Pilot screw out of adjustment (Chapter 3).
2 Pilot jet or air passage clogged. Remove and overhaul the carburetor (Chapter 3).
3 Air bleed holes clogged. Remove carburetor and blow out all passages (Chapter 3).
4 Air cleaner clogged, poorly sealed or missing.
5 Air cleaner-to-carburetor boot poorly sealed. Look for cracks, holes or loose clamps and replace or repair defective parts.
6 Float level too high or too low. Check and replace the float if necessary (Chapter 3).
7 Fuel tank air vent obstructed. Make sure that the air vent passage in the filler cap is open.
8 Carburetor intake joint loose. Check for cracks, breaks, tears or loose clamps or bolts. Repair or replace the rubber boot and its O-ring.

12 Compression low

1 Spark plug loose. Remove the plug and inspect the threads. Reinstall and tighten to the specified torque (Chapter 1).
2 Cylinder head not sufficiently tightened down. If the cylinder head is suspected of being loose, then there's a chance that the gasket and head are damaged if the problem has persisted for any length of time. The head nuts and bolts should be tightened to the proper torque in the correct sequence (Chapter 2).
3 Improper valve clearance. This means that the valve is not closing completely and compression pressure is leaking past the valve. Check and adjust the valve clearances (Chapter 1).
4 Cylinder and/or piston worn. Excessive wear will cause compression pressure to leak past the rings. This is usually accompanied by worn rings as well. A top end overhaul is necessary (Chapter 2).
5 Piston rings worn, weak, broken, or sticking. Broken or sticking piston rings usually indicate a lubrication or carburetion problem that causes excess carbon deposits or seizures to form on the pistons and rings. Top end overhaul is necessary (Chapter 2).
6 Piston ring-to-groove clearance excessive. This is caused by excessive wear of the piston ring lands. Piston replacement is necessary (Chapter 2).
7 Cylinder head gasket damaged. If the head is allowed to become loose, or if excessive carbon build-up on the piston crown and combustion chamber causes extremely high compression, the head gasket may leak. Retorquing the head is not always sufficient to restore the seal, so gasket replacement is necessary (Chapter 2).
8 Cylinder head warped. This is caused by overheating or improperly tightened head nuts and bolts. Machine shop resurfacing or head replacement is necessary (Chapter 2).
9 Valve spring broken or weak. Caused by component failure or wear; the spring(s) must be replaced (Chapter 2).
10 Valve not seating properly. This is caused by a bent valve (from over-revving or improper valve adjustment), burned valve or seat (improper carburetion) or an accumulation of carbon deposits on the seat (from carburetion, lubrication problems). The valves must be cleaned and/or replaced and the seats serviced if possible (Chapter 2).

13 Poor acceleration

1 Carburetor leaking or dirty. Overhaul the carburetor (Chapter 3).
2 Timing not advancing. The pulse generator or the ignition control module may be defective. If so, they must be replaced with new ones, as they can't be repaired.
3 Engine oil viscosity too high. Using a heavier oil than that recommended in Chapter 1 can damage the oil pump or lubrication system and cause drag on the engine.
4 Brakes dragging. Usually caused by debris which has entered the brake piston sealing boots (front brakes), corroded wheel cylinders

(front brakes), sticking brake cam (rear brakes) or from a warped drum or bent axle. Repair as necessary (Chapter 6).

Poor running or no power at high speed

14 Firing incorrect

1   Air cleaner restricted. Clean or replace element (Chapter 1).
2   Spark plug fouled, defective or worn out. See Chapter 1 for spark plug maintenance.
3   Spark plug cap or secondary (HT) wiring defective. See Chapters 1 and 4 for details of the ignition system.
4   Spark plug cap not in good contact. See Chapter 4.
5   Incorrect spark plug. Wrong type, heat range or cap configuration. Check and install correct plugs listed in Chapter 1. A cold plug or one with a recessed firing electrode will not operate at low speeds without fouling.
6   Ignition control module defective. See Chapter 4.
7   Ignition coil defective. See Chapter 4.

15 Fuel/air mixture incorrect

1   Pilot screw out of adjustment. See Chapter 3 for adjustment procedures.
2   Main jet clogged. Dirt, water or other contaminants can clog the main jets. Clean the fuel tap strainer and in-tank strainer, the float bowl area, and the jets and carburetor orifices (Chapter 3).
3   Main jet wrong size. The standard jetting is for sea level atmospheric pressure and oxygen content. See Chapter 3 for high altitude adjustments.
4   Throttle shaft-to-carburetor body clearance excessive. Refer to Chapter 3 for inspection and part replacement procedures.
5   Air bleed holes clogged. Remove and overhaul carburetor (Chapter 3).
6   Air cleaner clogged, poorly sealed, or missing.
7   Air cleaner-to-carburetor boot poorly sealed. Look for cracks, holes or loose clamps, and replace or repair defective parts.
8   Float level too high or too low. Check float level and replace the float if necessary (Chapter 3).
9   Fuel tank air vent obstructed. Make sure the air vent passage in the filler cap is open.
10   Carburetor intake joint loose. Check for cracks, breaks, tears or loose clamps or bolts. Repair or replace the rubber boots (Chapter 3).
11   Fuel tap clogged. Remove the tap and clean it (Chapter 1).
12   Fuel line clogged. Pull the fuel line loose and carefully blow through it.

16 Compression low

1   Spark plug loose. Remove the plug and inspect the threads. Reinstall and tighten to the specified torque (Chapter 1).
2   Cylinder head not sufficiently tightened down. If the cylinder head is suspected of being loose, then there's a chance that the gasket and head are damaged if the problem has persisted for any length of time. The head nuts and bolts should be tightened to the proper torque in the correct sequence (Chapter 2).
3   Improper valve clearance. This means that the valve is not closing completely and compression pressure is leaking past the valve. Check and adjust the valve clearances (Chapter 1).
4   Cylinder and/or piston worn. Excessive wear will cause compression pressure to leak past the rings. This is usually accompanied by worn rings as well. A top end overhaul is necessary (Chapter 2).
5   Piston rings worn, weak, broken, or sticking. Broken or sticking piston rings usually indicate a lubrication or carburetion problem that causes excess carbon deposits or seizures to form on the pistons and rings. Top end overhaul is necessary (Chapter 2).

6   Piston ring-to-groove clearance excessive. This is caused by excessive wear of the piston ring lands. Piston replacement is necessary (Chapter 2).
7   Cylinder head gasket damaged. If a head is allowed to become loose, or if excessive carbon build-up on the piston crown and combustion chamber causes extremely high compression, the head gasket may leak. Retorquing the head is not always sufficient to restore the seal, so gasket replacement is necessary (Chapter 2).
8   Cylinder head warped. This is caused by overheating or improperly tightened head nuts and bolts. Machine shop resurfacing or head replacement is necessary (Chapter 2).
9   Valve spring broken or weak. Caused by component failure or wear; the spring(s) must be replaced (Chapter 2).
10   Valve not seating properly. This is caused by a bent valve (from over-revving or improper valve adjustment), burned valve or seat (improper carburetion) or an accumulation of carbon deposits on the seat (from carburetion or lubrication problems). The valves must be cleaned and/or replaced and the seats serviced if possible (Chapter 2).

17 Knocking or pinging

1   Carbon build-up in combustion chamber. Use of a fuel additive that will dissolve the adhesive bonding the carbon particles to the crown and chamber is the easiest way to remove the build-up. Otherwise, the cylinder head will have to be removed and decarbonized (Chapter 2).
2   Incorrect or poor quality fuel. Old or improper grades of fuel can cause detonation. This causes the piston to rattle, thus the knocking or pinging sound. Drain old fuel and always use the recommended fuel grade.
3   Spark plug heat range incorrect. Uncontrolled detonation indicates the plug heat range is too hot. The plug in effect becomes a glow plug, raising cylinder temperatures. Install the proper heat range plug (Chapter 1).
4   Improper air/fuel mixture. This will cause the cylinder to run hot, which leads to detonation. Clogged jets or an air leak can cause this imbalance. See Chapter 3.

18 Miscellaneous causes

1   Throttle valve doesn't open fully. Adjust the cable slack (Chapter 1).
2   Clutch slipping. May be caused by improperly adjustment or loose or worn clutch components. Refer to Chapter 1 for adjustment or Chapter 2 for cable replacement and clutch overhaul procedures.
3   Timing not advancing.
4   Engine oil viscosity too high. Using a heavier oil than the one recommended in Chapter 1 can damage the oil pump or lubrication system and cause drag on the engine.
5   Brakes dragging. Usually caused by debris which has entered the brake piston sealing boot, or from a warped disc or bent axle. Repair as necessary.

Overheating

19 Engine overheats

1   Engine oil level low. Check and add oil (Chapter 1).
2   Wrong type of oil. If you're not sure what type of oil is in the engine, drain it and fill with the correct type (Chapter 1).
3   Air leak at carburetor intake joints. Check and tighten or replace as necessary (Chapter 3).
4   Fuel level low. Check and adjust if necessary (Chapter 3).
5   Worn oil pump or clogged oil passages. Replace pump or clean passages as necessary.
6   Clogged external oil line. Remove and check for foreign material (see Chapter 2).

7   Carbon build-up in combustion chambers. Use of a fuel additive that will dissolve the adhesive bonding the carbon particles to the piston crown and chambers is the easiest way to remove the build-up. Otherwise, the cylinder head will have to be removed and decarbonized (Chapter 2).
8   Operation in high ambient temperatures.
9   Electric shift system problems (450ES models). Check the system (Chapter 8).

20   Firing incorrect

1   Spark plug fouled, defective or worn out. See Chapter 1 for spark plug maintenance.
2   Incorrect spark plug (see Chapter 1).
3   Faulty ignition coil(s) (Chapter 4).

21   Fuel/air mixture incorrect

1   Pilot screw out of adjustment (Chapter 3).
2   Main jet clogged. Dirt, water and other contaminants can clog the main jets. Clean the fuel tap strainer and in-tank strainer, the float bowl area and the jets and carburetor orifices (Chapter 3).
3   Main jet wrong size. The standard jetting is for sea level atmospheric pressure and oxygen content. See Chapter 3 for high altitude settings.
4   Air cleaner poorly sealed or missing.
5   Air cleaner-to-carburetor boot poorly sealed. Look for cracks, holes or loose clamps and replace or repair.
6   Fuel level too low. Check float level and replace the float if necessary (Chapter 3).
7   Fuel tank air vent obstructed. Make sure that the air vent passage in the filler cap is open.
8   Carburetor intake joint loose. Check for cracks, breaks, tears or loose clamps or bolts. Repair or replace the rubber boot and its O-ring (Chapter 3).

22   Compression too high

1   Carbon build-up in combustion chamber. Use of a fuel additive that will dissolve the adhesive bonding the carbon particles to the piston crown and chamber is the easiest way to remove the build-up. Otherwise, the cylinder head will have to be removed and decarbonized (Chapter 2).
2   Improperly machined head surface or installation of incorrect gasket during engine assembly.

23   Engine load excessive

1   Clutch slipping. Can be caused by damaged, loose or worn clutch components. Refer to Chapter 2 for overhaul procedures.
2   Engine oil level too high. The addition of too much oil will cause pressurization of the crankcase and inefficient engine operation. Check Specifications and drain to proper level (Chapter 1).
3   Engine oil viscosity too high. Using a heavier oil than the one recommended in Chapter 1 can damage the oil pump or lubrication system as well as cause drag on the engine.
4   Brakes dragging. Usually caused by debris which has entered the brake piston sealing boots (front brakes), corroded wheel cylinders (front brakes), sticking brake cam (rear brakes) or from a warped drum or bent axle. Repair as necessary (Chapter 6).

24   Lubrication inadequate

1   Engine oil level too low. Friction caused by intermittent lack of lubrication or from oil that is overworked can cause overheating. The oil provides a definite cooling function in the engine. Check the oil level (Chapter 1).
2   Poor quality engine oil or incorrect viscosity or type. Oil is rated not only according to viscosity but also according to type. Some oils are not rated high enough for use in this engine. Check the Specifications section and change to the correct oil (Chapter 1).
3   Camshaft or journals worn. Excessive wear causing drop in oil pressure. Replace cam or cylinder head. Abnormal wear could be caused by oil starvation at high rpm from low oil level or improper viscosity or type of oil (Chapter 1).
4   Crankshaft and/or bearings worn. Same problems as paragraph 3. Check and replace crankshaft assembly if necessary (Chapter 2).

25   Miscellaneous causes

Modification to exhaust system. Most aftermarket exhaust systems cause the engine to run leaner, which makes it run hotter. When installing an accessory exhaust system, always rejet the carburetor.

Clutch problems

26   Clutch slipping

1   Change clutch friction plates worn or warped. Overhaul the change clutch assembly (Chapter 2).
2   Change clutch steel plates worn or warped (Chapter 2).
3   Change clutch spring(s) broken or weak. Old or heat-damaged spring(s) (from slipping clutch) should be replaced with new ones (Chapter 2).
4   Change clutch release mechanism defective. Replace any defective parts (Chapter 2).
5   Change clutch center or housing unevenly worn. This causes improper engagement of the plates. Replace the damaged or worn parts (Chapter 2).
6   Centrifugal clutch weight linings or drum worn (Chapter 2).

27   Clutch not disengaging completely

1   Change clutch improperly adjusted (400 and 450) (see Chapter 1).
2   Change clutch plates warped or damaged (400 and 450). This will cause clutch drag, which in turn will cause the machine to creep. Overhaul the clutch assembly (Chapter 2).
3   Sagged or broken change clutch spring(s). Check and replace the spring(s) (Chapter 2).
4   Engine oil deteriorated. Old, thin, worn out oil will not provide proper lubrication for the discs, causing the change clutch to drag. Replace the oil and filter (Chapter 1).
5   Engine oil viscosity too high. Using a thicker oil than recommended in Chapter 1 can cause the change clutch plates to stick together, putting a drag on the engine. Change to the correct viscosity oil (Chapter 1).
6   Change clutch housing seized on shaft. Lack of lubrication, severe wear or damage can cause the housing to seize on the shaft. Overhaul of the clutch, and perhaps transmission, may be necessary to repair the damage (Chapter 2).
7   Change clutch release mechanism defective. Worn or damaged release mechanism parts can stick and fail to apply force to the pressure plate. Overhaul the release mechanism (Chapter 2).
8   Loose change clutch center nut. Causes housing and center misalignment putting a drag on the engine. Engagement adjustment

continually varies. Overhaul the clutch assembly (Chapter 2).
9   Weak or broken centrifugal clutch springs (all models) (Chapter 2).

Gear shifting problems

28 Doesn't go into gear or lever doesn't return

1   400 and 450 - change clutch not disengaging. See Section 27.
2   Shift fork(s) bent or seized. May be caused by lack of lubrication. Overhaul the transmission (400 or 450) or sub-transmission (500) (Chapter 2).
3   Gear(s) stuck on shaft. Most often caused by a lack of lubrication or excessive wear in transmission bearings and bushings. Overhaul the transmission (Chapter 2).
4   Shift drum binding. Caused by lubrication failure or excessive wear. Replace the drum and bearing (Chapter 2).
5   Shift lever return spring weak or broken (Chapter 2).
6   Shift lever broken. Splines stripped out of lever or shaft, caused by allowing the lever to get loose. Replace necessary parts (Chapter 2).
7   Shift mechanism pawl broken or worn. Full engagement and rotary movement of shift drum results. Replace shaft assembly (Chapter 2).
8   Pawl spring broken. Allows pawl to float, causing sporadic shift operation. Replace spring (Chapter 2).
9   500 models - automatic transmission ball nut stuck at the end of its travel (see Chapter 2).
10   500 models - shift control mechanism problem (see Chapter 8).

29 Jumps out of gear

1   Shift fork(s) worn. Overhaul the transmission (Chapter 2).
2   Gear groove(s) worn. Overhaul the transmission (Chapter 2).
3   Gear dogs or dog slots worn or damaged. The gears should be inspected and replaced. No attempt should be made to service the worn parts.

30 Overshifts

1   Pawl spring weak or broken (Chapter 2).
2   Shift drum stopper lever not functioning (Chapter 2).

Abnormal engine noise

31 Knocking or pinging

1   Carbon build-up in combustion chamber. Use of a fuel additive that will dissolve the adhesive bonding the carbon particles to the piston crown and chamber is the easiest way to remove the build-up. Otherwise, the cylinder head will have to be removed and decarbonized (Chapter 2).
2   Incorrect or poor quality fuel. Old or improper fuel can cause detonation. This causes the pistons to rattle, thus the knocking or pinging sound. Drain the old fuel (Chapter 3) and always use the recommended grade fuel (Chapter 1).
3   Spark plug heat range incorrect. Uncontrolled detonation indicates that the plug heat range is too hot. The plug in effect becomes a glow plug, raising cylinder temperatures. Install the proper heat range plug (Chapter 1).
4   Improper air/fuel mixture. This will cause the cylinder to run hot and lead to detonation. Clogged jets or an air leak can cause this imbalance. See Chapter 3.

32 Piston slap or rattling

1   Cylinder-to-piston clearance excessive. Caused by improper assembly. Inspect and overhaul top end parts (Chapter 2).
2   Connecting rod bent. Caused by over-revving, trying to start a badly flooded engine or from ingesting a foreign object into the combustion chamber. Replace the damaged parts (Chapter 2).
3   Piston pin or piston pin bore worn or seized from wear or lack of lubrication. Replace damaged parts (Chapter 2).
4   Piston ring(s) worn, broken or sticking. Overhaul the top end (Chapter 2).
5   Piston seizure damage. Usually from lack of lubrication or overheating. Replace the pistons and bore the cylinder, as necessary (Chapter 2).
6   Connecting rod upper or lower end clearance excessive. Caused by excessive wear or lack of lubrication. Replace worn parts.

33 Valve noise

1   Incorrect valve clearances. Adjust the clearances by referring to Chapter 1.
2   Valve spring broken or weak. Check and replace weak valve springs (Chapter 2).
3   Camshaft or cylinder head worn or damaged. Lack of lubrication at high rpm is usually the cause of damage. Insufficient oil or failure to change the oil at the recommended intervals are the chief causes.

34 Other noise

1   Cylinder head gasket leaking.
2   Exhaust pipe leaking at cylinder head connection. Caused by improper fit of pipe, damaged gasket or loose exhaust flange. All exhaust fasteners should be tightened evenly and carefully. Failure to do this will lead to a leak.
3   Crankshaft runout excessive. Caused by a bent crankshaft (from over-revving) or damage from an upper cylinder component failure.
4   Engine mounting bolts or nuts loose. Tighten all engine mounting bolts and nuts to the specified torque (Chapter 2).
5   Crankshaft bearings worn (Chapter 2).
6   Camshaft chain tensioner defective. Replace according to the procedure in Chapter 2.
7   Camshaft chain, sprockets or guides worn (Chapter 2).

Abnormal driveline noise

35 Clutch noise

1   Change clutch housing/friction plate clearance excessive (Chapter 2).
2   Loose or damaged change clutch pressure plate and/or bolts (Chapter 2).
3   Broken centrifugal clutch springs (Chapter 2).

36 Transmission noise (400/450) or sub-transmission noise (500)

1   Bearings worn. Also includes the possibility that the shafts are worn. Overhaul the transmission (Chapter 2).
2   Gears worn or chipped (Chapter 2).
3   Metal chips jammed in gear teeth. Probably pieces from a broken clutch, gear or shift mechanism that were picked up by the gears. This will cause early bearing failure (Chapter 2).

4   Engine oil level too low. Causes a howl from transmission. Also affects engine power and clutch operation (Chapter 1).

37 Differential noise

1   Differential oil level low (Chapter 1).
2   Differential gear lash out of adjustment. Checking and adjustment require special tools and skills and should be done by a Honda dealer.
3   Differential gears damaged or worn. Overhaul requires special tools and skills and should be done by a Honda dealer.

Abnormal chassis noise

38 Suspension noise

1   Spring weak or broken. Makes a clicking or scraping sound.
2   Steering shaft bearings worn or damaged. Clicks when braking. Check and replace as necessary (Chapter 5).
3   Shock absorber fluid level incorrect. Indicates a leak caused by defective seal. Shock will be covered with oil. Replace shock (Chapter 5).
4   Defective shock absorber with internal damage. This is in the body of the shock and can't be remedied. The shock must be replaced with a new one (Chapter 5).
5   Bent or damaged shock body. Replace the shock with a new one (Chapter 5).

39 Driveaxle noise

1   Worn or damaged outer joint. Makes clicking noise in turns. Check for cut or damaged seals and repair as necessary (see Chapter 5).
2   Worn or damaged inner joint. Makes knock or clunk when accelerating after coasting. Check for cut or damaged seals and repair as necessary (see Chapter 5).

40 Brake noise

1   Brake linings worn or contaminated. Can cause scraping or squealing. Replace the shoes (Chapter 6).
2   Brake linings warped or worn unevenly. Can cause chattering. Replace the linings (Chapter 6).
3   Brake drum out of round. Can cause chattering. Replace brake drum (Chapter 6).
7   Loose or worn knuckle or rear axle bearings. Check and replace as needed (Chapter 5).

Temperature indicator light comes on

41 Engine lubrication or cooling system

1   High oil temperature due to operation in high ambient temperature. Shut the engine off and let it cool. Check the oil cooler for clogged fins or tubes and clean it as necessary.
2   Low coolant level (500). Check as described in Chapter 1.
3   Cooling system problem (500). Check as described in Chapter 2D.

42 Electrical system

1   Oil or coolant temperature sensor defective. Check the sensor

according to the procedure in Chapter 2D or 8. Replace it if it's defective.
2   Oil temperature indicator light circuit defective. Check for pinched, shorted, disconnected or damaged wiring (Chapter 8).
3   Oil cooler fan not working correctly (see Chapter 8).

Excessive exhaust smoke

43 White smoke

1   Piston oil ring worn. The ring may be broken or damaged, causing oil from the crankcase to be pulled past the piston into the combustion chamber. Replace the rings with new ones (Chapter 2).
2   Cylinders worn, cracked, or scored. Caused by overheating or oil starvation. If worn or scored, the cylinders will have to be rebored and new pistons installed. If cracked, the cylinder block will have to be replaced (see Chapter 2).
3   Valve oil seal damaged or worn. Replace oil seals with new ones (Chapter 2).
4   Valve guide worn. Perform a complete valve job (Chapter 2).
5   Engine oil level too high, which causes the oil to be forced past the rings. Drain oil to the proper level (Chapter 1).
6   Head gasket broken between oil return and cylinder. Causes oil to be pulled into the combustion chamber. Replace the head gasket and check the head for warpage (Chapter 2).
7   Abnormal crankcase pressurization, which forces oil past the rings. Clogged breather or hoses usually the cause (Chapter 2).

44 Black smoke

1   Air cleaner clogged. Clean or replace the element (Chapter 1).
2   Main jet too large or loose. Compare the jet size to the Specifications (Chapter 3).
3   Choke stuck, causing fuel to be pulled through choke circuit (Chapter 3).
4   Fuel level too high. Check the float level and replace the float if necessary (Chapter 3).
5   Inlet needle held off needle seat. Clean the float chamber and fuel line and replace the needle and seat if necessary (Chapter 3).

45 Brown smoke

1   Main jet too small or clogged. Lean condition caused by wrong size main jet or by a restricted orifice. Clean float chamber and jets and compare jet size to Specifications (Chapter 3).
2   Fuel flow insufficient. Fuel inlet needle valve stuck closed due to chemical reaction with old fuel. Float level incorrect; check and replace float if necessary. Restricted fuel line. Clean line and float chamber.
3   Carburetor intake tube loose (Chapter 3).
4   Air cleaner poorly sealed or not installed (Chapter 1).

Poor handling or stability

46 Handlebar hard to turn

1   Steering shaft nut too tight (Chapter 5).
2   Lower bearing or upper bushing damaged. Roughness can be felt as the bars are turned from side-to-side. Replace bearing and bushing (Chapter 5).
3   Steering shaft bearing lubrication inadequate. Caused by grease getting hard from age or being washed out by high pressure car washes. Remove steering shaft and replace bearing (Chapter 5).
4   Steering shaft bent. Caused by a collision, hitting a pothole or by

rolling the machine. Replace damaged part. Don't try to straighten the steering shaft (Chapter 5).
5   Front tire air pressure too low (Chapter 1).

47 Handlebar shakes or vibrates excessively

1   Tires worn or out of balance (Chapter 1 or 6).
2   Swingarm bearings worn. Replace worn bearings by referring to Chapter 6.
3   Wheel rim(s) warped or damaged. Inspect wheels (Chapter 6).
4   Wheel bearings worn. Worn front or rear wheel bearings can cause poor tracking. Worn front bearings will cause wobble (Chapter 6).
5   Wheel hubs installed incorrectly (Chapter 5 or Chapter 6).
6   Handlebar clamp bolts or bracket nuts loose (Chapter 5).
7   Steering shaft nut or bolts loose. Tighten them to the specified torque (Chapter 5).
8   Motor mount bolts loose. Will cause excessive vibration with increased engine rpm (Chapter 2).

48 Handlebar pulls to one side

1   Uneven tire pressures (Chapter 1).
2   Frame bent. Definitely suspect this if the machine has been rolled. May or may not be accompanied by cracking near the bend. Replace the frame (Chapter 5).
3   Wheel out of alignment. Caused by incorrect toe-in adjustment (Chapter 1) or bent tie-rod (Chapter 5).
4   Swingarm bent or twisted. Caused by age (metal fatigue) or impact damage. Replace the swingarm (Chapter 5).
5   Steering shaft bent. Caused by impact damage or by rolling the vehicle. Replace the steering stem (Chapter 5).

49 Poor shock absorbing qualities

1   Too hard:
a) Shock internal damage.
b) Tire pressure too high (Chapters 1 and 6).
2   Too soft:
a) Shock oil insufficient and/or leaking (Chapter 5).
d) Fork springs weak or broken (Chapter 5).

Braking problems

50 Front brakes are spongy, don't hold

1   Air in brake line. Caused by inattention to master cylinder fluid level or by leakage. Locate problem and bleed brakes (Chapter 6).
2   Linings worn (Chapters 1 and 6).
3   Brake fluid leak. See paragraph 1.
4   Contaminated linings. Caused by contamination with oil, grease, brake fluid, etc. Clean or replace linings. Clean drum thoroughly with brake cleaner (Chapter 6).

5   Brake fluid deteriorated. Fluid is old or contaminated. Drain system, replenish with new fluid and bleed the system (Chapter 6).
6   Master cylinder internal parts worn or damaged causing fluid to bypass (Chapter 6).
7   Master cylinder bore scratched by foreign material or broken spring. Repair or replace master cylinder (Chapter 6).
8   Drum warped. Replace drum (Chapter 6).

51 Brake lever or pedal pulsates

1   Axle bent. Replace axle (Chapter 5).
2   Wheel warped or otherwise damaged (Chapter 6).
3   Hub or axle bearings damaged or worn (Chapter 6).
4   Brake drum out of round. Replace brake drum (Chapter 6).

52 Brakes drag

1   Master cylinder piston seized. Caused by wear or damage to piston or cylinder bore (Chapter 6).
2   Lever balky or stuck. Check pivot and lubricate (Chapter 6).
3   Wheel cylinder or caliper piston seized in bore. Caused by wear or ingestion of dirt past deteriorated seal (Chapter 6).
4   Brake shoes damaged. Lining material separated from shoes. Usually caused by faulty manufacturing process or from contact with chemicals. Replace shoes (Chapter 6).
5   Shoes improperly installed (Chapter 6).
6   Rear brake pedal or lever free play insufficient (Chapter 1).
7   Rear brake springs weak. Replace brake springs (Chapter 6).

Electrical problems

53 Battery dead or weak

1   Battery faulty. Caused by sulfated plates which are shorted through sedimentation or low electrolyte level. Also, broken battery terminal making only occasional contact (Chapter 8).
2   Battery cables making poor contact (Chapter 8).
3   Load excessive. Caused by addition of high wattage lights or other electrical accessories.
4   Ignition switch defective. Switch either grounds/earths internally or fails to shut off system. Replace the switch (Chapter 8).
5   Regulator/rectifier defective (Chapter 8).
6   Stator coil open or shorted (Chapter 8).
7   Wiring faulty. Wiring grounded or connections loose in ignition, charging or lighting circuits (Chapter 8).

54 Battery overcharged

1   Regulator/rectifier defective. Overcharging is noticed when battery gets excessively warm or boils over (Chapter 8).
2   Battery defective. Replace battery with a new one (Chapter 8).
3   Battery amperage too low, wrong type or size. Install manufacturer's specified amp-hour battery to handle charging load (Chapter 8).

Chapter 1
Tune-up and routine maintenance

Contents

Specifications

Engine

Spark plugs (400 and 450 models)
- Type
  - Standard ..... NGK DPR7EA-9 or ND X22EPR-U9
  - Extended high speed riding ..... NGK DPR8EA-9 or ND X24EPR-U9
  - Cold climates (below 5-degrees C/41-degrees F) ..... NGK DPR6EA-9 or ND X24EPR-U9
- Gap ..... 0.8 to 0.9 mm (0.031 to 0.035 inch)

Spark plugs (500 models)
- Type
  - Standard ..... NGK IJR7A-9 or ND VX22BC
  - Optional ..... NGK IJR6A-9 or ND VX20BC
- Gap ..... 0.8 to 0.9 mm (0.031 to 0.035 inch)

Engine idle speed ..... 1400 +/- 100 rpm
Valve clearance (COLD engine, intake and exhaust) ..... 0.15 mm (0.006 inch)

Miscellaneous

Front brake shoe lining thickness (drum brakes)
- New ..... 4 mm (0.16 inch)
- Wear limit ..... 2 mm (0.08 inch)

Front brake wear limit (disc brakes) ..... Shown by indicator

Rear brake shoe lining thickness
- New ..... 5 mm (0.20 inch)
- Wear limit ..... Shown by indicator

Front brake lever freeplay
- Drum brake models ..... 25 to 30 mm (1 to 1-1/4 inch)
- Disc brake models ..... Not specified

Rear brake lever freeplay ..... 15 to 20 mm (5/8 to 3/4 inch)
Rear brake pedal freeplay ..... 15 to 20 mm (5/8 to 3/4 inch)
Reverse selector lever freeplay (400 and 450 models only) ..... 2 to 4 mm (1/16 to 1/8 inch)
Throttle lever freeplay ..... 3 to 8 mm (1/8 to 5/16 inch)
Choke freeplay ..... Not adjustable
Minimum tire tread depth ..... 4 mm (0.16 inch)

Tire pressures (cold)
- Minimum ..... 3.2 psi
- Standard ..... 3.6 psi
- Maximum ..... 4.0 psi
- Rear tires with cargo ..... 3.6 psi

Front wheel toe-out
- 400 models ..... 16 mm (5/8 inch)
- 450 models ..... 35 +/- 15 mm (1-3/8 +/- 9/16 inch)
- 500 models ..... 30 +/- 15 mm (1-3/16 +/- 9/16 inch)

Torque specifications

Oil drain plug	25 Nm (18 ft-lbs)
Oil filter cover bolts (400 and 450 models)	10 Nm (84 in-lbs)
Oil filter center bolt (500 models)	18 Nm (13 ft-lbs)
Clutch adjusting screw locknut (400 and 450 models only)	22 Nm (16 ft-lbs)
Timing hole cap	10 Nm (84 in-lbs)
Valve adjusting screw locknuts	17 Nm (144 in-lbs)
Spark plugs	
400 and 450 models	18 Nm (156 in-lbs)
500 models	22 Nm (16 ft-lbs)
Differential and final drive filler, drain and check plugs	12 Nm (108 in-lbs)
Tie rod locknuts	55 Nm (40 ft-lbs)

Recommended lubricants and fluids

Engine/transmission oil	
Type	API grade SF or SG multigrade oil meeting JASO standard MA
Viscosity	10W-40
Capacity	
Foreman	
With filter change	2.1 liters (2.21 US qt, 3.7 Imp pt)
Oil change only	2.0 liters (2.1 US qt, 3.52 Imp pt)
After engine overhaul	2.7 liters (2.84 US qt, 4.76 Imp pt)
Rubicon	
2001 through 2004 models, with oil and filter change	4.9 liters (5.2 US qt, 8.6 Imp pt)
2005 and later models, with oil and filter change	4.6 liters (4.9 US qt, 8.1 Imp pt)
Differential oil	
Type	Hypoid gear oil
Viscosity	SAE 80
Front differential capacity	
400 models	200 cc (6.76 US fl oz, 7.02 Imp oz)
450 models	
1998 through 2001	190 cc (6.4 US fl oz, 6.7 Imp oz)
2002 and later	241 cc (8.2 US fl oz, 8.5 Imp oz)
500 models	
2001 through 2004	185 cc (6.0 US fl oz, 6.5 Imp oz)
2005 and later	241 cc (8.2 US fl oz, 8.5 Imp oz)
Rear final drive capacity	
400 and 450 models	100 cc (3.4 US fl oz, 3.5 Imp oz)
500 models	
2001 through 2004	75 cc (2.5 US fl oz, 2.6 Imp oz)
2005 and later	90 cc (3.0 US fl oz, 3.2 Imp oz)
Brake fluid	DOT 3 or DOT 4

Miscellaneous

Wheel bearings	Medium weight, lithium-based multi-purpose grease (NLGI no. 3)
Swingarm pivot bearings	Medium weight, lithium-based multi-purpose grease (NLGI no. 3)
Cables and lever pivots	Chain and cable lubricant or 10W30 motor oil
Brake pedal/shift lever/throttle lever pivots	Chain and cable lubricant or 10W30 motor oil

1 Honda TRX400/450/500 Routine maintenance schedule

Routine maintenance intervals

Note: *The pre-ride inspection outlined in the owner's manual covers checks and maintenance that should be carried out on a daily basis. It's condensed and included here to remind you of its importance. Always perform the pre-ride inspection at every maintenance interval (in addition to the procedures listed). The intervals listed below are the shortest intervals recommended by the manufacturer for each particular operation during the model years covered in this manual. Your owner's manual may have different intervals for your model.*

Daily or before riding

Check the engine oil level
Check the coolant level (500)
Check the fuel level and inspect for leaks
Check the operation of both brakes - check the front brake fluid level and look for leakage; check the rear brake pedal and lever for correct freeplay
Check the tires for damage, the presence of foreign objects and correct air pressure
Check the throttle for smooth operation and correct freeplay
Make sure the steering operates smoothly
Check for proper operation of the headlight, taillight, indicator lights, speedometer and horn
Make sure the engine kill switch works properly
Check the driveaxle boots for damage or deterioration
Check the air cleaner drain tube and clean it if necessary
Make sure any cargo is properly loaded and securely fastened
Check all fasteners, including wheel nuts and axle nuts, for tightness
Check the underbody for mud or debris that could start a fire or interfere with vehicle operation

Every 600 miles/100 operating hours

Perform all of the daily checks plus:
Check front brake fluid level

Inspect the brakes
Check and adjust the valve clearances
Clean the air filter element (1)
Clean the air cleaner housing drain tube (2)
Check/adjust the throttle lever freeplay
Check choke operation
Check/adjust the idle speed
Change the engine oil and oil filter
Check the tightness of all fasteners
Inspect the suspension
Clean and gap the spark plug
Check/adjust the reverse selector cable freeplay (400 and 450 models)
Check the skid plates for looseness or damage
Adjust the clutch (400 and 450 models)
Check the exhaust system for leaks and check fastener tightness; clean the spark arrester
Inspect the wheels and tires
 1 *More often in dusty, sandy or snowy conditions.*
 2 *More often in wet or muddy conditions.*

Every 1200 miles/200 operating hours

Check the cleanliness of the fuel system and the condition of the fuel line
Clean the fuel tap strainer screen
Check the brake shoes for wear (1, 2)
Check differential and final drive oil level
Inspect the steering system and steering shaft bearing
 1 *More often in dusty, sandy or snowy conditions.*
 2 *More often in wet or muddy conditions.*

Every two years

Change the brake fluid
Change the differential and final drive oil
Change the coolant (500 models)

2.1 Decals on the vehicle include maintenance and safety information

3.3 The engine oil level must be between the upper and lower marks on the dipstick (400/450)

2   Introduction to tune-up and routine maintenance

Refer to illustration 2.1

This Chapter covers in detail the checks and procedures necessary for the tune-up and routine maintenance of your vehicle. Section 1 includes the routine maintenance schedule, which is designed to keep the machine in proper running condition and prevent possible problems. The remaining Sections contain detailed procedures for carrying out the items listed on the maintenance schedule, as well as additional maintenance information designed to increase reliability. Maintenance information is also printed on decals, which are mounted in various locations on the vehicle **(see illustration)**. Where information on the decals differs from that presented in this Chapter, use the decal information.

Since routine maintenance plays such an important role in the safe and efficient operation of your vehicle, it is presented here as a comprehensive check list. For the rider who does all of the maintenance, these lists outline the procedures and checks that should be done on a routine basis.

Deciding where to start or plug into the routine maintenance schedule depends on several factors. If you have a vehicle whose warranty has recently expired, and if it has been maintained according to the warranty standards, you may want to pick up routine maintenance as it coincides with the next mileage or calendar interval. If you have owned the machine for some time but have never performed any maintenance on it, then you may want to start at the nearest interval and include some additional procedures to ensure that nothing important is overlooked. If you have just had a major engine overhaul, then you may want to start the maintenance routine from the beginning. If you have

a used machine and have no knowledge of its history or maintenance record, you may desire to combine all the checks into one large service initially and then settle into the maintenance schedule prescribed.

The Sections which actually outline the inspection and maintenance procedures are written as step-by-step comprehensive guides to the actual performance of the work. They explain in detail each of the routine inspections and maintenance procedures on the check list. References to additional information in applicable Chapters is also included and should not be overlooked.

Before beginning any actual maintenance or repair, the machine should be cleaned thoroughly, especially around the oil filter housing, spark plug, cylinder head cover, side covers, carburetor, etc. Cleaning will help ensure that dirt does not contaminate the engine and will allow you to detect wear and damage that could otherwise easily go unnoticed.

3   Fluid levels - check

Engine oil
400 and 450 models

Refer to illustration 3.3

1   Park the vehicle in a level position, then start the engine and allow it to reach normal operating temperature. **Caution:** *Do not run the engine in an enclosed space such as a garage or shop.*
2   Stop the engine and allow the machine to sit undisturbed in a level position for about five minutes.
3   With the engine off, unscrew the dipstick from the left side of the crankcase **(see illustration)**. Pull it out, wipe it off with a clean rag, and reinsert it (let the dipstick rest on the threads; don't screw it back in). Pull the dipstick out and check the oil level on the dipstick scale. The oil level should be between the Maximum and Minimum level marks on the scale.
4   If the level is below the Minimum mark, add oil through the dipstick hole. Add enough oil of the recommended grade and type to bring the level up to the Maximum mark. Do not overfill.

500 models

Refer to illustration 3.7

5   Park the vehicle in a level position, then start the engine and let it idle for five minutes. Do not rev the engine during this time. **Note:** *In cold weather (below 10-degrees C/50-degrees F), let the engine idle for 10 minutes).*
6   Stop the engine.
7   With the engine off, unscrew the dipstick from the oil tank **(see illustration)**. Pull it out, wipe it off with a clean rag, and reinsert it (let the dipstick rest on the threads; don't screw it back in). Pull the dipstick out and check the oil level on the dipstick scale. The oil level should be

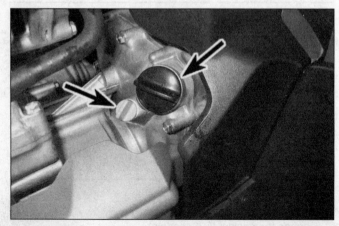

3.7 On 500 models, check oil level on the dipstick and add oil through the filler hole (arrows)

3.14 The brake fluid level must be above the Lower mark on the reservoir; remove the cover screws (arrows) to add fluid

3.22 Unscrew the filler plug (upper arrow) to check front differential oil level; unscrew the drain bolt (hidden, lower arrow) to change the oil

between the Maximum and Minimum level marks on the scale.

8   If the level is below the Minimum mark, unscrew the filler cap and add oil through the hole **(see illustration 3.7)**. Add enough oil of the recommended grade and type to bring the level up to the Maximum mark. Do not overfill.

9   As a check on the lubrication system, you can also check the oil level with the engine running. The oil pump should maintain the correct oil level. If it doesn't, and there is enough oil in the tank, there is a problem with the lubrication system.

10   To check with the engine running, park the vehicle in a level position and let the engine idle for several minutes. **Note:** *Don't make this check right after operating at high speeds or the oil level won't be correct.*

11   Measure the oil level with the dipstick as described in Step 7. The level should be above the stepped line on the end of the dipstick. If it isn't, and the oil level is correct with the engine off, there is a problem with the lubrication system such as a worn oil pump or clogged lines.

Brake fluid

Refer to illustration 3.14

12   In order to ensure proper operation of the hydraulic front drum brakes, the fluid level in the master cylinder reservoirs must be properly maintained.

13   With the vehicle parked in a level position, turn the handlebars until the top of the front brake master cylinder is as level as possible.

14   The fluid level is visible through the sight glass in the master cylinder reservoir. Make sure that the fluid level is above the Lower mark on the reservoir **(see illustration)**.

15   If the level is low, the fluid must be replenished. Before removing the master cylinder cap, place rags beneath the reservoir (to protect the paint from brake fluid spills) and remove all dust and dirt from the area around the cap.

16   Remove the cover screws, then lift off the cover, rubber diaphragm and float (if equipped). **Note:** *Don't operate the brake lever with the cover removed.*

17   Add new, clean brake fluid of the recommended type until the level is even with the cast line inside the master cylinder reservoir. Don't mix different brands of brake fluid in the reservoir, as they may not be compatible. Also, don't mix different specifications (DOT 3 with DOT 4).

18   Reinstall the float (if equipped), rubber diaphragm and cover. Tighten the cover screws securely.

19   Wipe any spilled fluid off the reservoir body.

20   If the brake fluid level was low in either check, inspect the front or rear brake system for leaks.

Differential and final drive oil

Refer to illustrations 3.22, 3.23a and 3.23b

21   Park the vehicle on a level surface.

22   If you're working on a front differential, remove the differential filler cap **(see illustration)**. Feel the oil level inside the differential; it should be up to the bottom of the filler hole threads. If not, add the recommended oil until it does.

23   If you're working on a rear differential, remove the oil level check bolt **(see illustration)**. Oil should flow from the hole. If it doesn't, remove the oil filler cap **(see illustration)**. Slowly pour oil into the filler cap hole

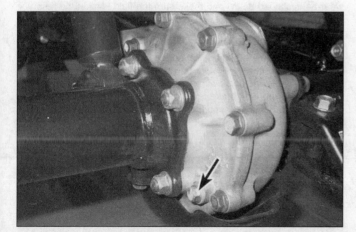

3.23a Unscrew the rear differential check bolt (arrow); if oil doesn't run out . . .

3.23b . . . unscrew the filler cap (arrow) and add oil until it runs out the check bolt hole

3.27a On 500 models, coolant should be between the lines on the reservoir

3.27b Remove the reservoir cap and add coolant through the hole

until it flows from the check bolt hole, then install the check bolt and filler cap.
24   Add oil if necessary of the type recommended in this Chapter's Specifications.
25   Reinstall the filler cap and tighten securely.

Coolant (500 models)

Refer to illustrations 3.27a and 3.27b

26   Warm the engine to normal operating temperature and park it on a level surface.
27   Check the coolant level in the reservoir tank **(see illustrations)**. It should be between the Upper and Lower lines. If it's low, add a 50/50 mixture of the recommended coolant and distilled water to bring it up to the correct level.
28   If the reservoir tank is completely empty, check the cooling system for leaks and bleed air from the system before topping up the reservoir (see Section 18 and Chapter 2D).

---

4   Battery - check

Refer to illustration 4.1

Warning: *Be extremely careful when handling or working around the battery. The electrolyte is very caustic and an explosive gas (hydrogen) is given off when the battery is charging.*

1   Remove the seat (see Chapter 7). Unbolt the battery bracket (if equipped) **(see illustration)** or remove the retaining strap.
2   Remove the screws securing the battery cables to the battery terminals (remove the negative cable first, positive cable last). Lift the battery out of the vehicle.
3   The battery is a sealed type which requires no maintenance. **Note:** *Do not attempt to remove the battery caps to check the electrolyte level or battery specific gravity.* Removal will damage the caps, resulting in electrolyte leakage and battery damage. All that should be done is to check that its terminals are clean and tight and that the casing is not damaged or leaking. See Chapter 8 for further details.
4   If the vehicle will be stored for an extended time, fully charge the battery, then disconnect the negative cable before storage.
5   Install the battery. Be sure to refer to safety precautions regarding battery installation in Chapter 8.

---

5   Brake system - general check

---

1   A routine general check of the brakes will ensure that any problems are discovered and remedied before the rider's safety is jeopardized.

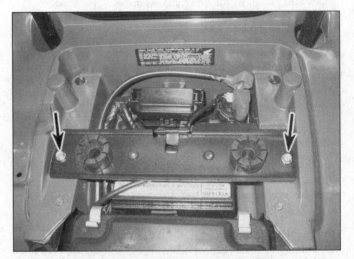

4.1 Unbolt the battery cover (arrows) or unhook the retaining strap, disconnect the cables (negative first), then lift the battery out of the vehicle

2   Check the brake levers and pedal for loose connections, excessive play, bends, and other damage. Replace any damaged parts with new ones (see Chapter 6).
3   Make sure all brake fasteners are tight. Check the brakes for wear as described below and make sure the fluid level in the reservoir is correct (see Section 3). Look for leaks at the hose connections and check for cracks in the hoses. If the lever is spongy, bleed the brakes as described in Chapter 6.
4   Make sure the brake light operates when the front brake lever is depressed. The front brake light switch is not adjustable. If it fails to operate properly, replace it with a new one (see Chapter 8).
5   Operate the rear brake lever and pedal. If operation is rough or sticky, refer to Section 13 and lubricate the cables.

Front brakes
Drum brakes

Refer to illustration 5.6

6   Remove the adjusting hole plug from the brake drum **(see illustration)**.
7   Look through the hole to inspect the thickness of the lining material on the brake shoes (use a flashlight if necessary). If it's worn to near the limit listed in this Chapter's Specifications, refer to Chapter 6 and replace the brake shoes.

5.6 Pull the rubber inspection plug out of the brake drum

5.8 If the pointer and indicator (arrows) align with each other, the pads are worn and should be replaced

5.9 If the pointer (lower arrow) aligns with the mark (upper arrow) when the rear brake is applied, it's time to replace the rear brake shoes

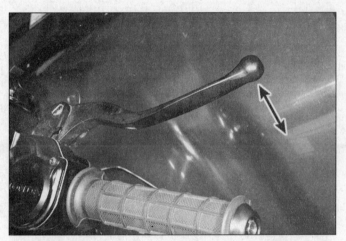

6.1 Measure the front drum brake lever freeplay at the lever tip

6.3a Insert a screwdriver through the access hole to turn the adjuster wheels . . .

Disc brakes

Refer to illustration 5.8

8   Check the alignment of the indicator and reference mark **(see illustration)**. If necessary, jack up the front end of the vehicle and remove the front wheel for better visibility. If the indicator aligns with the reference mark, the pads are worn and should be replaced (see Chapter 6).

Rear brakes

Refer to illustration 5.9

9   With the rear brake lever and pedal freeplay properly adjusted (see Section 6), check the wear indicator on the rear brake panel **(see illustration)**. If the pointer lines up with the indicator when the lever is pulled or the pedal is pressed, refer to Chapter 6 and replace the brake shoes.

6   Brake lever and pedal freeplay - check and adjustment

Front brake lever

Refer to illustrations 6.1, 6.3a and 6.3b

1   On drum brake models, squeeze the front brake lever and note how far the lever travels **(see illustration)**. If it exceeds the limit listed in this Chapter's Specifications, adjust the front brakes as described below. On disc brake models, there shouldn't be any freeplay. If there is, bleed the front brake and check the hydraulic lines for leaks (see Chapter 6).

2   Securely block the rear wheels so the vehicle can't roll. Jack up the front end and support it securely on jackstands.

3   There's an adjuster wheel at each wheel cylinder, located at the sides of the brake panel **(see illustrations)**. It's accessible through the adjusting hole plug **(see illustration 5.6)**.

4   To adjust the brakes, insert a screwdriver through the adjusting

6.3b . . . there's one on each wheel cylinder (brake drum removed for clarity)

6.7 Check the rear brake lever freeplay at the handlebar

6.8 The upper wingnut adjusts the lever; the lower wingnut adjusts the pedal

hole and turn the adjuster wheel until the tire can't be turned by hand, then back it off three notches. Spin the tire by hand to make sure the brake lining isn't dragging on the drum; if it is, back off the adjuster just enough so the dragging stops. Then align the hole with the second adjuster wheel and repeat the adjustment.

5   Push the adjusting hole cap securely into its hole with a screw-driver.

6   Repeat the adjustment on the other front wheel, then remove the jackstands and lower the vehicle.

Rear brakes

Refer to illustrations 6.7, 6.8 and 6.9

7   Check the rear brake lever play at the left handlebar in the same way as for front brake lever play **(see illustration)**. If it exceeds the limit listed in this Chapter's Specifications, adjust it as described below.

8   If freeplay isn't within specifications, turn the lower wingnut at the brake panel lever **(see illustration)**. **Note:** *Push the lever forward so its bushing clears the cutout in the wingnut, then turn the nut.* Make sure the cutout seats on the bushing after adjustment.

9   Check the play of the rear brake pedal **(see illustration)**. If it exceeds the limit listed in this Chapter's Specifications, adjust it with the upper wingnut at the brake panel **(see illustration 6.8)**.

7   Tires/wheels - general check

Refer to illustration 7.4

1   Routine tire and wheel checks should be made with the realization that your safety depends to a great extent on their condition.

2   Check the tires carefully for cuts, tears, embedded nails or other sharp objects and excessive wear. Operation of the vehicle with exces-sively worn tires is extremely hazardous, as traction and handling are directly affected. Measure the tread depth at the center of the tire and replace worn tires with new ones when the tread depth is less than that listed in this Chapter's Specifications.

3   Repair or replace punctured tires as soon as damage is noted. Do not try to patch a torn tire, as wheel balance and tire reliability may be impaired.

4   Check the tire pressures when the tires are cold and keep them properly inflated **(see illustration)**. Proper air pressure will increase tire life and provide maximum stability and ride comfort. Keep in mind that low tire pressures may cause the tire to slip on the rim or come off, while high tire pressures will cause abnormal tread wear and unsafe handling.

5   The steel wheels used on this machine are virtually maintenance free, but they should be kept clean and checked periodically for cracks,

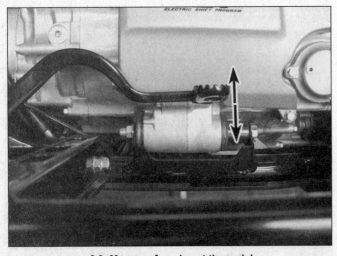

6.9 Measure freeplay at the pedal

7.4 Check tire pressure with a gauge that will read accurately at the low pressures used in ATV tires

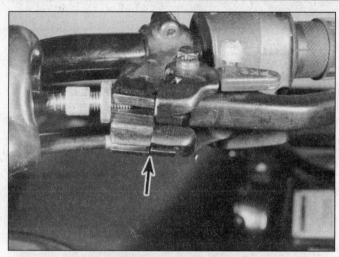

8.2 Measure freeplay at the gap between the reverse lock lever and its bracket (arrow)

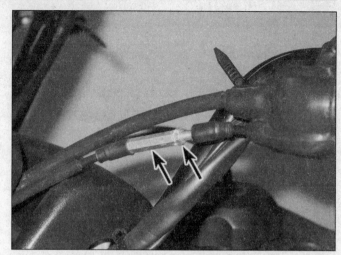

8.3 Loosen the locknut (right arrow) and turn the adjuster (left arrow) to adjust freeplay

bending and rust. Never attempt to repair damaged wheels; they must be replaced with new ones.

6   Check the valve stem locknuts to make sure they're tight. Also, make sure the valve stem cap is in place and tight. If it is missing, install a new one made of metal or hard plastic.

8   Reverse lock system (400 and 450 models) - check and adjustment

Refer to illustrations 8.2 and 8.3

1   Follow the reverse selector cable from its lever on the left handlebar to its lever on the right side of the engine. Check for kinks, bends, loose retainers or other problems and correct them as necessary.

2   Measure the gap between the reverse lock lever and its cable bracket at the handlebar **(see illustration)**. If it's not within the range listed in this Chapter's Specifications, adjust it.

3   To adjust the cable, loosen the locknut at the handlebar adjuster **(see illustration)**. Turn the adjusting nut to achieve the correct play at the handlebar, then tighten the locknut securely.

9   Clutch (400 and 450 models) - check and freeplay adjustment

Refer to illustration 9.2

1   The automatic clutch mechanism on these models disengages the change clutch automatically when the shift lever is operated, so there is no clutch lever (as is normal on motorcycles). If shifting gears becomes difficult, the clutch may be in need of adjustment.

2   Loosen the locknut on the front of the engine **(see illustration)**. carefully turn the adjusting screw counterclockwise until you feel resistance, then turn it back in 1/4 turn. Hold the screw in this position and tighten the locknut to the torque listed in this Chapter's Specifications.

10   Driveaxle boots - check

Refer to illustration 10.1

1   Check the driveaxle boots for cracks or damage, such as tears and cuts **(see illustration)**.

2   If any problems are found, refer to Chapter 5 and replace the boots.

9.2 Loosen the locknut and turn the screw as described in the text, then tighten the locknut

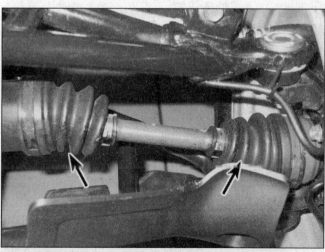

10.1 Check the driveaxle boots (arrows) for damage or deterioration

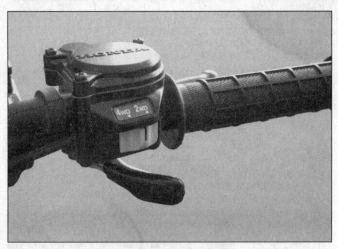

11.2 Measure throttle freeplay at the lever

11.3 Loosen the lockwheel (right arrow) and turn the adjuster
wheel (left arrow) to make fine adjustments in throttle freeplay

11   Throttle and choke operation/grip freeplay - check and adjustment

Throttle check

Refer to illustration 11.2

1   Make sure the throttle lever moves easily from fully closed to fully open with the front wheel turned at various angles. The grip should return automatically from fully open to fully closed when released. If the throttle sticks, check the throttle cable for cracks or kinks in the housings. Also, make sure the inner cable is clean and well-lubricated.
2   Check for a small amount of freeplay at the lever and compare the freeplay to the value listed in this Chapter's Specifications **(see illustration)**.

Throttle adjustment

Refer to illustrations 11.3 and 11.5

3   Freeplay adjustments can be made at the throttle lever end of the accelerator cable. Pull back the rubber boot and loosen the lockwheel on the cable **(see illustration)**. Turn the adjuster until the desired freeplay is obtained, then retighten the lockwheel.
4   If the freeplay can't be adjusted at the grip end, adjust the cable at the carburetor end. To do this, first remove the seat (see Chapter 7).
5   Loosen the locknut on the throttle cable **(see illustration)**.Turn the adjusting nut to set freeplay, then tighten the locknut securely.

12   Choke - operation check

1   Operate the choke lever on the left handlebar while you feel for smooth operation. If the lever doesn't move smoothly, refer to Section 13 and lubricate the choke cable.
2   Follow the cable from the handlebar to the starting enrichment valve on the carburetor **(see illustration 11.5)**. Check for kinks, bends, loose retainers or other problems and correct them as necessary.

13   Lubrication - general

Refer to illustration 13.3

1   Since the controls, cables and various other components of a vehicle are exposed to the elements, they should be lubricated periodically to ensure safe and trouble-free operation.
2   The throttle and brake levers, brake pedal, kickstarter pivot should be lubricated frequently. In order for the lubricant to be applied where it will do the most good, the component should be disassembled. However, if chain and cable lubricant is being used, it can be applied to the pivot joint gaps and will usually work its way into the areas where friction occurs. If motor oil or light grease is being used, apply it sparingly as it may attract dirt (which could cause the controls to bind or wear at an accelerated rate). **Note:** *One of the best lubricants for the control lever pivots is a dry-film lubricant (available from many sources by different names).*
3   The throttle, choke, brake and reverse cables should be removed

11.5 Here are the carburetor throttle cable locknut (A), adjuster
(B) and choke cable (C)

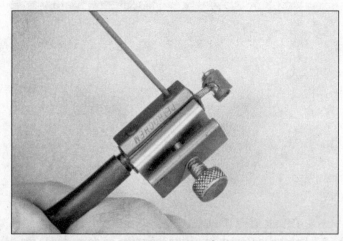

13.3 Lubricating a cable with a pressure lube adapter (make sure
the tool seats around the inner cable)

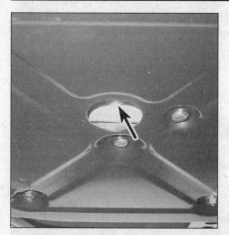

14.5a The 400/450 oil drain plug is on the underside of the crankcase (arrow)

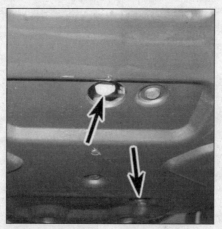

14.5b 500 models have two engine oil drain plugs (arrows)

14.6a On 400/450 models, remove the filter cover bolts (arrows). . .

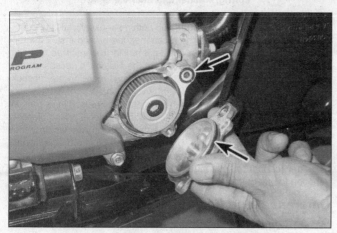

14.6b . . . pull off the cover and note the O-ring locations (arrows) . . .

14.6c . . . remove the filter and spring and wipe the remaining oil out of the filter housing; be sure the filter element's OUT SIDE mark faces outward on installation

and treated with a commercially available cable lubricant which is specially formulated for use on vehicle control cables. Small adapters for pressure lubricating the cables with spray can lubricants are available and ensure that the cable is lubricated along its entire length **(see illustration)**. When attaching the cable to the lever, be sure to lubricate the barrel-shaped fitting at the end with multi-purpose grease.

4   To lubricate the cables, disconnect them at the lower end, then lubricate the cable with a pressure lube adapter **(see illustration 13.3)**. See Chapter 2A (reverse selector cable), Chapter 3 (throttle and choke cables) or Chapter 6 (brake cables).

5   Refer to Chapter 5 for the following lubrication procedures:

a) Swingarm bearing and dust seals
b) Front driveaxle splines
c) Rear driveshaft pinion joint
d) Rear axle shaft splines

6   Refer to Chapter 6 for the following lubrication procedures:

a) Brake pedal pivot and seals
b) Front brake drum waterproof seals
c) Rear brake drum cover seal

14 Engine oil/filter and differential oil - change

Engine oil/filter

Refer to illustrations 14.5a, 14.5b, 14.6a, 14.6b, 14.6c, 14.7a and 14.7b

1   Consistent routine oil and filter changes are the single most impor-

tant maintenance procedure you can perform on a vehicle. The oil not only lubricates the internal parts of the engine, transmission and clutch, but it also acts as a coolant, a cleaner, a sealant, and a protectant. Because of these demands, the oil takes a terrific amount of abuse and should be replaced often with new oil of the recommended grade and type. Saving a little money on the difference in cost between a good oil and a cheap oil won't pay off if the engine is damaged. Honda recommends against using the following:

a) Oils with graphite or molybdenum additives
b) Non-detergent oils
c) Castor or vegetable based oils
d) Oil additives.

2   Before changing the oil and filter, warm up the engine so the oil will drain easily. Be careful when draining the oil, as the exhaust pipe, the engine and the oil itself can cause severe burns.

3   Park the vehicle over a clean drain pan.

4   Remove the dipstick/oil filler cap to vent the crankcase and act as a reminder that there is no oil in the engine.

5   Next, remove the drain plug(s) from the engine **(see illustrations)** and allow the oil to drain into the pan. Do not lose the sealing washer on the drain plug(s).

400 and 450 models

6   As the oil is draining, remove the oil filter cover bolts **(see illustration)**. Remove the cover, filter element and spring **(see illustrations)**. If additional maintenance is planned for this time period, check or service another component while the oil is allowed to drain completely. Wipe any remaining oil out of the filter housing area of the crankcase.

14.7a On 500 models, remove the cover center bolt (arrow) . . .

14.7b . . . pull off the cover with its O-ring, then remove the spring, washer and filter element

500 models

7   Unscrew the center bolt from the cover **(see illustration)**. Remove the cover, spring, washer and filter element **(see illustration)**. If additional maintenance is planned for this time period, check or service another component while the oil is allowed to drain completely. Wipe any remaining oil out of the filter housing area of the crankcase.
8   Check the condition of the drain plug threads and the sealing washer(s).

All models

9   If you're working on a 400 or 450, install the spring on its post, then install the filter element. **Caution:** *The OUT SIDE mark on the filter must face outward (away from the crankcase) or severe engine damage will occur.*
10   Install new O-rings on the crankcase (400 and 450) and on the filter cover (all models). Install the cover and tighten its bolt(s) to the torque listed in this Chapter's Specifications.
11   Slip a new sealing washer over the drain plug, then install and tighten the plug to the torque listed in this Chapter's Specifications. Avoid overtightening, as damage to the engine case will result.
12   Before refilling the engine, check the old oil carefully. If the oil was drained into a clean pan, small pieces of metal or other material can be easily detected. If the oil is very metallic colored, then the engine is experiencing wear from break-in (new engine) or from insufficient lubrication. If there are flakes or chips of metal in the oil, then something is drastically wrong internally and the engine will have to be disassembled for inspection and repair.
13   If there are pieces of fiber-like material in the oil on a 400 or 450 model, the change clutch is experiencing excessive wear and should be checked.

14.18 Remove the drain bolt (arrow) from the rear differential

14   If the inspection of the oil turns up nothing unusual, refill the crankcase to the proper level with the recommended oil and install the dipstick/filler cap. Start the engine and let it run for two or three minutes. Shut it off, wait a few minutes, then check the oil level. If necessary, add more oil to bring the level up to the upper level mark on the dipstick. Check around the drain plug and filter cover for leaks.
15   The old oil drained from the engine cannot be reused in its present state and should be disposed of. Check with your local refuse disposal company, disposal facility or environmental agency to see whether they will accept the oil for recycling. Don't pour used oil into drains or onto the ground. After the oil has cooled, it can be drained into a suitable container (capped plastic jugs, topped bottles, milk cartons, etc.) for transport to one of these disposal sites.

Differential and final drive oil

Refer to illustration 14.18

16   Place a protective cover under the front differential drain bolt so oil won't drip onto the frame rail. This can be a piece of cardboard or aluminum foil.
17   Place a drain pan beneath the differential.
18   Remove the oil filler plug, then the drain bolt and sealing washer **(see illustration 3.15 or the accompanying illustration)**. Let the oil drain for several minutes, until it stops dripping.
19   Clean the drain bolt and sealing washer. If the sealing washer is in good condition, it can be reused; otherwise, replace it.
20   Install the drain bolt and tighten it to the torque listed in this Chapter's Specifications.
21   Add oil of the type and amount listed in this Chapter's Specifications, then check the oil level as described in Section 3. Install the filler plug and tighten it to the torque listed in this Chapter's Specifications.
22   Refer to Step 15 above to dispose of the drained oil.

15 Air cleaner - filter element and drain tube cleaning

Element cleaning

Refer to illustrations 15.2, 15.3 and 15.4

1   Remove the seat (see Chapter 7).
2   Remove the clips that secure the filter cover and lift it off **(see illustration)**.
3   Loosen the clamping band at the front of the element, remove the holder and lift the element out **(see illustration)**.
4   Separate the foam element from the metal core **(see illustration)**.
5   Clean the element and core in a high flash point solvent, squeeze the solvent out of the foam and let the core and element dry completely. If you're working on a 500 model, remove the dust cover from the hole at the left side of the air cleaner housing and clean it with compressed

15.2 Pull back the clips (arrows) and lift off the cover

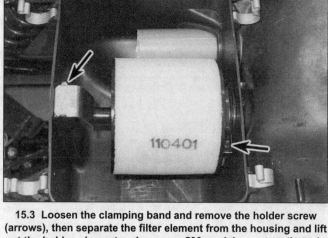

15.3 Loosen the clamping band and remove the holder screw (arrows), then separate the filter element from the housing and lift out the holder, element and core; on 500 models, remove the sub-air cleaner filter from the tube

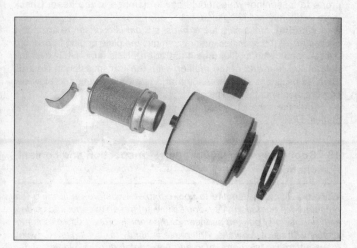

15.4 Separate the foam element from the metal core

15.9 Open the clip and pull the drain tube (arrow) off its fitting

air if necessary. Remove the sub-air cleaner filter from the tube at the front end of the air cleaner housing.

6   Soak the foam element in the amount and type of foam filter oil listed in this Chapter's Specifications, then squeeze it firmly to remove the excess oil.

7   Place the element on the core.

8   The remainder of installation is the reverse of the removal steps.

Drain tube cleaning

Refer to illustration 15.9

9   Check the drain tube for accumulated water and oil (see illustration). If oil or water has built up in the tube, squeeze its clamp, remove it from the air cleaner housing and clean it out. Install the drain tube on the housing and secure it with the clamp.

16 Fuel system - check and filter cleaning

Refer to illustrations 16.1, 16.5a, 16.5b and 16.9

Warning: *Gasoline is extremely flammable, so take extra precautions when you work on any part of the fuel system. Don't smoke or allow open flames or bare light bulbs near the work area, and don't work in a garage where a gas-type appliance (such as a water heater or clothes dryer) is present. Since gasoline is carcinogenic, wear protective gloves and if you spill any fuel on your skin, rinse it off immediately with soap and water. When you perform any kind of work on the fuel system, wear*

safety glasses and have a fire extinguisher suitable for class B type fires (flammable liquids) on hand.

1   Check the carburetor, fuel tank, the fuel tap and the line for leaks and evidence of damage (see illustration).

2   If carburetor gaskets are leaking, the carburetor should be disassembled and rebuilt by referring to Chapter 3.

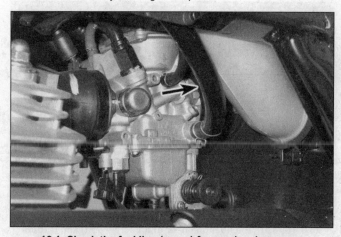

16.1 Check the fuel line (arrow) for cracks, damage or deterioration and replace it if there are any problems

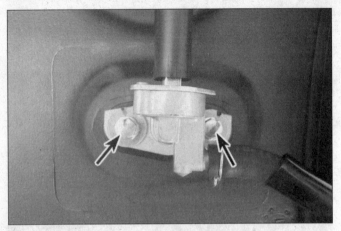

16.5a Remove the fuel tap bolts (arrows) . . .

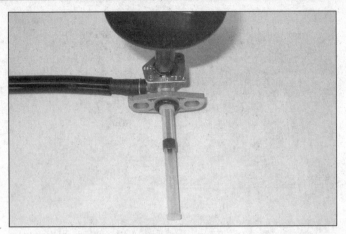

16.5b . . . remove the fuel tap, then pull off the O-ring and plastic strainer

3   If the fuel tap is leaking, tightening the screws may help. If leakage persists, the tap should be disassembled and repaired or replaced with a new one.

4   If the fuel line is cracked or otherwise deteriorated, replace it with a new one.

5   Place the fuel tap lever in the Off position. Remove the fuel tap bolts and remove the strainer and O-ring **(see illustrations)**.

6   Clean the strainer. If it's torn or otherwise damaged, replace it.

7   Installation is the reverse of the removal steps, with the following additions:

  a) *Install a new O-ring and tighten the nut to the torque listed in this Chapter's Specifications.*

  b) *Tighten the fuel tap bolts to the torque listed in this Chapter's Specifications.*

8   After installation, run the engine and check for fuel leaks.

9   If the vehicle will be stored for a month or more, remove and drain the fuel tank. Also loosen the float chamber drain screw and drain the fuel from the carburetor **(see illustration)**.

17 Exhaust system - inspection and spark arrester cleaning

Refer to illustration 17.3

1   Periodically check the exhaust system for leaks and loose fasteners. If tightening the holder nuts at the cylinder head fails to stop any leaks, replace the gasket with a new ones (a procedure which requires removal of the system).

2   The exhaust pipe flange nuts at the cylinder head are especially prone to loosening, which could cause damage to the head. Check them frequently and keep them tight.

3   **Warning:** *Make sure the exhaust system is cool before doing this procedure.* At the specified interval, remove the plate or plug from under the rear end of the muffler **(see illustration)**. Hold a rag firmly over the hole at the rear end of the muffler. With the transmission in Neutral, have an assistant start the engine and rev it a few times to blow out carbon, then shut the engine off.

4   After the exhaust system has cooled, install the plug. Tighten the plug securely.

18 Cooling system (500 models) - inspection and coolant change

Warning: *Allow the engine to cool completely before performing this maintenance operation. Also, don't allow antifreeze to come into contact with your skin or painted surfaces of the vehicle. Rinse off spills immediately with plenty of water. Antifreeze is highly toxic if ingested. Never leave antifreeze lying around in an open container or in puddles on the floor; children and pets are attracted by its sweet smell and may drink it. Check with local authorities about disposing of used antifreeze. Many communities have collection centers which will see that antifreeze is disposed of safely. Antifreeze is also combustible, so don't store or use it near open flames.*

1   The entire cooling system should be checked carefully at the recommended intervals. Look for evidence of leaks, check the condition of

16.9 Here are the float chamber drain screw (left) and throttle stop screw (right) (400/450 shown; 500 similar)

17.3 Unscrew the plug (arrow), then hold a rag against the muffler opening and rev the engine a few times to blow carbon out of the spark arrester

18.4 Check the coolant hoses for deterioration and leaks

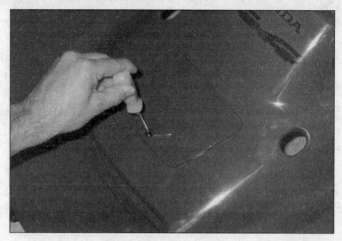

18.8a Remove the screw and lift the cover for access to the radiator cap

the coolant, check the radiator for clogged fins and damage and make sure the fan operates when required.

Inspection

Refer to illustrations 18.4, 18.8a and 18.8b

2   Remove the front fenders and fuel tank cover (see Chapter 7).
3   Remove the radiator grille and side plates (see Chapter 7).
4   Examine each of the rubber coolant hoses along its entire length. Look for cracks, abrasions and other damage **(see illustration)**. Squeeze each hose at various points. They should feel firm, yet pliable, and return to their original shape when released. If they are dried out or hard, replace them with new ones.
5   Check for evidence of leaks at each cooling system joint. Tighten the hose clamps carefully to prevent future leaks.
6   Check the radiator for evidence of leaks and other damage. Leaks in the radiator leave telltale scale deposits or coolant stains on the outside of the core below the leak. If leaks are noted, remove the radiator (refer to Chapter 2D) and have it repaired at a radiator shop or replace it with a new one. **Caution**: *Do not use a liquid leak stopping compound to try to repair leaks.*
7   Check the radiator fins for mud, dirt and insects, which may impede the flow of air through the radiator. If the fins are dirty, force water or low pressure compressed air through the fins from the backside. If the fins are bent or distorted, straighten them carefully with a screwdriver.
8   Remove the pressure cap cover **(see illustration)**. Remove the cooling system pressure cap by turning it counterclockwise until it reaches a stop. If you hear a hissing sound (indicating there is still pres-

sure in the system), wait until it stops. Now, press down on the cap with the palm of your hand and continue turning the cap counterclockwise until it can be removed **(see illustration)**. Check the condition of the coolant in the system. If it is rust colored or if accumulations of scale are visible, drain, flush and refill the system with new coolant as described below. Check the cap gaskets for cracks and other damage. Have the cap tested by a dealer service department or replace it with a new one. Install the cap by turning it clockwise until it reaches the first stop, then push down on the cap and continue turning until it can turn no further.
9   Check the antifreeze content of the coolant with an antifreeze hydrometer. Sometimes coolant may look like it's in good condition, but might be too weak to offer adequate protection. If the hydrometer indicates a weak mixture, drain, flush and refill the cooling system.
10   Start the engine and let it reach normal operating temperature, then check for leaks again. As the coolant temperature increases, the fan should come on automatically and the temperature should begin to drop. If it does not, refer to Chapter 2D and check the fan and fan circuit carefully. If the coolant level is consistently low, and no evidence of leaks can be found, have the entire system pressure checked by a dealer service department, repair shop or service station.

Coolant change

Refer to illustrations 18.11 and 18.13

11   With the radiator cap installed and tightened, place a drain pan beneath the drain plug at the bottom of the radiator **(see illustration)**.
12   Unscrew the drain plug. If the cooling system is airtight, coolant should only dribble out at this point. Make sure the drain pan is posi-

18.8b Here's the 500 radiator cap - DO NOT remove it when the engine is warm

18.11 Here's the radiator drain plug (500 models)

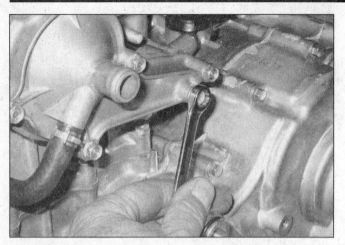

18.13 Here's the coolant drain plug on a 500 engine

19.1 Twist the spark plug cap back and forth to free it, then pull it off the plug

tioned correctly, then unscrew the radiator cap **(see illustration 18.8)**. Coolant should now flow freely.

13   Once coolant has stopped draining from the radiator, position the drain pan beneath the engine drain plug **(see illustration)**. Remove the plug and let the coolant drain into the pan.

14   Remove and drain the coolant reservoir. Refer to Chapter 2D for the reservoir removal procedure. Wash the reservoir out with water.

15   Flush the system with clean tap water by inserting a garden hose in the radiator filler neck. Allow the water to run through the system until it is clear when it exits the drain plug and bolt holes. If the radiator is extremely corroded, remove it by referring to Chapter 2D and have it cleaned at a radiator shop.

16   Check the drain plug and bolt gaskets. Replace them with new ones if necessary. Clean the holes, then install the drain plug and bolt and tighten them securely (but don't overtighten them and strip the threads).

17   Fill the cooling system with clean water mixed with a flushing compound. Make sure the flushing compound is compatible with aluminum components, and follow the manufacturer's instructions carefully.

18   Start the engine and allow it to reach normal operating temperature. Let it run for about ten minutes.

19   Stop the engine. Let the machine cool for a while, then cover the pressure cap with a heavy rag and turn it counterclockwise to the first stop, releasing any pressure that may be present in the system. Once the hissing stops, push down on the cap and remove it completely.

20   Drain the system once again.

21   Fill the system with clean water, then repeat Steps 11, 12 and 13.

22   Fill the drained system to the top of the filler neck with the proper coolant mixture (see this Chapter's Specifications).

23   With the transmission in Neutral and the radiator cap off, start the engine. Let it idle for two or three minutes to circulate the coolant, then rev the engine sharply three or four times to bleed out the air.

24   Shut the engine off, fill the coolant to the top of the filler neck again, then reinstall the radiator cap and tighten it.

25   Fill the reservoir tank to the correct level (see Section 3).

26   Check the system for leaks.

27   Do not dispose of the old coolant by pouring it down a drain. Instead, pour it into a heavy plastic container, cap it tightly and take it to an authorized disposal site or a service station.

19   Spark plug - replacement

Refer to illustrations 19.1, 19.5a and 19.5b

1   Twist the spark plug cap to break it free from the plug, then pull it off **(see illustration)**. If available, use compressed air to blow any accumulated debris from around the spark plug. Unscrew the plug with a spark plug socket.

2   Inspect the electrodes for wear. Both the center and side electrodes should have square edges and the side electrode should be of uniform thickness. Look for excessive deposits and evidence of a cracked or chipped insulator around the center electrode. Compare your

19.5a Spark plug manufacturers recommend using a wire type gauge when checking the gap - if the wire doesn't slide between the electrodes with a slight drag, adjustment is required

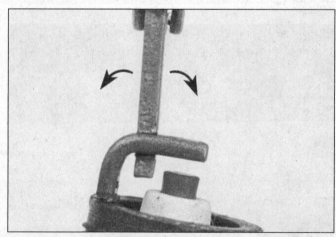

19.5b To change the gap, bend the side electrode only, as indicated by the arrows, and be very careful not to crack or chip the ceramic insulator surrounding the center electrode

20.5 Here are the 500 intake valve adjusting hole covers (arrows) . . .

20.6a On 500 models, remove the recoil starter access cover

spark plugs to the color spark plug reading chart. Check the threads, the washer and the ceramic insulator body for cracks and other damage.

3   If the electrodes are not excessively worn, and if the deposits can be easily removed with a wire brush, the plug can be regapped and reused (if no cracks or chips are visible in the insulator). If in doubt concerning the condition of the plug, replace it with a new one, as the expense is minimal.

4   Cleaning the spark plug by sandblasting is permitted, provided you clean the plug with a high flash-point solvent afterwards.

5   Before installing a new plug, make sure it is the correct type and heat range. Check the gap between the electrodes, as it is not preset. For best results, use a wire-type gauge rather than a flat gauge to check the gap (see illustration). If the gap must be adjusted, bend the side electrode only and be very careful not to chip or crack the insulator nose (see illustration). Make sure the washer is in place before installing the plug.

6   Since the cylinder head is made of aluminum, which is soft and easily damaged, thread the plug into the head by hand. Slip a short length of hose over the end of the plug to use as a tool to thread it into place. The hose will grip the plug well enough to turn it, but will start to slip if the plug begins to cross-thread in the hole - this will prevent damaged threads and the accompanying repair costs.

7   Once the plug is finger tight, the job can be finished with a socket. If a torque wrench is available, tighten the spark plug to the torque listed in this Chapter's Specifications. If you do not have a torque wrench,

tighten the plug finger tight (until the washer bottoms on the cylinder head) then use a wrench to tighten it an additional 1/4 turn. Regardless of the method used, do not over-tighten it.

8   Reconnect the spark plug cap.

20 Valve clearances - check and adjustment

Refer to illustrations 20.5, 20.6a, 20.6b, 20.9a and 20.9b

1   The engine must be completely cool for this maintenance procedure (below 35-degrees C/95-degrees F), so if possible let the machine sit overnight before beginning.

2   Refer to Section 4 and disconnect the cable from the negative terminal of the battery.

3   Refer to Chapter 3 and remove the fuel tank and heat shield.

4   Refer to Section 19 and remove the spark plug.

5   If you're working on a 400 or 450 model, remove the valve cover (see Chapter 2). If you're working on a 500, remove the adjusting hole covers (see illustration).

6   If you're working on a 500, remove the recoil starter access cover (see illustration). Unscrew the timing hole cap (just forward of the recoil starter pull rope) (see illustrations).

7   Position the piston at Top Dead Center (TDC) on the compression stroke. Do this by turning the crankshaft (pull on the recoil starter rope) until the mark on the rotor is aligned with the timing notch inside

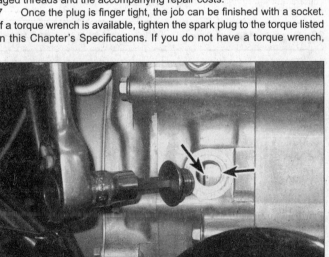

20.6b Align the notch on the crankcase cover (right arrow) with the TDC line on the alternator rotor inside the hole (left arrow) (this is a 400/450) . . .

20.6c . . . and this is a 500

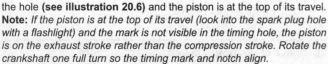

20.9a Measure valve clearance with a feeler gauge; to adjust it, loosen the locknut and turn the adjusting screw with a screwdriver (this is a 400/450) . . .

20.9b . . . and this is a 500

the hole **(see illustration 20.6)** and the piston is at the top of its travel. **Note:** *If the piston is at the top of its travel (look into the spark plug hole with a flashlight) and the mark is not visible in the timing hole, the piston is on the exhaust stroke rather than the compression stroke. Rotate the crankshaft one full turn so the timing mark and notch align.*

8   With the engine in this position, both of the valves can be checked.

9   To check, insert a feeler gauge of the thickness listed in this Chapter's Specifications between the valve stem and rocker arm **(see illustrations)**. Pull the feeler gauge out slowly - you should feel a slight drag. If there's no drag, the clearance is too loose. If there's a heavy drag, the clearance is too tight.

10   If the clearance is incorrect, loosen the adjuster locknut with a box wrench. Turn the adjusting screw with a screwdriver until the correct clearance is achieved, then tighten the locknut. **Note:** *On some models, it's necessary to insert the screwdriver through an access hole in the frame to adjust the intake valve (on the rear side of the engine).*

11   After adjusting, recheck the clearance with the feeler gauge to make sure it wasn't changed when the locknut was tightened.

12   Now measure the other valve, following the same procedure you used for the first valve. Make sure to use a feeler gauge of the specified thickness.

13   With both of the clearances within the Specifications, install the valve cover and timing hole cap. Use a new O-ring on the cap if the old one is hardened, deteriorated or damaged.

14   Install the fuel tank and heat shield and reconnect the cable to the negative terminal of the battery.

21 Idle speed - check and adjustment

1   Before adjusting the idle speed, make sure the valve clearances and spark plug gap are correct. Also, turn the handlebars back-and-forth and see if the idle speed changes as this is done. If it does, the throttle cable may not be adjusted correctly, or it may be worn out. Be sure to correct this problem before proceeding.

2   The engine should be at normal operating temperature, which is usually reached after 10 to 15 minutes of stop and go riding. Make sure the transmission is in Neutral.

3   Turn the throttle stop screw **(see illustration 16.9)** until the idle speed listed in this Chapter's Specifications is obtained.

4   Snap the throttle open and shut a few times, then recheck the idle speed. If necessary, repeat the adjustment procedure.

5   If a smooth, steady idle can't be achieved, the fuel/air mixture may be incorrect. Refer to Chapter 3 for additional carburetor information.

22 Fasteners - check

1   Since vibration of the machine tends to loosen fasteners, all nuts, bolts, screws, etc. should be periodically checked for proper tightness. Also make sure all cotter pins or other safety fasteners are correctly installed.

2   Pay particular attention to the following:

Spark plug
Engine oil drain plug(s)
Oil filter cover bolts
Gearshift lever
Brake pedal
Footpegs
Engine mount bolts
Shock absorber mount bolts
Front axle nuts
Rear axle nuts
Skid plate bolts

3   If a torque wrench is available, use it along with the torque specifications at the beginning of this, or other, Chapters.

23 Suspension - check

1   The suspension components must be maintained in top operating condition to ensure rider safety. Loose, worn or damaged suspension parts decrease the vehicle's stability and control.

2   Lock the front brake and push on the handlebars to compress the front shock absorbers several times. See if they move up-and-down smoothly without binding. If binding is felt, the shocks should be inspected as described in Chapter 5.

3   Check the tightness of all front suspension nuts and bolts to be sure none have worked loose.

4   Inspect the rear shock absorbers for fluid leakage and tightness of the mounting nuts and bolts. If leakage is found, the shock should be replaced.

5   Support the vehicle securely upright with its rear wheel off the ground. Grab the swingarm on each side, just ahead of the axle. Rock the swingarm from side to side - there should be no discernible movement at the rear. If there's a little movement or a slight clicking can be heard, make sure the swingarm pivot shafts are tight. If the pivot shafts are tight but movement is still noticeable, the swingarm will have to be removed and the bearings replaced as described in Chapter 5.

6   Inspect the tightness of the rear suspension nuts and bolts.

24   Steering system - inspection and toe-in adjustment

Inspection

1   This vehicle is equipped with a ball bearing at the lower end of the steering shaft and a hard rubber bushing at the upper end, which can become dented, rough or loose during normal use of the machine. In extreme cases, worn or loose parts can cause steering wobble that is potentially dangerous.

2   To check the bearings, block the rear wheels so the vehicle can't roll, jack up the front end and support it securely on jackstands.

3   Point the wheel straight ahead and slowly move the handlebars from side-to-side. Dents or roughness in the bearing or bushing will be felt and the bars will not move smoothly. **Note:** *Make sure any hesitation in movement is not being caused by the cables and wiring harnesses that run to the handlebars.*

4   If the handlebars don't move smoothly, or if they move horizontally, refer to Chapter 5 to remove and inspect the steering shaft bushing and bearing.

Toe-in adjustment

Refer to illustration 24.10

5   Roll the vehicle forward onto a level surface and stop it with the front wheels pointing straight ahead.

6   Make a mark at the front and center of each tire, even with the centerline of the front hub.

7   Measure the distance between the marks with a toe-in gauge or steel tape measure.

8   Have an assistant push the vehicle backward while you watch the marks on the tires. Stop pushing when the tires have rotated exactly one-half turn, so the marks are at the backs of the tires.

24.10 Hold and turn the tie rod by placing an open end wrench on the flats as shown; loosen the locknuts (arrows) so the tie rod can be turned

9   Again, measure the distance between the marks. Subtract the front measurement from the rear measurement to get toe-in.

10   If toe-in is not as specified in this Chapter's Specifications, hold each tie-rod with a wrench on the flats and loosen the locknuts **(see illustration)**. Turn the tie-rods an equal amount to change toe-in. When toe-in is set correctly, tighten the locknuts to the torque listed in this Chapter's Specifications.

Notes

Chapter 2 Part A
Engine, clutch and transmission (400 and 450 models)

Contents

Specifications

Note: *For wear tolerance and service limit specifications, refer to Chapter 2C.*

General
Bore
    400 models .... 86 mm (3.39 inches)
    450 models .... 90 mm (3.54 inches)
Stroke .... 68 mm (2.68 inches)
Displacement
    400 models .... 394.9 cc (24.1 cubic inches)
    450 models .... 432.6 cc (26.4 cubic inches)

Torque specifications
Valve cover bolts .... Not specified
Cylinder head
    Bolts .... Not specified
    Cap nuts .... 39 Nm (29 ft-lbs) (1)
Rocker assembly bolt .... 7 Nm (61 in-lbs)
Cam chain tensioner
    Cap screw .... 4 Nm (35 in-lbs)
    External tensioner mounting bolts .... 12 Nm (108 in-lbs)
    Tensioner slipper/mainshaft bearing retainer bolts .... Not specified
Cam sprocket bolts .... 20 Nm (14 ft-lbs)
Cylinder base bolts .... Not specified
Front crankcase cover bolts .... Not specified
Centrifugal clutch locknut .... 120 Nm (87 ft-lbs) (2)
Change clutch spring bolts .... 12 Nm (108 in-lbs)
Change clutch locknut .... 110 Nm (80 ft-lbs) (2)
Oil pump
    To-engine bolts .... Not specified
    Cover screw .... 4 Nm (35 in-lbs)

Torque specifications (continued)

Shift pedal pinch bolt	
1995 through 2001 models	16 Nm (144 in-lbs)
2002 and later models	20 Nm (168 in-lbs)
External shift linkage return spring pin	22 Nm (12 ft-lbs) (3)
Gearshift plate and drum shifter bolt	
400 models	
450 models	
2001 and earlier..	12 Nm (108 in-lbs (3)
2002 and later...	16 Nm (144 in-lbs)
Stopper arm bolt...	12 Nm (108 in-lbs)
Gearshift arm bolt	25 Nm (18 ft-lbs) (4)
Crankcase bolts..	Not specified

1) Use engine oil on the threads.
2) Use a new locknut with engine oil on the threads. Stake the locknut.
3) Use non-permanent thread locking agent on the threads.
4) Use a new lockwasher.

1   General information

The engine/transmission unit is of the air-cooled, single-cylinder four-stroke design. The two valves are operated by pushrods and solid lifters. The lifters are operated by a camshaft mounted in the crankcase, which in turn is chain driven off the crankshaft. The engine/transmission assembly is constructed from aluminum alloy. The crankcase is divided vertically.

The crankshaft centerline is parallel to the centerline of the vehicle.

The crankcase incorporates a wet sump, pressure-fed lubrication system which uses a gear-driven rotor-type oil pump, an oil filter and separate strainer screen and an oil temperature warning switch.

Power from the crankshaft is routed to the transmission via two clutches. The centrifugal clutch, which engages as engine speed is increased, connects the crankshaft to the change clutch, which is of the wet, multi-plate type. The change clutch transmits power to the transmission; it's engaged and disengaged automatically when the shift lever is moved from one gear position to another. The transmission has five forward gears and one reverse gear.

2   Operations possible with the engine in the frame

The components and assemblies listed below can be removed without having to remove the engine from the frame. If, however, a number of areas require attention at the same time, removal of the engine is recommended.

Valve cover
Cylinder head
Rocker arms and pushrods
Cylinder and piston
Gear selector mechanism external
components
Recoil starter
Starter motor
Starter reduction gears
Starter clutch
Alternator rotor and stator
Clutches (centrifugal clutch and change clutch)
Cam chain tensioner
Camshaft
Oil pump

3   Operations requiring engine removal

It is necessary to remove the engine/transmission assembly from the frame and separate the crankcase halves to gain access to the fol-

lowing components:

Crankshaft and connecting rod
Balancer
Transmission shafts
Shift drum and forks

4   Major engine repair - general note

1   It is not always easy to determine when or if an engine should be completely overhauled, as a number of factors must be considered.
2   High mileage is not necessarily an indication that an overhaul is needed, while low mileage, on the other hand, does not preclude the need for an overhaul. Frequency of servicing is probably the single most important consideration. An engine that has regular and frequent oil and filter changes, as well as other required maintenance, will most likely give many miles of reliable service. Conversely, a neglected engine, or one which has not been broken in properly, may require an overhaul very early in its life.
3   Exhaust smoke and excessive oil consumption are both indications that piston rings and/or valve guides are in need of attention. Make sure oil leaks are not responsible before deciding that the rings and guides are bad. Refer to Chapter 1 and perform a cylinder compression check to determine for certain the nature and extent of the work required.
4   If the engine is making obvious knocking or rumbling noises, the connecting rod and/or main bearings are probably at fault.
5   Loss of power, rough running, excessive valve train noise and high fuel consumption rates may also point to the need for an overhaul, especially if they are all present at the same time. If a complete tune-up does not remedy the situation, major mechanical work is the only solution.
6   An engine overhaul generally involves restoring the internal parts to the specifications of a new engine. During an overhaul the piston rings are replaced and the cylinder walls are bored and/or honed. If a rebore is done, then a new piston is also required. The crankshaft and connecting rod are permanently assembled, so if one of these components needs to be replaced both must be. Generally the valves are serviced as well, since they are usually in less than perfect condition at this point. While the engine is being overhauled, other components such as the carburetor and the starter motor can be rebuilt also. The end result should be a like-new engine that will give as many trouble-free miles as the original.
7   Before beginning the engine overhaul, read through all of the related procedures to familiarize yourself with the scope and requirements of the job. Overhauling an engine is not all that difficult, but it is time consuming. Plan on the vehicle being tied up for a minimum of two (2) weeks. Check on the availability of parts and make sure that any necessary special tools, equipment and supplies are obtained in advance.

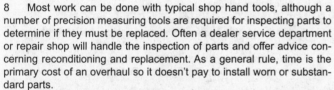

5.4 Remove the bolts and collars and take off the engine side covers (right side cover shown)

5.5 Disconnect the starter cable and two ground cables (arrows)

8   Most work can be done with typical shop hand tools, although a number of precision measuring tools are required for inspecting parts to determine if they must be replaced. Often a dealer service department or repair shop will handle the inspection of parts and offer advice concerning reconditioning and replacement. As a general rule, time is the primary cost of an overhaul so it doesn't pay to install worn or substandard parts.

9   As a final note, to ensure maximum life and minimum trouble from a rebuilt engine, everything must be assembled with care in a spotlessly clean environment.

5   Engine - removal and installation

Note: *Engine removal and installation should be done with the aid of an assistant to avoid damage or injury that could occur if the engine is dropped. A hydraulic floor jack should be used to support and lower the engine if possible (they can be rented at low cost).*

Removal

Refer to illustrations 5.4, 5.5, 5.13a, 5.13b and 5.13c

1   Drain the engine oil and disconnect the spark plug wire (see Chapter 1).

2   Remove the fuel tank, carburetor, air cleaner housing and exhaust system (see Chapter 3). The choke and throttle cables can be left connected. Plug the carburetor intake openings with rags.

3   Remove the front fenders (see Chapter 7).

4   Remove the bolts and collars and take the right and left side covers off the engine **(see illustration)**.

5   Disconnect the starter cable and two ground cables from the engine (it's secured by one of the starter mounting bolts **(see illustration)** (see Chapter 8).

6   Label and disconnect the following wires (refer to Chapters 4 or 8 for component location if necessary):

Ignition pulse generator
Alternator
Oil temperature, reverse and neutral switches
Speed sensor (1996 through 2001 models)
Control motor (electric shift models)

7   Disconnect the reverse cable (Section 16).

8   Remove the shift pedal (see Section 18).

9   Remove the front driveshaft and loosen the clamps on the rear driveshaft boot that connects the swingarm to the engine (see Chapter 5).

10   Disconnect the crankcase breather tube **(see illustration 9.4 in Chapter 3)**.

11   Disconnect the oil cooler hoses from the engine (see Section 13).

12   Support the engine securely from below.

13   Remove the engine mounting bolts, nuts and brackets at the top, lower left and lower right **(see illustrations)**.

14   Have an assistant help you lift the engine. As you lift, pull the engine forward to disengage the rear driveshaft from the engine. The driveshaft

5.13a Remove the engine mounts at the top . . .

5.13b . . . lower left . . .

5.13c . . . and lower right

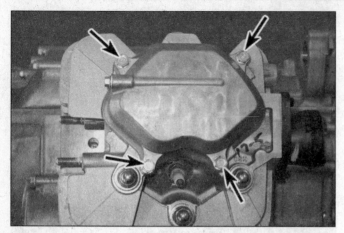

6.2 Remove the valve cover bolts (arrows) and lift off the cover . . .

6.3 . . . and remove the gasket and O-ring (arrow)

is mounted inside the left side of the swingarm (refer to Chapter 5 if necessary). Remove the engine to the left side of the vehicle.
15   Slowly lower the engine to a suitable work surface.

Installation

16   Check the rubber engine supports for wear or damage and replace them if necessary before installing the engine.
17   Coat the driveshaft splines with moly-based grease. Install the engine from the left side of the vehicle and move it rearward to engage the driveshaft with the engine (refer to Chapter 5 if necessary).
18   Lift the engine to align the mounting bolt holes, then install all of the brackets, bolts and nuts, but don't tighten them yet.
19   Install the lower left engine hanger bracket and rubber dampers, with the wide sides of the dampers facing the engine **(see illustration 5.13b)**. Install the bracket bolts and the hanger through-bolt and nut. Tighten the through-bolt and nut, then the bracket bolts, to the torque listed in this Chapter's Specifications.
20   Install the rubber dampers in the lower right engine mounting boss **(see illustration 5.13c)**. Install the collar, through-bolt and nut, then tighten the through-bolt and nut to the torque listed in this Chapter's Specifications.
21   Loosely install the upper engine hanger plate bracket, rubber dampers, through-bolt and nut **(see illustration 5.13a)**. Tighten the bracket bolts, then the through-bolt and nut, to the torques listed in this Chapter's Specifications.

22   The remainder of installation is the reverse of the removal steps, with the following additions:
   a) *Use new gaskets at all exhaust pipe connections.*
   b) *Adjust the throttle cable and reverse selector cable following the procedures in Chapter 1.*
   c) *Fill the engine with oil and check the differential oil level, also following the procedures in Chapter 1. Run the engine and check for leaks.*

6   Valve cover - removal and installation

Note: *The valve cover can be removed with the engine in the frame. If the engine has been removed, ignore the steps which don't apply.*

Removal

Refer to illustrations 6.2 and 6.3
1   Remove the fuel tank and its heat shield (see Chapter 4).
2   Remove the valve cover bolts and lift off the cover **(see illustration)**. If it won't come easily, tap it from the side with a rubber mallet. Be careful not to damage the gasket surfaces of the cover or cylinder head by prying the cover loose.
3   Remove the valve cover gasket and O-ring **(see illustration)**.
4   Clean all traces of old gasket from the surfaces of the valve cover and cylinder head. Check the valve cover for cracks or damaged sealing surfaces.

Installation

5   Install a new gasket and O-ring on the cylinder head. Install the valve cover bolts and tighten them evenly, in a criss-cross pattern. Tighten the bolts securely, but don't distort the valve cover or strip the threads.

7   Rocker arms, pushrods and cylinder head - removal and installation

Note: *Refer to Chapter 2C for inspection procedures.*

Removal

Refer to illustrations 7.5, 7.6a, 7.6b, 7.6c and 7.9
1   Remove the carburetor, intake manifold, exhaust pipe and fuel tank mounting brackets (see Chapter 4).
2   Remove the valve cover (see Section 6).
3   Place the piston at TDC on the compression stroke (see *Valve clearances - adjustment* in Chapter 1).
4   Disconnect the spark plug wire (see Chapter 1 if necessary).
5   Remove the two cylinder head bolts **(see illustration)**. Loosen the

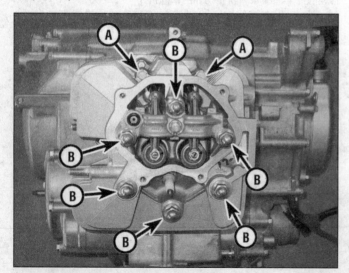

7.5 Remove the small bolts (A) first, then loosen the nuts (B) in a criss-cross pattern in two or three stages

7.6a Lift off the rocker assembly and locate the dowels (arrows)

7.6b Label the rocker arms, unscrew the rocker assembly bolt (arrow) . . .

cylinder head nuts in two or three stages, in a criss-cross pattern, then remove the nuts and washers. **Note:** *Don't remove the small bolt in the center of the rocker assembly. It holds the assembly together.*

6   Lift the rocker arm assembly off the cylinder head. Locate the dowels **(see illustration)**. They may have come off the rocker arm assembly or remained in the cylinder head. Label the rocker arms so they can be reinstalled in their original locations. Unscrew the rocker assembly bolt(s). Slide out the rocker shaft and remove the rocker arms **(see illustrations)**.

7   Label the pushrods so they can be reinstalled right-side up and in their original locations (exhaust or intake), then lift them from the engine **(see illustration 8.6)**.

8   Lift the cylinder head off the cylinder. If the head is stuck, tap around the side of the head with a rubber mallet to jar it loose, or use two wooden dowels inserted into the intake and exhaust ports to lever the head off. Don't attempt to pry the head off by inserting a screwdriver between the head and the cylinder block - you'll damage the sealing surfaces.

9   Cover the pushrod holes with a clean shop towel to prevent the entry of debris. Once this is done, remove the head gasket and the two dowel pins from the cylinder **(see illustration)**.

Installation

Refer to illustration 7.12

10   Install the two dowel pins, then lay the new gasket in place on the cylinder. Never reuse the old gasket and don't use any type of gasket sealant.

7.6c . . . pull out the rocker shaft and remove the rocker arms from the bracket

11   Carefully lower the cylinder head over the studs and dowels.

12   Install the pushrods. If you're reusing the old ones, return them to their original positions. Also be sure the ends of pushrods fit in the lifter pockets, not off to the side **(see illustration)**.

13   Make sure the rocker assembly dowels are in position **(see illus-**

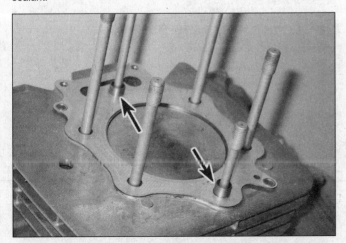

7.9 Lift the cylinder head off and remove the gasket and dowels (arrows)

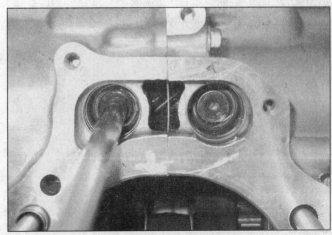

7.12 Be sure to install the pushrod ends in the pockets of the lifters, not off to the side

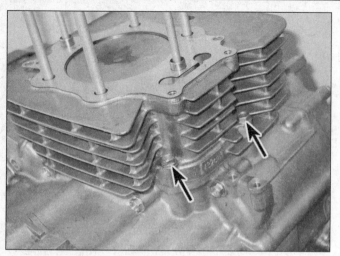

8.2 Remove the bolts that attach the cylinder to the crankcase (arrows)

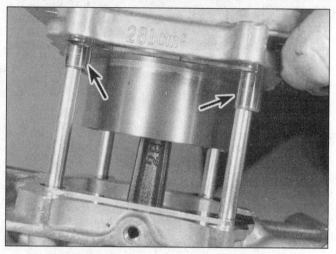

8.4 When you lift the cylinder off, the dowels (arrows) may come off with the cylinder or stay in the crankcase

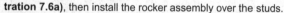

tration 7.6a), then install the rocker assembly over the studs.

14   Install the washers and cap nuts on the studs.

15   Tighten the cap nuts in two or three stages to the torque listed in this Chapter's Specifications, working in a criss-cross pattern.

16   Tighten the bolts to the torque listed in this Chapter's Specifications.

17   Install all parts removed for access.

18   Change the engine oil and adjust the valve clearances (see Chapter 1).

8   Cylinder - removal, inspection and installation

Removal

Refer to illustrations 8.2, 8.4 and 8.5

1   Remove the valve cover, rocker arms, pushrods and cylinder head (see Sections 6 and 7). Make sure the crankshaft is positioned at Top Dead Center (TDC).

2   Remove the cylinder base gasket and locate the dowel pins **(see illustration)**. The dowel pins may have come off with the cylinder head or still be in the crankcase.

3   Remove two bolts that secure the base of the cylinder to the crank-

case **(see illustration 8.2)**.

4   Lift the cylinder straight up to remove it **(see illustration)**. If it's stuck, tap around its perimeter with a soft-faced hammer (but don't tap on the cooling fins or they may break). Don't attempt to pry between the cylinder and the crankcase, as you'll ruin the sealing surfaces.

5   Locate the dowel pins (they may have come off with the cylinder or still be in the crankcase). Be careful not to let these drop into the engine. Stuff rags around the piston **(see illustration)** and remove the gasket and all traces of old gasket material from the surfaces of the cylinder and the crankcase.

6   Refer to Chapter 2C for inspection procedures.

Installation

Refer to illustrations 8.8 and 8.10

7   Lubricate the cylinder bore with plenty of clean engine oil. Apply a thin film of moly-based grease to the piston skirt.

8   Thoroughly clean the cylinder mating surface on the crankcase. Apply a small dab of silicone sealant to each of the three points where the crankcase seam meets the surface **(see illustration)**. Install the dowel pins, then lower a new cylinder base gasket over them.

9   Attach a piston ring compressor to the piston and compress the piston rings. A large hose clamp can be used instead - just make sure it doesn't scratch the piston, and don't tighten it too much.

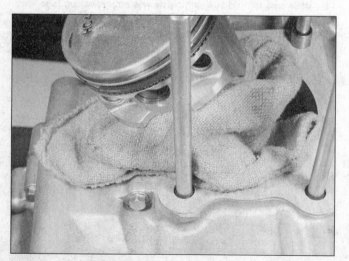

8.5 Pack clean rags into the crankcase opening to keep out debris

8.8 Install the cylinder base gasket and both dowels (arrows) on the crankcase

8.10 If you're very careful, the cylinder can be installed over the rings without a ring compressor, but a compressor is recommended

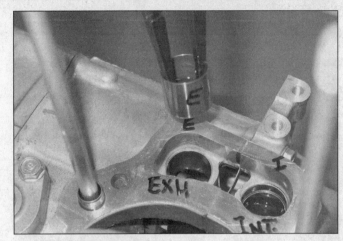

9.2 Measure the inside diameter of the lifter bores and compare it to the outside diameter of the lifters

10   Install the cylinder over the studs and carefully lower it down until the piston crown fits into the cylinder liner **(see illustration)**. Push down on the cylinder, making sure the piston doesn't get cocked sideways, until the bottom of the cylinder liner slides down past the piston rings. A wood or plastic hammer handle can be used to gently tap the cylinder down, but don't use too much force or the piston will be damaged.

11   Remove the piston ring compressor or hose clamp, being careful not to scratch the piston.

12   The remainder of installation is the reverse of the removal steps.

9   Valve lifters - removal and installation

Removal

Refer to illustration 9.2

1   Remove the valve cover, rocker arms and pushrods, cylinder head and cylinder (see Sections 6 and 7).

2   Label the lifters so they can be returned to their correct bores **(see illustration)**. Lift the lifters out.

3   Refer to Chapter 2C for inspection procedures.

Installation

4   Lubricate the lifters on the camshaft contact surfaces, sides and pushrod pockets with molybdenum disulfide grease. Install the lifters in their bores.

5   The remainder of installation is the reverse of the removal steps.

10   Centrifugal clutch - removal, inspection and installation

Removal

Refer to illustrations 10.5a, 10.5b, 10.6, 10.7a, 10.7b and 10.8

1   Drain the engine oil (see Chapter 1).

2   Disconnect the oil cooler hoses (see Section 13).

3   Remove the right engine cover **(see illustration 5.4)**.

4   If you're working on an electric shift 450 model, remove the front driveshaft and shift control motor (see Chapters 5 and 8).

5   Remove the front crankcase cover bolts **(see illustration)**. Separate the cover from the engine, taking care not to damage the gasket surfaces. Remove the cover gasket and O-ring and locate the three dowel pins **(see illustration)**. The dowels may have come off with the cover or stayed in the engine.

10.5a Remove the cover bolts (arrows), take off the cover . . .

10.5b . . . locate the dowels (arrows) and remove the gasket and O-ring

10.6 Grind or file away the staked portion of the locknut lip (arrow)

10.7a Hold the clutch with a tool like this one

10.7b Unscrew the nut and remove the washer; its OUT SIDE mark faces (if equipped) away from the engine

10.8 If the clutch won't come off easily, remove it with a puller like this one

10.9 While holding the drum, it should be possible to turn the weight assembly only in the direction of the arrow; if it turns both ways or neither way, remove it and inspect the one-way clutch

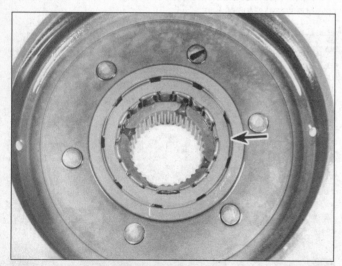

10.11 Lift the one-way clutch (arrow) out of the drum and check it for wear and damage

6   Grind or file away the staked portion of the clutch nut, taking care not to get metal particles in the engine (**see illustration**).
7   Hold the clutch with a removal tool so it won't turn (**see illustration**). Remove the nut, then the washer (**see illustration**).
8   Pull the centrifugal clutch weight assembly and drum off the crankshaft. If it won't come easily, use a special tool (Honda part no. 07933-HB3000A or equivalent) (**see illustration**).

Inspection

Refer to illustrations 10.9, 10.11, 10.12, 10.13a, 10.13b, 10.13c, 10.13d, 10.14, 10.21, 10.22, 10.23, 10.26a and 10.26b

9   Hold the drum in one hand and try to rotate the weight assembly with the other hand (**see illustration**). It should rotate counterclockwise only. If it rotates both ways or neither way, disassemble the centrifugal clutch for further inspection.
10   Lift the weight assembly out of the drum.
11   Lift the one-way clutch out of the drum (**see illustration**). Check the one-way clutch rollers for signs of wear or scoring. The rotors should be unmarked with no signs of wear such as pitting or flat spots. Replace the one-way clutch if it's worn.
12   Measure the thickness of the lining material on the weights at the

10.12 Measure the thickness of the friction material at the three thick points on each weight (arrows)

10.13a Pry the snap-rings loose from the posts

10.13b Lift off the outer plate . . .

10.13c . . . the clutch spring (arrow) . . .

10.13d . . . and the inner plate; the lip on the inner plate (arrow) faces away from the weight assembly

three thickest points **(see illustration)**. If it's thinner than the minimum listed in this Chapter's Specifications, replace the weights as a set.

13   Pry the clips off the drive plate posts **(see illustration)**. Lift off the outer plate, clutch spring and inner plate **(see illustrations)**.

14   Check the springs for breakage and the weights for wear or damage and replace them as necessary. If the weights need to be removed from the drive plate, unhook the springs **(see illustration)** and lift the weights off the posts.

15   Measure the inside diameter of the drum and replace if it it's greater than the limit listed in this Chapter's Specifications.

16   Measure the free length of the clutch weight springs and replace them if they've stretched to longer than the limit listed in this Chapter's Specifications.

17   Check the drive plate posts for wear or damage and replace the drive plate if problems are found.

18   Place the clutch spring on a flat surface (such as a piece of glass) with its concave side down. Measure the height of the spring center from the surface with a vernier caliper. If the spring has been flattened to less than the limit listed in this Chapter's Specifications, replace it.

19   Place the weights in the drive plate with their OUT SIDE marks facing upward **(see illustration 10.14)**. Install the springs, noting how their ends are located.

20   Place the inner plate on the weights with its lip upward **(see illustration 10.13d)**.

10.14 Remove the springs and slip the weights off the drive plate posts; the OUT SIDE mark on each weight faces away from the drive plate

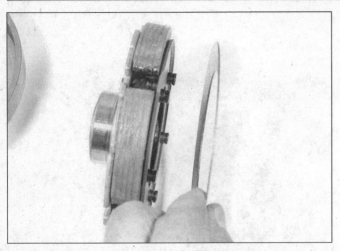

10.21 Install the clutch spring with its concave side toward the weight assembly

10.22 Install the outer plate with its locating pins (arrows) facing away from the weight assembly

21 Place the clutch spring on the inner plate with its concave side toward the plate **(see illustration)**.

22 Place the outer plate on the clutch spring with its dimples upward **(see illustration)**.

23 Place a pair of C-clamps or similar clamps on the outer plate and tighten them until the circlip grooves in the posts are exposed, then squeeze the clips onto the posts with pliers **(see illustration)**.

24 Install the one-way clutch in the drum with its OUT SIDE marking facing out **(see illustration 10.13d)**. Lubricate the one-way clutch with engine oil.

25 Install the weight assembly in the drum **(see illustration 10.9)**.

26 Rotate the inner race of the ball bearing inside the cover with a finger. If the bearing is rough, loose or noisy, remove it with a blind hole puller, then drive in a new bearing with a bearing driver or socket that bears against the bearing outer race **(see illustrations)**.

Installation

27 Slip the centrifugal clutch onto the crankshaft. Engage the drum splines with the splines on the crankshaft. Rotate the weight assembly slightly and align the drive plate splines with the primary gear, then push the centrifugal clutch all the way on.

28 Install the washer **(see illustration 10.7b)**.

29 Oil the threads and seating surface of a new locknut, then install the locknut. Hold the clutch with a holding tool and tighten the nut to the torque listed in this Chapter's Specifications.

10.23 Place a pair of clamps on the assembly and compress it so the post grooves are exposed, then squeeze the snap-rings into place with a pair of pliers

30 Stake the lip of the locknut with a hammer and punch **(see illustration 10.6)**.

31 Make sure the dowels are in position and install a new gasket **(see illustration 10.5b)**.

10.26a Remove the cover bearing if necessary with a slide hammer and blind hole puller . . .

10.26b . . . and drive in a new one with a driver or socket the same diameter as the bearing outer race

11.2a Slide the thrust washer and lifter lever (arrows) off the shaft . . .

11.2b . . . remove the ball retainer, noting how the spring fits on it . . .

11.2c . . . and remove the lifter cam; on installation, be sure the O-ring (right arrow) is reinstalled and the lifter cam fits over the pin (left arrow)

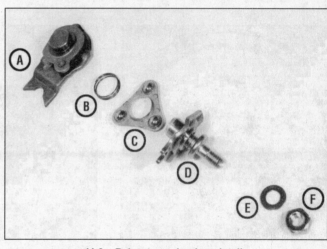

11.3a Release mechanism details

A	Lifter cam	D	Adjuster bolt
B	Spring	E	Washer
C	Ball retainer	F	Adjuster bolt locknut

32   Thread the cover bolts into their holes (see illustration 10.5a). Tighten the cover bolts in two or three stages, in a criss-cross pattern.
33   The remainder of installation is the reverse of the removal steps.
34   Refill the engine oil (see Chapter 1).

11 Change clutch - removal, inspection and installation

Release mechanism

Removal

Refer to illustrations 11.2a, 11.2b and 11.2c

1   Remove the front crankcase cover (Section 10).
2   Unscrew the clutch adjusting nut completely and remove its washer (see Chapter 1). Remove the release mechanism components from the crankcase and the cover (see illustrations).

Inspection

Refer to illustrations 11.3a and 11.3b

3   Check for visible wear or damage at the contact points of the lever and cam and the friction points of the cam, ball retainer and lifter plate

(see illustrations). Check the spring for bending or distortion. Replace any parts that show problems. Replace the lifter plate O-ring in the crankcase cover whenever it's removed.

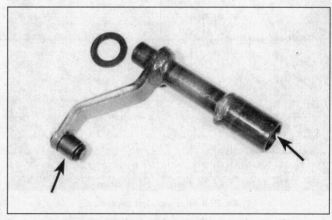

11.3b Check the clutch lever for a worn roller (left arrow) and damaged splines (right arrow)

11.7a Hold the clutch with a tool like this one . . .

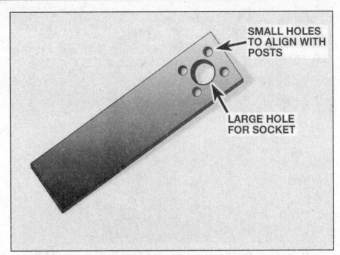

SMALL HOLES TO ALIGN WITH POSTS

LARGE HOLE FOR SOCKET

11.7b . . . or you can make a holding tool from flat steel stock

11.8a Remove the four bolts and the lifter plate (arrow) . . .

11.8b . . . and remove the pressure plate springs

11.8c Grind or file away the staked portion of the locknut (arrow), then unscrew it

11.8d Pull off the clutch center . . .

Installation

4   Installation is the reverse of the removal steps, with the following additions:

a) *Make sure the lifter plate engages the pin inside the crankcase cover* (**see illustration 11.2c**).

b) *Make sure the lever engages the cam* (**see illustration 11.2a**).

5   Refill the engine oil and adjust the clutch (see Chapter 1).

Clutch

Removal

Refer to illustrations 11.7a, 11.7b and 11.8a through 11.8i

6   Remove the front crankcase cover and the centrifugal clutch (Section 10). Remove the release mechanism as described above.

7   Note that if an air wrench is not available, the clutch needs to be prevented from rotating while removing the locknut. The Honda service tool (part no. 07HGB-001010A or 07HGB-001010B) resembles a steering wheel puller and is attached to the spring posts on the pressure plate (**see illustration**). It is then held with a breaker bar while the nut is loosened with a socket. A similar tool can be fabricated from metal stock (**see illustration**).

8   Refer to the accompanying illustrations to remove the clutch components (**see illustrations**).

11.8e ... remove the outer friction plate ...

11.8f ... then the metal plate, then remove the remaining friction and metal plates

11.8g Remove the pressure plate from the clutch housing ...

11.8h ... then remove the thrust washer and clutch housing ...

11.8i ... and the clutch outer guide

11.9 Clutch inspection points

A Pressure plate posts	D Clutch housing bearing
B Pressure plate friction	surface
surface	E Primary driven gear
C Clutch housing slots	

Inspection

Refer to illustrations 11.9, 11.11, 11.12, 11.13, 11.16 and 11.17

9   Check the bolt posts and the friction surface on the pressure plate for damaged threads, scoring or wear (see illustration). Replace the pressure plate if any defects are found.

10   Check the edges of the slots in the clutch housing for indentations made by the friction plate tabs (see illustration 11.9). If the indenta-

tions are deep they can prevent clutch release, so the housing should be replaced with a new one. If the indentations can be removed easily with a file, the life of the housing can be prolonged to an extent. Also,

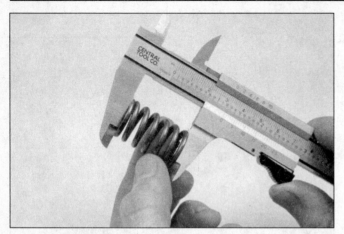

11.11 Measure the clutch spring free length

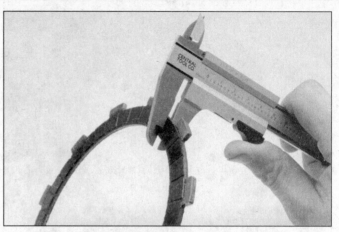

11.12 Measure the thickness of the friction plates

check the driven gear teeth for cracks, chips and excessive wear and the springs on the back side for breakage. If the gear is worn or damaged or the springs are broken, the clutch housing must be replaced with a new one. Check the bearing surface in the center of the clutch housing for score marks, scratches and excessive wear.

11   Measure the free length of the clutch springs **(see illustration)** and compare the results to this Chapter's Specifications. If the springs have sagged, or if cracks are noted, replace them with new ones as a set.

12   If the lining material of the friction plates smells burnt or if it is glazed, new parts are required. If the metal clutch plates are scored or discolored, they must be replaced with new ones. Measure the thickness of the friction plates **(see illustration)** and replace with new parts any friction plates that are worn.

13   Lay the metal plates, one at a time, on a perfectly flat surface (such as a piece of plate glass) and check for warpage by trying to slip a feeler gauge between the flat surface and the plate **(see illustration)**. The feeler gauge should be the same thickness as the maximum warp listed in this Chapter's Specifications. Do this at several places around the plate's circumference. If the feeler gauge can be slipped under the plate, it is warped and should be replaced with a new one.

14   Check the tabs on the friction plates for excessive wear and mushroomed edges. They can be cleaned up with a file if the deformation is not severe. Check the friction plates for warpage as described in Step 14.

15   Check the clutch outer guide for score marks, heat discoloration and evidence of excessive wear **(see illustration 11.8i)**. Measure its inner and outer diameter and compare them to the values listed in the Chapter 2C Specifications (a dealer can do this if you don't have preci-

11.13 Check the metal plates for warpage

sion measuring equipment). Replace the outer guide if it's worn beyond the specified limits. Also measure the end of the transmission mainshaft where the outer guide rides; if it's worn to less than the limit listed in the Chapter 2C Specifications, replace the mainshaft (Section 20).

16   Check the clutch lifter plate for wear and damage. Rotate the inner race of the bearing and check for roughness, looseness or excessive noise **(see illustration)**.

17   Check the splines of the clutch center for wear or damage and replace the clutch center if problems are found **(see illustration)**.

11.16 Check the ball bearing in the center of the lifter plate for roughness, looseness or noise

11.17 Check the clutch center splines for wear or damage

11.20a Install a friction plate first, then a metal plate, then alternate the remaining friction and metal plates . . .

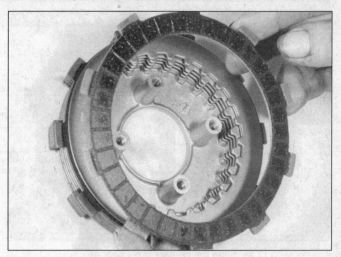

11.20b . . .a friction plate goes on last

11.21a Install the clutch center . . .

11.21b . . . then install the assembly on the mainshaft

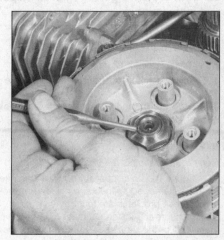

11.24 Stake the new locknut

Installation

Refer to illustrations 11.20a, 11.20b, 11.21a, 11.21b, 11.24 and 11.25

18   Lubricate the inner and outer surfaces of the clutch outer guide with moly-based grease and install it on the crankshaft.

19   Install the clutch housing and thrust washer on the mainshaft **(see illustration 11.8h)**.

20   Coat the friction plates with engine oil. Install a friction plate on the disc, followed by a metal plate, then alternate the remaining friction and metal plates until they're all installed (there are six friction plates and five metal plates). Friction plates go on first and last, so the friction material contacts the metal surfaces of the clutch center and the pressure plate **(see illustrations)**.

21   Install the clutch center over the posts, then install the assembly in the clutch housing **(see illustrations)**.

22   Install the washer on the mainshaft **(see illustration 11.8d)**.

23   Coat the threads of a new locknut with clean engine oil and install it on the mainshaft. Hold the clutch with one of the methods described in Step 7 and tighten the locknut to the torque listed in this Chapter's Specifications.

24   Stake the locknut with a hammer and punch **(see illustration)**.

25   Install the clutch springs and the lifter plate **(see illustration)**. Tighten the bolts next to the grooves first, then tighten the other two bolts to the torque listed in this Chapter's Specifications.

26   The remainder of installation is the reverse of the removal steps.

11.25 Install the springs and lifter plate and install the bearing in the lifter plate if it was removed

12.2a Slide the primary drive gear off . . .

12.2b . . . and remove the thrust washer (arrow)

12 Primary drive gear - removal, inspection and installation

Removal

Refer to illustrations 12.2a and 12.2b

1   Remove the centrifugal clutch and change clutch (Sections 10 and 11).
2   Slide the primary drive gear off the crankshaft and remove the washer **(see illustrations)**.

Inspection

Refer to illustrations 12.4 and 12.5

3   Check the drive gear for obvious damage such as a worn inner bushing, damaged splines and chipped or broken teeth. Replace it if any of these problems are found.
4   Measure the inside diameter of the bushing at the outer end and inner end of the gear **(see illustration)**. A Honda dealer or machine shop can do this if you don't have precision measuring equipment. If either bushing is worn beyond the diameter listed in the Chapter 2C Specifications, replace the gear.
5   Measure the crankshaft at the two points where the bushings ride **(see illustration)**. If either point is worn to less than the diameter listed in the Chapter2C Specifications, replace the crankshaft (see Chapter 2C).

Installation

6   Installation is the reverse of the removal steps.

13 Oil pump and cooler - removal, inspection and installation

Oil pump

Removal

Refer to illustrations 13.1 and 13.2

1   Remove the front crankcase cover and centrifugal clutch (Section 10). If the cover O-ring and dowel pin stay with the oil pump, remove them **(see illustration)**.
2   If you're planning to disassemble the pump, remove its snap-ring and washer now, while the pump is on the engine **(see illustration)** (this can also be done later, but it will be easier while the pump is still bolted in position). Remove the oil pump mounting bolts and take the pump off the engine.
3   Remove the mounting bolts, then pull the pump out of the engine **(see illustration 13.2)**.
4   Refer to Chapter 2C for inspection procedures.

Installation

5   Installation is the reverse of removal, with the following additions:

12.4 Measure the diameter of the bushings (arrow); there's one inside each end of the gear

12.5 Measure the points on the crankshaft where the primary drive gear rides (arrows)

13.1 Remove the front cover dowel and O-ring (arrows) if they stay in the oil pump

13.2 Remove the pump mounting bolts (arrows)

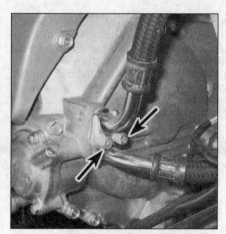

13.7 Unscrew the Allen bolts (arrows), remove the retainer plate, pull the oil lines out of the front crankcase cover and remove the O-rings

13.8 Unbolt the hose retainer and oil cooler brackets (arrows), then remove the oil cooler and hoses

13.9a Remove the hose retainer bolts and detach the hoses from the oil cooler . . .

a) Engage the oil pump shaft with the balancer shaft when you install the pump on the engine. Tighten the oil pump bolts securely, but don't overtighten them and strip the threads.

b) Make sure the front cover dowel and O-ring are in position (see illustration 13.1).

c) Install the washer so its internal flat aligns with the flat on the oil pump shaft. Install the snap-ring with its chamfered edge toward the oil pump (against the washer).

Oil cooler

Removal

Refer to illustrations 13.7, 13.8, 13.9a and 13.9b

6 Drain the engine oil and remove the front fender (see Chapters 1 and 7)

7 Unscrew the Allen bolts and remove the retainer plate, then pull the oil lines out of the front crankcase cover and remove the O-rings **(see illustration)**.

8 Unbolt the hose retainer and oil cooler brackets from the frame and remove the oil cooler from the vehicle together with the hoses **(see illustration)**.

9 Remove the hose retainer bolts and detach the hoses from the oil cooler, then remove the O-rings **(see illustrations)**.

Inspection

10 Check the oil cooler for signs of leakage, especially at the hose joints. It's a good idea to replace the O-rings whenever they're removed,

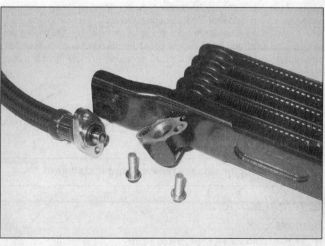

13.9b . . . then remove the O-rings

14.1 Unscrew the tensioner cap and remove the O-ring

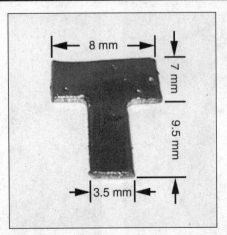

14.2a This tensioner holding tool can be made from a piece of 0.039 inch (1 mm) feeler gauge stock

14.2b Use the tool to turn the tensioner to the retracted position, then slip the tool into the tensioner to hold it there

14.10 Unbolt the main bearing retainer/tensioner assembly (right arrows) and pull off the slipper (left arrow)

but they should be definitely be replaced if they're compressed, brittle or deteriorated.

11   Check the hoses for deterioration, and look closely for leakage or cracks at the joints where the hose meets the metal fitting. Replace the hoses if there are any doubts about their condition - a hose failure will cause a sudden catastrophic loss of oil pressure.

12   Check the oil cooler fins for clogging or bending. Clean out any debris with a garden hose or low-pressure compressed air. Carefully straighten any bent fins with a small screwdriver, taking care not to puncture the oil passages.

Installation

13   Installation is the reverse of the removal steps. Use new O-rings and tighten the mounting bolts securely, but don't overtighten them and strip the threads.

---

14   Cam chain tensioner - removal and installation

External tensioner

Removal

Refer to illustrations 14.1, 14.2a and 14.2b

1   Remove the tensioner cap screw and O-ring **(see illustration)**.

2   Make a tensioner holding tool from a piece of thin steel **(see illustration)**. Insert the narrow part of the tool into the tensioner shaft through the cap bolt hole and turn it clockwise to retract the tensioner piston, then insert the tool all the way into the shaft to lock it. Remove the tensioner bolts and lift it out of the engine **(see illustration)**. **Caution:** *The tensioner piston locks in place as it extends. If the tensioner piston is allowed to extend while it is out of the engine, the piston must be retracted before the bolts are tightened. If the bolts are tightened without retracting the tensioner piston, the piston will be forced against the tensioner slipper, damaging the tensioner or possibly the cam chain.*

3   Remove the cap bolt and sealing washer from the tensioner body and wash them with solvent.

Installation

4   Clean all old gasket material from the tensioner body and engine.

5   Lubricate the friction surfaces of the components with moly-based grease.

6   If the tensioner piston is extended, turn the tensioner shaft clockwise with the special tool to retract the tensioner piston into the body, then push the tool all the way into lock the piston in the retracted position **(see illustration 14.2b)**.

7   Install a new tensioner gasket and position the tensioner body on the engine. Coat the threads of the tensioner bolts with non-permanent thread locking agent and install the bolts, tightening them to the torque listed in this Chapter's Specifications.

8   Pull the tool out of the cap screw hole. Install the cap screw with a new sealing washer and tighten it to the torque listed in this Chapter's Specifications.

Internal tensioner and slipper

Removal

Refer to illustration 14.10

9   Remove the front crankcase cover, centrifugal clutch and change clutch (see Sections 10 and 11).

10   Unbolt the main bearing retainer/tensioner assembly from the crankcase **(see illustration)**.

11   If you need to remove the tensioner slipper, remove the oil pump (see Section 13), then take the slipper off the crankcase **(see illustration 14.10)**.

Inspection

Refer to illustration 14.12

12   Check the friction surfaces on the internal tensioner and slipper for wear or damage **(see illustration)**. Replace them if problems are found.

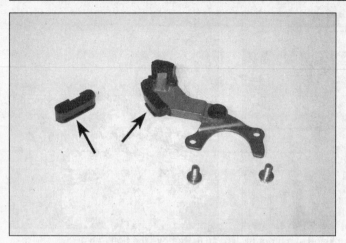

14.12 Check the friction surfaces on the tensioner
and slipper (arrows)

15.5a The dimple on the sprocket aligns with the cast pointer
on the crankcase (arrows) when the piston is at TDC on the
compression stroke (bolts removed for clarity) . . .

Installation

13   Installation is the reverse of the removal steps. Tighten the bearing retainer/slipper assembly bolts to the torque listed in this Chapter's Specifications.

---

15 Camshaft, chain and sprocket - removal and installation

Removal

Refer to illustrations 15.5a, 15.5b, 15.7 and 15.8

1   Refer to the valve adjustment procedure in Chapter 1 and position the piston at top dead center (TDC) on its compression stroke.
2   Remove the valve cover, rocker arms, pushrods, cylinder head, cylinder and valve lifters (see Sections 6, 7 and 9).
3   Remove the front crankcase cover, centrifugal clutch and change clutch (see Sections 10 and 11).
4   Remove the external camshaft chain tensioner (see Section 14).
5   Verify that the crankshaft and piston are still at TDC on the compression stroke. When this occurs, the dimple on the camshaft sprocket will align with the cast mark on the crankcase **(see illustrations)**.
6   Remove the sprocket bolts and take the sprocket off the camshaft **(see illustration 15.5a)**. Disengage the sprocket from the chain and remove the chain from the crankshaft.
7   Unbolt the camshaft bearing retainer and take it off the crankcase **(see illustration)**.

15.5b . . . if the dimple is 180-degrees away from the pointer
(arrow), rotate the crankshaft one full turn, which will rotate the
camshaft one-half turn and bring the marks into alignment

8   Note the alignment of the camshaft and crankcase timing marks, then pull the camshaft out of the engine **(see illustration)**.
9   Refer to Chapter 2C for inspection procedures.

15.7 Remove the camshaft bearing retainer bolt (arrow) and
remove the retainer . . .

15.8 . . . then slip the camshaft out of the engine

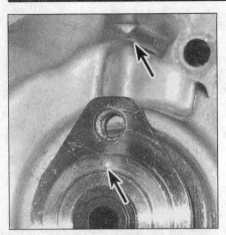

15.11 Align the camshaft mark with the crankcase pointer (arrows)

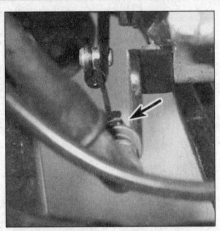

16.1 Pull the cable back and slip it out of the bracket (arrow), then rotate the cable to align it with the lever slot and slip it out of the lever

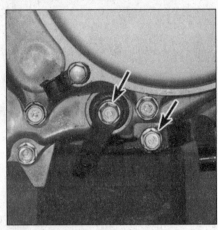

16.6 Remove the bolt (left arrow) and take the lever off; if necessary, unbolt the cable retainer (right arrow)

Installation

Refer to illustration 15.11

10   Make sure the piston is at TDC on the compression stroke (see the valve adjustment procedure in Chapter 1).

11   Lubricate the cam bearing journals with engine oil and the lobes with molybdenum disulfide grease. Place the camshaft in its bores with the lobes downward. When the camshaft is correctly installed, the punch mark on the sprocket flange will align with the cast pointer on the crankcase **(see illustration)**.

12   Install the bearing retainer, aligning its notch with the cast rib on the crankcase **(see illustration 15.7)**. Apply non-permanent thread locking agent to the threads of the retainer bolt and tighten it to the torque listed in this Chapter's Specifications.

13   Engage the camshaft sprocket with the chain, then install the chain and sprocket so the sprocket bolt hole with a punch mark next to it aligns with the crankcase pointer **(see illustration 15.5a)**.

14   Apply non-permanent thread locking agent to the threads of the sprocket bolt next to the punch mark. Install it and tighten it to the torque listed in this Chapter's Specifications.

15   Apply non-permanent thread locking agent to the threads of the remaining sprocket bolt, install it and tighten it to the torque listed in this Chapter's Specifications.

16   Recheck the position of the timing marks on the sprocket and crankcase **(see illustration 16.5a)**. Recheck the crankshaft timing mark to make sure it's still at the TDC position (see *Valve clearance - check*

and adjustment in Chapter 1). **Caution:** *Don't run the engine with the marks out of alignment or severe engine damage could occur.*

17   Install the valve lifters (see Section 9).

18   Install the cylinder, cylinder head, pushrods and rocker arms (see Sections 6 and 7).

19   Adjust the valve clearances (see Chapter 1).

20   The remainder of installation is the reverse of removal.

16   Reverse lock mechanism - cable replacement, removal, inspection and installation

Cable replacement

Refer to illustration 16.1

1   Pull the cable housing out of the bracket, slip the cable out of the bracket slot, then rotate the cable to align it with the slot in the lever and slip the cable out of the lever **(see illustration)**.

2   Pull the cable housing out of the handlebar bracket. Rotate the cable out of the bracket, then align the cable with the slot in the bracket and slip the cable end down out of the bracket.

3   Note the location of the cable along the frame. Detach it from its retainers and install the new cable in the same location, making sure to secure it with all of the retainers.

4   Reconnect the ends of the cable at the handlebar, lower bracket and lever. Refer to Chapter 1 and adjust the cable.

Removal

Refer to illustrations 16.6, 16.8 and 16.9

5   Disconnect the reverse cable as described above.

6   Remove the bolt and take the lever off the shaft **(see illustration)**.

7   Remove the recoil starter and rear crankcase cover (Section 17 and Chapter 8).

8   Slip the washer off the reverse shaft **(see illustration)**.

9   Hold the reverse arm with a screwdriver and pull the reverse shaft out of the crankcase **(see illustration)**.

Inspection

10   Inspect the shaft and lever components and replace any worn or damaged parts. Leave the snap-ring on the shaft unless the shaft, snap-ring or spring needs to be replaced.

Installation

Refer to illustration 16.11

11   Installation is the reverse of the removal steps, with the following

16.8 Slip the washer (arrow) off the reverse shaft

16.9 Hold the reverse arm with a screwdriver and pull the reverse shaft out of the crankcase

16.11 The OUT mark on the lever faces away from the engine

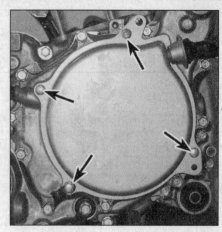

17.1 Remove the cover bolts (arrows) and take the recoil starter off the engine

addition: Install the reverse stopper arm with its OUT mark facing away from the engine (see illustration). Tighten its bolt securely, but don't overtighten and strip the threads.

---

17 Recoil starter - removal and installation

Removal

Refer to illustration 17.1

1   Unbolt the recoil starter from the rear of the engine (see illustration).

Inspection

Refer to illustrations 17.2, 17.3, 17.4, 17.5 and 17.6

2   Remove the nut and lift off the ratchet cover with the clip (see illustration).

3   Note how the ratchet and spring are installed, then lift them off the starter (see illustration).

4   Untie the knot in the starter rope. Carefully release the rope into the starter and remove the pull handle (see illustration).

5   Note how the rope is wound onto the pulley (counterclockwise, viewed from the ratchet side), then unwind it and pull the knot out of the pocket (see illustration).

17.2 Remove the nut (arrow) and lift off the ratchet cover with the clip

6   **Warning:** *Whenever you handle the recoil spring, wear eye protection and heavy gloves to avoid injury if the spring uncoils suddenly. If the spring is in good condition, leave it installed. If it's broken, carefully*

17.3 Note how the ratchet and spring are installed, then lift them off the starter

17.4 Untie the knot, carefully release the rope into the starter and remove the pull handle

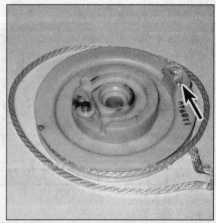

17.5 Note how the rope is wound onto the pulley (counterclockwise, viewed from the ratchet side), then unwind it and pull the knot out of the pocket (arrow)

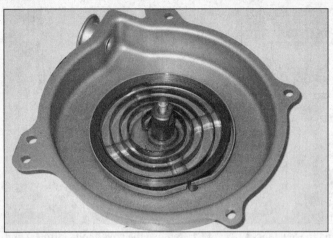

17.6 Wearing eye protection and heavy gloves, carefully remove the recoil spring from the cover only if necessary

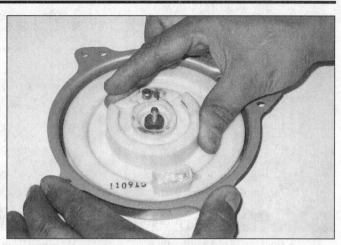

17.10 With the rope in the pulley notch, turn the pulley 2-1/2 turns counterclockwise to preload the spring, then install the handle and tie a square knot in the rope

remove it from the cover (**see illustration**).

7   Check all other parts for wear or damage and replace worn or damaged parts.

Installation

Refer to illustrations 17.10 and 17.12

8   If you removed the spring, reinstall it, hooking the end into the notch in the cover (**see illustration 17.6**).

9   Lubricate the pulley shaft in the cover with multi-purpose grease. Install the pulley in the cover, making sure the pulley engages the inner end of the recoil spring.

10   Place the rope in the pulley notch, then turn the pulley 2-1/2 turns counterclockwise to preload the recoil spring (**see illustration**). Guide the end of the rope through the cover hole and pull handle, then tie a square knot in the end of the rope to secure it.

11   Lubricate the ratchet with multi-purpose grease, then install the ratchet and spring (**see illustration 17.3**).

12   If the clip was removed from the ratchet cover, install it, then install the ratchet cover on the spring cover (**see illustration**). Install the nut to secure the ratchet cover.

13   Hold the cover down on a work surface and pull the rope two or three times to make sure the recoil mechanism works properly.

14   The remainder of installation is the reverse of the removal steps. Tighten the recoil starter bolts securely, but don't overtighten them and strip the threads.

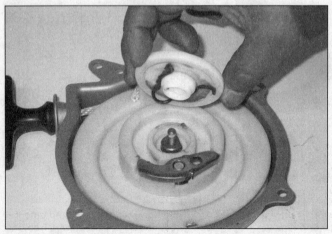

17.12 Install the clip and ratchet cover, then secure them with the nut

18   External shift mechanism - removal, inspection and installation

Shift pedal

1   The shift pedal is used on all except 450ES models.

Removal

2   Look for alignment marks on the end of the shift pedal and shift shaft. If they aren't visible, make your own marks with a sharp punch.

3   Remove the shift pedal pinch bolt and slide the pedal off the shaft.

Inspection

4   Check the shift pedal for wear or damage such as bending. Check the splines on the shift pedal and shaft for stripping or step wear. Replace the pedal or shaft if these problems are found.

Installation

5   Install the shift pedal. Line up its punch marks and tighten the pinch bolt to the torque listed in this Chapter's Specifications.

External shift linkage

Removal

Refer to illustrations 18.8a, 18.8b, 18.9, 18.10, 18.11, 18.12 and 18.13

6   Remove the centrifugal and change clutches (Sections 10 and 11), and the alternator and rear crankcase cover (Chapter 8).

7   Remove the shift pedal (if equipped) as described above.

8   In the rear crankcase cover, bend back the lockwasher tab and unscrew the bolt (**see illustration**). Pull out the spindle and remove the gearshift arm (**see illustration**).

9   On the engine, slide the thrust washer and pull the sub-gear-shift arm off the spindle, noting how the arm fits between the ends of the return spring (**see illustration**). Pull up on the shift arm spring far enough to disconnect it from the gearshift plate, then slide the master shift arm off the shaft.

10   Unbolt the guide plate, then remove it and the gearshift plate (**see illustration**). If you haven't already done so, remove the washer from the sub-gearshift spindle.

11   Push the stopper arm away from the drum shifter, then pull the drum shifter out (**see illustration**). Be careful not to lose the drum shifter dowel. **Note:** *The transmission is in Neutral when the dowel is aligned with the cast pointer on the crankcase.*

12   Note how the stopper arm spring fits against the crankcase rib and over the stopper arm (**see illustration**). Unbolt the stopper arm and remove it together with the spring.

13   Pull the sub-gearshift spindle out of the rear crankcase, noting the location of the washer (**see illustration**).

18.8a Bend back the lockwasher and unscrew the bolt . . .

18.8b . . . then pull out the spindle and remove the gearshift arm

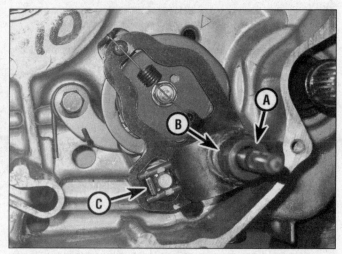

18.9 Slide the thrust washer (A) and sub-gearshift arm (B) off the shaft; note how the arm's tab fits between the spring ends (C)

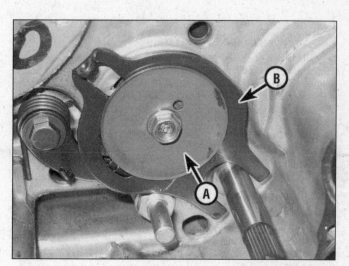

18.10 Unbolt the guide plate (A) and remove the gearshift plate (B)

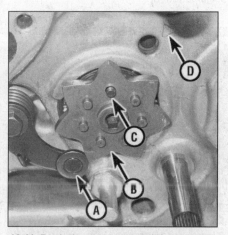

18.11 Push the stopper arm (A) down and pull out the drum shifter (B); the dowel (C) aligns with the crankcase pointer (D) to indicate Neutral

18.12 Note how the spring ends are arranged (arrows), then unbolt the stopper arm and take it off

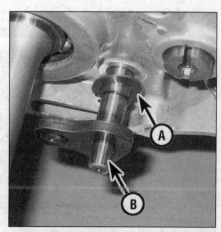

18.13 Note the location of the washer (A) and pull the sub-gearshift spindle (B) out of the crankcase

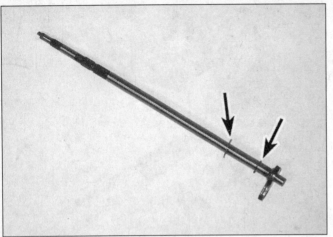

18.15 Inspect the spindle, as well as its snap-ring and thrust washer (arrows)

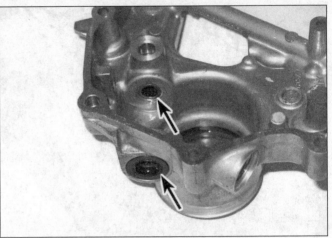

18.17 Inspect the seal and needle bearings (arrows) and replace them if necessary

Inspection

Refer to illustrations 18.15 and 18.17

14   Check the drum shifter and replace it if it's worn or damaged.

15   Check the sub-gearshift spindle for bends and damage to the splines **(see illustration)**. If the shaft is bent, you can attempt to straighten it, but if the splines are damaged it will have to be replaced.

16   Make sure the return spring pin isn't loose **(see illustration 18.12)**. If it is, unscrew it, apply a non-hardening locking compound to the threads, then reinstall it and tighten it to the torque listed in this Chapter's Specifications.

17   Inspect, and replace if necessary, the seal and needle roller bearings in the alternator cover **(see illustration)**.

Installation

Refer to illustrations 18.22 and 18.28

18   If the reverse stopper arm has been removed, install it before you reinstall the sub-gearshift spindle (see Section 16).

19   Install the washer and sub-gearshift spindle **(see illustration 18.13)**.

20   Place the return spring on the stopper arm **(see illustration 18.12)**, then install the stopper arm and tighten the bolt to the torque listed in this Chapter's Specifications. Make sure the end of the return spring is positioned against the crankcase rib.

21   Install the dowel pin in its hole in the shift drum, then pull the stopper arm out of the way and place the drum shifter over the dowel.

22   Install the gearshift plate, positioning its inner tangs around the drum shifter pins **(see illustration)**. Install the shift guide plate, making sure its tab fits into the notch in the drum shifter.

23   Apply non-permanent thread locking agent to the threads of the drum shifter bolt, then install it through the shift guide plate into the drum shifter and tighten it to the torque listed in this Chapter's Specifications. **Note:** *The transmission in is Neutral when the small round hole in the plate is aligned with the cast pointer on the crankcase (the same pointer that aligns with the drum shifter dowel pin when the transmission is in Neutral).*

24   Slip the gearshift master arm onto the spindle. Engage the master arm's pin with the gearshift plate slot, then hook the spring between the master arm and gearshift plate.

25   Install the return spring and position its ends on each side of the master arm's tab and the return spring pin.

26   Install the sub-gearshift spindle arm, placing its tab between the ends of the return spring.

27   Note that there are wide splines in the sub-gearshift spindle arm and on the spindle. Align these as you install the sub-gearshift spindle arm.

28   Install the thrust washer on the sub-gearshift spindle arm, aligning its flat with the spindle **(see illustration)**.

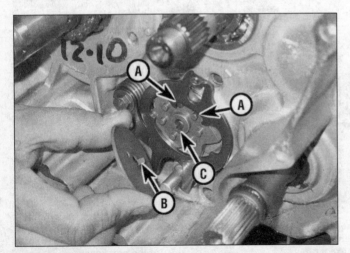

18.22 Position the inner tangs of the gearshift plate around two of the pins (A); engage the shift guide plate tab (B) with the notch in the drum shifter (C)

18.28 Align the flats on the thrust washer and spindle (arrow)

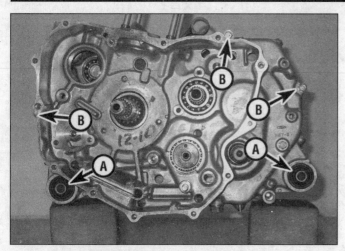

19.11 Drive out the engine hanger bushings (A) and remove the three front side crankcase bolts (B)

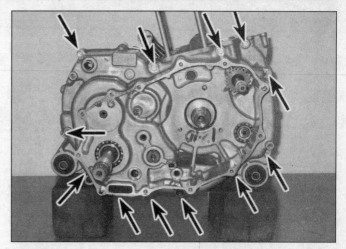

19.12 Loosen the rear crankcase bolts (arrows) in two or three stages, then remove them

29 The remainder of installation is the reverse of the removal steps.
30 Check the engine oil level and add some, if necessary (see Chapter 1).

19 Crankcase - disassembly and reassembly

1 To examine and repair or replace the crankshaft, connecting rod, bearings and transmission components, the crankcase must be split into two parts.

Disassembly

Refer to illustrations 19.11, 19.12 and 19.14

2 Remove the engine from the vehicle (see Section 5).
3 Remove the carburetor (see Chapter 3).
4 Remove the alternator rotor, starter clutch and starter motor (see Chapter 8).
5 Remove the centrifugal clutch (see Section 10) and the change clutch (Section 11).
6 Remove the external shift mechanism (see Section 18).
7 Remove the reverse lock mechanism (see Section 16).
8 Remove the valve cover, rocker arms and pushrods, cylinder head, cylinder and piston (see Sections 6, 7, 8 and Chapter 2C).
9 Remove the oil pump (Section 13).
10 Check carefully to make sure there aren't any remaining components that attach the front and rear halves of the crankcase together.
11 From the front side of the crankcase, remove the output shaft O-ring. Remove the dust seals from the engine hanger bushings if you haven't already done so. Drive the bushings out of the crankcase, then remove the three crankcase bolts that are accessible from the front side **(see illustration)**.
12 Loosen the rear crankcase bolts in two or three stages, in a criss-cross pattern **(see illustration)**. Remove the bolts and label them; they are different lengths.
13 Set the crankcase on a work surface with the rear aside down, then lift the front half off the rear half. Don't pry against the mating surfaces or they'll develop leaks.
14 Remove the two crankcase dowels **(see illustration)**.
15 Refer to Sections 19 and 20 and Chapter 2C for information on the internal components of the crankcase.

Reassembly

16 Remove all traces of old gasket and sealant from the crankcase mating surfaces with a sharpening stone or similar tool. Be careful not to let any fall into the case as this is done and be careful not to damage the mating surfaces.

17 Check to make sure the two dowel pins are in place in their holes in the mating surface of the left crankcase half **(see illustration 19.14)**.
18 Pour some engine oil over the transmission gears, the crankshaft bearing surface and the shift drum. Don't get any oil on the crankcase mating surface.
19 Install a new gasket on the crankcase mating surface.
20 Carefully place the front crankcase half onto the rear crankcase half. While doing this, make sure the transmission shafts, shift drum, crankshaft and balancer fit into their ball bearings in the front crankcase half.
21 Install the rear crankcase half bolts in the correct holes and tighten them so they are just snug. Then tighten them in two or three stages, in a criss-cross pattern, to the torque listed in this Chapter's Specifications.
22 Tighten the three bolts in the front half of the crankcase to the torque listed in this Chapter's Specifications.
23 Turn the transmission mainshaft to make sure it turns freely. Also make sure the crankshaft turns freely.
24 The remainder of installation is the reverse of removal.

20 Transmission shafts and shift drum - removal, inspection and installation

Note: *When disassembling the transmission shafts, place the parts on a long rod or thread a wire through them to keep them in order and facing the proper direction.*

19.14 Remove the crankcase dowels (arrows) and gasket

20.2 Slip the copper washer (arrow) off the countershaft and lift out first gear

20.3a Lift the thrust washer (arrow) and reverse idler gear off its shaft

Removal and disassembly

Refer to illustrations 20.2, 20.3a, 20.3b, 20.4, 20.5a, 20.5b, 20.6a, 20.6b and 20.7

1   Remove the engine, then separate the case halves (see Sections 5 and 19).

2   Remove the copper washer from the countershaft, then lift off the countershaft first gear and its bushing **(see illustration)**.

3   Remove the thrust washer and lift the reverse idler gear off its shaft **(see illustration)**. Pull out the shift fork shaft, remove the shift forks, then lift the shift drum out of the case **(see illustration)**. Finally, lift out the final drive shaft and gear.

4   Lift the mainshaft and countershaft out of the transmission together **(see illustration)**.

5   Slide the components off the mainshaft and place them in order on a long rod or piece of wire (such as a straightened coat hanger) **(see illustrations)**.

6   Slide the components off the countershaft (noting that the thrust washer, first gear and bushing were already removed) and place them in order on a long rod or piece of wire (such as a straightened coat hanger) **(see illustrations)**. Don't remove the washer from the narrow end of the countershaft unless you're planning to install a new one.

7   Slide the components off the reverse idler shaft and place them in order on a long rod or piece of wire (such as a straightened coat hanger) **(see illustration)**.

Inspection

Refer to illustration 20.10

8   Wash all of the components in clean solvent and dry them off.

9   Inspect the shift fork grooves in the countershaft first/reverse shifter, mainshaft third gear and countershaft fourth gear. If a groove is worn or scored, replace the affected part and inspect its corresponding shift fork.

10   Check the shift forks for distortion and wear, especially at the fork ears **(see illustration)**. Measure the thickness of the fork ears and compare your findings with this Chapter's Specifications. If they are discolored or severely worn they are probably bent. Inspect the guide pins for excessive wear and distortion and replace any defective parts with new ones.

11   Measure the inside diameter of the forks and the outside diameter of the fork shaft and compare to the values listed in this Chapter's Specifications. Replace any parts that are worn beyond the limits. Check the shift fork shaft for evidence of wear, galling and other damage. Make sure the shift forks move smoothly on the shafts. If the shafts are worn or bent, replace them with new ones.

12   Check the edges of the grooves in the shift drum for signs of excessive wear.

13   Spin the shift drum bearing with fingers. Replace the bearing if it's rough, loose or noisy.

14   Check the gear teeth for cracking and other obvious damage.

20.3b Pull out the shift fork shaft (A), remove the shift forks (B), then lift out the shift drum (C) and final drive shaft (D)

20.4 Lift out the mainshaft and countershaft together

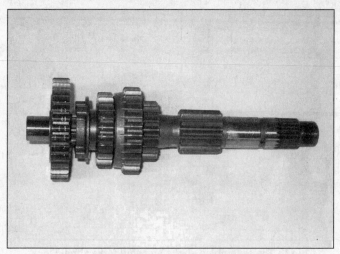

20.5a This is the assembled mainshaft . . .

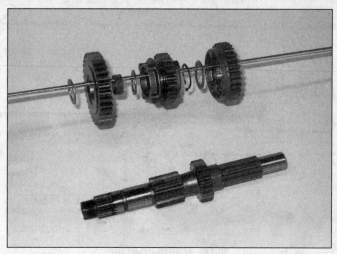

20.5b . . . slip off the components and place them in order on a long rod

20.6a This is the assembled countershaft . . .

20.6b . . . slip off the components and place them in order on a long rod; don't remove the special washer from the shaft unless you plan to replace it with a new one

20.7 Slip the components off the reverse idler shaft and place them in order on a long rod

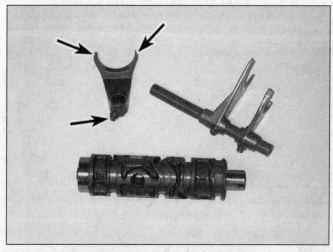

20.10 The fork ears and pins (arrows) are common wear points; check the shift drum grooves for wear

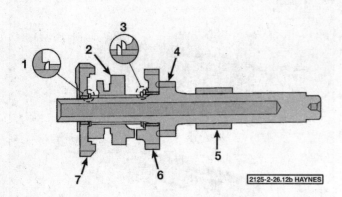

2125-2-26.12b HAYNES

20.18a   Mainshaft details

1	Washer	5	First gear
2	Third gear	6	Fourth gear
3	Snap-ring and spline washer	7	Fifth gear
4	Second gear (integral with shaft)		

20.18b The assembled shafts and shift forks should look like this when they're installed

Check the bushing and surface in the inner diameter of the freewheeling gears for scoring or heat discoloration. Replace damaged parts.

15   Inspect the engagement dogs and dog holes on gears so equipped for excessive wear or rounding off. Replace the paired gears as a set if necessary.

16   Check the mainshaft needle bearing in the crankcase for wear or heat discoloration and replace them if necessary (see Chapter 2C).

Assembly and installation

Refer to illustrations 20.18a, 20.18b and 20.18c

18   Assembly and installation are the basically the reverse of the disassembly procedure, but take note of the following points:

a) *Oil holes in bushings must be aligned with the corresponding oil hole in the shaft the bushing is installed on.*

b) *Thrust washers have a rounded edge and a flat edge. The rounded edge faces toward the direction of thrust (that is, toward the gear whose thrust is being controlled)* **(see illustration)**.

c) *Use a new snap-ring to secure the spline washer, fourth gear and bushing to the mainshaft* **(see illustration 26.12a)**. *Install the snap-ring and spline washer with their rounded edges toward fourth gear.*

d) *Lubricate the components with engine oil before assembling them.*

20.18c   Place the reverse idler shaft pin in the crankcase notch (arrows)

e) *After assembling the countershaft and mainshaft, check the gears to make sure they mesh correctly before installing the shafts in the crankcase* **(see illustration)**.

f) *Place the reverse idler shaft pin in the crankcase notch* **(see illustration)**.

Chapter 2 Part B
Engine, clutch and transmission (500 models)

Contents

Specifications

Note: *For wear tolerance and service limit specifications, refer to Chapter 2C.*

General
Bore	92 mm (3.62 inches)
Stroke	75 mm (2.95 inches)
Displacement	499 cc (30.4 cubic inches)

Torque specifications
Rocker assembly cap nuts	53 Nm (39 ft-lbs)
Rocker assembly bolts	Not specified
Cylinder head bolts	Not specified
Cam chain tensioner	
Cap screw	Not specified
Mounting bolts	Not specified
Cylinder base bolts	Not specified
Front crankcase cover oil feed pipe cap	18 Nm (13 ft-lbs)

Torque specifications (continued)

Crankcase cover bolts	Not specified
Centrifugal clutch locknut	118 Nm (87 ft-lbs) (1)
Primary driven gear bolts	17 Nm (144 inch-lbs)
Oil pump sprocket bolt	12 Nm (108 inch-lbs)
Oil pressure relief valve (external)	34 Nm (25 ft-lbs)
Shift linkage pinch bolt	Not specified
Shift linkage pivot bolt	27 Nm (20 ft-lbs)
Shift linkage tie-rod locknuts	10 Nm (84 inch-lbs)
Shift drum center bolt	27 Nm (20 ft-lbs) (2)
Shift lever housing cover bolt	5 Nm (43 inch-lbs)
External shift linkage stopper arm bolt	12 Nm (108 inch-lbs) (2)
Crankcase bolts	Not specified
Oil pump-to-engine bolts	Not specified
Automatic transmission unit mounting bolts	Not specified

1. *Use a new locknut with engine oil on the threads and seating surface. Stake the locknut.*
2. *Use non-permanent thread locking agent on the threads.*

1   General information

The engine/transmission unit is of the liquid-cooled, single-cylinder four-stroke design. The four valves are operated by pushrods and solid lifters. The lifters are operated by a camshaft mounted in the crankcase, which in turn is chain driven off the crankshaft. The engine/transmission assembly is constructed from aluminum alloy. The crankcase is divided vertically.

The crankshaft centerline is parallel to the centerline of the vehicle.

The crankcase incorporates a dry sump, pressure-fed lubrication system which uses a gear-driven rotor-type oil pump, an oil filter and separate strainer screen and an oil temperature warning switch.

Power from the crankshaft is routed to the transmissions via a centrifugal clutch, which engages as engine speed is increased. The sub-transmission allows the rider to select a gear range (high, low, neutral or reverse). The automatic transmission, mounted inside the crankcase, is a continuously variable swash plate design. It can operate in two modes: continuously variable or Electric Shift Program (ESP). The ESP mode allows the rider to select between five preset transmission output ratios, using switches on the left handlebar. This gives the feel of a conventional gear-type transmission.

2   Operations possible with the engine in the frame

The components and assemblies listed below can be removed without having to remove the engine from the frame. If, however, a number of areas require attention at the same time, removal of the engine is recommended.

Valve cover
Cylinder head
Rocker arms and pushrods
Cylinder and piston
Gear selector mechanism external components
Recoil starter
Starter motor
Starter reduction gears
Starter clutch
Alternator rotor and stator
Centrifugal clutch
Cam chain tensioner
Camshaft
Oil pump

3   Operations requiring engine removal

It is necessary to remove the engine/transmission assembly from the frame and separate the crankcase halves to gain access to the following components:

Crankshaft and connecting rod
Balancer
Sub-transmission
Automatic transmission unit

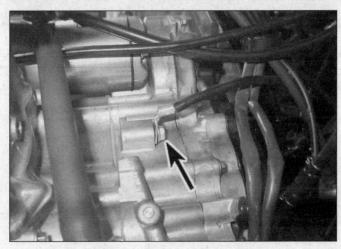

5.5a Disconnect this ground cable (arrow) . . .

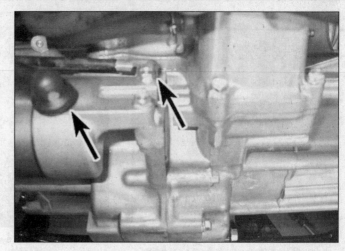

5.5b . . . as well as a second ground cable and the starter cable (arrows)

4   Major engine repair - general note

1   It is not always easy to determine when or if an engine should be completely overhauled, as a number of factors must be considered.

2   High mileage is not necessarily an indication that an overhaul is needed, while low mileage, on the other hand, does not preclude the need for an overhaul. Frequency of servicing is probably the single most important consideration. An engine that has regular and frequent oil and filter changes, as well as other required maintenance, will most likely give many miles of reliable service. Conversely, a neglected engine, or one which has not been broken in properly, may require an overhaul very early in its life.

3   Exhaust smoke and excessive oil consumption are both indications that piston rings and/or valve guides are in need of attention. Make sure oil leaks are not responsible before deciding that the rings and guides are bad. Refer to Chapter 1 and perform a cylinder compression check to determine for certain the nature and extent of the work required.

4   If the engine is making obvious knocking or rumbling noises, the connecting rod and/or main bearings are probably at fault.

5   Loss of power, rough running, excessive valve train noise and high fuel consumption rates may also point to the need for an overhaul, especially if they are all present at the same time. If a complete tune-up does not remedy the situation, major mechanical work is the only solution.

6   An engine overhaul generally involves restoring the internal parts to the specifications of a new engine. During an overhaul the piston rings are replaced and the cylinder walls are bored and/or honed. If a rebore is done, then a new piston is also required. The crankshaft and connecting rod are permanently assembled, so if one of these components needs to be replaced both must be. Generally the valves are serviced as well, since they are usually in less than perfect condition at this point. While the engine is being overhauled, other components such as the carburetor and the starter motor can be rebuilt also. The end result should be a like-new engine that will give as many trouble-free miles as the original.

7   Before beginning the engine overhaul, read through all of the related procedures to familiarize yourself with the scope and requirements of the job. Overhauling an engine is not all that difficult, but it is time consuming. Plan on the vehicle being tied up for a minimum of two (2) weeks. Check on the availability of parts and make sure that any necessary special tools, equipment and supplies are obtained in advance.

8   Most work can be done with typical shop hand tools, although a number of precision measuring tools are required for inspecting parts to determine if they must be replaced. Often a dealer service department or repair shop will handle the inspection of parts and offer advice concerning reconditioning and replacement. As a general rule, time is the primary cost of an overhaul so it doesn't pay to install worn or substandard parts.

9   As a final note, to ensure maximum life and minimum trouble from a rebuilt engine, everything must be assembled with care in a spotlessly clean environment.

5   Engine - removal and installation

Note: *Engine removal and installation should be done with the aid of an assistant to avoid damage or injury that could occur if the engine is dropped. A hydraulic floor jack should be used to support and lower the engine if possible (they can be rented at low cost).*

Removal

Refer to illustrations 5.5a, 5.5b, 5.12a through 5.12e

1   Drain the engine oil and coolant and disconnect the spark plug wire (see Chapter 1).

2   Remove the fuel tank, carburetor, air cleaner housing and exhaust system (see Chapter 3). The choke and throttle cables can be left connected. Plug the carburetor intake openings with rags.

3   Remove the mudguards and inner fenders (see Chapter 7).

4   Disconnect the breather hose from the crankcase.

5   Disconnect the starter cable and two ground cable from the engine (one starter cable is secured by one of the starter mounting bolts **(see illustrations)**.

6   Label and disconnect the following wires and free them from any retainers (refer to Chapters 4 or 8 for component location if necessary):

   Ignition pulse generator

   Alternator

   Oil temperature sensor

   Coolant temperature sensor

   Shift control motor

   Angle sensor

   Gear position switch

7   Remove the front driveshaft and loosen the clamps on the rear driveshaft boot that connects the swingarm to the engine (see Chapter 5).

8   With the sub-transmission in Neutral, detach the gearshift arm from the spindle (see Section 22). Lift the free end of the tie-rod to position the tie-rod out of the way of engine removal.

9   Disconnect the coolant hoses from the engine (see Chapter 2D).

10   Disconnect the oil tank hoses from the engine (see Section 17).

11   Support the engine securely from below.

12   Remove the engine mounting bolts, nuts and brackets at the top,

5.12a Remove the top engine mount through-bolt (arrow), as well as the two bolts that attach the bracket to the engine

5.12b Remove the lower left engine mount through-bolt . . .

5.12c . . . and the lower right engine mount through-bolt

lower left and lower right **(see illustrations)**.

13   Have an assistant help you lift the engine. As you lift, pull the engine forward to disengage the rear driveshaft from the engine. The driveshaft is mounted inside the left side of the swingarm (refer to Chapter 5 if necessary). Remove the engine to the left side of the vehicle.

14   Slowly lower the engine to a suitable work surface.

Installation

15   Check the rubber engine supports for wear or damage and replace them if necessary before installing the engine. The lips of the mounting bushing dust seals face outward.

16   Coat the driveshaft splines with moly-based grease. Install the engine from the left side of the vehicle and move it rearward to engage the driveshaft with the engine (refer to Chapter 5 if necessary).

17   Lift the engine to align the mounting bolt holes, then install all of the brackets, bolts and nuts, but don't tighten them yet.

18   Install the lower left engine hanger bracket and its rubber dampers, with the wide sides of the dampers facing the engine **(see illustration 5.12b)**. Install the bracket bolts and the hanger through-bolt and nut. Tighten the through-bolt and nut, then the bracket bolts, to the torque listed in this Chapter's Specifications.

19   Install the rubber dampers in the lower right engine mounting boss **(see illustration 5.12c)**. Install the collar, through-bolt and nut, then tighten the through-bolt and nut to the torque listed in this Chapter's Specifications.

20   Loosely install the upper engine hanger plate bracket, rubber

dampers, through-bolt and nut **(see illustration 5.12a)**. Tighten the bracket bolts, then the through-bolt and nut, to the torques listed in this Chapter's Specifications.

21   The remainder of installation is the reverse of the removal steps, with the following additions:

a) *Use new gaskets at all exhaust pipe connections.*

b) *Adjust the throttle cable and reverse selector cable following the procedures in Chapter 1.*

c) *Fill the engine with oil and check the differential oil level, also following the procedures in Chapter 1. Run the engine and check for leaks.*

6   Rocker assembly, pushrods and lifters - removal and installation

Note: *The rocker assembly can be removed with the engine in the frame. If the engine has been removed, ignore the steps which don't apply.*

Removal

Refer to illustrations 6.3, 6.5, 6.7a, 6.7b and 6.9

1   Remove the fuel tank and its heat shield. Disconnect the throttle and choke cables from the carburetor (see Chapter 3). Drain the cooling system and disconnect the upper radiator hose (see Chapters 1 and 2C).

2   Disconnect the spark plug cable and remove the valve adjusting hole covers (see Chapter 1).

5.12d With the help of an assistant, turn the engine 1/4-turn clockwise (viewed from above) . . .

5.12e . . . tilt it to the rear and remove it from the left side of the vehicle

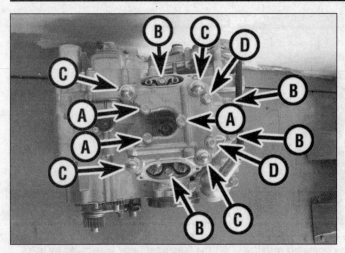

6.3 Rocker assembly and cylinder head nuts and bolts

A   Rocker assembly mounting bolts (with sealing washers)
B   Rocker assembly mounting bolts (without sealing washers)
C   Cylinder head nuts (with sealing washers)
D   Rocker shaft retaining bolts (with sealing washers)

3   Loosen the bolts and nuts that secure the rocker assembly evenly in two or three stages, then remove them (see illustration). Note that the three center bolts and all of the nuts have sealing washers.
4   Lift the rocker assembly off the studs. If it's stock, tap it gently with a rubber mallet to break the gasket seal. Don't pry against the mating surfaces or they'll leak.
5   Once the assembly is off, locate the dowels (see illustration). They may have come off with the assembly or stayed in the cylinder head.
6   Lift the pushrods out of their bores. Label the pushrods so they can be returned to their original locations.
7   To remove the rocker arms from the assembly, unscrew the shaft retaining bolts and remove their sealing washers (see illustration). Push the rocker shafts out of the assembly, using a flat-bladed screwdriver in the slots in the ends of the shafts (see illustration). Label the shafts so they can be returned to their original locations, then remove the rocker arms and put them on their shafts.
8   Place a clean shop rag over the cylinder head to prevent foreign material from falling into the engine, then clean all traces of old gasket from the surfaces of the valve cover and cylinder head.
9   Pull the lifters out of their bores with a magnet (see illustration).
10   Refer to Chapter 2C for inspection procedures.

6.5 Here are the dowel locations (arrows) - in this case, one dowel came off with the rocker assembly

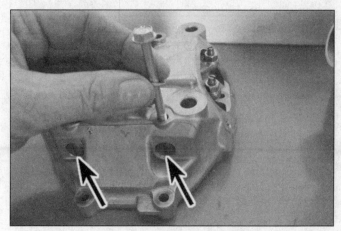

6.7a Remove the rocker shaft retaining bolts and sealing washers; use the screwdriver slots (arrows) to twist the rocker shafts as you remove them

Installation

11   Install a new gasket and O-ring on the cylinder head. Install the valve cover bolts and tighten them evenly, in a criss-cross pattern. Tighten the bolts securely, but don't distort the valve cover or strip the threads.

6.7b Label the rocker arms so they can be returned to their original locations, remove the shafts and lift the rocker arms out

6.9 Label and remove the lifters (arrows), using a magnet if necessary; on assembly, be sure to install the pushrod ends in the pockets of the lifters, not off to the side

7.7 Remove the cylinder head bolts (arrows)

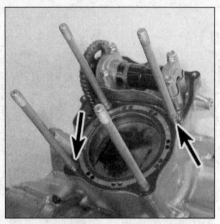

7.9 When you lift the cylinder head off, the dowels (arrows) may come off with the cylinder or stay in the crankcase; remove the old gasket

8.1 Remove the cap screw and washer; the tensioner body is secured by bolts (arrows) (lower bolt hidden)

7 Cylinder head - removal and installation

Removal

Refer to illustrations 7.7 and 7.9

1   Remove the rocker assembly, pushrods and valve lifters (see Section 6).

1   Remove the carburetor and exhaust pipe (see Chapter 3). If necessary for access, remove the intake manifold.

3   Place the piston at TDC on the compression stroke (see Valve clearances - adjustment in Chapter 1).

4   Disconnect the spark plug wire (see Chapter 1 if necessary).

5   Disconnect the coolant bypass hoses from the cylinder head. Disconnect the engine coolant temperature sensor wire. Remove the thermostat and water pump (see Chapter 3).

6   Remove the upper engine mount (see Section 5).

7   Remove the cylinder head bolts **(see illustration)**.

8   Lift the cylinder head off the cylinder. If the head is stuck, tap around the side of the head with a rubber mallet to jar it loose, or use two wooden dowels inserted into the intake and exhaust ports to lever the head off. Don't attempt to pry the head off by inserting a screwdriver between the head and the cylinder block - you'll damage the sealing surfaces.

9   Remove the head gasket from the cylinder **(see illustration)**. Locate the two dowel pins (they may have stayed in the cylinder or come off with the head).

Installation

10   Install the two dowel pins, then lay the new gasket in place on the cylinder. Never reuse the old gasket and don't use any type of gasket sealant.

11   Carefully lower the cylinder head over the studs and dowels.

12   Tighten the bolts to the torque listed in this Chapter's Specifications.

13   The remainder of installation is the reverse of the removal steps.

14   Install all parts removed for access.

15   Change the engine oil, top off the coolant and adjust the valve clearances (see Chapter 1).

8 Cam chain tensioner - removal and installation

Removal

Refer to illustrations 8.1, 8.2a and 8.2b

1   Remove the tensioner cap screw and washer **(see illustration)**.

2   Insert a screwdriver into the tensioner shaft through the cap bolt hole and turn it clockwise to retract the tensioner piston, then lock the screwdriver in position with a pair of locking pliers **(see illustration)**. Remove the tensioner bolts and lift it out of the engine **(see illustration)**. **Caution:** *The tensioner piston locks in place as it extends. If*

8.2a Turn the screwdriver clockwise to retract the tensioner piston, then clamp the screwdriver with locking pliers

8.2b Remove the tensioner body and gasket from the engine; be sure to retract the tensioner piston before you reinstall it

9.3 Position the cam sprocket so its paint mark is at the closest point to the gasket surface

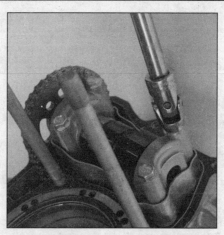

9.5a Unscrew the four holder bolts . . .

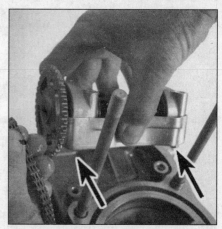

9.5b . . . disengage the sprocket from the cam chain and lift the holder, noting the locations of the dowels (arrows) (one dowel hidden)

the tensioner piston is allowed to extend while it is out of the engine, the piston must be retracted before the bolts are tightened. If the bolts are tightened without retracting the tensioner piston, the piston will be forced against the tensioner slipper, damaging the tensioner or possibly the cam chain.

Installation

3 Clean all old gasket material from the tensioner body and engine.
4 Lubricate the friction surfaces of the components with moly-based grease.
5 If the tensioner piston is extended, turn the tensioner shaft clockwise with the special tool to retract the tensioner piston into the body, then push the tool all the way into lock the piston in the retracted position.
6 Install a new tensioner gasket and position the tensioner body on the engine. Coat the threads of the tensioner bolts with non-permanent thread locking agent and install the bolts, tightening them to the torque listed in this Chapter's Specifications.
7 Pull the tool out of the cap screw hole. Install the cap screw with a new sealing washer and tighten it to the torque listed in this Chapter's Specifications.

9 Camshaft and sprocket - removal and installation

Removal

Refer to illustrations 9.3, 9.5a, 9.5b, 9.5c and 9.6
1 Refer to the valve adjustment procedure in Chapter 1 and position the piston at top dead center (TDC) on its compression stroke.
2 Remove the rocker assembly, pushrods, valve lifters and cylinder head (see Sections 6 and 7).
3 Verify that the crankshaft and piston are still at TDC on the compression stroke. When this occurs, the paint mark on the camshaft sprocket will be at its closest point to the cylinder gasket surface (see illustration).
4 Retract the chain tensioner piston as described in Steps 1 and 2 of Section 8.
5 Remove the holder bolts (see illustration). Hold the cam chain so it won't fall into the crankcase, lift the holder and disengage the sprocket from the chain (see illustration). Tie the chain up with wire so it won't fall into the crankcase (see illustration).
6 Locate the holder dowels (see illustration). They may have come off with the holder or stayed in the cylinder.
7 Refer to Chapter 2C for inspection procedures.

9.5c Support the cam chain with a piece of wire so it doesn't fall into the engine

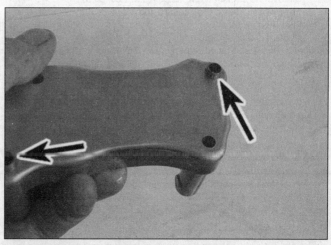

9.6 There are two holder dowels (arrows) - in this case, both came off with the holder

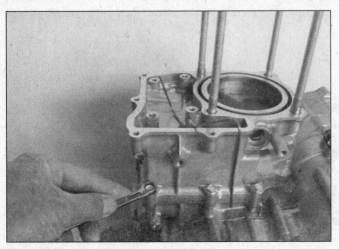

10.4 Remove the bolts that secure the cylinder to the crankcase

11.5a Unscrew the feed pipe cap with an Allen wrench, then remove the cap and its O-ring (if equipped)

Installation

8   Make sure the piston is at TDC on the compression stroke (see the valve adjustment procedure in Chapter 1).

9   Lubricate the cam bearing journals with engine oil and the lobes with molybdenum disulfide grease. Tilt the holder to engage the sprocket with the chain, making sure that the sprocket index line will align with the top surface of the cylinder after installation **(see illustration 9.3)**. Place the camshaft holder on the cylinder over the dowels and recheck to make sure the index line is still aligned correctly.

10   Install the holder bolts and tighten them evenly to the torque listed in this Chapter's Specifications.

11   The remainder of installation is the reverse of the removal steps.

12   Adjust the valve clearances (see Chapter 1).

10 Cylinder - removal and installation

Removal

Refer to illustration 10.4

1   Remove the valve cover, rocker arms, pushrods and cylinder head (see Sections 6 and 7). Make sure the crankshaft is positioned at Top Dead Center (TDC).

2   Remove the cam chain tensioner (see Section 8).

3   Remove the camshaft and holder (see Section 9).

4   Remove four bolts that secure the base of the cylinder to the crankcase **(see illustration)**.

5   Lift the cylinder straight up to remove it. If it's stuck, tap around its perimeter with a soft-faced hammer. Don't attempt to pry between the cylinder and the crankcase, as you'll ruin the sealing surfaces.

6   Locate the dowel pins (they may have come off with the cylinder or still be in the crankcase). Be careful not to let these drop into the engine. Stuff rags around the piston and remove the gasket and all traces of old gasket material from the surfaces of the cylinder and the crankcase.

7   Refer to Chapter 2C for inspection procedures.

Installation

8   Lubricate the cylinder bore with plenty of clean engine oil. Apply a thin film of moly-based grease to the piston skirt.

9   Thoroughly clean the cylinder mating surface on the crankcase. Install the dowel pins, then lower a new cylinder base gasket over them.

10   Attach a piston ring compressor to the piston and compress the piston rings. A large hose clamp can be used instead - just make sure it doesn't scratch the piston, and don't tighten it too much.

11   Install the cylinder over the studs and carefully lower it down until the piston crown fits into the cylinder liner **(see illustration 8.10 in Chapter 2A)**. Push down on the cylinder, making sure the piston doesn't get cocked sideways, until the bottom of the cylinder liner slides down past the piston rings. A wood or plastic hammer handle can be used to gently tap the cylinder down, but don't use too much force or the piston will be damaged.

12   Remove the piston ring compressor or hose clamp, being careful not to scratch the piston.

13   The remainder of installation is the reverse of the removal steps.

11 Front crankcase cover - removal, inspection and installation

Removal

Refer to illustrations 11.5a, 11.5b, 11.7, 11.9a, 11.9b and 11.10

1   Remove the front mudguards and inner fenders (see Chapter 7).

2   Remove the gearshift linkage (see Section 22).

3   Remove the oil tank (see Section 17).

4   Remove the left engine cover, then unbolt its bracket.

5   Unscrew the cap that retains the oil feed pipe in the crankcase cover, then remove the pipe and its O-ring **(see illustrations)**.

6   Remove the shift control motor (see Chapter 8).

11.5b Remove the oil feed pipe and its O-ring

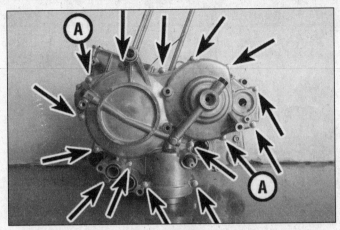

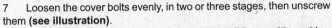

11.7 Remove the cover bolts (arrows); locations marked A have dowels

7 Loosen the cover bolts evenly, in two or three stages, then unscrew them (see illustration).
8 Take the cover off the engine. If it's stuck, tap it loose with a rubber mallet. Do not pry against the sealing surfaces or they'll be damaged.
9 Locate the dowels and O-rings (see illustration). Pull out the oil joint pipe so its O-rings can be inspected (see illustration).
10 If necessary, remove the control motor reduction gear from its shaft (see illustration).

Inspection

11 Spin the cover bearings with fingers and check them for rough, loose or noisy movement. If defects are found, replace the bearings, referring to crankcase bearing procedures in Chapter 2C.
12 Pry the gearshift spindle oil seal out of the cover. Press in a new seal with a socket or bearing driver the same diameter as the seal. Coat the seal lip with clean engine oil.
13 Check the O-rings and replace them if there's any doubt about their condition. It's a good idea to replace the O-rings whenever the cover is removed.

Installation

14 If the control motor reduction gear was removed, apply clean engine oil to the shaft and gear teeth, then install the gear.
15 Install the oil joint pipe and O-rings.
16 Install the cover O-rings and make sure the cover dowels are in position.
17 Coat the cover mating surface with silicone sealant, Install the cover and tighten its bolts evenly, in two or three stages, to the torque listed in this Chapter's Specifications.
18 The remainder of installation is the reverse of the removal steps.

11.10 If necessary, remove the shift control motor reduction gear

11.9a Remove the double O-ring

11.9b Remove the oil supply pipe and its O-rings

12 Centrifugal clutch - removal, inspection and installation

Removal

Refer to illustrations 12.2, 12.4a and 12.4b

1 Remove the front crankcase cover (see Section 12).
2 Grind or file away the staked portion of the clutch nut, taking care not to get metal particles in the engine (see illustration).

12.2 Grind or file away the staked portion of the nut (arrow)

12.4a If the clutch won't come off easily, use a puller like this one

12.4b Remove the clutch and the thrust washer behind it

13.2 Remove the primary driven gear bolts (arrows) and take the gear off

3   Hold the clutch with a removal tool so it won't turn **(see illustrations 16.7a and 16.7b in Chapter 2A)**. Remove the nut, then the washer.

4   Pull the centrifugal clutch weight assembly and drum off the crankshaft. If it won't come easily, use a special tool (Honda part no. 07ZMC-HN20100 or equivalent) **(see illustration)**. Remove the thrust washer behind the clutch **(see illustration)**.

Inspection

5   This is the same as for 400/450 models (see Chapter 2A).

Installation

6   Slip the centrifugal clutch onto the crankshaft. Engage the drum splines with the splines on the crankshaft. Rotate the weight assembly slightly and align the drive plate splines with the primary gear, then push the centrifugal clutch all the way on.

7   Install the washer **(see illustration 12.4b)**.

8   Oil the threads of a new locknut, then install the locknut. Hold the clutch with a holding tool and tighten the nut to the torque listed in this Chapter's Specifications.

9   Stake the lip of the locknut with a hammer and punch **(see illustration 12.2)**.

10   The remainder of installation is the reverse of the removal steps.

11   Refill the engine oil (see Chapter 1).

---

13   Primary driven gear - removal, inspection and installation

Removal

Refer to illustration 13.2

1   Remove the centrifugal clutch (Section 12).

2   Unbolt the primary driven gear from the automatic transmission unit and take it off **(see illustration)**. **Note:** *If necessary, slip the centrifugal clutch back on and wedge a copper washer or penny between the drive gear on the clutch hub and the driven gear to keep the gear from turning while the bolts are removed.*

Inspection

3   Check the driven gear for obvious damage such as chipped or broken teeth. Replace it if any of these problems are found.

Installation

4   Installation is the reverse of the removal steps. Tighten the driven gear bolts to the torque listed in this Chapter's Specifications.

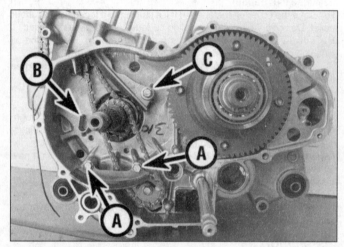

14.2 Unbolt the oil baffle (A), lift the chain guide out of its pocket (B) and unbolt the remaining chain guide (C)

14   Cam chain and guides - removal and installation

Refer to illustration 14.2

1   Remove the rocker assembly, pushrods, lifters, cylinder head, cylinder, front crankcase cover, centrifugal clutch and oil pump chain (Sections 6, 7, 10, 12 and 14).

2   Unbolt the oil baffle from the crankcase **(see illustration)**.

3   Unbolt the sprocket from the oil pump, then remove the sprocket and oil pump chain.

4   Slip the cam chain off the crankshaft.

5   Lift the unbolted guide out of its pocket and unbolt the other cam chain guide **(see illustration 14.2)**.

6   Check all parts for wear and damage and replace as needed.

7   Installation is the reverse of the removal steps.

15   Oil pressure relief valve - removal, inspection and installation

Note: *This procedure applies to the external relief valve. There's another relief valve inside the oil pump.*

Refer to illustration 15.1

1   Unscrew the check valve bolt (it's on the right side of the front

15.1 Unscrew the check valve bolt (arrow) from the front crankcase cover

16.2 Remove the retaining bolts (arrows) and disconnect the hoses from the cooler

crankcase cover) **(see illustration)**.
2   Remove the spring from the valve bore and pull out the valve, using a magnet if necessary.
3   Check the valve and spring for wear and damage and replace them as needed.
4   Installation is the reverse of the removal steps. Use a new sealing washer and tighten the check valve to the torque listed in this Chapter's Specifications.

16 Oil cooler - removal, inspection and installation

Removal
Refer to illustration 16.2
1   Remove the radiator grille and front fender (see Chapter 7).
2   Unbolt the oil cooler tubes from the oil cooler and pull them out **(see illustration)**.
3   Unbolt the oil cooler and lift it off the vehicle.

Inspection
4   Check the oil cooler for signs of leakage, especially at the hose joints. It's a good idea to replace the O-rings whenever they're removed, but they should be definitely be replaced if they're compressed, brittle or deteriorated.
5   Check the hoses for deterioration, and look closely for leakage or

cracks at the joints where the hose meets the metal fitting. Replace the hoses if there are any doubts about their condition - a hose failure will cause a sudden catastrophic loss of oil pressure.
6   Check the oil cooler fins for clogging or bending. Clean out any debris with a garden hose or low-pressure compressed air. Carefully straighten any bent fins with a small screwdriver, taking care not to puncture the oil passages.

Installation
7   Installation is the reverse of the removal steps. Use new O-rings and tighten the mounting bolts securely, but don't overtighten them and strip the threads.

17 Oil tank and feed pump strainer - removal, inspection and installation

Tank and feed pump strainer
Refer to illustrations 17.2, 17.3, 17.4a, 17.4b, 17.5a, 17.5b, 17.5c and 17.6
1   Remove the front mudguards and inner fenders (see Chapter 7).
2   Disconnect the oil temperature sensor connector from the sensor on the tank **(see illustration)**.
3   Unbolt the oil tubes from the tank and pull them out **(see illustration)**.

17.2   Disconnect the oil temperature sensor connector from the sensor

17.3   Unbolt the oil tubes from the tank and pull them out

17.4a Remove the oil tank mounting bolts and lift the tank off

17.4b Remove the joint collar and O-rings

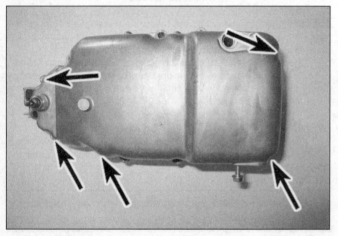

17.5a Remove the tank assembly bolts from the front side of the
tank (arrows) (three bolts hidden) . . .

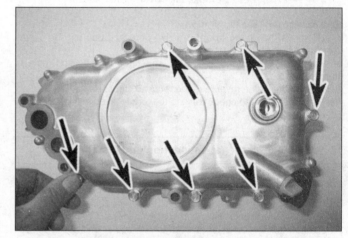

17.5b . . . and from the rear half (arrows), then separate the
tank halves . . .

4   Working from the front of the engine, remove the oil tank mounting bolts (see illustration). Lift the tank off the vehicle and remove the joint collar and O-rings (see illustration).
5   Remove the tank assembly bolts from the front and rear sides of the tank (see illustrations). Separate the tank halves and locate the O-ring (see illustration).

6   Remove the feed pump strainer screen from the tank (see illustration). Clean it in solvent and dry it with compressed air.
7   Remove all traces of old sealant from the tank half mating surfaces. Clean the inside of the tank with solvent, blow it dry and reinstall the strainer.
8   Coat the mating surfaces with a thin layer of silicone sealant and

17.5c . . . remove the O-ring . . .

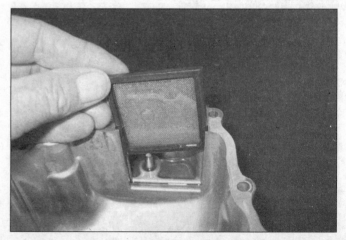

17.6 . . . and remove the feed pump strainer screen from
the tank

18.2 Unbolt the sub-scavenge oil strainer (left arrow) and remove it, then unbolt the main scavenge strainer (right arrow) and pull it out

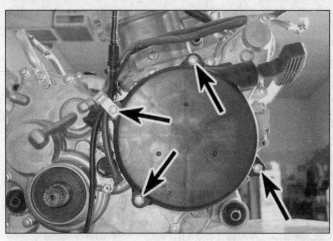

19.1 Remove the bolts (arrows) and take the recoil starter off the engine

reassemble the tank. Install the bolts in both sides and tighten them evenly. Tighten the bolts securely, but don't overtighten and strip the threads.

9   The remainder of installation is the reverse of the removal steps. Use new O-rings on the oil tubes.

18 Scavenge pump strainer - removal and installation

Refer to illustration 18.2

1   Remove the alternator cover (see Chapter 8).

2   Unbolt the secondary strainer and pull it out, then unbolt the main strainer and slide it out **(see illustration)**.

3   Clean the strainers in solvent and dry them with compressed air.

4   Installation is the reverse of the removal steps.

19 Recoil starter - removal, inspection and installation

Removal

Refer to illustration 19.1

1   Unbolt the recoil starter from the rear of the engine **(see illustration)**.

Inspection and installation

2   These are the same as for 400/450 models ((see Chapter 2A).

20 Shift lever and linkage - removal, inspection and installation

Removal

Refer to illustration 20.2

1   Remove the cover from the fuel tank and remove the reverse switch from the bottom of the linkage (see Chapters 3 and 7).

2   Unscrew the drain plug from the bottom of the shift lever box to let out any water **(see illustration)**.

3   Remove the left front mudguard and the front fenders (see Chapter 7).

4   Remove the pinch bolt from the gearshift arm. Remove the bolt completely, don't just loosen it. Remove the pivot bolt, together with its O-ring and washer.

5   Slide the shift linkage off the pivot post and spindle. If necessary, remove the cotter pin, washer and slide shaft and detach the linkage from the shift lever housing.

6   Remove the shift lever mounting bolts and take it off the vehicle.

Inspection

Refer to illustrations 20.7a and 20.7b

7   Unbolt the cover **(see illustration)**. Take off the cover and shift lever housing **(see illustration)**.

8   Check for wear on the tip of the detent plunger, its contact surface in the lever housing and the lock pin **(see illustration 20.7b)**. Replace worn components. Check the oil seals for wear or damage. It's a good

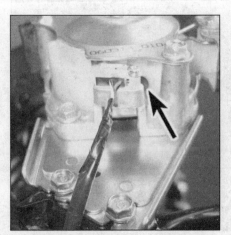

20.2 Remove the drain plug (arrow) from the bottom of the shift lever box

20.7a Unbolt the cover

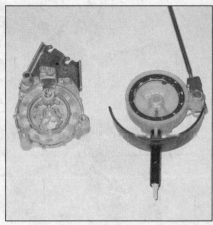

20.7b Take off the cover and shift lever housing

20.17 With the cotter pin and washer removed, make sure the slide pin (arrow) is centered in its slot

21.4 Loosen the rear crankcase cover bolts (arrows) in two or three stages, them remove the bolts and cover

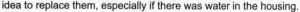

idea to replace them, especially if there was water in the housing.

9   Remove the detent plunger and lubricate it with molybdenum disulfide grease. Also lubricate the lock pin and the friction surfaces of the base bracket and shift lever housing.

10   Reverse the disassembly steps to reassemble the housing.

Installation

Refer to illustration 20.17

11   Install the shift lever housing on the vehicle. Tighten its mounting bolts securely, but don't overtighten them and strip the threads.

12   Install the reverse switch (see Chapter 8).

13   Check the lengths of the upper and lower tie-rods. If they're not within the range listed in this Chapter's Specifications, loosen the lock-nuts, turn the tie-rods to adjust their lengths and tighten the locknuts.

14   Place the shift lever in Neutral.

15   With the gearshift arm in the Neutral position, slip the gearshift arm onto the spindle, aligning the wide spindle tooth with the gearshift arm groove. Install the pinch bolt and tighten it securely, but don't over-tighten it and strip the threads.

16   Install new O-rings on the linkage arm pivot bolt. Position the link-age arm next to its pivot point, then install the bolt and tighten it to the torque listed in this Chapter's Specifications.

17   If you removed the cotter pin and slide shaft to separate the link-age from the shift lever housing, place the linkage end in its installed position. The slide shaft holes in the rod end and housing should be

aligned **(see illustration)**. If not, loosen the locknuts and rotate the upper linkage rod to align the holes, then tighten the locknut. Coat the shaft with molybdenum disulfide grease and install it. Install the washer and a new cotter pin.

18   The remainder of installation is the reverse of the removal steps.

21   Rear crankcase cover - removal and installation

Refer to illustrations 21.4 and 21.5

1   Remove the engine from the vehicle (see Section 5).

2   Remove the alternator cover, starter and reduction gears, vehicle speed sensor and gear position switch (see Chapter 8).

3   Remove the engine side cover and bracket.

4   Loosen the rear crankcase cover bolts in two or three stages, in a criss-cross pattern **(see illustration)**. When they're all loose, remove them.

5   Locate the oil passage collar, its O-ring and the dowel pins **(see illustration)**. They may have come off with the cover or stayed in the engine.

6   Inspect the cover bearings and seal, referring to procedures in Chapter 2C. Blow out the cover oil passages with compressed air.

7   Remove all traces of sealant form the mating surfaces on the cover and engine.

8   Make sure the dowel pins are in place. Install the oil passage col-

21.5 Locate the dowels (A) - in this case, the lower dowel came off with the cover - and the oil passage and O-ring (B)

22.2 Slide the output shaft and driven gear (arrows) out, then separate them

22.3 Note how the shaft forks (arrows) engage the shift drum and gears, then remove the shaft and forks

22.4a Line up the index line on the gearshift spindle with the pointer on the shift drum (arrows)

lar with a new O-ring, lubricated with clean engine oil.

9   Coat the cover mating surface on the engine with silicone sealant. Install the cover and its bolts. Tighten the bolts evenly, in a criss=cross pattern, to the torque listed in this Chapter's Specifications.

10   The remainder of installation is the reverse of the removal steps.

22 External shift mechanism - removal and installation

Removal

Refer to illustrations 22.2, 22.3, 22.4a, 22.4b, 22.5a and 22.5b

1   Remove the rear crankcase cover (see Section 21).

2   Slide the output shaft and driven gear out of the crankcase and remove the driven gear from the output shaft **(see illustration)**.

3   Note the shift forks are installed **(see illustration)**. Pull the fork shaft out of the crankcase and remove the forks.

4   Rotate the shift drum to align its pointer with the index line on the gearshift spindle **(see illustrations)**.

5   Press the stopper arm against its spring with a screwdriver and pull the shift drum out of the crankcase **(see illustration)**. Once the shift drum is out, let the stopper arm move to the left until it stops **(see illustration)**.

22.4b Here's a close-up of the shift drum pointer (arrow)

6   Unbolt the retainer plate and remove the gearshift spindle **(see illustration 22.5b)**.

7   Unbolt the stopper arm and remove it, together with its spring.

8   Refer to Chapter 2C for inspection procedures.

22.5a Push the stopper arm against its spring until it clears the shift drum and pull the shift drum out (shift drum removed for clarity)

22.5b Once the shift drum is out, release the stopper arm, then unbolt the retainer plate (arrow) and pull the gearshift spindle out

23.2 Slip the washers off of the reverse idler shaft and countershaft (arrows)

23.3 Locate the mainshaft O-ring and remove it if it stayed in the automatic transmission unit

Installation

9   Installation is the reverse of the removal steps, with the following additions:

   a) *Use non-permanent thread locking agent on the threads of the stopper arm bolt and tighten the bolt to the torque listed in this Chapter's Specifications.*

   b) *Install the gearshift spindle and tighten its bolt to the torque listed in this Chapter's Specifications, then align it as described in Step 4 when installing the shift drum.*

   c) *Turn the shift drum clockwise so its slot is vertical to place it in the Neutral position before installing the shift forks.*

   d) *Install the shift forks with their numbers outward (away from the engine). Lubricate the fork shaft with clean engine oil.*

   e) *Install the output shaft, then install its gear with the long side of the hub facing away from the engine.*

23 Sub-transmission - removal and installation

Refer to illustrations 23.2, 23.3, 23.4 and 23.6

1   Remove the rear crankcase cover and external shift linkage (see Sections 21 and 22).

2   Slip the washers off of the reverse idler shaft and countershaft **(see illustration)**.

3   Pull the mainshaft out of the engine (it's installed in the automatic

transmission unit). Look for the mainshaft O-ring **(see illustration)**. It may come off with the mainshaft or stay in the automatic transmission unit.

4   Pull the countershaft and reverse idler gear out of the crankcase together, then separate them **(see illustration)**.

5   Pull the reverse idler shaft out of the crankcase and remove its washer.

6   Disassemble the countershaft and lay the parts in order on a clean workbench **(see illustration)**.

7   Refer to Chapter 2C for inspection procedures.

8   Assemble the countershaft. The rounded side of the thrust washer between the reverse/low shift and reverse gear faces away from the engine. The rounded side of the drive gear thrust washer faces toward the engine.

9   Installation is the reverse of the removal steps.

24 Crankcase - disassembly and reassembly

1   To examine and repair or replace the oil pump, crankshaft, connecting rod, balancer, bearings and automatic transmission unit, the crankcase must be split into two parts.

Disassembly

Refer to illustrations 24.13, 24.14, 24.15 and 24.16

2   Remove the engine from the vehicle (see Section 5).

3   Remove the carburetor (see Chapter 3).

23.4 Pull the countershaft and reverse idler gear out of the crankcase together, then separate them

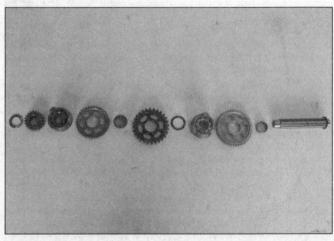

23.6 Countershaft components

24.13 Remove five bolts (arrows) from the rear crankcase half . . .

24.14 . . . and 12 bolts (arrows) from the front crankcase half

4　Remove the alternator rotor, starter clutch and starter motor (see Chapter 8).

5　Remove the centrifugal clutch (see Section 12).

6　Remove the external shift mechanism (see Section 22).

7　Remove the sub-transmission (see Section 23).

8　Remove the rocker assembly and pushrods, cylinder head, cylinder and piston (see Sections 6, 7 and 9 and Chapter 2D).

9　Remove the angle sensor and its connecting shaft (see Chapter 8).

10　Remove the oil pump drive chain and sprocket, then remove the cam chain and tensioner (see Sections 8 and 14).

11　Check carefully to make sure there aren't any remaining components that attach the front and rear halves of the crankcase together.

12　Remove the primary driven gear (see Section 13).

13　Loosen the five rear crankcase bolts in two or three stages, in a criss-cross pattern (see illustration).

14　Turn the crankcase over and remove the twelve front crankcase bolts (see illustration).

15　Lift the front half off the rear half (see illustration). Don't pry against the mating surfaces or they'll develop leaks.

16　Remove the two crankcase dowels and two O-rings (see illustration).

17　Refer to Sections 25 and 26 and Chapter 2C for information on the internal components of the crankcase.

Reassembly

18　Make sure the inner race is in position on the crankshaft (see illustration 24.16b).

19　Remove all traces of old gasket and sealant from the crankcase mating surfaces with a sharpening stone or similar tool. Be careful not to let any fall into the case as this is done and be careful not to damage the mating surfaces.

20　Check to make sure the two dowel pins and two O-rings are in place in their holes in the mating surface of the left crankcase half (see illustration 24.16b).

21　Coat the crankcase mating surface with silicone sealant.

22　Carefully place the front crankcase half onto the rear crankcase half. While doing this, make sure the automatic transmission unit and crankshaft fit into their ball bearings in the front crankcase half.

23　Install the front crankcase half bolts in the correct holes and tighten them so they are just snug. Then tighten them in two or three stages, in a criss-cross pattern, to the torque listed in this Chapter's Specifications.

24　Tighten the five bolts in the rear half of the crankcase to the torque listed in this Chapter's Specifications.

25　Make sure the crankshaft turns freely.

26　The remainder of installation is the reverse of removal.

24.16a Lift the front case half from the rear case half . . .

24.16b . . . and locate the dowels and O-rings
(upper dowel hidden)

25.2 Remove the five dark mounting bolts (the three light-colored bolts hold the pump halves together) . . .

25.3 Take the pump out of the crankcase and remove the O-rings (arrows)

25 Oil pump - removal and installation

Removal

Refer to illustrations 25.2 and 25.3

1 Remove the engine, then separate the case halves (see Sections 5 and 24).
2 Unbolt the oil pump and take it out of the case **(see illustration)**.
3 Remove the oil pump O-rings **(see illustration)**.
4 Refer to Chapter 2C for inspection procedures.
5 Installation is the reverse of the removal steps. Use new O-rings, coated with clean engine oil. Tighten the pump mounting bolts in a criss-cross pattern. Tighten the bolts securely, but don't overtighten them and strip the threads.

26 Automatic transmission unit - removal, inspection and installation

Removal

Refer to illustrations 26.2a and 26.2b

1 Remove the engine, then separate the case halves (see Sections 5 and 25).

2 Locate the automatic transmission unit dowel pin **(see illustrations)**. It may come off with the transmission unit or stay in the crankcase.
3 Remove the transmission unit mounting bolts and lift it out of the crankcase **(see illustration 26.2a)**.

Inspection

4 Check the unit for visible damage. It can't be disassembled; if problems are found, it must be replaced as a unit.
5 Rotate the transmission shaft and check for rough or noisy rotation. Replace the transmission unit if any problems are found.
6 It's possible for the ball nut to rotate to the end of the shaft and become stuck. If this happens, you should be able to free it by rocking the gear back and forth with a screwdriver. The gear can be reached by removing the shift control motor if the crankcase is still assembled.

Installation

7 Installation is the reverse of the removal steps. Be sure the dowel pin is in position. Tighten the bolts in a criss-cross pattern. Tighten the bolts securely, but don't overtighten them and strip the threads.

26.2a Remove the transmission unit mounting bolts; there's a dowel at location A . . .

26.2b . . . between the transmission unit and crankcase (lower arrow) - the ball nut (upper arrow) may become stuck if it travels to the end of the threaded rod

Chapter 2 Part C
General engine overhaul procedures

Contents

Specifications

400 and 450 models

Rocker arms and lifters

Rocker arm inside diameter
Standard .... 12.000 to 12.018 mm (0.4724 to 0.4731 inch)
Limit .... 12.05 mm (0.474 inch)
Rocker shaft outside diameter
Standard .... 11.964 to 11.984 mm (0.4710 to 0.4718 inch)
Limit .... 11.92 mm (0.469 inch)
Shaft-to-arm clearance
Standard .... 0.016 to 0.054 mm (0.0006 to 0.0021 inch)
Limit .... 0.08 mm (0.003 inch)
Valve lifter diameter (intake and exhaust)
Standard .... 22.467 to 22.482 mm (0.8845 to 0.8851 inch)
Limit .... 22.46 mm (0.884 inch)
Valve lifter bore diameter (intake and exhaust)
Standard .... 22.451 to 22.526 mm (0.8862 to 0.8868 inch)
Limit .... 22.54 mm (0.887 inch)

Camshaft

Lobe height limit
Intake .... 36.25 mm (1.427 inch)
Exhaust .... 36.10 mm (1.421 inch)

Cylinder head, valves and valve springs

Cylinder head warpage limit	0.10 mm 0.004 inch)
Valve stem runout	Not specified

Valve stem diameter
Intake
Standard .... 5.475 to 5.490 mm (0.2156 to 0.2161 inch)
Limit .... 5.45 mm (0.215 inch)
Exhaust
Standard .... 5.455 to 5.470 mm (0.2148 to 0.2154 inch)
Limit .... 5.43 mm (0.214 inch)

Valve guide inside diameter (intake and exhaust)
Standard .... 5.500 to 5.512 mm (0.2165 to 0.2170 inch)
Limit .... 5.525 mm (0.2177 inch)

Valve seat width (intake and exhaust)
Standard .... 1.2 mm (0.05 inch)
Limit .... 1.5 mm (0.06 inch)

Valve spring free length
400 models
Inner spring
Standard .... 36.31 m (1.430 inch)
Limit .... 35.2 mm (1.39 inch)
Outer spring
Standard .... 41.34 mm (1.628 inch)
Limit .... 40.0 mm (1.57 inch)
450 models
Inner spring
Standard .... 36.85 m (1.451 inch)
Limit .... 35.84 mm (1.411 inch)
Outer spring
Standard .... 41.67 mm (1.641 inch)
Limit .... 40.42 mm (1.591 inch)

Cylinder

Bore diameter
400 models
Standard .... 86.000 to 86.010 mm (3.3858 to 3.3862 inch)
Limit .... 86.10 mm (3.390 inches)
450 models
Standard .... 90.000 to 90.010 mm (3.543 to 3.544 inches)
Limit .... 90.10 mm (3.547 inches)
Taper and out-of-round limits .... 0.10 mm (0.004 inch)
Surface warpage limit .... 0.10 mm (0.004 inch)

Pistons

Piston diameter
400 models
Standard .... 85.965 to 85.985 mm (3.3844 to 3.3852 inch)
Limit .... 85.90 mm (3.382 inches)
450 models
Standard .... 89.945 to 89.965 mm (3.5411 to 3.5419 inches)
Piston-to-cylinder clearance
Standard .... 0.15 to 0.45 mm (0.0006 to 0.0018 inch)
Limit .... 0.10 mm (0.004 inch)
Oversize pistons and rings available .... + 0.25 mm (0.010 inch), 0.5 mm (0.020 inch), 0.75 mm (0.030 inch), 1.00 mm (0.040 inch)

Piston pin bore

In piston
Standard .... 19.002 to 19.008 mm (0.7481 to 0.7483 inch)
Limit .... 19.04 mm (0.750 inch)
In connecting rod
Standard .... 19.020 to 19.041 mm (0.7488 to 0.7496 inch)
Limit .... 19.07 mm (0.751 inch)
Piston pin outer diameter
Standard .... 18.994 to 19.000 mm (0.7478 to 0.7480 inch)
Limit .... 18.96 mm (0.746 inch)
Piston pin-to-piston clearance
Standard .... 0.002 to 0.014 mm (0.0001 to 0.0006 inch)
Limit .... 0.012 mm (0.0039 inch)

Ring side clearance
  Top
    Standard .... 0.03 to 0.06 mm (0.001 to 0.002 inch)
    Limit .... 0.09 mm (0.004 inch)
  Second
    Standard .... 0.015 to 0.045 mm (0.0006 to 0.0018 inch)
    Limit .... 0.09 mm (0.004 inch)
Ring end gap
  Top
    Standard .... 0.15 to 0.30 mm (0.006 to 0.012 inch)
    Limit .... 0.5 mm (0.02 inch)
  Second
    Standard .... 0.30 to 0.45 mm (0.012 to 0.018 inch)
    Limit .... 0.60 mm (0.02 inch)
  Oil
    Standard .... 0.20 to 0.70 mm (0.01 to 0.03 inch)
    Limit .... Not specified

Centrifugal clutch
Drum internal diameter
  Standard .... 140.0 mm (5.51 inches)
  Limit .... 140.2 mm (5.52 inches)
Weight lining thickness
  Standard .... 3.0 mm (0.12 inch)
  Limit .... 2.0 mm (0.08 inch)
Clutch spring height
  Standard .... 3.1 mm (0.122 inch)
  Limit .... 2.95 mm (0.116 inch)
Clutch weight spring free length
  Standard .... 21.6 mm (0.85 inch)
  Limit .... 22.5 mm (0.89 inch)

Change clutch
Spring free length
  Standard .... 32.1 mm (1.26 inch)
  Limit .... 31.0 mm (1.22 inch)
Friction plate thickness
  Standard .... 2.62 to 2.78 mm (0.103 to 0.109 inch)
  Limit .... 2.3 mm (0.09 inch)
Friction and metal plate warpage limit .... 0.20 mm (0.008 inch)
Clutch outer guide outside diameter
  Standard .... 27.959 to 27.980 mm (1.1007 to 1.1016 inch)
  Limit .... 27.92 mm (1.099 inch)
Clutch outer guide inside diameter
  Standard .... 22.000 to 22.021 mm (0.8661 to 0.8670 inch)
  Limit .... 22.05 mm (0.868 inch)
Diameter of outer guide friction surface on mainshaft
  Standard .... 21.972 to 21.993 mm (0.8650 to 0.8659 inch)
  Limit .... 21.93 mm (0.863 inch)
Primary drive gear
Inside diameter
  Standard .... 27.000 to 27.021 mm (1.0630 to 1.0638 inch)
  Limit .... 27.05 mm (1.065 inch)
Diameter of friction surface on crankshaft
  Standard .... 26.959 to 26.980 mm (1.0614 to 1.0622 inch)
  Limit .... 26.93 mm (1.060 inch)

Oil pump
Outer rotor to body clearance
  Standard .... 0.15 to 0.21 mm (0.006 to 0.008 inch)
  Limit .... 0.25 mm (0.010 inch)
Inner to outer rotor clearance
  Standard .... 0.15 mm (0.006 inch) or less
  Limit .... 0.20 mm (0.008 inch)
Side clearance (rotors to straightedge)
  Standard .... 0.02 to 0.09 mm (0.001 to 0.004 inch)
  Limit .... 0.11 mm (0.004 inch)

Shift drum and forks

Fork inside diameter
  Standard .... 13.000 to 13.021 mm (0.5118 to 0.5126 inch)
  Limit .... 13.04 mm (0.513 inch)
Fork shaft outside diameter
  Standard .... 12.966 to 12.984 mm (0.5105 to 0.5112 inch)
  Limit .... 12.96 mm (0.510 inch)
Fork ear thickness
  Standard .... 4.93 to 5.00 mm (0.194 to 0.197 inch)
  Limit .... 4.50 mm (0.177 inch)

Transmission

Gear inside diameters
  Mainshaft fourth
    Standard .... 25.000 to 25.021 mm (0.9843 to 0.9851 inch)
    Limit .... 25.05 mm (0.986 inch)
  Mainshaft fifth
    Standard .... 20.020 to 20.041 mm (0.7882 to 0.7890 inch)
    Limit .... 20.07 mm (0.790 inch)
  Countershaft first, second, third
    Standard .... 28.020 to 28.041 mm (1.1031 to 1.1040 inch)
    Limit .... 28.07 mm (1.105 inch)
  Countershaft reverse
    Standard .... 28.021 to 28.041 mm (1.1032 to 1.1040 inch)
    Limit .... 28.07 mm (1.105 inch)
Reverse idler
  Standard .... 18.000 to 18.021 mm (0.7087 to 0.7095 inch)
  Limit .... 18.05 mm (0.711 inch)
Bushing diameters
  Mainshaft fourth outside diameter
    Standard .... 24.959 to 24.980 mm (0.9826 to 0.9835 inch)
    Limit .... 24.93 mm (0.981 inch)
  Mainshaft fourth inside diameter
    Standard .... 22.000 to 22.021 mm (0.8661 to 0.8670 inch)
    Limit .... 22.05 mm (0.868 inch)
  Mainshaft fifth outside diameter
    Standard .... 19.966 to 19.984 mm (0.7861 to 0.7868 inch)
    Limit .... 19.93 mm (0.785 mm)
  Mainshaft fifth inside diameter
    Standard .... 17.016 to 10.034 mm (0.6699 to 0.6706 inch)
    Limit .... 17.06 mm (0.672 inch)
  Countershaft first outside diameter
    Standard .... 27.984 to 28.005 mm (1.1017 to 1.1026 inch)
    Limit .... 27.93 mm (1.100 inch)
  Countershaft second outside diameter
    Standard .... 27.979 to 28.000 mm (1.1015 to 1.1024 inch)
    Limit .... 27.93 mm (1.100 inch)
  Countershaft reverse outside diameter
    Standard .... 27.979 to 28.00 mm (1.1015 to 1.1024 inch)
    Limit .... 27.93 mm (1.100 inch)
Gear-to-bushing clearances
  Mainshaft fourth
    Standard .... 0.020 to 0.062 mm (0.0008 to 0.0024 inch)
    Limit .... 0.10 mm (0.004 inch)
  Mainshaft fifth
    Standard .... 0.016 to 0.055 mm (0.0006 to 0.0022 inch)
    Limit .... 0.10 mm (0.004 inch)
  Countershaft first
    Standard .... 0.015 to 0.057 mm (0.0006 to 0.0022 inch)
    Limit .... 0.10 mm (0.004 inch)
  Countershaft second and reverse
    Standard .... 0.020 to 0.062 mm (0.0008 to 0.0024 inch)
    Limit .... 0.10 mm (0.00 inch)
  Countershaft third
    Standard .... 0.015 to 0.057 mm (0.0006 to 0.0022 inch)
    Limit .... 0.10 mm (0.004 inch)
  Reverse idler
    Standard .... 0.016 to 0.055 mm (0.0006 to 0.0022 inch)
    Limit .... 0.10 mm (0.004 inch)

Shaft diameters
  Mainshaft fourth gear surface
    Standard .... 21.959 to 21.980 mm (0.8645 to 0.8654 inch)
    Limit .... 21.93 mm (0.863 inch)
  Mainshaft fifth gear surface
    Standard .... 16.983 to 16.994 mm (0.6686 to 0.6691 inch)
    Limit .... 16.95 mm (0.667 inch)
  Reverse idler gear surface
    Standard .... 13.966 to 13.984 mm (0.5498 to 0.5506 inch)
    Limit .... 13.93 mm (0.548 inch)
Shaft-to-bushing clearances
  Mainshaft fourth
    Standard .... 0.020 to 0.062 mm (0.0008 to 0.0024 inch)
    Limit .... 0.10 mm (0.004 inch)
  Mainshaft fifth
    Standard .... 0.022 to 0.051 mm (0.0009 to 0.0020 inch)
    Limit .... 0.10 mm (0.004 inch)
  Reverse idler
    Standard .... 0.016 to 0.059 mm (0.0006 to 0.0023 inch)
    Limit .... 0.10 mm (0.004 inch)

Crankshaft

Connecting rod side clearance
  Standard .... 0.05 to 0.65 mm (0.002 to 0.026 inch)
  Limit .... 0.80 mm (0.031 inch)
Connecting rod big end radial clearance
  Standard .... 0.006 to 0.018 mm (0.0002 to 0.0007 inch)
  Limit .... 0.05 mm (0.002 inch)
Runout limit .... 0.05 mm (0.002 inch)

500 models

Rocker arms and lifters

Rocker arm inside diameter
  Standard .... 12.000 to 12.018 mm (0.4724 to 0.4731 inch)
  Limit .... 12.05 mm (0.474 inch)
Rocker shaft outside diameter
  Standard .... 11.964 to 11.984 mm (0.4710 to 0.4718 inch)
  Limit .... 11.92 mm (0.469 inch)
Shaft-to-arm clearance
  Standard .... 0.016 to 0.054 mm (0.0006 to 0.0021 inch)
  Limit .... 0.08 mm (0.003 inch)
Valve lifter diameter (intake and exhaust) .... Not specified
Valve lifter bore diameter (intake and exhaust) .... Not specified

Camshaft

Lobe height limit
  Intake .... 33.960 to 34.120 mm (1.3370 to 1.3433 inch)
  Exhaust .... 34.196 to 34.356 mm (1.346 to 1.352 inch)

Cylinder head, valves and valve springs

Cylinder head warpage limit .... 0.10 mm 0.004 inch)
Valve stem runout.. Not specified
Valve stem diameter
  Intake
    Standard .... 5.475 to 5.490 mm (0.2156 to 0.2161 inch)
    Limit .... 5.45 mm (0.215 inch)
  Exhaust
    Standard .... 5.455 to 5.470 mm (0.2148 to 0.2154 inch)
    Limit .... 5.43 mm (0.214 inch)
Valve guide inside diameter (intake and exhaust)
  Standard .... 5.500 to 5.512 mm (0.2165 to 0.2170 inch)
  Limit .... 5.525 mm (0.2177 inch)
Valve seat width (intake and exhaust)
  Standard .... 1.0 to 1.1 mm (0.039 to 0.043 inch)
  Limit .... 1.4 mm (0.059 inch)

Cylinder head, valves and valve springs (continued)

Valve spring free length
    Inner spring
        Standard .... 38.82 mm (1.528 inch)
        Limit .... 37.8 mm (1.49 inch)
    Outer spring
        Standard .... 51.17 mm (1.2.015 inch)
        Limit .... 49.0 mm (1.93 inch)

Cylinder

Bore diameter
    Standard .... 92.000 to 92.010 mm (3.6220 to 3.6224 inch)
    Limit .... 92.10 mm (3.626 inches)
Taper and out-of-round limits .... 0.10 mm (0.004 inch)
Surface warpage limit... 0.10 mm (0.004 inch)

Pistons

Piston diameter
    Standard .... 91.965 to 91.985 mm (3.6207 to 3.6214 inch)
    Limit .... 91.90 mm (3.618 inches)
Piston-to-cylinder clearance
    With standard piston (limit) .... 0.10 mm (0.004 inch)
    With oversize piston... 0.15 to 0.45 mm (0.0006 to 0.0018 inch)
Oversize pistons and rings available... + 0.25 mm (0.010 inch), 0.5 mm (0.020 inch)
Piston pin bore
    In piston
        Standard .... 20.002 to 20.008 mm (0.7875 to 0.7877 inch)
        Limit .... 20.04 mm (0.789 inch)
    In connecting rod
        Standard .... 20.020 to 20.041 mm (0.7882 to 0.7890 inch)
        Limit .... 20.07 mm (0.790 inch)
Piston pin outer diameter
    Standard .... 19.994 to 20.000 mm (0.7872 to 0.7874 inch)
    Limit .... 19.96 mm (0.786 inch)
Piston pin-to-piston clearance
    Standard .... 0.002 to 0.014 mm (0.0001 to 0.0006 inch)
    Limit .... 0.012 mm (0.0039 inch)
Ring side clearance (top and second)
    Standard .... 0.03 to 0.06 mm (0.001 to 0.002 inch)
    Limit .... 0.09 mm (0.004 inch)
Ring end gap
    Top
        Standard .... 0.15 to 0.30 mm (0.006 to 0.012 inch)
        Limit .... 0.5 mm (0.02 inch)
    Second
        Standard .... 0.30 to 0.45 mm (0.012 to 0.018 inch)
        Limit .... 0.60 mm (0.02 inch)
    Oil ring side rails
        Standard .... 0.20 to 0.70 mm (0.01 to 0.03 inch)
        Limit .... Not specified

Centrifugal clutch

Drum internal diameter
    Standard .... 150.0 to 150.2 mm (5.906 to 5.913 inches)
    Limit .... 150.4 mm (5.92 inches)
Weight lining thickness
    Standard .... 3.0 mm (0.12 inch)
    Limit .... 2.0 mm (0.08 inch)
Clutch spring height
    Standard .... 3.72 mm (0.146 inch)
    Limit .... 3.6 mm (0.140 inch)
Clutch weight spring free length
    Standard .... 23.2 mm (0.91 inch)
    Limit .... 24.1 mm (0.95 inch)

Oil pump

Outer rotor to body clearance
    Standard .... 0.12 to 0.22 mm (0.005 to 0.009 inch)
    Limit .... 0.25 mm (0.010 inch)

Inner to outer rotor clearance
    Standard .... 0.15 mm (0.006 inch) or less
    Limit .... 0.20 mm (0.008 inch)
Side clearance (rotors to straightedge)
    Standard .... 0.02 to 0.09 mm (0.001 to 0.004 inch)
    Limit .... 0.11 mm (0.004 inch)

Shift drum and forks

Fork inside diameter
    Standard .... 11.000 to 11.021 mm (0.4331 to 0.4339 inch)
    Limit .... 13.04 mm (0.513 inch)
Fork shaft outside diameter
    Standard .... 10.966 to 10.984 mm (0.4317 to 0.4324 inch)
    Limit .... 10.96 mm (0.431 inch)
Fork ear thickness
    Standard .... 4.93 to 5.00 mm (0.194 to 0.197 inch)
    Limit .... 4.50 mm (0.177 inch)

Sub-transmission

Gear inside diameters
  High, low, reverse
    Standard .... 28.020 to 28.041 mm (1.1031 to 1.1040 inch)
    Limit .... 28.07 mm (1.105 inch)
  Reverse idler
    Standard .... 14.000 to 14.018 mm (0.5512 to 0.5519 inch)
    Limit .... 14.04 mm (0.553 inch)
Bushing diameters
  High and reverse
    Outside diameter
      Standard.. 27.979 to 28.000 mm (1.1015 to 1.1024 inch)
      Limit... 27.93 mm (1.100 inch)
    Inside diameter
      Standard.. 25.000 to 25.013 mm (0.9483 to 0.9848 inch)
      Limit... 25.04 mm (0.986 inch)
  Low
    Outside diameter
      Standard.. 27.984 to 28.005 mm (1.1017 to 1.1026 inch)
      Limit... 27.93 mm (1.100 mm)
Gear-to-bushing clearances
  High, reverse
    Standard .... 0.020 to 0.062 mm (0.0008 to 0.0024 inch)
    Limit .... 0.10 mm (0.004 inch)
  Low
    Standard .... 0.015 to 0.057 mm (0.0006 to 0.0022 inch)
    Limit .... 0.10 mm (0.004 inch)
Reverse idler shaft diameter
    Standard .... 13.966 to 13.984 mm (0.5498 to 0.5506 inch)
    Limit .... 13.93 mm (0.548 inch)
Reverse idler gear to shaft clearance
    Standard .... 0.016 to 0.052 mm (0.0006 to 0.0020 inch)
    Limit .... 0.10 mm (0.004 inch)

Crankshaft

Connecting rod side clearance
    Standard .... 0.05 to 0.65 mm (0.002 to 0.026 inch)
    Limit .... 0.80 mm (0.031 inch)
Connecting rod big end radial clearance
    Standard .... 0.006 to 0.018 mm (0.0002 to 0.0007 inch)
    Limit .... 0.05 mm (0.002 inch)
Runout limit .... 0.15 mm (0.006 inch)

3.5 A compression gauge with a fitting for the spark plug hole is preferred over the type that requires hand pressure to maintain the seal

1   General information

Included in this portion of Chapter 2 are general inspection and overhaul procedures. The information includes advice concerning preparation for an overhaul and the purchase of replacement parts, as well as inspection procedures which will tell you if a part must be conditioned or replaced.

The Specifications included in this Part are only those necessary for the inspection and overhaul procedures which follow. Refer to earlier parts of Chapter 2 for additional Specifications.

2   Major engine repair - general note

1   It is not always easy to determine when or if an engine should be completely overhauled, as a number of factors must be considered.
2   High mileage is not necessarily an indication that an overhaul is needed, while low mileage, on the other hand, does not preclude the need for an overhaul. Frequency of servicing is probably the single most important consideration. An engine that has regular and frequent oil and filter changes, as well as other required maintenance, will most likely give many miles of reliable service. Conversely, a neglected engine, or one which has not been broken in properly, may require an overhaul very early in its life.
3   Exhaust smoke and excessive oil consumption are both indications that piston rings and/or valve guides are in need of attention. Make sure oil leaks are not responsible before deciding that the rings and guides are bad. Refer to Chapter 1 and perform a cylinder compression check to determine for certain the nature and extent of the work required.
4   If the engine is making obvious knocking or rumbling noises, the connecting rod and/or main bearings are probably at fault.
5   Loss of power, rough running, excessive valve train noise and high fuel consumption rates may also point to the need for an overhaul, especially if they are all present at the same time. If a complete tune-up does not remedy the situation, major mechanical work is the only solution.
6   An engine overhaul generally involves restoring the internal parts to the specifications of a new engine. During an overhaul the piston rings are replaced and the cylinder walls are bored and/or honed. If a rebore is done, then a new piston is also required. The crankshaft and connecting rod are permanently assembled, so if one of these components needs to be replaced both must be. Generally the valves are serviced as well, since they are usually in less than perfect condition at this point. While the engine is being overhauled, other components such as the carburetor and the starter motor can be rebuilt also. The end result

should be a like-new engine that will give as many trouble-free miles as the original.
7   Before beginning the engine overhaul, read through all of the related procedures to familiarize yourself with the scope and requirements of the job. Overhauling an engine is not all that difficult, but it is time consuming. Plan on the vehicle being tied up for a minimum of two (2) weeks. Check on the availability of parts and make sure that any necessary special tools, equipment and supplies are obtained in advance.
8   Most work can be done with typical shop hand tools, although a number of precision measuring tools are required for inspecting parts to determine if they must be replaced. Often a dealer service department or repair shop will handle the inspection of parts and offer advice concerning reconditioning and replacement. As a general rule, time is the primary cost of an overhaul so it doesn't pay to install worn or substandard parts.
9   As a final note, to ensure maximum life and minimum trouble from a rebuilt engine, everything must be assembled with care in a spotlessly clean environment.

3   Cylinder compression - check

Refer to illustration 3.5
1   Among other things, poor engine performance may be caused by leaking valves, incorrect valve clearances, a leaking head gasket, or worn piston, rings and/or cylinder wall. A cylinder compression check will help pinpoint these conditions and can also indicate the presence of excessive carbon deposits in the cylinder head.
2   The only tools required are a compression gauge and a spark plug wrench. Depending on the outcome of the initial test, a squirt-type oil can may also be needed.
3   Start the engine and allow it to reach normal operating temperature, then remove the spark plug (see Chapter 1, if necessary). Work carefully - don't strip the spark plug hole threads and don't burn your hands.
4   Disable the ignition by disconnecting the primary (low tension) wires from the coil (see Chapter 4). Be sure to mark the locations of the wires before detaching them.
5   Install the compression gauge in the spark plug hole **(see illustration)**. Hold or block the throttle wide open.
6   Crank the engine over a minimum of four or five revolutions (or until the gauge reading stops increasing) and observe the initial movement of the compression gauge needle as well as the final total gauge reading. Compare the results to the value listed in this Chapter's Specifications.
7   If the compression built up quickly and evenly to the specified amount, you can assume the engine upper end is in reasonably good mechanical condition. Worn or sticking piston rings and worn cylinders will produce very little initial movement of the gauge needle, but compression will tend to build up gradually as the engine spins over. Valve and valve seat leakage, or head gasket leakage, is indicated by low initial compression which does not tend to build up.
8   To further confirm your findings, add a small amount of engine oil to the cylinder by inserting the nozzle of a squirt-type oil can through the spark plug hole. The oil will tend to seal the piston rings if they are leaking.
9   If the compression increases significantly after the addition of the oil, the piston rings and/or cylinder are definitely worn. If the compression does not increase, the pressure is leaking past the valves or the head gasket. Leakage past the valves may be due to insufficient valve clearances, burned, warped or cracked valves or valve seats or valves that are hanging up in the guides.
10   If compression readings are considerably higher than specified, the combustion chamber is probably coated with excessive carbon deposits. It is possible (but not very likely) for carbon deposits to raise the compression enough to compensate for the effects of leakage past rings or valves. Refer to Chapter 2A or 2B, remove the cylinder head and carefully decarbonize the combustion chamber.

4.2 On 500 models, engine oil pressure can be checked by removing this plug and threading an oil pressure gauge into the hole

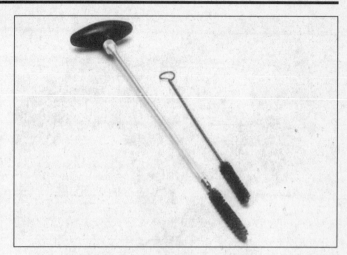

5.2 A selection of brushes is required for cleaning holes and passages in the engine components

4   Engine oil pressure (500 models) - check

Note: *This procedure applies to 500 models, which have a dry sump lubrication system. Honda does not provide oil pressure specifications or a test procedure for 400 or 450 models, which have a wet sump lubrication system.*
Refer to illustration 4.2

1   Check the engine oil level and add some if necessary (see Chapter 1).
2   With the engine off, unscrew the oil gallery plug and washer **(see illustration)**. Thread an external oil pressure gauge into the hole (it has 10 X 1.25 mm threads).
3   Start the engine. Note the oil pressure readings at idle and at 5000 rpm and compare them to the values listed in this Chapter's Specifications. If the readings are low, check the oil pressure relief valve (see Chapter 2B). If the valve is good, remove and clean the oil strainers. If this doesn't solve the problem, you'll to remove the engine and disassemble the crankcase to inspect the oil pump (see Chapter 2C).

5   Engine disassembly and reassembly - general information

Refer to illustrations 5.2 and 5.3

1   Before disassembling the engine, clean the exterior with a degreaser and rinse it with water. A clean engine will make the job easier and prevent the possibility of getting dirt into the internal areas of the engine.
2   In addition to the precision measuring tools mentioned earlier, you will need a torque wrench, a valve spring compressor, oil gallery brushes **(see illustration)**, a piston ring removal and installation tool, a piston ring compressor and a clutch holder tool (described in Section 11 and Chapter 2A). Some new, clean engine oil of the correct grade and type, some engine assembly lube (or moly-based grease) and a tube of RTV (silicone) sealant will also be required.
3   An engine support stand make from short lengths of 2 x 4's bolted together will facilitate the disassembly and reassembly procedures **(see illustration)**. If you have an automotive-type engine stand, an adaptor plate can be made from a piece of plate, some angle iron and some nuts and bolts.
4   When disassembling the engine, keep "mated" parts together (including gears, drum shifter pawls, etc.) that have been in contact with each other during engine operation. These "mated" parts must be reused or replaced as an assembly.
5   Engine/transmission disassembly on 400/450 models should be done in the following general order with reference to the appropriate Sections.

Remove the valve cover, rocker arms and pushrods
Remove the cylinder head
Remove the cylinder and valve lifters
Remove the piston
Remove the clutches
Remove the oil pump
Remove the cam chain tensioner and camshaft
Remove the external shift mechanism
Remove the alternator rotor and starter clutch
Separate the crankcase halves
Remove the shift drum/forks
Remove the transmission shafts/gears
Remove the crankshaft, connecting rod and balancer

6   Engine/transmission disassembly on 500 models should be done in the following general order with reference to the appropriate Sections.

Remove the rocker assembly, pushrods and lifters
Remove the cylinder head
Remove the cam chain tensioner and camshaft
Remove the cylinder
Remove the piston
Remove the centrifugal clutch
Remove the cam chain tensioner and camshaft
Remove the shift lever and external shift mechanism
Remove the sub-transmission

5.3 An engine stand can be made from short lengths of lumber and lag bolts or nails

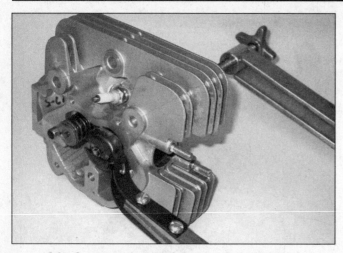

8.9a Compress the spring, remove the keepers and release the compressor

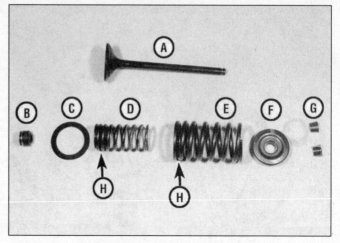

8.9b Valve and related components

A	Valve stem	E	Outer valve spring
B	Oil seal	F	Valve spring retainer
C	Spring seat	G	Keepers
D	Inner valve spring	H	Tightly wound coils

Remove the alternator rotor and starter clutch
Separate the crankcase halves
Remove the oil pump
Remove the automatic transmission unit
Remove the crankshaft, connecting rod and balancer

7   Reassembly is accomplished by reversing the general disassembly sequence.

6   Rocker assembly and pushrods - inspection

1   Check the rocker arms for wear at the pushrod contact surfaces and at the tips of the valve adjusting screws. Try to twist the rocker arms from side-to-side on the shafts. If they're loose on the shafts or if there's visible wear, replace them.
2   Measure the outer diameter of each rocker shaft and the inner diameter of the rocker arms with a micrometer and compare the measurements to the values listed in this Chapter's Specifications. If rocker arm-to-shaft clearance is excessive, replace the rocker arm or shaft, whichever is worn.
3   Check the pushrod ends for wear or scoring. Roll the pushrods on a flat surface such as a piece of plate glass and check them for bending. Replace the pushrods if problems are visible. Don't disassemble them.
4   Coat the rocker shaft(s) and rocker arm bores with moly-based grease. Install the rocker arms and shaft(s), making sure the rocker arms are returned to their original locations if you're reusing the old ones. As you install the rocker shaft(s), align the rocker shaft hole with the bolt hole, using the screwdriver slot in the end of the shaft to twist it in its bore. Install the rocker assembly bolt(s) and tighten to the torque listed in this Chapter's Specifications.

7   Valves/valve seats/valve guides - servicing

1   Because of the complex nature of this job and the special tools and equipment required, servicing of the valves, the valve seats and the valve guides (commonly known as a valve job) is best left to a professional.
2   The home mechanic can, however, remove and disassemble the head, do the initial cleaning and inspection, then reassemble and deliver the head to a dealer service department or properly equipped vehicle repair shop for the actual valve servicing. Refer to Section 8 for those procedures.
3   The dealer service department will remove the valves and springs, recondition or replace the valves and valve seats, replace the valve guides, check and replace the valve springs, spring retainers and keep-

ers (as necessary), replace the valve seals with new ones and reassemble the valve components.
4   After the valve job has been performed, the head will be in like-new condition. When the head is returned, be sure to clean it again very thoroughly before installation on the engine to remove any metal particles or abrasive grit that may still be present from the valve service operations. Use compressed air, if available, to blow out all the holes and passages.

8   Cylinder head and valves - disassembly, inspection and reassembly

Pre-disassembly inspection

1   Check the cylinder head gasket and the mating surfaces on the cylinder head and cylinder for leakage, which could indicate warpage. Refer to Section 8 and check the flatness of the cylinder head.
2   Clean all traces of old gasket material from the cylinder head and cylinder. Be careful not to let any of the gasket material fall into the crankcase, the cylinder bore or the bolt holes.

Disassembly

Refer to illustrations 8.9a and 8.9b

3   As mentioned in the previous Section, valve servicing and valve guide replacement should be left to a dealer service department or vehicle repair shop. However, disassembly, cleaning and inspection of the valves and related components can be done (if the necessary special tools are available) by the home mechanic. This way no expense is incurred if the inspection reveals that service work is not required at this time.
4   To properly disassemble the valve components without the risk of damaging them, a valve spring compressor is absolutely necessary. If the special tool is not available, have a dealer service department or vehicle repair shop handle the entire process of disassembly, inspection, service or repair (if required) and reassembly of the valves.
5   Remove the carburetor intake tube from the cylinder head (see Chapter 3).
6   Before the valves are removed, scrape away any traces of gasket material from the head gasket sealing surface. Work slowly and do not nick or gouge the soft aluminum of the head. Gasket removing solvents,

which work very well, are available at most ATV shops and auto parts stores.

7   Carefully scrape all carbon deposits out of the combustion chamber area. A hand held wire brush or a piece of fine emery cloth can be used once most of the deposits have been scraped away. Do not use a wire brush mounted in a drill motor, or one with extremely stiff bristles, as the head material is soft and may be eroded away or scratched by the wire brush.

8   Before proceeding, arrange to label and store the valves along with their related components so they can be kept separate and reinstalled in the same valve guides they are removed from (again, plastic bags work well for this).

9   Compress the valve spring(s) on the first valve with a spring compressor, then remove the keepers/collets and the retainer from the valve assembly (see illustration). Do not compress the spring(s) any more than is absolutely necessary. Carefully release the valve spring compressor and remove the spring(s), spring seat and valve from the head (see illustration). If the valve binds in the guide (won't pull through), push it back into the head and deburr the area around the keeper groove with a very fine file or whetstone.

10   Repeat the procedure for the remaining valves. Remember to keep the parts for each valve together so they can be reinstalled in the same location.

11   Once the valves have been removed and labeled, pull off the valve stem seals with pliers and discard them (the old seals should never be reused).

12   Next, clean the cylinder head with solvent and dry it thoroughly. Compressed air will speed the drying process and ensure that all holes and recessed areas are clean.

13   Clean all of the valve springs, keepers/collets, retainers and spring seats with solvent and dry them thoroughly. Do the parts from one valve at a time so that no mixing of parts between valves occurs.

14   Scrape off any deposits that may have formed on the valve, then use a motorized wire brush to remove deposits from the valve heads and stems. Again, make sure the valves do not get mixed up.

Inspection

Refer to illustrations 8.16, 8.17, 8.18, 8.19, 8.20a, 8.20b, 8.21a and 8.21b

15   Inspect the head very carefully for cracks and other damage. If cracks are found, a new head will be required. Check the cam bearing surfaces for wear and evidence of seizure. Check the camshaft for wear as well (see Section 14).

16   Using a precision straightedge and a feeler gauge, check the head gasket mating surface for warpage. Lay the straightedge lengthwise, across the head and diagonally (corner-to-corner), intersecting the head bolt holes, and try to slip a feeler gauge under it, on either side of each

8.16 Check the gasket surface for flatness with a straightedge and feeler gauge in the directions shown

combustion chamber (see illustration). The feeler gauge thickness should be the same as the cylinder head warpage limit listed in this Chapter's Specifications. If the feeler gauge can be inserted between the head and the straightedge, the head is warped and must either be machined or, if warpage is excessive, replaced with a new one.

17   Examine the valve seats in each of the combustion chambers. If they are pitted, cracked or burned, the head will require valve service that is beyond the scope of the home mechanic. Measure the valve seat width (see illustration) and compare it to this Chapter's Specifications. If it is not within the specified range, or if it varies around its circumference, valve service work is required.

18   Clean the valve guides to remove any carbon buildup, then measure the inside diameters of the guides (at both ends and the center of the guide) with a small hole gauge and a micrometer (see illustration). Record the measurements for future reference. The guides are measured at the ends and at the center to determine if they are worn in a bell-mouth pattern (more wear at the ends). If they are, guide replacement is an absolute must.

19   Carefully inspect each valve face for cracks, pits and burned spots. Check the valve stem and the keeper groove area for cracks (see illustration). Rotate the valve and check for any obvious indication that it is bent. Check the end of the stem for pitting and excessive wear and make sure the bevel is the specified width. The presence of any of the above conditions indicates the need for valve servicing.

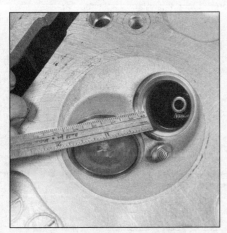
8.17 Measuring valve seat width

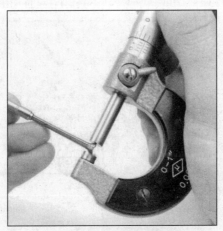
8.18 Measure the valve guide inside diameter with a hole gauge, then measure the gauge with a micrometer

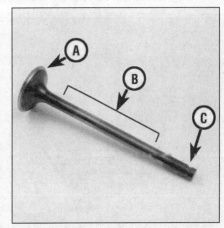
8.19 Check the valve face (A), stem (B) and keeper groove (C) for wear and damage

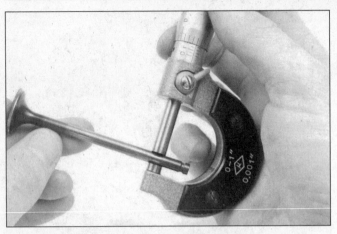

8.20 Measuring valve stem diameter

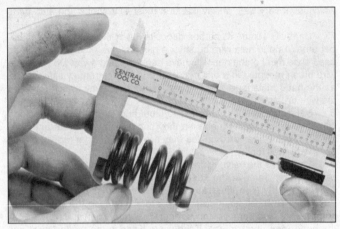

8.21a Measuring the free length of the valve springs

20   Measure the valve stem diameter **(see illustration)**. If the diameter is less than listed in this Chapter's Specifications, the valves will have to be replaced with new ones. Also check the valve stem for bending. Set the valve in a V-block with a dial indicator touching the middle of the stem (see illustration). Rotate the valve and look for a reading on the gauge (which indicates a bent stem). If the stem is bent, replace the valve.

21   Check the end of each valve spring for wear and pitting. Measure the free length **(see illustration)** and compare it to this Chapter's Specifications. Any springs that are shorter than specified have sagged and should not be reused. Stand the spring on a flat surface and check it for squareness **(see illustration)**.

22   Check the spring retainers and keepers/collets for obvious wear and cracks. Any questionable parts should not be reused, as extensive damage will occur in the event of failure during engine operation.

23   If the inspection indicates that no service work is required, the valve components can be reinstalled in the head.

Reassembly

Refer to illustrations 8.25, 8.26a, 8.27b, 8.28 and 8.29

24   If the valve seats have been ground, the valves and seats should be lapped before installing the valves in the head to ensure a positive seal between the valves and seats. This procedure requires coarse and fine valve lapping compound (available at auto parts stores) and a valve lapping tool. If a lapping tool is not available, a piece of rubber or plastic hose can be slipped over the valve stem (after the valve has been installed in the guide) and used to turn the valve.

25   Apply a small amount of coarse lapping compound to the valve face **(see illustration)**, then slip the valve into the guide. **Note:** *Make*

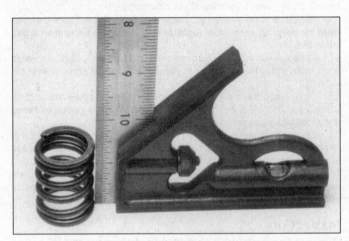

8.21b Checking the valve springs for squareness

sure the valve is installed in the correct guide and be careful not to get any lapping compound on the valve stem.

26   Attach the lapping tool (or hose) to the valve and rotate the tool between the palms of your hands. Use a back-and-forth motion rather than a circular motion. Lift the valve off the seat and turn it at regular intervals to distribute the lapping compound properly. Continue the lapping procedure until the valve face and seat contact area is of uniform width and unbroken around the entire circumference of the valve face and seat **(see illustrations)**. Once this is accomplished, lap the valves

8.25 Apply the lapping compound very sparingly, in small dabs, to the valve face only

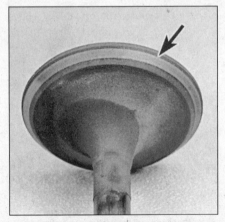

8.26a After lapping, the valve face should exhibit a uniform, unbroken contact pattern (arrow) . . .

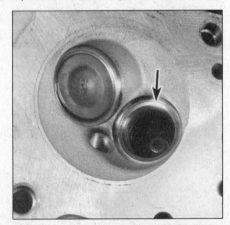

8.26b . . . and the seat (arrow) should be the specified width with a smooth, unbroken appearance

8.28 Push the oil seal onto the valve guide (arrow)

8.29 A small dab of grease will help hold the keepers/collets in place on the valve while the spring compressor is released

9.1 Check the cylinder top surface for warpage in the directions shown

again with fine lapping compound.

27 Carefully remove the valve from the guide and wipe off all traces of lapping compound. Use solvent to clean the valve and wipe the seat area thoroughly with a solvent soaked cloth. Repeat the procedure for the remaining valves.

28 Lay the spring seat in place in the cylinder head, then install new valve stem seals on both of the guides **(see illustration)**. Use an appropriate size deep socket to push the seals into place until they are properly seated. Don't twist or cock them, or they will not seal properly against the valve stems. Also, don't remove them again or they will be damaged.

29 Coat the valve stems with assembly lube or moly-based grease, then install one of them into its guide. Next, install the spring seat, springs and retainers, compress the springs and install the keepers/collets. Note: Install the springs with the tightly wound coils at the bottom (next to the spring seat). When compressing the springs with the valve spring compressor, depress them only as far as is absolutely necessary to slip the keepers/collets into place. Apply a small amount of grease to the keepers/collets **(see illustration)** to help hold them in place as the pressure is released from the springs. Make certain that the keepers/collets are securely locked in their retaining grooves.

30 Support the cylinder head on blocks so the valves can't contact the workbench top, then very gently tap each of the valve stems with a soft-faced hammer. This will help seat the keepers in their grooves.

31 Once all of the valves have been installed in the head, check for proper valve sealing by pouring a small amount of solvent into each of the valve ports. If the solvent leaks past the valve(s) into the combustion chamber area, disassemble the valve(s) and repeat the lapping procedure, then reinstall the valve(s) and repeat the check. Repeat the procedure until a satisfactory seal is obtained.

9 Cylinder - inspection

Refer to illustration 9.1

Caution: *Don't attempt to separate the liner from the cylinder.*

1 Check the top surface of the cylinder for warpage, using the same method as for the cylinder head (see Section 8). Measure along the sides and diagonally across the stud holes **(see illustration)**.

2 Check the cylinder walls carefully for scratches and score marks.

3 Using the appropriate precision measuring tools, check the cylinder's diameter at the top, center and bottom of the cylinder bore, parallel to the crankshaft axis. Next, measure the cylinder's diameter at the same three locations across the crankshaft axis. Compare the results to this Chapter's Specifications. If the cylinder walls are tapered, out-

of-round, worn beyond the specified limits, or badly scuffed or scored, have the cylinder rebored and honed by a dealer service department or an ATV repair shop. If a rebore is done, oversize pistons and rings will be required as well.

4 As an alternative, if the precision measuring tools are not available, a dealer service department or repair shop will make the measurements and offer advice concerning servicing of the cylinder.

5 If it's in reasonably good condition and not worn to the outside of the limits, and if the piston-to-cylinder clearance can be maintained properly, then the cylinder does not have to be rebored; honing is all that is necessary.

6 To perform the honing operation you will need the proper size flexible hone with fine stones as shown in *Maintenance techniques, tools and working facilities* at the front of this book, or a "bottle brush" type hone, plenty of light oil or honing oil, some shop towels and an electric drill motor. Hold the cylinder in a vise (cushioned with soft jaws or wood blocks) when performing the honing operation. Mount the hone in the drill motor, compress the stones and slip the hone into the cylinder. Lubricate the cylinder thoroughly, turn on the drill and move the hone up and down in the cylinder at a pace which will produce a fine crosshatch pattern on the cylinder wall with the crosshatch lines intersecting at approximately a 60-degree angle. Be sure to use plenty of lubricant and do not take off any more material than is absolutely necessary to produce the desired effect. Do not withdraw the hone from the cylinder while it is running. Instead, shut off the drill and continue moving the hone up and down in the cylinder until it comes to a complete stop, then compress the stones and withdraw the hone. Wipe the oil out of the cylinder and repeat the procedure on the remaining cylinder. Remember, do not remove too much material from the cylinder wall. If you do not have the tools, or do not desire to perform the honing operation, a dealer service department or ATV repair shop will generally do it for a reasonable fee.

7 Next, the cylinder must be thoroughly washed with warm soapy water to remove all traces of the abrasive grit produced during the honing operation. Be sure to run a brush through the bolt holes and flush them with running water. After rinsing, dry the cylinder thoroughly and apply a coat of light, rust-preventative oil to all machined surfaces.

10 Piston - removal, inspection and installation

1 The piston is attached to the connecting rod with a piston pin that is a slip fit in the piston and rod.

2 Before removing the piston from the rod, stuff a clean shop towel into the crankcase hole, around the connecting rod. This will prevent the circlips from falling into the crankcase if they are inadvertently dropped.

10.3a The IN mark on top of the piston faces the intake (rear) side of the engine

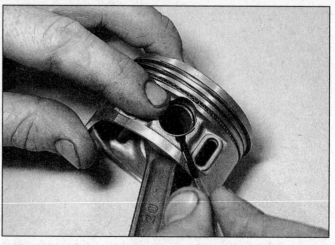

10.3b Wear eye protection and pry the circlip out of its groove with a pointed tool

Removal

Refer to illustrations 10.3a, 10.3b, 10.4a and 10.4b

3   The piston should have an IN mark on its crown that goes toward the intake (rear) side of the engine **(see illustration)**. If this mark is not visible due to carbon buildup, scribe an arrow into the piston crown before removal. Support the piston and pry the circlip out with a pointed tool **(see illustration)**.

4   Push the piston pin out from the opposite end to free the piston from the rod **(see illustration)**. You may have to deburr the area around the groove to enable the pin to slide out (use a triangular file for this procedure). If the pin won't come out, you can fabricate a piston pin removal tool from a long bolt, a nut, a piece of tubing and washers **(see illustration)**.

Inspection

Refer to illustrations 10.6, 10.13, 10.14 and 10.16

5   Before the inspection process can be carried out, the pistons must be cleaned and the old piston rings removed.

6   Using a piston ring removal and installation tool, carefully remove the rings from the pistons **(see illustration)**. Do not nick or gouge the pistons in the process.

7   Scrape all traces of carbon from the tops of the pistons. A hand-held wire brush or a piece of fine emery cloth can be used once the majority of the deposits have been scraped away. Do not, under any

circumstances, use a wire brush mounted in a drill motor to remove deposits from the pistons; the piston material is soft and will be eroded away by the wire brush.

8   Use a piston ring groove cleaning tool to remove any carbon deposits from the ring grooves. If a tool is not available, a piece broken off the old ring will do the job. Be very careful to remove only the carbon deposits. Do not remove any metal and do not nick or gouge the sides of the ring grooves.

9   Once the deposits have been removed, clean the pistons with solvent and dry them thoroughly. Make sure the oil return holes below the oil ring grooves are clear.

10   If the pistons are not damaged or worn excessively and if the cylinders are not rebored, new pistons will not be necessary. Normal piston wear appears as even, vertical wear on the thrust surfaces of the piston and slight looseness of the top ring in its groove. New piston rings, on the other hand, should always be used when an engine is rebuilt.

11   Carefully inspect each piston for cracks around the skirt, at the pin bosses and at the ring lands.

12   Look for scoring and scuffing on the thrust faces of the skirt, holes in the piston crown and burned areas at the edge of the crown. If the skirt is scored or scuffed, the engine may have been suffering from overheating and/or abnormal combustion, which caused excessively high operating temperatures. The oil pump should be checked thoroughly. A hole in the piston crown, an extreme to be sure, is an indication that abnormal combustion (pre-ignition) was occurring. Burned areas at the

10.4a Push the piston pin partway out, then pull it the rest of the way

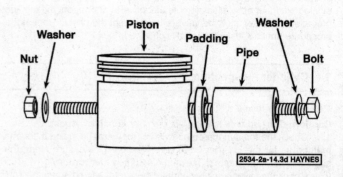

2534-2a-14.3d HAYNES

10.4b The piston pin should come out with hand pressure - if it doesn't, this removal tool can be fabricated from readily available parts

10.6 Remove the piston rings with a ring removal and installation tool

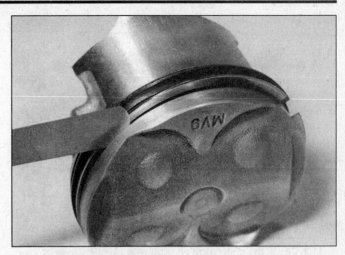

10.13 Measure the piston ring-to-groove clearance with a feeler gauge

edge of the piston crown are usually evidence of spark knock (detonation). If any of the above problems exist, the causes must be corrected or the damage will occur again.

13   Measure the piston ring-to-groove clearance (side clearance) by laying a new piston ring in the ring groove and slipping a feeler gauge in beside it **(see illustration)**. Check the clearance at three or four locations around the groove. Be sure to use the correct ring for each groove; they are different. If the clearance is greater then specified, new pistons will have to be used when the engine is reassembled.

14   Check the piston-to-bore clearance by measuring the bore (see Section 9) and the piston diameter **(see illustration)**. Measure the piston across the skirt on the thrust faces at a 90-degree angle to the piston pin, at the specified distance up from the bottom of the skirt. Subtract the piston diameter from the bore diameter to obtain the clearance. If it is greater than specified, the cylinder will have to be rebored and a new oversized piston and rings installed. If the appropriate precision measuring tools are not available, the piston-to-cylinder clearance can be obtained, though not quite as accurately, using feeler gauge stock. Feeler gauge stock comes in 12-inch lengths and various thicknesses and is generally available at auto parts stores. To check the clearance, slip a piece of feeler gauge stock of the same thickness as the specified piston clearance into the cylinder along with appropriate piston. The cylinder should be upside down and the piston must be positioned exactly as it normally would be. Place the feeler gauge between the piston and cylinder on one of the thrust faces (90-degrees to the piston pin bore). The piston should slip through the cylinder (with the feeler gauge in

place) with moderate pressure. If it falls through, or slides through easily, the clearance is excessive and a new piston will be required. If the piston binds at the lower end of the cylinder and is loose toward the top, the cylinder is tapered, and if tight spots are encountered as the piston/feeler gauge is rotated in the cylinder, the cylinder is out-of-round. Be sure to have the cylinder and piston checked by a dealer service department or a repair shop to confirm your findings before purchasing new parts.

15   Apply clean engine oil to the pin, insert it into the piston and check for freeplay by rocking the pin back-and-forth. If the pin is loose, a new piston and possibly new pin must be installed.

16   Repeat Step 15, this time inserting the piston pin into the connecting rod **(see illustration)**. If the pin is loose, measure the pin diameter and the pin bore in the rod (or have this done by a dealer or repair shop). A worn pin can be replaced separately; if the rod bore is worn, the rod and crankshaft must be replaced as an assembly.

17   Refer to Section 11 and install the rings on the pistons.

Installation

Refer to illustration 10.18

18   Install the piston with its IN mark toward the intake side (rear) of the engine. Lubricate the pin and the rod bore with moly-based grease. Install a new circlip in the groove in one side of the piston (don't reuse the old circlips). Push the pin into position from the opposite side and install another new circlip. Compress the circlips only enough for them to fit in the piston. Make sure the clips are properly seated in the grooves **(see illustration)**.

10.14 Measure the piston diameter with a micrometer

10.16 Slip the piston pin into the rod and try to rock it back-and-forth to check for looseness

10.18 Make sure both piston pin circlips are securely seated in the piston grooves

11.2 Check the piston ring end gap with a feeler gauge at the bottom of the cylinder

11.4 If the end gap is too small, clamp a file in a vise and file the ring ends (from the outside in only) to enlarge the gap slightly

11 Piston rings - installation

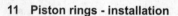

Refer to illustrations 11.2, 11.4, 11.7a, 11.7b, and 11.7c

1   Before installing the new piston rings, the ring end gaps must be checked.

2   Insert the top (No. 1) ring into the bottom of the first cylinder and square it up with the cylinder walls by pushing it in with the top of the piston. The ring should be about one-half inch above the bottom edge of the cylinder. To measure the end gap, slip a feeler gauge between the ends of the ring **(see illustration)** and compare the measurement to the Specifications.

3   If the gap is larger or smaller than specified, double check to make sure that you have the correct rings before proceeding.

4   If the gap is too small, it must be enlarged or the ring ends may come in contact with each other during engine operation, which can cause serious damage. The end gap can be increased by filing the ring ends very carefully with a fine file **(see illustration)**. When performing this operation, file only from the outside in.

5   Repeat the procedure for the second compression ring (ring gap is not specified for the oil ring rails or spacer).

6   Once the ring end gaps have been checked/corrected, the rings can be installed on the piston.

7   The oil control ring (lowest on the piston) is installed first. It is composed of three separate components. Slip the spacer into the groove, then install the upper side rail **(see illustrations)**. Do not use a piston ring installation tool on the oil ring side rails as they may be dam-

11.7a Installing the oil ring expander - make sure the ends don't overlap

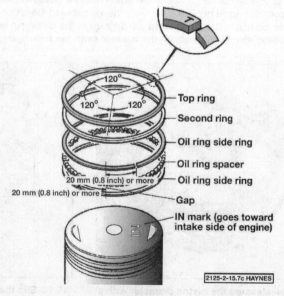

11.7c Ring details

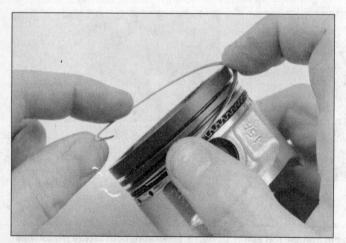

11.7b Installing an oil ring side rail - don't use a ring installation tool to do this

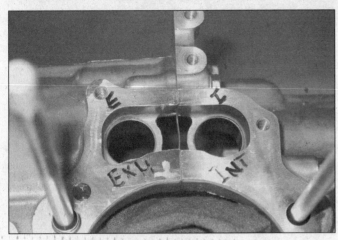

12.2 Label the bores and lifters, then pull the lifters out (use a magnet if necessary)

13.1 On 400/450 models, remove the screw (arrow) and take off the pump cover

aged. Instead, place one end of the side rail into the groove between the spacer expander and the ring land. Hold it firmly in place and slide a finger around the piston while pushing the rail into the groove (taking care not to cut your fingers on the sharp edges). Next, install the lower side rail in the same manner.

8   After the three oil ring components have been installed, check to make sure that both the upper and lower side rails can be turned smoothly in the ring groove.

9   Install the no. 2 (middle) ring next. It can be readily distinguished from the top ring by its cross-section shape (see illustration 11.7c). Do not mix the top and middle rings.

10   To avoid breaking the ring, use a piston ring installation tool and make sure that the identification mark is facing up (see illustration 11.7c). Fit the ring into the middle groove on the piston. Do not expand the ring any more than is necessary to slide it into place.

11   Finally, install the no. 1 (top) ring in the same manner. Make sure the identifying mark is facing up. Be very careful not to confuse the top and second rings. Besides the different profiles, the top ring is narrower than the second ring.

12   Once the rings have been properly installed, stagger the end gaps, including those of the oil ring side rails (see illustration 11.7c).

12   Valve lifters - inspection

Refer to illustration 12.2

1   Check the lifters for wear, galling, scoring or the bluish tint that

indicates overheating. Check the camshaft contact surfaces, the sides and the pockets that contain the pushrod ends. If any problems can be seen, replace the lifters.

2   If there's any doubt about lifter wear, measure lifter diameter with a micrometer. Measure the internal diameter of the lifter bores, using a hole gauge and micrometer (see illustration). If the lifter measurements are not within the range listed in this Chapter's Specifications, replace the lifters. If the bores are worn, replace the crankcase.

13   Oil pump - inspection

Refer to illustrations 13.1, 13.2a, 13.2b, 13.4a, 13.4b and 13.4c

1   If you're working on a 400 or 450 model, remove the screw and take off the pump cover (see illustration). Remove the rotors and shaft.

2   If you're working on a 500 model, unscrew the pump assembly bolts. Disassemble the pump and lay the parts in order on a clean workbench (see illustration).

3   Wash all the components in solvent, then dry them off. Check the pump body, the rotors and the cover for scoring and wear. If any damage or uneven or excessive wear is evident, replace the pump. If you are rebuilding the engine, it's a good idea to install a new oil pump.

4   Place the rotors in their bores. Measure the clearance between the outer rotor and body, and between the inner and outer rotors, with a

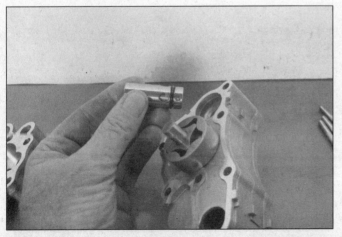

13.2a On 500 models, remove the cover bolts, separate the pump halves and remove the relief valve . . .

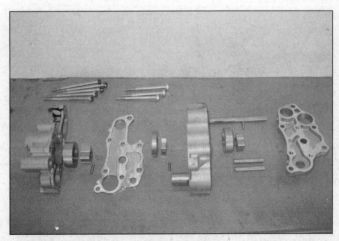

13.2b . . . and lay the pump components out for inspection

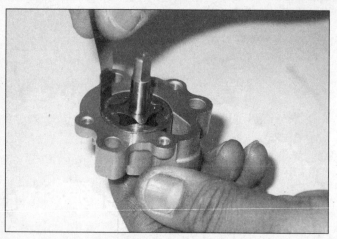

13.4a Use a feeler gauge to measure the outer
rotor-to-body clearance . . .

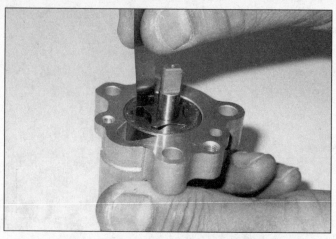

13.4b . . . and the inner-to-outer rotor clearance

feeler gauge **(see illustrations)**. Place a straightedge across the pump body and rotors and measure the gap with a feeler gauge **(see illustration)**. If any of the clearances are beyond the limits listed in this Chapter's Specifications, replace the pump.

8   Reassemble the pump by reversing the disassembly steps, with the following additions:

a) *Before installing the cover, pack the cavities between the rotors with petroleum jelly - this will ensure the pump develops suction quickly and begins oil circulation as soon as the engine is started.*

b) *If you're working on a 400 or 450, tighten the pump cover screw to the torque listed in this Chapter's Specifications. If you're working on a 500, tighten the cover bolts securely, but don't overtighten them and strip the threads.*

14   Camshaft, chain and sprockets - inspection

Refer to illustrations 14.2a, 14.2b, 14.2c and 14.4

Note: *Before replacing the camshaft or crankcase because of damage, check with local machine shops specializing in ATV or motorcycle engine work. In the case of the camshaft, it may be possible for cam lobes to be welded, reground and hardened, at a cost far lower than that of a new camshaft. If the bearing surfaces in the crankcase are damaged, it may be possible for them to be bored out to accept bearing inserts. Due to the cost of a new crankcase it is recommended that all options be explored before condemning it as trash!*

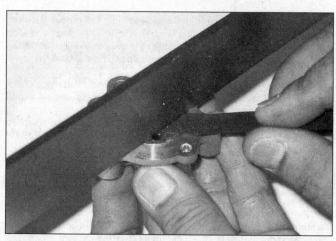

13.4c Lay a straightedge across the rotors and pump body and
measure the gap with a feeler gauge

1   Inspect the cam bearing surfaces inside the crankcase (400/450) or holder (500), using a flashlight if necessary. Look for score marks, deep scratches and evidence of spalling (a pitted appearance).

2   Check the camshaft lobes for heat discoloration (blue appearance), score marks, chipped areas, flat spots and spalling **(see illustrations)**. Measure the height of each lobe with a micrometer **(see illus-**

14.2a Spin the camshaft bearing and check it for roughness,
looseness and noise

14.2b Check the cam lobes for wear - here's a good example of
damage which will require replacement (or repair)
of the camshaft

14.2c Measure the height of the cam lobes with a micrometer

14.4 With the base of the exhaust lobe upright, pressing on the left side should cause the decompressor lobe to lock above the exhaust lobe base; pressing on the right side should lower the decompressor lobe below the exhaust lobe base

tration) and compare the results to the minimum lobe height listed in this Chapter's Specifications. If damage is noted or wear is excessive, the camshaft must be replaced. Also, be sure to check the condition of the valve lifters and their bores as described in Section 12.

3   Spin the ball bearing on the end of the camshaft and check it for roughness, looseness and noise **(see illustration 14.2a)**. If there's any problem with the bearing, replace the camshaft and bearing as an assembly.

4   Check the operation of the compression release mechanism **(see illustration)**. Hold the camshaft with the base of the exhaust lobe upright (see illustration). Press on the exhaust lobe. Pressing on the left side should cause the decompressor lobe to lock above the level of the exhaust lobe base. Pressing on the right side should lower the decompressor lobe below the level of the exhaust lobe base.

5   Except in cases of oil starvation, the camshaft chain wears very little. If the chain has stretched excessively, which makes it difficult to maintain proper tension, replace it with a new one. To remove the chain from the crankshaft sprocket, refer to Chapter 2A or 2B.

6   Check the sprocket for wear, cracks and other damage, replacing it if necessary. If the sprocket is worn, the chain is also worn, and possibly the sprocket on the crankshaft. If wear this severe is apparent, the entire engine should be disassembled for inspection.

7   If you're working on a 400 0r 450, check the internal chain tensioner and slipper (see Chapter 2A). If you're working on a 500, check the chain guides (see Chapter 2B). If they are worn or damaged, replace them.

15   Crankcase components - inspection and servicing

Refer to illustrations 15.3a and 15.3b

1   Separate the crankcase (Chapter 2A or 2B) and remove the following:

a) *Transmission shafts and gears (400/450) or automatic transmission unit (500)*
b) *Final drive shaft and gear (400/450)*
c) *Crankshaft and main bearings*
d) *Shift drum and forks (400/450)*
e) *Balancer*
f) *Oil strainer screen (400/450)*

2   Clean the crankcase halves thoroughly with new solvent and dry them with compressed air. All oil passages should be blown out with compressed air and all traces of old gasket sealant should be removed from the mating surfaces. Caution: Be very careful not to nick or gouge the crankcase mating surfaces or leaks will result. Check both crankcase sections very carefully for cracks and other damage.

3   Check the bearings in the case halves **(see illustrations)**. If they don't turn smoothly, replace them. For bearings that aren't accessible

15.3a Inspect the bearings in the front crankcase half (400/450 shown) . . .

from the outside, a blind hole puller will be needed for removal (these can be rented). Drive the remaining bearings out with a bearing driver or a socket having an outside diameter slightly smaller than that of the bearing outer race. Before installing the bearings, allow them to sit in the freezer overnight, and about fifteen-minutes before installation, place the case half in an oven, set to about 200-degrees F, and allow

15.3b . . . and in the rear half (400/450 shown)

16.2a Press the crankshaft out of the rear crankcase half . . .

16.2b . . . if the bearing stays on the crankshaft, remove it with the press and a bearing splitter

it to heat up. The bearings are an interference fit, and this will ease installation. **Warning:** *Before heating the case, wash it thoroughly with soap and water so no explosive fumes are present. Also, don't use a flame to heat the case.* Install the ball bearings with a socket or bearing driver that bears against the bearing outer race. Install the needle roller bearing with a shouldered drift that fits inside the bearing to keep it from collapsing while the shoulder applies pressure to the outer race.

4　　If any damage is found that can't be repaired, replace the crankcase halves as a set.

5　　Assemble the case halves (see Chapter 2A or 2B) and check to make sure the crankshaft and the transmission shafts turn freely.

16　Crankshaft and balancer - removal, inspection and installation

Note: *The procedures in this section require a press and special tools. If you don't have the necessary equipment or suitable substitutes, have the crankshaft removed and installed by a Honda dealer.*

Removal

Refer to illustrations 16.2a and 16.2b

1　　Remove the engine, separate the crankcase halves and remove the transmission (see Chapter 2A or 2B).

2　　Place the rear crankcase half in a press and press out the crank-

shaft, removing the balancer at the same time **(see illustration)**. The ball bearing may remain in the crankcase or come out with the crankshaft. If it stays on the crankshaft, remove it with the press and a bearing splitter **(see illustration)**. Discard the bearing, no matter what its apparent condition, and use a new one on installation.

Inspection

Refer to illustrations 16.3, 16.4, 16.6 and 16.7

3　　Measure the side clearance between connecting rod and crankshaft with a feeler gauge **(see illustration)**. If it's more than the limit listed in this Chapter's Specifications, replace the crankshaft and connecting rod as an assembly.

4　　Set up the crankshaft in V-blocks with a dial indicator contacting the big end of the connecting rod **(see illustration)**. Move the connecting rod up-and-down against the indicator pointer and compare the reading to the value listed in this Chapter's Specifications. If it's beyond the limit, replace the crankshaft and connecting rod as an assembly.

5　　Check the crankshaft gear, sprockets and bearing journals for visible wear or damage, such as chipped teeth or scoring. If any of these conditions are found, replace the crankshaft and connecting rod as an assembly.

6　　Set the crankshaft in a pair of V-blocks, with a dial indicator contacting each end **(see illustration)**. Rotate the crankshaft and note the runout. If the runout at either end is beyond the limit listed in this Chapter's Specifications, replace the crankshaft and connecting rod as an assembly.

16.3 Check the connecting rod side clearance with a feeler gauge

16.4 Check the connecting rod radial clearance with a dial indicator

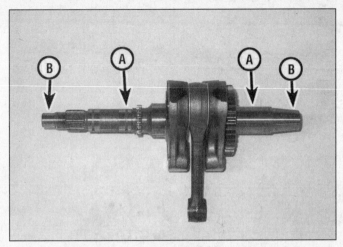

16.6 Place a V-block on each side of the crankshaft (A) and measure runout 6 mm in from the ends (B)

16.7 Check the balancer gear and bearing journals for wear or damage

7   Check the balancer gear and bearing journals for visible wear or damage and replace the balancer if any problems are found (see illustration).

Installation

400 and 450 models

Refer to illustrations 16.10, 16.11, 16.12 and 16.14

8   Install the balancer bearing and crankshaft bearing in the front crankcase half (see Chapter 2A).

9   Install the crankshaft and balancer in the front crankcase half. The balancer drive gear on the crankshaft and the balancer driven gear on the balancer have lines stamped in their outer edges. These are timing marks, which must be aligned with each other when the crankshaft and balancer are installed. **Note:** *It's important to align the timing marks exactly throughout this procedure. Severe engine vibration will occur if the crankshaft and balancer are out of time.*

10   Thread a puller adapter (Honda part no. 07931-KF00200 in the US or 07965-VM00300 in other markets) into the end of the crankshaft (see illustration).

11   Temporarily install the rear crankcase half on the front crankcase (see illustration).

12   Install a crankshaft puller (Honda tools 09731-ME4000A (US) or 9765-VM00200 (other markets) over the crankshaft and install the spe-

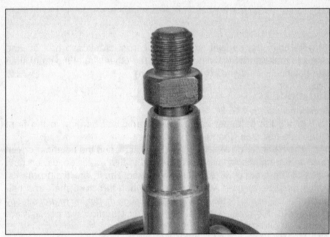

16.10 Thread the special tool adapter into the end of the crankshaft . . .

cial nut (7931-HB3020A) (see illustration).

13   Hold the puller shaft with one wrench and turn the nut with another wrench to pull the crankshaft into the center race of the ball bearing.

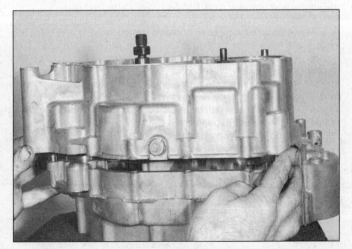

16.11 . . . install the left crankcase half without bolts . . .

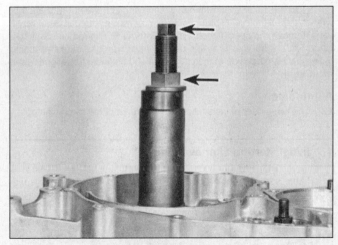

16.12 . . . and install the puller on the crankshaft adapter and crankcase half; hold the shaft (upper arrow) with a wrench and turn the nut to pull the crankshaft into the bearing

16.14 Make sure the balancer timing marks (arrows) are aligned (400/450 models)

16.21 On 500 models, align the timing marks, then install the balancer and crankshaft together - after they're installed, make sure the marks on the other side of the balancer and crankshaft line up

14   Remove the special tools. Lift the front crankcase half off and check to make sure the timing marks on the other side of the crankshaft and balancer are aligned **(see illustration)**.

500 models

Refer to illustration 16.21

15   Install the balancer bearing and crankshaft bearing in the front crankcase half (see Chapter 2B).

16   The balancer drive gear on the crankshaft and the balancer driven gear on the balancer have lines stamped in their outer edges, on both sides of the crankshaft and balancer gear. These are timing marks, which must be aligned with each other when the crankshaft and balancer are installed. **Note:** *It's important to align the timing marks exactly throughout this procedure. Severe engine vibration will occur if the crankshaft and balancer are out of time.*

17   With the timing marks aligned, install the balancer and crankshaft together into the rear case half.

18   Thread a puller adapter (Honda part no. 07931-KF00200 in the US or 07965-VM00300 in other markets) into the end of the crankshaft **(see illustration 16.10)**.

19   Install a crankshaft puller (Honda tools 09731-ME4010B (US) or 9765-VM00200 (other markets) over the crankshaft and install the special nut (7931-HB3020A).

20   Hold the puller shaft with one wrench and turn the nut with another wrench to pull the crankshaft into the center race of the ball bearing.

21   Remove the special tools. The timing marks aligned before installation will not be visible at this point. Check to make sure the timing marks on the other side of the crankshaft and balancer are aligned **(see illustration)**.

All models

22   The remainder of installation is the reverse of the removal steps.

17   Initial start-up after overhaul

1   Make sure the engine oil level is correct, then remove the spark plug from the engine. Place the engine kill switch in the Off position and

unplug the primary (low tension) wires from the coil.

2   Turn on the key switch and crank the engine over with the starter several times to build up oil pressure. Reinstall the spark plug, connect the wires and turn the switch to On.

3   Make sure there is fuel in the tank, then operate the choke.

4   Start the engine and allow it to run at a moderately fast idle until it reaches operating temperature. **Caution:** *If the oil temperature light doesn't go off, or it comes on while the engine is running, stop the engine immediately.*

5   Check carefully for oil leaks and make sure the transmission and controls, especially the brakes, function properly before road testing the machine. Refer to Section 18 for the recommended break-in procedure.

6   Upon completion of the road test, and after the engine has cooled down completely, recheck the valve clearances (see Chapter 1).

18   Recommended break-in procedure

1   Any rebuilt engine needs time to break-in, even if parts have been installed in their original locations. For this reason, treat the machine gently for the first few miles to make sure oil has circulated throughout the engine and any new parts installed have started to seat.

2   Even greater care is necessary if the cylinder has been rebored or a new crankshaft has been installed. In the case of a rebore, the engine will have to be broken in as if the machine were new. This means greater use of the transmission and a restraining hand on the throttle for the first few operating days. There's no point in keeping to any set speed limit - the main idea is to vary the engine speed, keep from lugging (laboring) the engine and to avoid full-throttle operation. These recommendations can be lessened to an extent when only a new crankshaft is installed. Experience is the best guide, since it's easy to tell when an engine is running freely.

3   If a lubrication failure is suspected, stop the engine immediately and try to find the cause. If an engine is run without oil, even for a short period of time, irreparable damage will occur.

Chapter 2 Part D
Cooling system (500 models)

Contents

Specifications

General

Coolant type and mixture ratio	See Chapter 1
Coolant capacity	See Chapter 1
Radiator cap pressure rating	108 to 137 kPa (16 to 20 psi)
Thermostat rating	
Opening temperature	80 to 84-degrees C (176 to 183-degrees F)
Fully open at	95-degrees C (203-degrees F)
Valve travel (when fully open)	Not less than 8 mm (5/16-inch)

1   General information

1   The 500 Rubicon models covered by this manual are equipped with a liquid cooling system, which utilizes a water/antifreeze mixture to carry away excess heat produced during the combustion process. The cylinder is surrounded by a water jackets, through which the coolant is circulated by the water pump. The pump is mounted on the front side of the cylinder head and is driven by the camshaft. When the engine is warm, the coolant is pulled into the engine from the bottom of the radiator, circulates through the water jacket and cylinder head coolant passages, then passes up through a hose into the top of the radiator. The hot coolant then flows down through into the radiator (which is mounted on the frame downtubes to take advantage of maximum air flow), where it is cooled by the passing air, through another hose and back to the water pump, where the cycle is repeated. When the engine is cold, the thermostat closes and the coolant circulates through the engine but doesn't pass through the radiator.

2   An electric fan, mounted behind the radiator and automatically controlled by a thermostatic switch, provides a flow of cooling air through the radiator when the vehicle is not moving or is moving at low speed. Under certain conditions, the fan may come on even after the engine is stopped, and the ignition switch is off, and may run for several minutes.

3   The coolant temperature sending unit senses the temperature of the coolant and controls the coolant temperature gauge light on the instrument cluster as well as the fan.

4   The entire system is sealed and pressurized. The pressure is controlled by a valve which is part of the radiator cap. Pressurizing the coolant raises the boiling point, which prevents premature boiling of the coolant. An overflow hose, connected between the radiator and reservoir tank, directs coolant to the tank when the radiator cap valve is opened by excessive pressure. The coolant is automatically siphoned back to the radiator as the engine cools.

5   Many cooling system inspection and service procedures are considered part of routine maintenance and are included in Chapter 1.

Warning: *Do not allow antifreeze to come in contact with your skin or painted surfaces of the vehicle. Rinse off spills immediately with plenty of water. Antifreeze is highly toxic if ingested. Never leave antifreeze lying around in an open container or in puddles on the floor; children and pets are attracted by its sweet smell and may drink it. Check with local authorities about disposing of used antifreeze. Many communities have collection centers which will see that antifreeze is disposed of safely.*

Warning: *Do not remove the pressure cap from the thermostat housing when the engine and radiator are hot. Scalding hot coolant and steam may be blown out under pressure, which could cause serious injury. To open the pressure cap, wait until the engine has cooled. When the engine has cooled, place a thick rag, like a towel, over the radiator cap; slowly rotate the cap counterclockwise to the first stop. This procedure allows any residual pressure to escape. When the steam has stopped escaping, press down on the cap while turning counterclockwise and remove it.*

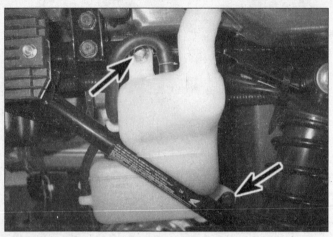

3.2 Disconnect the siphon hose from the underside of the tank, then remove the trim plug (lower arrow) and bolt (upper arrow)

4.8a Disconnect the breather hose (left arrow) to remove the fan; the fan is secured by three nuts (right arrows - one nut hidden)

2 Radiator cap - check

If problems such as overheating and loss of coolant occur, check the entire system as described in Chapter 1. The radiator cap opening pressure should be checked by a dealer service department or service station equipped with the special tester required to do the job. If the cap is defective, replace it with a new one.

3 Coolant reservoir - removal and installation

Refer to illustration 3.2
1   Unscrew the cap from the reservoir tank so the tank will fit through the body panel.
2   Pry up the center pin of the trim clip, then pull it out **(see illustration)**. Unscrew the bolt.
3   Remove the tank from the vehicle and disconnect the siphon hose. Pour the coolant into a suitable container.
4   Installation is the reverse of the removal steps. Fill the tank with the specified coolant (see Chapter 1).

4 Cooling fan and coolant temperature sender - check and replacement

Check

1   If the engine is overheating and the cooling fan isn't coming on, first check the fuse (see Chapter 8). If the fuse is blown, check the fan circuit for a short to ground (see the *Wiring diagrams* at the end of this book). If the fuse is good, right front mudguard and inner fender (see Chapter 7) and disconnect the fan electrical connector. Using two jumper wires, apply battery voltage to the terminals in the fan motor side of the electrical connector. If the fan doesn't work, replace the motor.
2   If the fan does come on, the problem lies in the thermostatic fan switch or the wiring that connects the components. Remove the jumper wires and reconnect the electrical connector to the fan.
3   The engine coolant temperature sender is mounted in the thermostat housing. Disconnect the electrical connector from the switch and ground the black/blue wire to the engine with a jumper wire. Turn the ignition key to On. If the fan comes on, the circuit to the motor is good, and the sender is probably defective. Remove it from the vehicle and test it as described below.
4   If the fan doesn't come on, locate the engine control module (see Chapter 8). Unplug its five-pin black connector and ground the connector's green/black wire with a jumper wire. Turn the ignition key to On. If the fan comes on, check for a break or bad connection in the black/blue wire that runs from the temperature sensor to the engine control module.

4.8b The fan bracket is secured to the radiator by three bolts (upper bolt shown; two lower bolts hidden)

5   If the fan motor doesn't start in Step 4, disconnect the fan motor electrical connector. With the ignition key turned to On, check for voltage between the blue wire terminal in the harness side of the connector and ground. If there's no voltage, check the blue wire for a break or bad connection. If there is voltage, check the green/black wire for a break or bad connection. If the wiring is good, the fan motor is probably defective. Replace it as described below.
6   To test the sender off the vehicle, remove it (see Section 5). Immerse the sender in a pan of coolant (50/50 mixture of antifreeze and water). **Warning:** *Antifreeze is poisonous. Do not use a cooking pan.* Tie the sender up with wire so it doesn't touch the sides of the pan, and keep the wires out of the coolant. Connect an ohmmeter between the sender wire terminals. Heat the coolant and compare the resistance reading to the values listed in this Chapter's Specifications as the coolant heats. If the readings are out of the specified range by more than 10 per cent, replace the sender.

Replacement

Fan motor
Refer to illustrations 4.8a and 4.8b
Warning: *The engine must be completely cool before beginning this procedure.*
7   Disconnect the cable from the negative terminal of the battery and remove the radiator (see Section 7).
8   Disconnect the breather hose from the fan motor **(see illustration)**. Unbolt the fan bracket from the radiator **(see illustration)**. Separate the fan and bracket from the radiator.

5.5a Remove the thermostat housing bolts (arrows) . . .

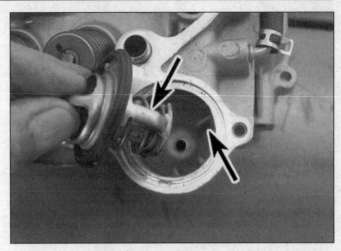

5.5b . . . lift off the housing and remove the thermostat (on installation, align the thermostat boss with the stopper in the housing (arrows) . . .

9   Remove the nut that retains the fan to the fan motor and remove the fan from the motor.

10   Remove the nuts that attach the fan motor to the bracket and detach the motor from the bracket **(see illustration 4.8a)**.

11   Installation is the reverse of the removal steps.

Coolant temperature sender

Warning: *The engine must be completely cool before beginning this procedure.*

12   Apply non-permanent thread locking agent to the threads of the new unit, but don't get any on the sensor head.

13   Unscrew the sending unit from the thermostat housing. Quickly install the new unit. Tighten it securely, but don't overtighten it and strip the threads.

14   Connect the electrical connector to the sending unit. Check, and if necessary, add coolant to the system (see Chapter 1).

Engine oil temperature sender

15   These models also use an engine oil temperature sender, which activates the temperature warning light on the instrument panel. Testing and replacement procedures are basically the same as those for 400 and 450 models, described in Chapter 8.

***

5   Thermostat - removal, check and installation

Warning: *The engine must be completely cool before beginning this procedure.*

Removal

Refer to illustrations 5.5a, 5.5b and 5.5c

1   If the thermostat is functioning properly, the engine should warm up to the normal operating temperature quickly and then stay there, only rising above the normal position occasionally when the engine gets abnormally hot. If the engine does not reach normal operating temperature quickly, or if it overheats, the thermostat should be removed and checked, or replaced with a new one.

2   Refer to Chapter 1 and drain the cooling system.

3   Remove the fuel tank cover and air cleaner intake tube (see Chapter 3).

4   Remove the thermostat cover from the housing.

5   Remove the thermostat from the housing **(see illustrations)**.

6   Check the thermostat O-ring for leakage. It should be replaced with a new one whenever the thermostat is removed.

Check

7   Remove any coolant deposits, then visually check the thermostat

for corrosion, cracks and other damage. If it was open when it was removed, the thermostat is defective.

8   To check the thermostat operation, submerge it in a container of the specified coolant (50/50 antifreeze and water) along with a thermometer. The thermostat should be suspended so it does not touch the sides of the container. **Warning**: *Antifreeze is poisonous. Do not use a cooking pan to test the thermostat.*

9   Gradually heat the water in the container with a hot plate or stove and check the temperature when the thermostat first starts to open.

10   Compare the opening temperature to the values listed in this Chapter's Specifications.

11   Continue heating the water until the valve is fully open.

12   Measure how far the thermostat valve has opened and compare to the value listed in this Chapter's Specifications.

13   If these specifications are not met, or if the thermostat doesn't open while the water is heated, replace it with a new one.

Installation

14   Install the thermostat into the housing.

15   Install a new O-ring in the groove in the thermostat cover.

16   Place the cover on the housing and install the bolts, tightening them securely.

17   The remainder of installation is the reverse of the removal steps. Fill the cooling system with the recommended coolant (see Chapter 1).

5.5c . . . and remove the sealing ring

6.3 Free the accessory socket connector (left arrow) from the retainer; disconnect the siphon hose and upper hose (right arrows) and the lower hose (hidden)

6.6 Remove the baffle from each side of the radiator

6   Radiator - removal and installation

Refer to illustrations 6.3 and 6.6

Warning: *The engine must be completely cool before beginning this procedure.*

1 Drain the cooling system (see Chapter 1).
2 Remove the oil cooler (see Chapter 2C).
3 Unplug the fan motor connector and free the electrical connector accessory harness from its retainer on the fan bracket **(see illustration)**.
4 Pry the siphon hose off the nipple in the radiator filler neck. Disconnect the breather hose from the fan motor.
5 Loosen the radiator hose clamps **(see illustration 6.3)**. Work the hoses free from the fittings, taking care not to damage the fittings in the process.
6 Remove the baffle from each side of the radiator **(see illustration)**. Remove the radiator bolts and lift the radiator out.
7 Inspect the mounting bushings. Replace them if they're cracked or deteriorated.
8 Installation is the reverse of the removal steps, with the following additions:
  a) *Don't forget to connect the electrical connector and reposition the accessory harness in its retainer.*
  b) *Fill the cooling system with the recommended coolant (see Chapter 1).*

7   Water pump - check, removal, inspection and installation

Warning: *The engine must be completely cool before beginning this procedure.*

Check

1 Visually check the area around the water pump for coolant leaks. Try to determine if the leak is simply the result of a loose hose clamp or deteriorated hose.
2 Check for coolant leakage at the weep hole in the underside of the pump **(see illustration)**. If coolant has been leaking from the hole, the mechanical seal is leaking and the pump should be replaced with a new one.

Removal and inspection

Refer to illustrations 7.4, 7.5a and 7.5b

3 Drain the coolant following the procedure in Chapter 1.
4 Disconnect the lower radiator hose and both bypass hoses from the pump **(see illustration)**.
5 Remove the pump mounting bolts **(see illustration)**. Work the pump free of the engine (wiggle it back and forth as you pull it out). Pull

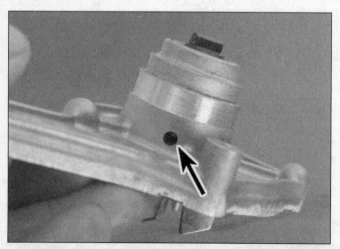

7.2 If coolant has been leaking from the weep hole, the mechanical seal is leaking and the pump must be replaced

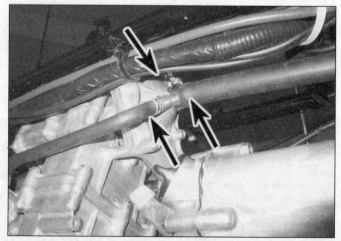

7.4 Disconnect the bypass hoses (left arrows; upper hose hidden) and the radiator hose (right arrow)

7.5a Remove the mounting bolts (A) to remove the pump; remove the assembly bolts (B) to separate the pump halves

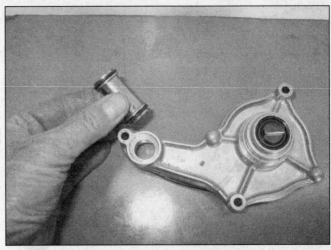

7.5b This passage (with two O-rings) fits between the water pump and cylinder head

the coolant tube out of the engine (if it didn't come out with the pump) **(see illustration)**.

6   Remove the two bolts that hold the pump together **(see illustration 7.5a)**. Separate the pump halves and remove the O-ring.

7   Check the impeller blades for corrosion. If they are heavily corroded, replace the water pump and flush the system thoroughly (it would also be a good idea to check the internal condition of the radiator).

8   If the pump is good, install a new O-ring and assemble the pump halves. Tighten the bolts securely, but don't overtighten them and strip the threads.

Installation

9   Make sure the weep hole is clear **(see illustration 7.2)**.

10   Installation is the reverse of the removal steps. Use new O-rings between the water pump housing and engine and on the coolant tube. Do not use oil or grease on the O-rings.

Notes

Chapter 3
Fuel and exhaust systems

Contents

Specifications

General
Fuel type .... Unleaded or low lead gasoline (petrol) subject to local regulations; minimum octane 91 RON (87 pump octane)

Carburetor
Identification mark

400 models
- 1995 .... VE92A
- 1996 and 1997 .... VE92B
- 1998
  - Except California VE92D
  - California VE92C
- 1999 and later VE92C

450 models
- 1998 through 2001 .... VE93A
- 2002 .... VE93C

500 models
- 2001 through 2003 .... VE6AB
- 2004 .... VE6AC
- 2005 and later (US and Canada) VE6AE
- 2005 and later (except US and Canada) VE6AF

Jet sizes and settings
Main jet
- Standard 130
- High altitude
  - 400 models 125
  - 450 models 120
  - 500 models
    - 2001 through 2004 158
    - 2005 and later 162

Jet needle clip position
- 400 and 450 models .... Third groove from top
- 500 models
  - 2001 through 2004 .... Second groove from top
  - 2005 and later .... Not specified

Slow jet 45

Pilot screw standard setting (sea level to 5000 feet, turns out from lightly seated position)
- 400 models
  - 1995 through 1997 .... 2-1/4
  - 1998 and late
    - Initial setting 3
    - Final setting .... 3/4 turn out from lean drop setting
- 450 models
  - Initial setting 2-5/8
  - Final setting .... 1/2 turn out from lean drop setting

Jet sizes and settings (continued)

500 models
    2001 through 2003
        Initial setting 2-5/8
        Final setting .... 1 turn out from lean drop setting
    2004
        Initial setting 2-3/4
        Final setting .... 1 turn out from lean drop setting
    2005 and later (US and Canada)
        Initial setting 2
        Final setting .... 3/4 turn out from lean drop setting
    2005 and later (except US and Canada) 1-3/4
        Final setting .... 3/4 turn out from lean drop setting
Pilot screw high altitude setting (3000 to 8000 feet, turns in from final sea level setting)
    400 models 3/4
    450 models .... Same as sea level setting
    500 models
        2001 through 2004 .... 7/8
        2005 and later... 1/4
Float level
    400 and 450 models .... 18.5 mm (0.73 inch)
    500 models
        2001 through 2003 .... 18.5 mm (0.73 inch)
        2004 and later.. 15.9 mm (0.63 inch)
Carburetor heater electrical resistance .... 13 to 15 ohms

Torque settings

Carburetor cover screw
    400 and 450 models .... 3.5 Nm (30 in-lbs)
    500 models .... Not specified
Starting enrichment valve nut
    400 models .... 2.5 Nm (22 in-lbs)
    450 models .... 3 Nm (24 in-lbs)
    500 models
        2001 through 2004 .... 2 Nm (17 in-lbs)
        2005 and later... 2.3 Nm (20 in-lbs)
Throttle drum cover screws (500 models)
    2001 through 2004 .... 2 Nm (17 in-lbs)
    2005 and later .... 1.5 Nm (13 in-lbs)

---

1   General information

    The fuel system consists of the fuel tank, fuel tap, filter screen, carburetor and connecting lines, hoses and control cables.

    The carburetor used on these vehicles is a constant vacuum unit with a butterfly-type throttle valve. For cold starting, an enrichment circuit is actuated by a cable and the choke lever mounted on the left handlebar.

    The exhaust system consists of a pipe and muffler/silencer with a spark arrester function.

    Many of the fuel system service procedures are considered routine maintenance items and for that reason are included in Chapter 1.

2   Fuel tank - removal and installation

Warning: *Gasoline is extremely flammable, so take extra precautions when you work on any part of the fuel system. Don't smoke or allow open flames or bare light bulbs near the work area, and don't work in a garage where a natural gas-type appliance (such as a water heater or clothes dryer) is present. Since gasoline is carcinogenic, wear protective gloves when there is a possibility of being exposed to fuel, and if you spill any fuel on your skin, rinse it off immediately with soap and water. Mop up any spills immediately and do not store fuel-soaked rags where they could ignite. When you perform any kind of work on the fuel system, wear safety glasses and have an extinguisher suitable for a class B type fire (flammable liquids) on hand.*

Removal

Refer to illustrations 2.3, 2.4 and 2.5

1   Turn the fuel tap to Off.
2   Remove the seat, left and right side covers and the fuel tank cover (see Chapter 7).
3   Remove the mounting bolts at the front of the fuel tank **(see illustration)**.
4   Remove the tank seal and unhook the mounting band on each side at the rear of the tank **(see illustration)**.
5   Lift the tank and disconnect the fuel line from the fuel tap **(see illustration)**. Lift the tank off the vehicle together with the fuel tap.

Installation

Refer to illustration 2.6

6   Before installing the tank, check the condition of the tank mounts, seal and rubber mounting bands - if they're hardened, cracked, or show any other signs of deterioration, replace them **(see illustration 2.4 and the accompanying illustration)**.
7   When installing the tank, reverse the removal procedure. Do not pinch any control cables or wires.

3   Fuel tank - cleaning and repair

1   All repairs to the fuel tank should be carried out by a professional who has experience in this critical and potentially dangerous work. Even after cleaning and flushing of the fuel system, explosive fumes can remain and ignite during repair of the tank.

2.3 Remove the mounting bolts at the front of the fuel tank (arrows)

2.4 Remove the tank seal (upper arrow) and unhook the mounting band on each side (lower arrow)

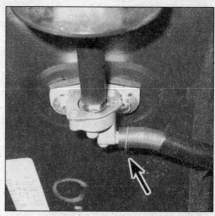

2.5 Lift the tank and disconnect the fuel line from the tap (arrow)

2   If the fuel tank is removed from the vehicle, it should not be placed in an area where sparks or open flames could ignite the fumes coming out of the tank. Be especially careful inside garages where a natural gas-type appliance is located, because the pilot light could cause an explosion.

4   Idle fuel/air mixture adjustment

Normal adjustment
Refer to illustration 4.3

1   Idle fuel/air mixture on these vehicles is preset at the factory and should not need adjustment unless the carburetor is overhauled or the pilot screw, which controls the mixture adjustment, is replaced.
2   The engine must be properly tuned up before making the adjustment (valve clearances set to specifications, spark plug in good condition and properly gapped).
3   To make an initial adjustment, turn the pilot screw clockwise until it seats lightly, then back it out the number of turns listed in this Chapter's Specifications **(see illustration). Caution:** *Turn the screw just far enough to seat it lightly. If it's bottomed hard, the screw or its seat may be damaged, which will make accurate mixture adjustments impossible.*
4   Warm up the engine to normal operating temperature. Shut it off and connect a tune-up tachometer, following the tachometer manufacturer's instructions.
5   Restart the engine and compare idle speed to the value listed in the Chapter 1 Specifications. Adjust it if necessary.

1995 through 1997 models
6   Turn the pilot screw clockwise (in) just until the engine speed drops

or the engine starts to run roughly. Note how many turns were required.
7   Turn the pilot screw counterclockwise, again until the engine starts to slow down or run roughly. Note how many turns were required.
8   Turn the pilot screw clockwise to a point halfway between the points in Steps 6 and 7.

1998 and later models
9   Turn the pilot screw a little at a time, in or out, to obtain the highest possible idle speed. Once you've done this, reset the idle to the specified idle speed using the throttle stop screw.
10   Turn the pilot screw in (clockwise) slowly until engine speed drops 100 rpm below the specified idle speed.
11   Back the pilot screw out (counterclockwise) the final fraction of a turn listed in this Chapter's Specifications.

High altitude adjustment
12   If the vehicle is normally used at altitudes from sea level to 5000 feet (1500 meters), use the normal main jet and pilot screw setting. If it's used at altitudes between 3000 and 8000 feet (1000 and 2500 meters), the main jet and pilot screw setting must be changed to compensate for the thinner air. **Caution:** *Don't use the vehicle for sustained operation below 5000 feet (15 meters) with the main jet and pilot screw at the high altitude settings or the engine may overheat and be damaged.*
13   Refer to Section 7 and change the main jet to the high altitude jet listed in this Chapter's Specifications.
14   If you're working on a 400 model, set the pilot screw to the standard setting, then turn it in the additional amount listed in this Chapter's Specifications (this step doesn't apply to 450 models).
15   With the vehicle at high altitude, refer to Chapter 1 and adjust the idle speed.

2.6 Inspect the tank mounts and replace them if they're damaged or deteriorated

4.3 The pilot screw (arrow) adjusts idle fuel/air mixture

6.6 Loosen the clamping band on the intake manifold (arrow)

6.7a On 450 and 500 models, disconnect the carburetor heater connector (arrow) (450 shown)

6.7b If you're working on a 500, disconnect the throttle position sensor

5   Carburetor overhaul - general information

1   Poor engine performance, hesitation, hard starting, stalling, flooding and backfiring are all signs that major carburetor maintenance may be required.

2   Keep in mind that many so-called carburetor problems are really not carburetor problems at all, but mechanical problems within the engine or ignition system malfunctions. Try to establish for certain that the carburetor is in need of maintenance before beginning a major overhaul.

3   Check the fuel tap and its strainer screen, the in-tank fuel strainer, the fuel lines, the intake manifold clamps, the O-ring between the intake manifold and cylinder head, the vacuum hoses, the air filter element, the cylinder compression, the spark plug and the ignition timing before assuming that a carburetor overhaul is required. If the vehicle has been unused for more than a month, refer to Chapter 1, drain the float chamber and refill the tank with fresh fuel.

4   Most carburetor problems are caused by dirt particles, varnish and other deposits which build up in and block the fuel and air passages. Also, in time, gaskets and O-rings shrink or deteriorate and cause fuel and air leaks which lead to poor performance.

5   When the carburetor is overhauled, it is generally disassembled completely and the parts are cleaned thoroughly with a carburetor cleaning solvent and dried with filtered, unlubricated compressed air. The fuel and air passages are also blown through with compressed air to force out any dirt that may have been loosened but not removed by the solvent. Once the cleaning process is complete, the carburetor is reassembled using new gaskets, O-rings and, generally, a new inlet needle valve and seat.

6   Before disassembling the carburetor, make sure you have a carburetor rebuild kit (which will include all necessary O-rings and other parts), some carburetor cleaner, a supply of rags, some means of blowing out the carburetor passages and a clean place to work.

6   Carburetor - removal and installation

Warning: *Gasoline is extremely flammable, so take extra precautions when you work on any part of the fuel system. Don't smoke or allow open flames or bare light bulbs near the work area, and don't work in a garage where a natural gas-type appliance (such as a water heater or clothes dryer) is present. Since gasoline is carcinogenic, wear protective gloves when there is a possibility of being exposed to fuel, and if you spill any fuel on your skin, rinse it off immediately with soap and water. Mop up any spills immediately and do not store fuel-soaked rags where they could ignite. When you perform any kind of work on the fuel system, wear safety glasses and have an extinguisher suitable for a class B type fire (flammable liquids) on hand.*

Removal
Refer to illustrations 6.6, 6.7a, 6.7b, 6.8, 6.10a and 6.10b

1   Remove the seat (see Chapter 7).

400 models

2   Remove the lower right side cover (see Chapter 7).

3   If you're working on a 1997 or later 400 model, remove the rubber plate that covers the air intake snorkel, loosen the air intake clamp at the carburetor and remove the clips that secure the air cleaner housing to the frame (see Section 9).

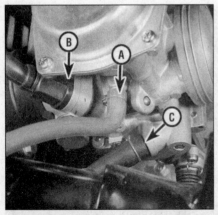

6.8 Disconnect the vent hose (A), unscrew the starting enrichment valve (B) and disconnect the fuel line (C)

6.10a Remove the bolts (arrows) . . .

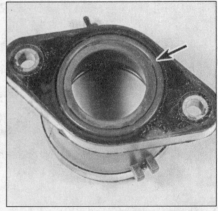

6.10b . . . then detach the manifold tube and inspect its O-ring (arrow)

7.2a Remove the air cutoff valve (if equipped), its jet and O-rings (left arrow) and the passage O-ring (right arrow)

7.2b Remove the four screws securing the vacuum chamber cover to the carburetor body (arrows)

7.2c Lift the cover off and remove the piston spring; note the location of the tab (arrow) which fits into a notch

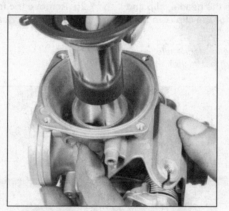

7.2d Peel the diaphragm away from its groove in the carburetor body, being careful not to tear it, and lift out the diaphragm/piston assembly

7.2e Push in on the needle jet holder and turn it 90-degrees counterclockwise with an 8 mm socket . . .

450 models

4   Remove the seat and side covers (see Chapter 7).
5   Remove the air cleaner housing (see Section 9).

All models

6   Loosen the clamping band on the intake manifold tube **(see illustration)**. Work the carburetor free of the manifold and lift it up.
7   If you're working on a 450 or 500 model, disconnect the carburetor heater **(see illustration)**. If you're working on a 500, disconnect the throttle position sensor connector **(see illustration)**.
8   Disconnect the vent hose from the carburetor **(see illustration)**. Unscrew the starting enrichment valve nut and pull the valve out of the carburetor body. Follow the fuel line from the tap to the carburetor and disconnect it.
9   Refer to Section 10 and disconnect the throttle cable from the carburetor body. The carburetor can now be removed.
10   Check the intake manifold tube for cracks, deterioration or other damage. If it has visible defects, or if there's reason to suspect its O-ring is leaking, remove it and inspect the O-ring **(see illustrations)**.
11   After the carburetor has been removed, stuff clean rags into the intake tube (or the intake port in the cylinder head, if the tube has been removed) to prevent the entry of dirt or other objects.

Installation

12   Refer to Sections 10 and 11 and connect the throttle and choke cables to the carburetor.
13   Connect the fuel hose to the carburetor and connect the air vent tube.
14   Slip the clamping band onto the intake tube. Position the pin on

the band in the intake tube groove. Position the carburetor in the intake tube and tighten the clamping band screw to the torque listed in this Chapter's Specifications.
15   Adjust the throttle freeplay (see Chap-ter 1).
16   The remainder of installation is the reverse of the removal steps.

7   Carburetor - disassembly, cleaning and inspection

Warning: *Gasoline is extremely flammable, so take extra precautions when you work on any part of the fuel system. Don't smoke or allow open flames or bare light bulbs near the work area, and don't work in a garage where a natural gas-type appliance (such as a water heater or clothes dryer) is present. Since gasoline is carcinogenic, wear protective gloves when there is a possibility of being exposed to fuel, and if you spill any fuel on your skin, rinse it off immediately with soap and water. Mop up any spills immediately and do not store fuel-soaked rags where they could ignite. When you perform any kind of work on the fuel system, wear safety glasses and have an extinguisher suitable for a class B type fire (flammable liquids) on hand.*

Disassembly

Refer to illustrations 7.2a through 7.2t

1   Remove the carburetor from the machine as described in Section 6. Set it on a clean working surface. If you're working on a 450 or 500 model, remove the carburetor heater (see Section 13).
2   Refer to the accompanying illustrations to disassemble the carburetor **(see illustrations)**.

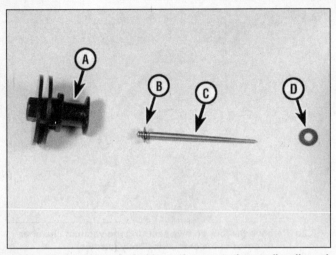

7.2f . . . then remove the holder and separate the needle, clip and washer from the piston; standard position for the clip is in the third groove

a)   Holder   c)   Jet needle
b)   Clip   d)   Washer

7.2g Remove the four screws retaining the float chamber to the carburetor body (arrows) . . .

7.2h . . . then detach the float chamber and remove its O-ring

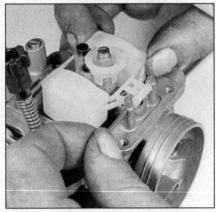

7.2i Remove the float chamber baffle, push the float pivot pin out and detach the float (and fuel inlet valve needle) from the carburetor body

7.2j Turn the pilot screw in, counting the number of turns until it bottoms lightly, and record the number for use when installing the screw . . .

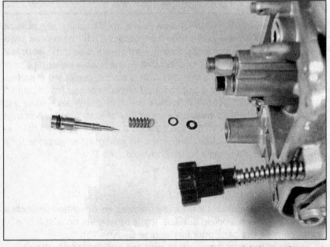

7.2k . . . then remove the pilot screw along with its spring, washer and O-ring

7.2l Unscrew the starter jet

7.2m Unscrew the slow jet and pull it out . . .

7.2n . . . noting that the narrow end goes in first

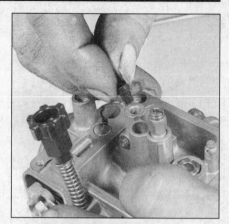

7.2o Remove the rubber plug from its passage

7.2p Unscrew the main jet from the needle jet holder . . .

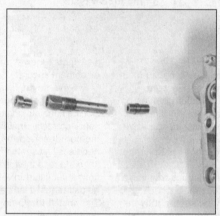

7.2q . . . then unscrew the needle jet holder and remove the needle jet

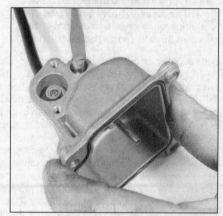

7.2r Remove the float chamber drain screw and its O-ring

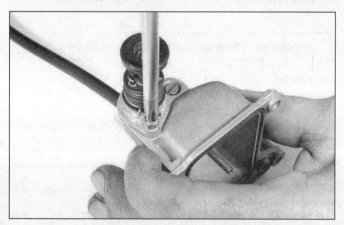

7.2s Remove the primer knob mounting screws . . .

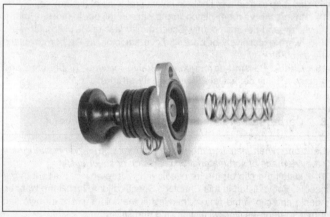

7.2t . . . then remove the primer knob and spring

Cleaning

Caution: *Use only a carburetor cleaning solution that is safe for use with plastic parts (be sure to read the label on the container).*

3   Submerge the metal components in the carburetor cleaner for approximately thirty minutes (or longer, if the directions recommend it).

4   After the carburetor has soaked long enough for the cleaner to loosen and dissolve most of the varnish and other deposits, use a brush to remove the stubborn deposits. Rinse it again, then dry it with compressed air. Blow out all of the fuel and air passages in the main and upper body. **Caution:** *Never clean the jets or passages with a piece of wire or a drill bit, as they will be enlarged, causing the fuel and air metering rates to be upset.*

Inspection

Refer to illustration 7.15

5   Check the operation of the primer knob. If it doesn't move smoothly, replace it, along with the return spring. If the rubber components of the knob are deteriorated or damaged, remove the clips, disassemble the knob and replace them.

6   Check the tapered portion of the pilot screw for wear or damage. Replace the pilot screw if necessary.

7   Check the carburetor body, float chamber and vacuum chamber cover for cracks, distorted sealing surfaces and other damage. If any defects are found, replace the faulty component, although replacement of the entire carburetor will probably be necessary (check with your

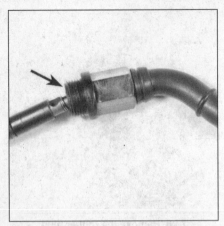

7.15 Check the starting enrichment valve for wear and damage and replace it if necessary; apply a thin coat of multipurpose grease to the end of the valve threads (arrow) on installation

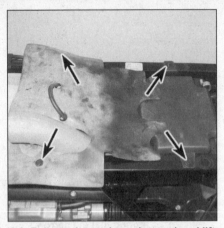

9.2 Release the retainers (arrows) and lift off the rubber plate

9.3 Loosen the clamping band on the carburetor intake tube (arrow)

parts supplier for the availability of separate components).

8   Check the jet needle for straightness by rolling it on a flat surface (such as a piece of glass). Replace it if it's bent or if the tip is worn.

9   Check the tip of the fuel inlet valve needle. If it has grooves or scratches in it, it must be replaced. Push in on the rod in the other end of the needle, then release it - if it doesn't spring back, replace the valve needle.

10   Check the O-rings on the float chamber and the drain plug (in the float chamber). Replace them if they're damaged.

11   Operate the throttle shaft to make sure the throttle butterfly valve opens and closes smoothly. If it doesn't, replace the carburetor.

12   Check the floats for damage. This will usually be apparent by the presence of fuel inside one of the floats. If the floats are damaged, they must be replaced.

13   Check the diaphragm for splits, holes and general deterioration. Holding it up to a light will help to reveal problems of this nature.

14   Insert the vacuum piston in the carburetor body and see that it moves up-and-down smoothly. Check the surface of the piston for wear. If it's worn excessively or doesn't move smoothly in the bore, replace the carburetor.

15   Check the starting enrichment valve for wear or damage and replace it if any defects are found **(see illustration)**.

8   Carburetor - reassembly and float height check

Caution: *When installing the jets, be careful not to over-tighten them - they're made of soft material and can strip or shear easily.*

1   Install the clip on the jet needle if it was removed. Place it in the needle groove listed in this Chapter's Specifications. Install the washer, needle and clip in the piston, then install the holder, press it down and turn it 90-degrees clockwise with an 8 mm socket.

2   Install the pilot screw (if removed) along with its spring, washer and O-ring, turning it in until it seats lightly. Now, turn the screw out the number of turns that was previously recorded.

3   Install the diaphragm/vacuum piston assembly into the carburetor body. Lower the spring into the piston. Seat the bead of the diaphragm into the groove in the top of the carburetor body, making sure the diaphragm isn't distorted or kinked **(see illustration 7.2c)**. This is not always an easy task. If the diaphragm seems too large in diameter and doesn't want to seat in the groove, place the vacuum chamber cover over the carburetor diaphragm, insert your finger into the throat of the carburetor and push up on the vacuum piston, holding it almost all the way up. Push down gently on the vacuum chamber cover - it should drop into place, indicating the diaphragm has seated in its groove. Once this occurs, install at least two of the vacuum chamber cover screws before you let go of the piston.

4   Install the remaining vacuum chamber cover screws and tighten all of them securely.

5   Reverse the disassembly steps to install the jets and rubber plug.

6   Invert the carburetor. Attach the fuel inlet valve needle to the float. Set the float into position in the carburetor, making sure the valve needle seats correctly. Install the float pivot pin. To check the float level, hold the carburetor so the float hangs down, then tilt it back until the valve needle is just seated. Measure the distance from the float chamber gasket surface to the top of the float and compare your measurement to the float level listed in this Chapter's Specifications. There's no means of adjustment; if it isn't as specified, replace the float and needle valve.

7   Install the O-ring into the groove in the float chamber. Place the float chamber on the carburetor and install the screws, tightening them securely.

8   Install the spring and primer knob, taking care to locate the diaphragm correctly.

9   Air cleaner housing - removal and installation

Removal

400/450 models

Refer to illustrations 9.2, 9.3, 9.4 and 9.5

1   Refer the seat, side covers and fuel tank cover (see Chapter 7).

2   If you're working on a 1998 or later model, pull up the center pins of the rubber plate retainers, then lift off the rubber plate **(see illustration)**.

3   Loosen the clamp and detach the air intake tube from the carburetor **(see illustration)**.

4   If you're working on a 1998 or later model, detach the crankcase breather hose from the engine **(see illustration)**.

5   Pull the molded clip portion of the intake duct off the frame **(see illustration)**.

6   Remove the two air cleaner housing retaining pins. Lift the air cleaner housing out of the frame, together with the intake duct and carburetor connecting tube.

500 models

7   Remove the seat, the rubber heat shield beneath it and the fuel tank cover (see Chapter 7).

8   Follow the hose from the air cleaner housing to the carburetor and disconnect it.

9   Loosen the clamps that secure the air intake duct to the carburetor and air cleaner housing, then work the duct free and remove it.

10   Remove the housing from the vehicle.

All models

11   Installation is the reverse of the removal steps.

9.4 On 1998 and later models, disconnect the breather hose (arrow) from the crankcase

9.5 Unclip the air intake duct from the frame

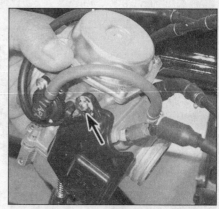

10.3a Remove the throttle pulley cover screw (arrow) and lift off the cover

10.3b Loosen the locknut and adjusting nut (arrows) and slip the cable out of the slot, then align the cable with the slot in the throttle pulley and slip it out

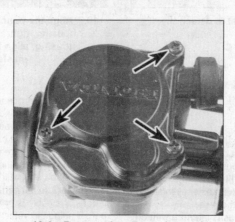

10.4a Remove the screws (arrows) and lift the cover and gasket off the throttle housing

10.4b Bend back the lockwasher tab (arrow), remove the nut and lockwasher . . .

10 Throttle cable and housing - removal, installation and adjustment

1   The throttle on these vehicles is operated by a thumb lever on the right handlebar.

Removal

Refer to illustrations 10.3a, 10.3b, 10.4a, 10.4b, 10.4c, 10.4d and 10.6

2   Remove the carburetor (see Section 6).

3   Remove the throttle housing cover from the carburetor **(see illustration)**. Loosen the locknut and adjusting nut to create slack in the cable, then rotate the throttle pulley, align the cable with the pulley slot and slip the cable out of the pulley **(see illustration)**. Slip the cable out of the bracket slot to complete disconnection at the carburetor end.

4   Remove the cover from the throttle housing on the handlebar, remove the lever components and disconnect the cable **(see illustrations)**.

5   Remove the cable, noting how it's routed.

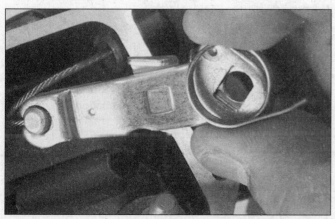

10.4c . . . then lift off the lever and spring . . .

10.4d . . . align the lever slot (arrow) with the cable and slip the cable out

10.6 Remove the clamp screws (arrows) to detach the throttle housing

10.7 Align the punch mark on the handlebar (under the throttle housing, right arrow) with the outer end of the throttle housing; align the throttle housing line with the brake master cylinder seam (left arrows)

6   If necessary, remove the throttle housing clamp screws and detach the throttle housing from the handlebar **(see illustration)**.

Installation

Refer to illustration 10.7

7   If the throttle housing was removed, install it on the handlebar and tighten its clamp screws loosely. Position the housing so its outer end is aligned with the handlebar punch mark **(see illustration)**. Align the cast line on the housing with the seam of the brake master cylinder and clamp. Install the clamp and screws and tighten them securely.

8   Route the cable into place. Make sure it doesn't interfere with any other components and isn't kinked or bent sharply.

9   Lubricate the end of the cable with multi-purpose grease and connect it to the throttle pulley at the carburetor. Pass the inner cable through the slot in the bracket, then seat the cable housing in the bracket. Install the carburetor on the engine (see Section 6). Make sure all cable retainers are securely installed.

10   Reverse the disconnection steps to connect the throttle cable to the handlebar lever, noting how the spring is installed **(see illustration 10.4c)**. Operate the lever and make sure it returns to the idle position by itself under spring pressure. **Warning:** *If the lever doesn't return by itself, find and solve the problem before continuing with installation. A stuck lever can lead to loss of control of the vehicle.*

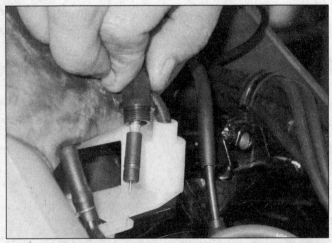

11.2 Unscrew the cable and remove the starting enrichment valve from the carburetor

Adjustment

11   Follow the procedure outlined in Chapter 1, Throttle operation/grip freeplay - check and adjustment, to adjust the cable.

12   Turn the handlebars back and forth to make sure the cables don't cause the steering to bind.

13   Once you're sure the cable operates properly, install the covers on the throttle housing and carburetor.

14   With the engine idling, turn the handlebars through their full travel (full left lock to full right lock) and note whether idle speed increases. If it does, the cable is routed incorrectly. Correct this dangerous condition before riding the vehicle.

11   Choke cable - removal and installation

Removal

Refer to illustrations 11.2, 11.3a, 11.3b and 11.3c

1   Remove the seat and fuel tank (see Chapter 7 and Section 2).

2   Unscrew the cable, together with the starting enrichment valve, from the carburetor **(see illustration)**.

3   At the left handlebar, remove the clip that secures the choke cable to the switch housing **(see illustration)**. Slip the cable out of the slots in the housing and lever **(see illustrations)**.

4   Detach the cable from any clips and remove it, noting how it's routed.

Installation

5   Installation is the reverse of the removal steps. Make sure the cable is securely fastened in its clips.

6   Install the fuel tank and all of the other components that were previously removed.

12   Exhaust system - removal and installation

Refer to illustrations 12.2, 12.4a, 12.4b, 12.6a and 12.6b

1   Refer to Chapter 7 and remove the right side cover.

2   Remove the exhaust pipe holder nuts and slide the holder off the mounting studs **(see illustration)**.

3   If necessary, unbolt the heat shield and remove it from the exhaust pipe.

4   Loosen the muffler clamp bolts and remove the mounting bolts **(see illustrations)**.

5   Pull the exhaust system forward, separate the pipe from the cylin-

11.3a Remove the cable clip (arrow) . . .

11.3b . . . and slip the cable end out of the housing slot (arrow) . . .

11.3c . . . and the lever slot (arrow)

12.2 Remove the holder nuts (arrows) and slip the holder off the studs

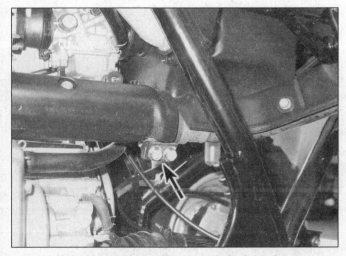

12.4a Loosen the muffler clamp bolts (arrow) . . .

12.4b . . . and remove the muffler mounting bolts (arrows)

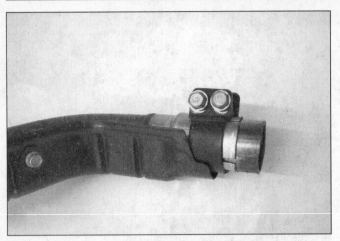

12.6a Install a new gasket at the muffler joint . . .

12.6b . . . and in the exhaust port

der head and remove the system from the machine.
6   Installation is the reverse of removal, with the following additions:

 a) *Be sure to install new gaskets at the muffler clamp and cylinder head* **(see illustrations)**.
 b) *Tighten the muffler mounting bolts and heat shield bolts securely, but don't overtighten them and strip the threads .*

13 Carburetor heater (450 and 500 models) - removal and installation

Refer to illustration 13.3
1   Disconnect the carburetor connector **(see illustration 6.7)**.
2   Connect an ohmmeter between the terminals and measure the resistance. If it's not within the range listed in this Chapter's Specifications, replace the carburetor heater as described below.
3   With rags handy to catch spilled fuel, unscrew the carburetor heater from the float bowl **(see illustration)**. Remove the heater and spacer.
4   Installation is the reverse of the removal steps. Use a new sealing washer.

13.3 On 450 and 500 models, unscrew the carburetor heater and remove the collar (arrow)

Chapter 4
Ignition system

Contents

Specifications

Ignition coil peak voltage (minimum)	100 volts
Pulse generator peak voltage (minimum)	0.7 volts
Ignition timing	
At idle	13-degrees BTDC
At full advance (4500 rpm)	30-degrees BTDC

Torque specifications

Pulse generator screws or Allen bolts	6 Nm (52 in-lbs)*
Timing hole cap	See Chapter 1

*Apply non-permanent thread locking agent to the bolt threads.

1 General information

These vehicles are equipped with a battery operated, fully transistorized, breakerless ignition system. The system consists of the following components:

Pulse generator
Ignition control module (ICM)
Battery and fuse
Ignition coil
Spark plug
Engine kill (stop) and main (key) switches
Primary and secondary (HT) circuit wiring

The transistorized ignition system functions on the same principle as a DC ignition system with the pulse generator and ICM performing the tasks previously associated with the breaker points and mechanical advance system. As a result, adjustment and maintenance of ignition components is eliminated (with the exception of spark plug replacement).

Because of their nature, the individual ignition system components can be checked but not repaired. If ignition system troubles occur, and the faulty component can be isolated, the only cure for the problem is to replace the part with a new one. Keep in mind that most electrical parts, once purchased, can't be returned. To avoid unnecessary expense, make very sure the faulty component has been positively identified before buying a replacement part.

2 Ignition system - check

Refer to illustrations 2.5 and 2.13
Warning: *Because of the very high voltage generated by the ignition system, extreme care should be taken when these checks are performed.*
1   If the ignition system is the suspected cause of poor engine performance or failure to start, a number of checks can be made to isolate the problem.
2   Make sure the ignition kill (stop) switch is in the Run or On position.

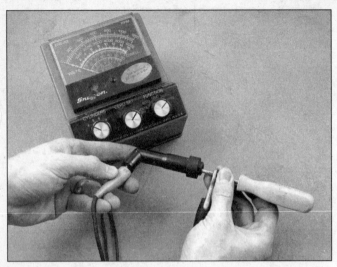

2.5 Unscrew the spark plug cap from the plug wire and measure
its resistance with an ohmmeter

2.13 A simple spark gap testing fixture can be made from a
block of wood, two nails, a large alligator clip, a screw
and a piece of wire

Engine will not start

3   Refer to Chapter 1 and disconnect the spark plug wire. Connect
the wire to a spare spark plug and lay the plug on the engine with the
threads contacting the engine. If necessary, hold the spark plug with
an insulated tool. Crank the engine over and make sure a well-defined,
blue spark occurs between the spark plug electrodes. **Warning:** *Don't
remove the spark plug from the engine to perform this check - atomized
fuel being pumped out of the open spark plug hole could ignite, causing
severe injury!*
4   If no spark occurs, the following checks should be made:
5   Unscrew the spark plug cap from the plug wire and check the cap
resistance with an ohmmeter **(see illustration)**. If the resistance is infinite, replace it with a new one.
6   Make sure all electrical connectors are clean and tight. Check all
wires for shorts, opens and correct installation.
7   Check the battery voltage with a voltmeter. If the voltage is less
than 12-volts, recharge the battery.
8   Check the ignition fuse and the fuse connections (see Chapter 8).
If the fuse is blown, replace it with a new one; if the connections are
loose or corroded, clean or repair them.
9   Refer to Section 3 and check the ignition coil primary and secondary resistance.
10   Refer to Section 4 and check the pulse generator resistance.
11   If the preceding checks produce positive results but there is still no
spark at the plug, refer to Section 5 and check the ICM.

Engine starts but misfires

12   If the engine starts but misfires, make the following checks before
deciding that the ignition system is at fault.
13   The ignition system must be able to produce a spark across a
seven millimeter (1/4-inch) gap (minimum). A simple test fixture **(see
illustration)** can be constructed to make sure the minimum spark gap
can be jumped. Make sure the fixture electrodes are positioned seven
millimeters apart.
14   Connect one of the spark plug wires to the protruding test fixture
electrode, then attach the fixture's alligator clip to a good engine ground
(earth).
15   Crank the engine over with the key in the On position and see
if well-defined, blue sparks occur between the test fixture electrodes.
If the minimum spark gap test is positive, the ignition coil is functioning properly. If the spark will not jump the gap, or if it is weak (orange
colored), refer to Steps 5 through 11 of this Section and perform the
component checks described.

3   Ignition coil - check, removal and installation

Check

1   In order to determine conclusively that the ignition coils are defective, they should be tested by an authorized Honda dealer service
department which is equipped with the special electrical tester required
for this check.
2   Honda doesn't provide ignition coil resistance specifications for
these models. Instead, it recommends testing the coil peak primary
voltage with one of the following:

a) *Imrie diagnostic tester model 625*
b) *Digital multimeter (minimum impedance 10 meg-ohms per DC
volt) and [peak voltage adapter (Honda part no. 07HGJ-0020100
or equivalent)*

If you don't have one of these special tools, have the coil tested by a
Honda dealer. If you do have the right equipment, the procedure is as
follows.
3   Place the transmission in Neutral and disconnect the spark plug
wire from the plug (see Chapter 1). Connect another spark plug to the
cap and lay it on a bare metal part of the engine so it's grounded.
4   Leave the ignition coil wires connected for this step. Connect the
peak voltage tester negative terminal to the ignition coil black/yellow
wire terminal. Connect the tester positive terminal to body ground (bare
metal on the engine). The meter must be on its "10 M-ohms/DCV" setting or it won't produce an accurate or meaningful measurement.
5   Set the engine start switch to Run and crank the engine with the
starter. Compare the tester reading to the value listed in this Chapter's
Specifications.
6   There are four possible outcomes: peak voltage is adequate, peak
voltage is too low, there is no voltage, or peak voltage is satisfactory but
there is still no spark at the spark plug.

a) *If peak voltage is adequate, the ignition coil is operating satisfactorily.*
b) *If peak voltage is low, go to Step 7.*
c) *If there is no voltage , go to Step 15.*
d) *If peak voltage is satisfactory, but there is no spark at the plug, go
to Step 20.*

Peak voltage is low

7   First, check the peak voltage adapter connections by repeating
Step 5 with the tester connections reversed. If the indicated voltage is
now above the specified minimum, the coil is OK (the adapter connections were incorrect the first time you measured coil peak voltage).

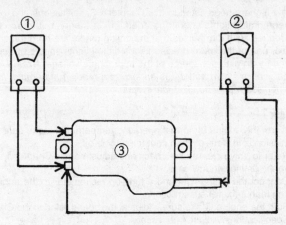

3.4 Ignition coil test

1   *Measure primary winding resistance*
2   *Measure secondary winding resistance*
3   *Ignition coil*

4.2 The ignition control module is mounted under the front fender at the center of the vehicle (arrow) (450 shown)

8   Check your multimeter's impedance setting. It should be at "10 M-ohms/DCV." If it isn't, change to the correct stetting and repeat Step 5.
9   If the battery is undercharged, the cranking speed might be too low. Charge the battery (see Chapter 8).
10   The sampling timing of the tester and measured pulse are not synchronized. The ignition system is operating satisfactorily if the measured peak voltage is higher than the specified minimum peak voltage at least once (this only applies to the peak voltage tester, not to a multimeter used with the peak voltage adapter).
11   There is a bad connection or broken wire In the ignition system (see the wiring diagrams at the end of Chapter 8). Check the wiring between the alternator and ICM.
12   The ignition pulse generator is defective (see Section 4).
13   The ignition coil is defective (substitute a known good coil and recheck).
14   If everything in Steps 7 through 13 is satisfactory, the ignition control module is defective (see Section 6).

No peak voltage

15   Verify the tester connections and setting as described in Steps 7 and 8 above.
16   Test the engine kill switch and ignition switch (see Chapter 8).
17   Check the ICM green/white (ground) wire for a break or poor connection.
18   Check the ignition pulse generator (see Section 4).
19   If everything in Steps 15 through 18 is OK, the ignition coil module may be defective (see Section 5).

Peak voltage satisfactory but no spark at the plug

20   The spark plug or plug wire may be defective (see Chapter 1).
21   Secondary ignition current might be "leaking" somewhere between the coil and spark plug.
22   If the plug and wire are good and there's no secondary current leak, the ignition coil is probably defective. Substitute a known good coil or have it tested by a Honda dealer before replacing it.

Removal and installation

23   Refer to Chapter 3 and remove the fuel tank and heat shield.
24   Disconnect the spark plug wire from the plug. After labeling them with tape to aid in reinstallation, disconnect the coil primary circuit electrical connectors.
25   Slip the rubber coil mount off its blade, then remove the coil from the mount.
26   Installation is the reverse of removal. Make sure the primary circuit electrical connectors are attached to the proper terminals. Just in case you forgot to mark the wires, the black/yellow wire connects to the positive terminal and the green wire connects to the negative terminal.

4   Pulse generator - check, removal and installation

Check

Refer to illustration 4.2

1   Testing the pulse generator on these models is done by checking the peak voltage. It requires the special tester described in Section 3.
2   Locate the ignition control module at the front of the vehicle (**see illustration**). If you're working on a 400 or 450, locate the four-pin connector. If you're working on a 500, locate the 21-pin connector.
3   Connect the tester positive probe to the connector blue-yellow wire terminal. Connect the negative probe to the green/white wire terminal (400 and 450) or ground (500). **Note:** *Leave the wiring connector connected. Connect the tester by backprobing the terminals on the harness side of the connector.*
4   Place the transmission in Neutral and disconnect the spark plug wire from the plug (see Chapter 1). Connect another spark plug to the cap and lay it on a bare metal part of the engine so it's grounded.
5   Set the engine start switch to Run and crank the engine with the starter. Compare the peak voltage reading to the value listed in this Chapter's Specifications.
6   If voltage is less then the peak voltage listed in this Chapter's Specifications, locate the 5-pin round alternator connector on the right side of the vehicle beneath the rear fender. Disconnect the connector. If you're working on a 400 or 450, connect the tester between the blue/yellow and green/white wire terminals. If you're working on a 500, connect the tester between the blue/yellow wire terminal and ground.
7   Measure peak voltage as described in Step 4.
8   If the reading in Step 4 (at the ICM connector) is not within the Specifications, but the reading in Step 6 (at the alternator connector) is within the Specifications, check the wiring for a break or poor connection, referring to the wiring diagrams in Chapter 8.
9   If the reading is incorrect at both connectors (ICM and alternator), perform Steps 7 through 13 in Section 3. If these steps don't locate the problem, replace the pulse generator.

Removal

10   Remove the alternator cover and disconnect the pulse generator connector, if you haven't already done so (see Chapter 8).
11   Free the pulse generator wire from the groove in the pulse generator body.
12   Unscrew the pulse generator Allen bolts and remove the pulse generator.

Installation

13   Installation is the reverse of the removal procedure, with the fol-

lowing addition: Apply non-permanent thread locking agent to the pulse generator screws or Allen bolts and tighten them to the torque listed in this Chapter's Specifications.

14   Refer to Chapter 8 and reinstall the alternator cover.

5   Ignition control module (ICM) - check, removal and installation

1   The ICM can only be checked by process of elimination; that is, after all other possible causes of ignition problems have been checked and eliminated, the ICM is probably at fault.

2   Perform the checks in Sections 2 through 4 to test other parts of the ignition system. If all of these test OK, the ICM is probably at fault. However, since a new ICM can't be returned once purchased, it's a good idea to have a dealer service department or other qualified shop check the ignition system before buying a new ICM.

6   Ignition timing - general information and check

General information

1   Ignition timing need be checked only if you're troubleshooting a problem such as loss of power. Since the ignition timing can't be adjusted and since none of the ignition system parts is subject to mechanical wear, there's no need for regular checks.

2   The ignition timing is checked with the engine running, both at idle

and at a higher speed listed in this Chapter's Specifications. Inexpensive neon timing lights should be adequate in theory, but in practice may produce such dim pulses that the timing marks are hard to see. If possible, one of the more precise xenon timing lights should be used, powered by an external source of the appropriate voltage. **Note:** *Don't use the vehicle's own battery as an incorrect reading may result from stray impulses within the electrical system.*

Check

3   Warm the engine to normal operating temperature, make sure the transmission is in Neutral, then shut the engine off.

4   Refer to Valve clearance - check and adjustment in Chapter 1 and remove the timing window cap.

5   Connect the timing light and a tune-up tachometer to the engine, following manufacturer's instructions.

6   Start the engine. Make sure it idles at the speed listed in the Chapter 1 Specifications. Adjust if necessary.

7   Point the timing light into the timing window. At idle, the line next to the F mark on the alternator rotor should align with the notch at the side of the timing window.

8   Raise engine by turning the throttle stop screw (see Chapter 1). The timing mark on the alternator rotor should move in relation to the notch.

9   If the timing is incorrect and all other ignition components have tested as good, the ICM may be defective. Have it tested by a dealer service department or other qualified shop.

10   When the check is complete, grease the timing window O-ring, then install the O-ring and cap and disconnect the test equipment.

Chapter 5
Steering, suspension and final drive

Contents

Specifications

Shock absorbers

Front spring length
    400 models
        Standard .... 215.3 mm (8.48 inches)
        Minimum .... 211.0 mm (8.3 inches)
    450 and 500 models .... Not specified
Rear spring length
    400 models
        Standard .... 208.5 mm (8.21 inches)
        Minimum .... 204.3 mm (8.04 inches)
    450 and 500 models .... Not specified
Tie-rod ball-joint spacing
    400 models .... 349.5 mm (13.76 inches)
    450 models .... 369 mm (14.5 inches)
    500 models
        2001 through 2004 .... 387 mm (15.2 inches)
        2005 and later .... 382 +/- 1 mm (15.0 inches +/- 0.04 inch)
Rear axle runout (maximum)
    400 and 450 models .... 3.0 mm (0.12 inch)
    500 models .... Not specified

Torque specifications

Handlebars
    Grip end bolts .... Not specified
    Handlebar bracket bolts .... Not specified
    Handlebar bracket lower nuts .... 40 Nm (29 ft-lbs) (1)
Tie-rod stud nuts .... 54 Nm (40 ft-lbs) (1)
Tie-rod locknuts .... 54 Nm (40 ft-lbs)
Steering shaft nut .... 110 Nm (80 ft-lbs)
Steering shaft upper bracket bolts .... 32 Nm (24 ft-lbs)
Front shock absorbers .... 44 Nm (33 ft-lbs) (1)
Rear shock absorbers
    400 and 450 models
        Upper nut .... 39 Nm (29 ft-lbs) (1)
        Lower bolt/nut .... 44 Nm (33 ft-lbs) (1)
    500 models
        Upper nut
            2001 through 2004 models .... 34 Nm (25 ft-lbs) (1)
            2005 and later models .... 40 Nm (30 ft-lbs) (1)
        Lower bolt/nut .... 44 Nm (33 ft-lbs) (1)
Front suspension arm pivot bolt nuts .... 44 Nm (33 ft-lbs) (1)

Torque specifications (continued)

Ball-joint nuts
    400 models .... 30 to 36 Nm (22 to 26 ft-lbs)
    450 models
        1998 through 2001 .... 30 Nm (22 ft-lbs)
        2002 and later... 33 Nm (24 ft-lbs)
Breather tube retainer bolts (400 and 450 models)........................... 12 Nm (9 ft-lbs)
Brake hose retaining nuts (400 and 450 models)................................ 15 Nm (11 ft-lbs)
Brake hose retaining bolts (500 models).. 12 Nm (108 in-lbs)
Front differential
    Front bracket and mounting bolts/nuts.. 22 Nm (16 ft-lbs)
    Upper mounting bolts/nuts .... 44 Nm (33 ft-lbs) (2)
Front driveshaft cover bolts .... Not specified
Front driveaxle (hub) nuts
    400 models .... 80 to 100 Nm (58 to 72 ft-lbs)
    All others .... 78 Nm (58 ft-lbs)
Rear axle housing bolts/nuts .... 44 Nm (33 ft-lbs)
Rear differential mounting nuts... 44 Nm (33 ft-lbs)
Rear differential skid plate bolts .... 32 Nm (24 ft-lbs)
Swingarm
    Left pivot bolt... 112 Nm (83 ft-lbs)
    Right pivot bolt
        1995 through 2001 .... 4 Nm (36 in-lbs)
        2002 and later... 10 Nm (84 in-lbs)
    Right pivot bolt locknut... 112 Nm (83 ft-lbs)

1. *Use new nuts; don't reuse the old ones.*
2. *On 2005 and later 500 models, replace the nut with a new one each time it's removed.*

1   General information

The front suspension on all models consists of an upper and lower control arm on each side of the vehicle. A shock absorber with concentric coil spring is installed between the upper suspension arm and the frame.

The rear suspension on all models consists of shock absorbers with concentric coil springs and a steel swingarm. Final drive is by a shaft, which passes through an integral tube on the swingarm.

The steering system consists of knuckles mounted at the outer ends of the front suspension and connected to a steering shaft by tie rods. The steering shaft is turned by handlebars.

2   Handlebars - removal, inspection and installation

1   The handlebars are a one-piece tube. The tube fits into a bracket, which is integral with the steering shaft. If the handlebars must be removed for access to other components, such as the steering shaft, simply remove the bolts and slip the handlebars off the bracket. It's not necessary to disconnect the cables, wires or brake hose, but it is a good idea to support the assembly with a piece of wire or rope, to avoid unnecessary strain on the cables, wires and the brake hose.

2   If the handlebars are to be removed completely, refer to Chapter 3 for the throttle housing removal procedure, Chapter 6 for the master cylinder removal procedure and Chapter 8 for the switch removal procedure.

Removal

Refer to illustrations 2.3, 2.4a, 2.4b, 2.5 and 2.6

3   If you plan to remove one of the grips, remove its bolt while the handlebars are still bolted to the bracket **(see illustration)**. The grips are glued to the handlebars, so you may have to cut them off.

4   Pry out the trim cover and remove the handlebar cover screws **(see illustrations)**.

5   Remove the handlebar bracket bolts and lift off the brackets **(see illustration)**. Lift the handlebar out of the bracket.

2.3 The grips are secured to the handlebars by a bolt and adhesive

2.4a Pry up the trim piece . . .

2.4b . . . and remove the screws (arrows)

2.5 Unbolt the brackets (arrows) to free the handlebar

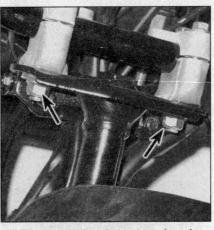

2.6 Remove the bracket nuts and washers (arrows); discard the nuts and use new ones on installation

2.8 Line up punch mark on the handlebar (arrow) with the bracket parting line

3.3a Remove the bolts (arrows) and lift off the bracket . . .

3.3b . . . to expose the bushing; the Up mark and arrow must be upright when the bushing is installed

3.5a Remove the cotter pin and nut, then detach the steering arm from the shaft

6   To remove the brackets, remove their mounting nuts and washers from below (see illustration). Discard the nuts and use new ones on installation.

Inspection

7   Check the handlebar and brackets for cracks and distortion and replace them if any undesirable conditions are found.

Installation

Refer to illustration 2.8

8   Installation is the reverse of the removal steps, with the following additions:

a) *If the bracket nuts were removed, install new nuts and tighten them to the torque listed in this Chapter's Specifications.*

b) *When installing the handlebar to the brackets, line up the punch mark on the handlebar with the bracket seams (see illustration). Tighten the front bracket bolts securely, then tighten the rear bracket bolts. There will be a small gap at the rear of each bracket (between the upper and lower parts of the bracket) when the bolts are correctly tightened. Don't try to close the gap by over-tightening the rear bolts, or the brackets will break*

c) *If a grip was removed, clean the handlebar and apply cement (Honda Hand Grip Cement or equivalent) to the inside of the grip. Let the cement cure for three to five minutes, then slide the grip onto the handlebar and twist it to spread the cement. Let the cement dry for an hour, then install the grip end bolt.*

3   Steering shaft - removal, inspection, bearing replacement and installation

Removal

Refer to illustrations 3.3a, 3.3b, 3.5a and 3.5b

1   Remove the handlebars and their bracket (Section 2).
2   Remove the front fender (see Chapter 7).
3   Unbolt the steering shaft bracket from the frame to expose the bushing (see illustrations).
4   Refer to Section 6 and disconnect the inner ends of the tie-rods.
5   Remove the cotter pin and steering shaft nut (see illustration). Remove the steering arm from the shaft (see illustration).
6   Remove the steering shaft from the vehicle.

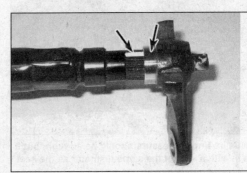

3.5b Align the wide splines on the arm and shaft (arrows) when installing the arm

3.11a Pry out the seal above the bearing . . .

3.11b . . . and the below the bearing . . .

3.12 . . . and remove the snap-ring, then the bearing

Inspection

7 Clean all the parts with solvent and dry them thoroughly, using compressed air, if available.

8 Check the steering shaft bushing for wear, deterioration or damage (see illustration 3.3b). Replace it if there's any doubt about its condition.

9 Check the steering shaft for bending or other signs of damage. Inspect the steering arm as well. Do not attempt to repair any steering components. Replace them with new parts if defects are found.

10 Insert a finger into the steering shaft bearing and turn the inner race. If it's rough, loose or noisy, replace it as described below.

Bearing replacement

Refer to illustrations 3.11a, 3.11b, 3.12 and 3.14

11 Pry the upper and lower grease seals out of the bearing housing in the frame (see illustrations).

12 Remove the snap-ring from on top of the bearing (see illustration), then remove the bearing through the top of the housing.

13 Pack a new bearing with high-quality grease (preferably a moly-based grease). Position the bearing in the housing with its sealed side up and tap it into place with a bearing driver or socket that bears against the bearing outer race.

14 Install the snap-ring. Coat the lips of new upper and lower grease seals with grease, then install them in the housing (see illustration).

Installation

15 Installation is the reverse of removal, with the following additions:

a) *Pack the steering shaft bushing's internal cavities with grease. Install it with its UP mark upward (see illustration 3.3b).*

b) *Align the wide splines on the steering arm and shaft, then install the steering arm (see illustration 3.5b).*

c) *Lubricate the threads and flange of the steering shaft nut with grease.*

d) *Use new cotter pins and tighten all fasteners to the torques listed in this Chapter's Specifications.*

4 Shock absorbers - removal and installation

Front shock absorbers

Refer to illustration 4.2

1 Securely block both rear wheels so the vehicle won't roll. Refer to Chapter 6 and remove the front wheels.

2 Remove the mounting nut and bolt from the bottom of the shock, then from the top (see illustration). Lift the shock out. Discard the mounting nuts and use new ones on installation.

3 Installation is the reverse of the removal steps. Use new nuts (don't re-use the old ones) and tighten the nuts and bolts to the torque listed in this Chapter's Specifications.

Rear shock absorbers

Refer to illustration 4.6

4 Securely block both front wheels so the vehicle can't toll. Jack up the rear end and support it securely with the rear wheels off the ground.

5 If you're removing the right shock absorber, remove the muffler for access (see Chapter 3).

6 Remove the mounting bolts and nuts at the bottom of the shock,

3.14 Press the seals in; finger pressure should be enough, but if not, tap the seals in with a socket the same diameter as the seal

4.2 The lower bolt head faces forward on all models; the upper bolt head faces forward on 400/450 models and rearward on 500 models - use new nuts

4.6 Remove the nut and bolt from the bottom of the shock absorber, then the nut from the top (arrows; left shock shown)

then at the top **(see illustration)**. Lift the shock out of the vehicle. Discard the nuts and use new ones on installation.

Rear shock absorber installation

7   Installation is the reverse of the removal steps. Use new nuts. Tighten the nuts and bolts to the torque listed in this Chapter's Specifications.

5   Shock absorbers - disassembly, inspection and reassembly

Refer to illustrations 5.1, 5.2 and 5.3
Warning: *Before overhauling the shocks, read through the procedure, paying special attention to the steps involved in compressing the spring. If you don't have access to the special tools needed, take the job to a Honda dealer or other shop equipped with the necessary special tools.*
1   Place the shock absorber in a spring compressor (Honda tool 07GME-0010000 with 07967-KC10100) **(see illustration)**. The purpose of the compressor is to compress the spring safely, so it can't fly out and cause injury.
2   Compress the spring just enough so the spring stopper can be removed **(see illustration)**.
3   Release the spring compressor and take off the spring guide, spring and washer **(see illustration)**.
4   Measure the free length of the spring. If it's less than the value listed in this Chapter's Specifications, replace it.
5   Check the shock absorber for oil leaks where the rod meets the body. Check the rod for wear or damage and replace it if any problems are found.
6   Check the spring guide (and seat guide, if equipped) for wear or

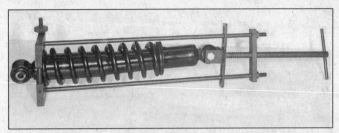

5.1 Place the shock absorber in a spring compressor

5.2 Compress the spring enough to remove the spring seat stopper

damage and replace them as necessary.
7   Check the spring seat stopper and washer for wear and damage and replace them as necessary.
8   Install the washer, spring and guide on the shock absorber. Position the spring so its tightly wound coils will be upward when the shock is installed.
9   Compress the spring with the special tool and install the spring seat stopper. Release the spring and make sure the stopper holds it securely.

6   Tie-rods - removal, inspection and installation

Removal
Refer to illustrations 6.1, 6.2 and 6.3
1   Remove the cotter pin from the nut at the outer end of the tie-rod **(see illustration)**.

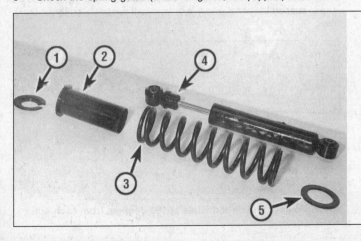

5.3 Front shock absorber details (typical; rear shock similar)

6.1 Straighten the cotter pin and pull it out of the tie-rod nut . . .

6.2 . . . prevent the stud from turning with an open-end wrench and unscrew the nut, then detach the stud from the steering knuckle

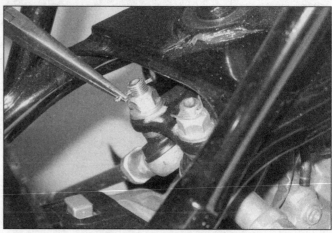

6.3 Remove the cotter pins and nuts and detach the inner ends of the tie-rods from the steering arm

2   Hold the tie-rod flat with a wrench and undo the nut **(see illustration)**. Separate the tie-rod stud from the knuckle.
3   Repeat Steps 1 and 2 to disconnect the inner end of the tie rod **(see illustration)**. Discard the nuts and use new ones on installation.

Inspection
Refer to illustration 6.5
4   Check the tie-rod shaft for bending or other damage and replace it if any problems are found. Don't try to straighten the shaft.
5   Check the ball-joint boot for cracks or deterioration **(see illustration)**. Twist and rotate the threaded stud. It should move easily, without roughness or looseness. If the boot or stud show any problems, unscrew the ball-joint from the tie-rod and install a new one. **Note:** *The silver-colored locknut and ball-joint labeled "L" go on the end of the tie-rod nearest the wrench flats. The gold-colored locknut and unlabeled ball-joint go on the other end.*

Installation
Refer to illustration 6.7
6   Measure the distance from each locknut to the end of the threads and compare it with the value listed in this Chapter's Specifications **(see illustration 6.5)**. If it's incorrect, loosen the locknut and reposition the locknut and ball-joint on the threads.
7   Position the ball-joint at each end of the tie-rod so the studs face

180-degrees away from each other **(see illustration)**.
8   The remainder of installation is the reverse of the removal steps, with the following additions:

a) *Use new ball-joint nuts (don't re-use the old ones). Tighten the new nuts to the torque listed in this Chapter's Specifications.*
b) *Use new cotter pins and bend them to hold the nuts securely.*
c) *Check front wheel toe-in and adjust as necessary (see Chapter 1).*

---

7   Steering knuckles - removal, inspection, and installation

---

Removal
Refer to illustrations 7.5, 7.6 and 7.7
1   Separating the ball-joint(s) from the knuckle requires either a special Honda separator tool or its equivalent. Equivalent automotive tools can be rented, but they must be small enough for use on these vehicles. An automotive tie-rod separator tool, rather than a ball-joint separator, may be the correct size. If the correct special tools aren't available, the knuckle can be removed as an assembly with the suspension arms. This assembly can then be taken to a Honda dealer for ball-joint removal (and knuckle bearing replacement if necessary).
2   Securely block both rear wheels so the vehicle won't roll. Loosen the front wheel nuts with the tires still on the ground, then jack up the front end, support it securely on jackstands and remove the front wheels.
3   Refer to Section 6 and disconnect the outer end of the tie-rod from the knuckle.
4   Remove the front brake panel or caliper (see Chapter 6). The front brake hose can be left connected, but be careful not to twist it and be sure to support the panel with wire or rope so it doesn't hang by the brake hose.

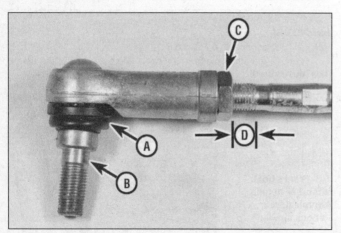

6.5 Check the boot for cracks or deterioration and make sure the stud moves easily, without roughness or looseness

A	Boot	D	Distance from locknut to
B	Stud		end of threads
C	Locknut		

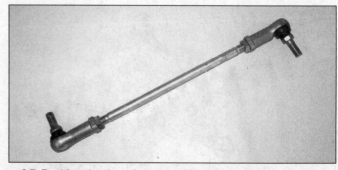

6.7 Position the tie-rod studs at 180-degrees from each other

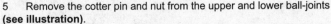

7.5 Remove the cotter pins and nuts (arrows) . . .

7.6 . . . and detach the ball-joint from the knuckle with the special tool or an aftermarket equivalent (shown)

5   Remove the cotter pin and nut from the upper and lower ball-joints (see illustration).

6   Separate the lower ball-joint from the knuckle with Honda tool 07MAC-SL00200 or equivalent (see illustration). If you're using the Honda tool, lubricate the puller jaw and the pressure bolt threads with multi-purpose grease. Slip the tool into position, taking care not to damage the rubber boot, and turn the adjusting bolt so the jaws are parallel. Tighten the pressure bolt by hand, make sure the jaws are still parallel (readjust the pressure bolt if necessary), then tighten the pressure bolt with a wrench until the ball-joint stud pops out of the knuckle.

7   If there isn't room to fit the separator tool onto the upper ball-joint, loosen the nut and tap on the knuckle boss with a mallet where the stud passes through it (see illustration). This should loosen the stud so it can be removed from the knuckle.

Inspection

Refer to illustration 7.8

8   Check the knuckle carefully for cracks, bending or other damage. Replace it if any problems are found. If the vehicle has been in a collision or has been bottomed hard, it's a good idea to have the knuckle magnafluxed by a machine shop to check for hidden cracks. Check the ball-joint boot for cracks or deterioration (see illustration). Twist and rotate the threaded stud. It should move easily, without roughness or looseness. If the boot or stud show any problems, refer to Section 8 or Section 9 and replace the ball-joint.

9   Turn the knuckle bearing inner race with a finger (see illustration 7.8). If it's rough, loose or noisy, refer to Section 8 and replace it. Replace the bearing grease seals if they show signs of leakage or wear.

Installation

10   Installation is the reverse of the removal steps, with the following additions: Use new cotter pins and tighten the ball-joint nut(s) to the torque listed in this Chapter's Specifications.

8   Steering knuckle bearing and lower ball-joint replacement

Bearing replacement

1   Pry out the bearing grease seals (see illustration 7.8).

2   Remove the bearing snap-ring from the outer side of the knuckle. Drive the bearing out of the knuckle with a bearing driver or socket that bears against the bearing outer race.

3   Pack a new bearing with grease, then drive it in with the same tool used for removal. Seat the bearing securely, then install the snap-ring and make sure it fits completely into its groove.

4   Tap in new grease seals with a bearing driver or socket the same diameter as the seals. Make sure the seals seat squarely in their bores, then lubricate the seal lips with grease.

Ball-joint replacement

Refer to illustration 8.5

Note: *This procedure requires a press and special support tools (Honda 07WMF-HN00100 and 07946-1870100 or equivalent). If you don't have them, take the knuckle to a Honda dealer for ball-joint replacement.*

5   Remove the ball-joint snap-ring (see illustration).

7.7 Tapping on the boss where the ball-joint stud passes through it is another way to free the ball-joint

7.8 Inspect the ball-joint boot and knuckle bearing (arrows)

8.5 Remove the ball-joint snap-ring (arrow)

9.3 Detach the brake hose retainer, breather hose retainer and the shock absorber lower end from the suspension arm (arrows)

9.6a Note which way the bolt heads face and remove the upper arm pivot bolts and nuts (arrows) . . .

9.6b . . . and do the same thing to remove the lower arm

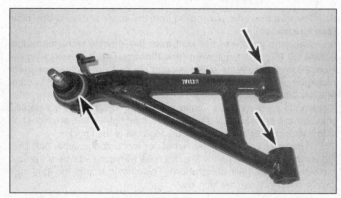

9.8 Inspect the pivot bushings and the ball-joint (arrows)

6   Place the knuckle in a press with the ball-joint stud upward. Place the driver portion of the removal tool under the ball-joint and the hollow portion over the stud and press the ball-joint out.

7   Place the new ball-joint on the press plate and place the knuckle over the stud.

8   Place the support tool over the stud so the stud will fit into the tool when the ball-joint is pressed on. Press the ball-joint into the knuckle; if it won't go easily, stop and make sure the support tool is aligned correctly.

9   Install the snap-ring and make sure it seats completely in its groove.

9   Suspension arms - removal, inspection, ball-joint replacement and installation

Note: *This procedure describes removal and installation of the upper and lower suspension arms. If you plan to remove only the upper or lower arm, ignore the steps which don't apply.*

Removal

Refer to illustrations 9.3, 9.6a and 9.6b

1   Securely block both rear wheels so the vehicle won't roll. Loosen the front wheel nuts with the tires still on the ground, then jack up the front end, support it securely on jackstands and remove the front wheels.

2   Refer to Section 7 and detach the steering knuckle from the suspension arm(s). The tie-rod doesn't have to be detached from the knuckle.

3   Detach the brake hose retainer and breather hose from the upper suspension arm **(see illustration)**.

4   Note which way the lower shock absorber nut faces and remove it **(see illustration 9.3)**.

5   Remove the bolt and detach the lower end of the shock absorber from the upper arm.

6   Remove the nuts and bolts at the inner end of the upper and lower suspension arms **(see illustrations)** and pull the suspension arms out. Discard the nuts and use new ones on installation.

Inspection

Refer to illustration 9.8

7   Check the suspension arm(s) for bending, cracks or other damage. Replace damaged parts. Don't attempt to straighten them.

9.10 Remove the snap-ring (arrow), then press out the lower ball-joint

10.5 The suspension arms and knuckle can be removed together if you don't have a ball-joint separator tool

10.6a Pull on the joint (not on the shaft) to free the circlip (arrow) from the differential . . .

10.6b . . . and use a pry bar to help separate the joint from the differential

8   Check the rubber bushings at the inner end of the suspension arm for cracks, deterioration or wear of the metal insert **(see illustration)**. Check the pivot bolts for wear as well. Replace the suspension arm if any problems are visible.

9   Check the ball-joint boot for cracks or deterioration. Twist and rotate the threaded stud **(see illustration 9.8)**. It should move easily, without roughness or looseness.

Ball-joint replacement

Refer to illustration 9.10

10   Remove the snap-ring **(see illustration)**, then replace the lower ball-joint using the methods and tools described in Section 8.

Installation

11   Installation is the reverse of the removal steps, with the following additions:

  a) *Use new nuts on the suspension arm pivot bolts and the shock absorber lower bolt.*

  b) *Tighten the nuts and bolts slightly while the vehicle is jacked up, then tighten them to the torque listed in this Chapter's Specifications while the vehicle's weight is resting on the wheels.*

10   Front driveaxles - removal and installation

Removal

Refer to illustrations 10.5, 10.6a and 10.6b

1   Securely block both rear wheels so the vehicle won't roll. Loosen the front wheel nuts with the tires still on the ground, then jack up the front end, support it securely on jackstands and remove the front wheels.

2   Remove the front brake drum and disconnect the breather tube from the brake panel (see Chapter 5).

3   Remove the cotter pin from the lower ball-joint nut, then loosen the nut but don't remove it yet.

4   Separate the lower ball-joint from the knuckle (see Section 7).

5   Freeing the outer end of the driveaxle from the knuckle requires that the knuckle be pulled outward off of the outer end of the driveaxle. If you have the necessary ball-joint separator tool, you can use it to separate the ball-joint studs from the knuckle, which will free the knuckle to be pulled outward (see Section 7). If you don't have the ball-joint tool, the inner ends of the suspension arms can be unbolted (see Section 9) and the suspension arms and knuckle pulled outward as a unit **(see illustration)**.

6   The inner end of the driveaxle is held in the final drive unit by a circlip **(see illustration)**. With the outer end of the driveaxle free of the knuckle, grasp the joint at the inner end firmly so it won't be pulled apart, then pry the driveaxle out of the final drive unit **(see illustration)**. **Caution:** *Pull the driveaxle straight out (don't let it tilt up, down or sideways) to prevent damage to the oil seal in the final drive unit.*

Installation

7   Installation is the reverse of the removal steps. After installing the driveaxle in the final drive unit, tug outward on it to make sure the circlip is locked in place. Tighten the hub nut to the torque listed in the Chapter 6 Specifications.

11   Front driveaxle - boot replacement and CV joint overhaul

Inner CV joint and boot

Disassembly

Refer to illustrations 11.3, 11.4, 11.6 and 11.8

1   Remove the driveaxle from the vehicle (see Section 10).

2   Mount the driveaxle in a vise. The jaws of the vise should be lined with wood or rags to prevent damage to the axleshaft.

3   Pry the boot clamp retaining tabs up with a small screwdriver and slide the clamps off the boot **(see illustration)**.

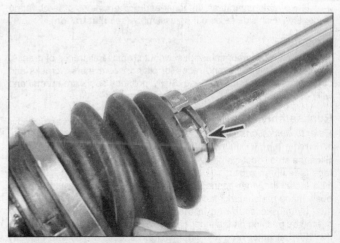

11.3 Pry the boot clamp retaining tabs (arrow) up with a small screwdriver, open the clamps and slide them off the boot

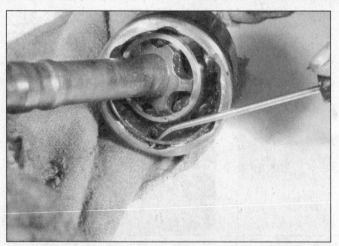

11.4 Pry the wire ring ball retainer out of the outer race

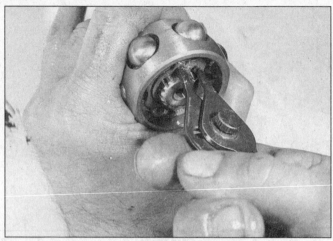

11.6 Remove the snap-ring from the end of the axle

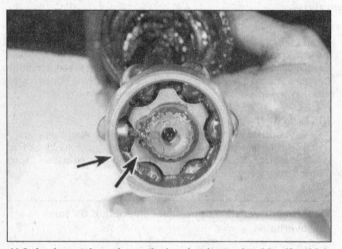

11.8 Apply match marks on the bearing (arrows) to identify which side faces out during reassembly

11.10 Wrap the splined area of the axle with tape to prevent damage to the boot when installing it

4   Slide the boot back on the axleshaft and pry the wire ring ball retainer from the outer race **(see illustration)**.

5   Pull the outer race off the inner bearing assembly.

6   Remove the snap-ring from the groove in the axleshaft with a pair of snap-ring pliers **(see illustration)**.

7   Slide the inner bearing assembly off the axleshaft.

8   Make match marks on the inner and outer portions of the bearing to identify which side faces out on assembly **(see illustration)**.

Inspection

9   Clean the components with solvent to remove all traces of grease. Inspect the cage, balls and races for pitting, score marks, cracks and other signs of wear and damage. Shiny, polished spots are normal and will not adversely affect CV joint performance.

Reassembly

Refer to illustrations 11.10, 11.16, 11.17a and 11.17b

10   Wrap the axleshaft splines with tape to avoid damaging the boot. Slide the small boot clamp and boot onto the axleshaft, then remove the tape **(see illustration)**.

11   Install the inner bearing assembly on the axleshaft with the previously made matchmarks facing outward.

12   Install the snap-ring in the groove. Make sure it's completely seated by pushing on the inner bearing assembly.

13   Fill the outer race and boot with the specified type and quantity of CV joint grease (normally included with the new boot kit). Pack the inner bearing assembly with grease, by hand, until grease is worked

completely into the assembly.

14   Slide the outer race down onto the inner race and install the wire ring retainer.

15   Wipe any excess grease from the axle boot groove on the outer race. Seat the small diameter of the boot in the recessed area on the axleshaft. Push the other end of the boot onto the outer race.

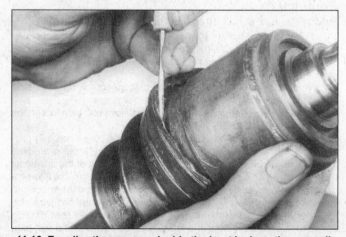

11.16 Equalize the pressure inside the boot by inserting a small, dull screwdriver between the boot and the outer race

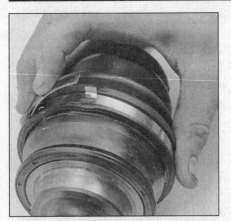

11.17a To install the new clamps, bend the tang down and . . .

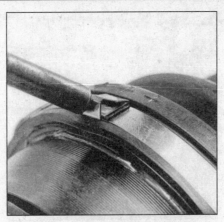

11.17b . . . fold the tabs over to hold it in place

11.21 Slide the boot away from the joint and off the axleshaft

16   Equalize the pressure in the boot by inserting a dull screwdriver between the boot and the outer race **(see illustration)**. Don't damage the boot with the tool.
17   Install the boot clamps **(see illustrations)**.
18   Install a new circlip on the inner CV joint stub axle.
19   Install the driveaxle as described in Section 10.

Outer CV joint and boot

Disassembly

Refer to illustration 11.21
20   Following Steps 1 through 8, remove the inner CV joint from the axleshaft.
21   Remove the outer CV joint boot clamps, using the technique described in Step 3. Slide the boot off the axleshaft **(see illustration)**.

Inspection

Refer to illustration 11.23
22   Thoroughly wash the inner and outer CV joints in clean solvent and blow them dry with compressed air, if available. **Note:** *Because the outer joint cannot be disassembled, it is difficult to wash away all the old grease and to rid the bearing of solvent once it's clean. But it is imperative that the job be done thoroughly, so take your time and do it right.*
23   Bend the outer CV joint housing at an angle to the driveaxle to expose the bearings, inner race and cage **(see illustration)**. Inspect the bearing surfaces for signs of wear. If the bearings are damaged or worn, replace the driveaxle.

Reassembly

24   Slide the new outer boot onto the driveaxle. It's a good idea to

wrap vinyl tape around the spline of shaft to prevent damage to the boot **(see illustration 11.10)**. When the boot is in position, add the specified amount of grease (included in the boot replacement kit) to the outer joint and the boot (pack the joint with as much grease as it will hold and put the rest into the boot). Slide the boot on the rest of the way and install the new clamps **(see illustrations 11.17a and 11.17b)**.
25   Proceed to clean and install the inner CV joint and boot by following Steps 9 through 18, then install the driveaxle as outlined in Section 10.

12   Front differential and driveshaft - removal, inspection and installation

Removal

Refer to illustrations 12.6, 12.8, 12.9 and 12.10
1   Refer to Section 10 and remove one of the front driveaxles.
2   Remove the front fender (see Chapter 7).
3   If you're working on a 2002 or later 400 or 450 model, disconnect the electrical connectors for the front final clutch and speed sensors. These are located with the electrical units between the front shock absorbers (see Chapter 8 if necessary).
4   Disconnect the differential breather hose.
5   On 1995 through 2001 400 and 450 models, remove the cover from the front driveshaft. The cover is secured by a bolt and two retainers. To remove the retainers, refer to Section 1 of Chapter 7.
6   Remove the nut from the upper mounting bolt and remove the bolt and collar **(see illustration)**.

11.23 After the old grease has been rinsed away and the solvent has been blown out with compressed air, rotate the outer joint housing through its full range of motion and inspect the bearing surfaces for wear and damage - if any of the balls, the race or the cage look damaged, replace the driveaxle and outer joint assembly

12.6 Remove the upper mounting bolt, nut and collar . . .

A)   *Upper mounting bolt, collar and nut*
B)   *Front mounting bolt and bracket*

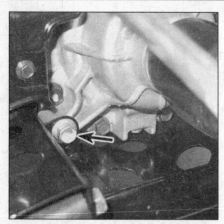

12.8 . . . then remove the rear mounting bolt and nut (arrow), followed by the front mounting bracket and bolt

12.9 Pull the differential forward to separate the driveshaft from the engine

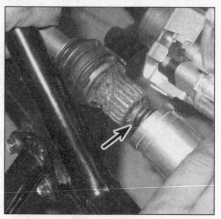

12.10 Pull out the driveshaft and remove the spring (arrow)

7   Remove the forward mounting bolt, then unbolt the mounting bolt bracket from the frame **(see illustration 12.6)**.

8   Remove the rear mounting bolt and nut **(see illustration)**.

9   Pull the differential forward to disengage the driveshaft coupling from the engine **(see illustration)**, then lift out the differential and driveshaft. As you remove the differential, separate the remaining driveaxle from it.

10   Pull the driveshaft coupling off the driveshaft and remove the spring **(see illustration)**. Pull the driveshaft out of the differential.

Inspection

Refer to illustrations 12.13a and 12.13b

11   Roll the O-rings off the ends of the driveshaft boots, then slide the boots off the shaft. Check the boots for wear, damage and deterioration and replace them if these conditions are found.

12   Check the driveshaft for bending and for worn or damaged splines. Replace it if these conditions are found.

13   Check the oil seals at the driveaxle holes and the driveshaft hole for signs of leakage. Look into the driveaxle holes and check for obvious signs of wear and for damage such as broken gear teeth **(see illustration)**. Turn the pinion (where the driveshaft enters the differential) by hand to rotate the gears so they can be inspected and listened to. If the pinion does not have internal threads, slip the driveshaft back in and use it as a handle if necessary. If it has internal threads, thread a bolt into the pinion, then turn the bolt with a socket to turn the pinion **(see illustration)**

14   Differential overhaul is a complicated procedure that requires several special tools, for which there are no readily available substitutes. If

there's visible wear or damage, or if the differential's rotation is rough or noisy, take it to a Honda dealer for disassembly and further inspection.

Installation

15   Install the boots on the ends of the driveshaft, using new O-rings.

16   Make sure the circlip is in place on the front end of the driveshaft.

17   Lubricate the lips of the driveaxle seals and the driveshaft seal, as well as the splines of the driveshaft, with moly-based multi-purpose grease.

18   Place the differential in the frame, slightly forward of its installed position.

19   Slip the driveshaft into the differential, making sure the circlip engages securely. Be careful not to bend back the rubber boot.

20   Slip the coupling onto the rear end of the driveshaft, making sure to install the spring. Push the coupling inside the rubber boot so the boot's O-ring aligns with the groove in the coupling.

21   Slide the differential back and slip the driveshaft onto the engine shaft. As you reposition the differential, install the driveaxle that was disconnected but not removed from the vehicle.

22   Install the rear mounting nut and bolt and tighten them to the torque listed in this Chapter's Specifications.

23   Install the upper mounting bolt, collar and nut and tighten them to the torque listed in this Chapter's Specifications.

24   Install the front mounting bracket and tighten its bolt securely.

25   Install the front mounting bolt and nut and tighten them to the torque listed in this Chapter's Specifications.

26   The remainder of installation is the reverse of the removal steps.

27   Fill the differential with the recommended oil (see Chapter 1).

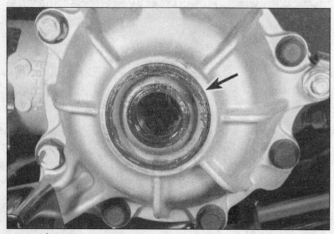

12.13a Check the driveshaft oil seal on each side of the differential (arrow) for wear or signs of leakage

12.13b If the pinion has internal threads, thread a bolt into the pinion, then turn the bolt with a socket to rotate the gears

13.4 Remove the bolts (arrows) and lower the skid plate away from the differential

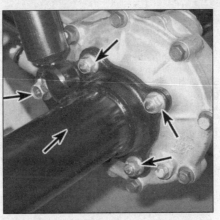

13.5 Remove the lower shock absorber bolt and axle housing nuts (arrows) (one nut hidden)

13.6 Note which way the chamfered side of the collar faces, then slide it off the shaft

13   Rear axle shaft and housings - removal, inspection and installation

Removal

Refer to illustrations 13.4, 13.5, 13.6, 13.7, 13.8a and 13.8b

1   Securely block the front wheels so the vehicle won't roll. Loosen the rear wheel nuts with the vehicle on the ground. Jack up the rear end and support it securely, positioning the jackstands so they won't obstruct removal of the axle.

2   Remove the rear wheels and their hubs (see Chapter 6).

3   Remove the brake drum cover, brake drum and brake panel (see Chapter 6). The brake shoes need not be removed from the panel.

4   Remove the skid plate from under the rear differential **(see illustration)**.

5   Unbolt the lower end of the left shock absorber, then remove and discard the nuts that secure the axle housing to the left side of the differential **(see illustration)**. Pull the axle housing off the differential and remove the O-ring.

6   Slide the collar off the left end of the axle shaft **(see illustration)**.

7   Clean any foreign material from the left side of the axle so it won't be pulled into the final drive unit during removal. Tap on the left end of the axle with a soft faced hammer to free it, then pull it out of the axle housing **(see illustration)**.

8   If you need to remove the right axle housing, unbolt the lower end of the right shock absorber (see Section 4). Remove and discard the nuts that secure it to the swingarm and differential **(see illustration)**. Remove the axle housing and its O-ring **(see illustration)**.

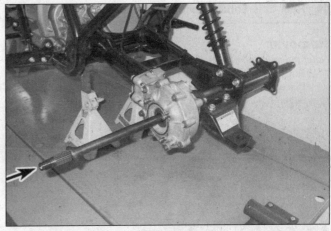

13.7 Tap on the left end of the axle shaft (arrow) and pull it out of the differential

Inspection

9   Check the axle for obvious damage, such as step wear of the splines or bending, and replace it as necessary.

10   Install the wheel hubs on the axle. Place the axle in V-blocks and set up a dial indicator contacting the center of the axle shaft. Rotate the axle and compare runout to the value listed in this Chapter's Specifications. If runout is excessive, replace the axle.

13.8a Remove the nuts that secure the right axle housing to the differential and swingarm (arrows)

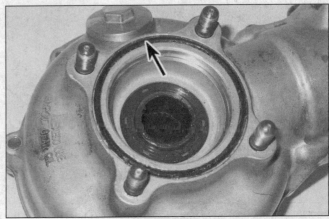

13.8b Pull the axle housing off the studs and remove the O-ring (arrow)

Installation

11   If the right axle housing was removed, coat a new O-ring with multipurpose grease and install it on the differential. Position the axle housing, being careful not to knock the O-ring out of position. Then install the axle housing on the differential and swingarm. Install new nuts and tighten them to the torque listed in this Chapter's Specifications.

12   Lubricate the axle splines with multipurpose grease.

13   Install the axle from the right side of the vehicle, aligning the splines of the axle with those of the final drive unit.

14   Coat a new O-ring with grease and install it on the left side of the differential. Install the left axle housing, using new nuts, and tighten them to the torque listed in this Chapter's Specifications.

15   Install the rear brake panel, drum and drum cover (see Chapter 6).

16   Install the collar on the right side of the axle, making sure it faces the proper direction **(see illustration 13.6)**.

17   The remainder of installation is the reverse of the removal steps.

18   Check oil level in the rear differential and add oil as necessary (see Chapter 1).

---

14   Rear differential - removal, inspection and installation

Removal

Refer to illustrations 14.2a, 14.2b and 14.2c

1   Remove the axle shaft and both axle housings (Section 13).

2   Disconnect the breather tube and remove the nuts that secure the

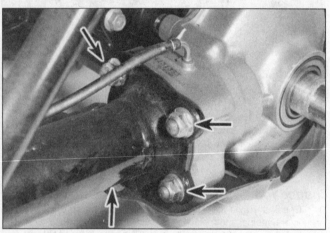

14.2a   Disconnect the breather tube and remove the four nuts (arrows; one nut hidden)

final drive unit to the swingarm **(see illustration)**. Pull the unit rearward to detach it and lift it away from the swingarm, then remove the spring and O-ring **(see illustrations)**. Discard the nuts and use new ones on installation.

Inspection

Refer to illustration 14.3

3   Look into the axle holes and check for obvious signs of wear and for damage such as broken gear teeth **(see illustration)**. Also check the seals for signs of leakage. Turn the pinion by hand (slip the driveshaft back on and use it as a handle if necessary) **(see illustration)**.

4   Differential overhaul is a complicated procedure that requires several special tools, for which there are no readily available substitutes. If there's visible wear or damage, or if the differential's rotation is rough or noisy, take it to a Honda dealer for disassembly and further inspection.

Installation

5   Make sure the driveshaft spring is in place in the driveshaft, then lubricate a new O-ring with oil and install it on the swingarm **(see illustrations 14.2c and 14.2b)**.

6   Slide the final differential studs through the holes in the swingarm, align the driveshaft with the final drive pinion and push the differential into position.

7   Install new differential nuts and tighten them slightly. Connect the breather hose.

8   Install the right axle housing on the differential and swingarm and tighten its nuts to the torque listed in this Chapter's Specifications (see Section 13).

9   Tighten the differential nuts to the torque listed in this Chapter's Specifications.

10   The remainder of installation is the reverse of the removal steps.

---

15   Swingarm bearings - check

1   Refer to Chapter 6 and remove the rear wheels, then refer to Section 4 and remove the rear shock absorbers.

2   Grasp the rear of the swingarm with one hand and place your other hand at the junction of the swingarm and the frame. Try to move the rear of the swingarm from side-to-side. Any wear (play) in the bearings should be felt as movement between the swingarm and the frame at the front. The swingarm will actually be felt to move forward and backward at the front (not from side-to-side). If any play is noted, the bearings should be replaced with new ones (see Section 21).

3   Next, move the swingarm up and down through its full travel. It should move freely, without any binding or rough spots. If it does not move freely, refer to Section 17 for servicing procedures.

14.2b   Pull the final drive unit away from the swingarm and remove the O-ring (arrow)

14.2c   Remove the spring from the end of the driveshaft

14.3   Rotate the pinion (arrow) and check for rough or noisy movement

16.8 Loosen the boot clamps so the boot can be detached from the engine as the swingarm is removed

16.9 Detach the breather hoses from the top of the swingarm

16 Swingarm - removal and installation

1   If the swingarm is being removed just for bearing replacement or driveshaft removal, the brake panel, final drive and rear axle need not be removed from the swingarm. **Note:** *Loosening and tightening the pivot bolt locknut on the right side of the swingarm requires a special wrench for which there is no alternative. If you don't have the special Honda tool or an exact equivalent, the locknut must be unscrewed (and later tightened) by a Honda dealer.*

Removal

Refer to illustrations 16.8, 16.9, 16.10, 16.11, 16.12a, 16.12b, 16.2c and 16.12d

2   Raise the rear end of the vehicle off the ground with a jack. Support the vehicle securely so it can't be knocked over while it's jacked up.
3   Remove the mudguards from the lower front edges of the rear fender (see Chapter 7).
4   Remove the rear wheels (see Chapter 6).
5   Refer to Section 4 and unbolt the lower ends of the shock absorbers from the swingarm.
6   Disconnect both rear brake cables (see Chapter 6).
7   If you're planning to remove the rear axle, differential or brake panel, do it now (see Section 13, Section 14 or Chapter 6).
8   On the left side of the swingarm, loosen the clamps that secure the rubber boot **(see illustration)**.
9   If you've removed the differential and brake panel, free the breather

16.10 Pry the plastic cap from each side of the swingarm

tubes from their retainer on top of the swingarm **(see illustration)**.
10   Pry the plastic pivot cap from each side of the swingarm **(see illustration)**.
11   Unscrew the pivot bolt from the left side of the vehicle with a socket and a 17 mm Allen bolt bit **(see illustration)**. These are available from tool stores.
12   On the right side of the vehicle, prevent the pivot bolt from turning with the 17 mm Allen bolt bit and unscrew the pivot bolt locknut with the special Honda tool (tool number 07908-4690003) **(see illustrations)**. Once the locknut is loose, unscrew the pivot bolt.
13   Pull the swingarm back and away from the vehicle, separating the

16.11 Unscrew the left pivot bolt with a 17 mm Allen bolt bit

16.12a This tool is used to loosen the pivot bolt locknut as well as to tighten it to the correct torque

16.12b Insert the Allen bolt bit in the right pivot bolt . . .

16.12c . . . and place the special tool on the locknut; loosen the locknut with the special tool . . .

16.12d . . . then unscrew the locknut and pivot bolt

16.16 The tab labeled HNO or HM7 should be upright when the clamps are tightened

driveshaft from the engine as you pull.

14   Check the pivot bearings in the swingarm for dryness or deterioration (see Section 17). If they're in need of lubrication or replacement, refer to Section 17.

Installation
Refer to illustration 16.16

15   If the driveshaft was removed from the swingarm, install it. Lubricate the driveshaft splines with molybdenum disulfide grease.

16   If the boot was removed from the swingarm, install it with its tab marked "HNO" or "HM7" upward **(see illustration)**.

17   Lift the swingarm into position in the frame. Align the splines of the driveshaft with those of the engine and align the pivot bolt holes in the swingarm with those in the frame.

18   Install the pivot bolt in the left side of the swingarm. Use the 17 mm Allen bolt bit to tighten it to the torque listed in this Chapter's Specifications.

19   Install the pivot bolt in the right side of the swingarm and tighten it to the torque listed in this Chapter's Specifications.

20   Raise and lower the swing arm several times, moving it through its full travel to seat the bearings and pivot bolts.

21   Retighten the pivot bolt in the right side of the swingarm to the torque listed in this Chapter's Specifications.

22   Hold the pivot bolt from turning with the 17 mm Allen bolt bit and use the locknut wrench to tighten the locknut to the torque listed in this Chapter's Specifications. **Note:** *The reading shown on the torque wrench is lower than the actual locknut torque because the special tool*

increases the leverage of the torque wrench.

23   Slip the boot onto the engine. Make sure its tab labeled HNO or HM7 is upright **(see illustration 16.16)**. Position the screws on the boot clamps so they align with the tabs on the boot. The forward clamp screw aligns with the outer boot tab. The rear clamp screw aligns with the upper boot tab. Tighten the clamps.

24   The remainder of installation is the reverse of the removal steps.

17   Swingarm bearings - replacement

1   The swingarm pivot shafts ride on ball bearings (1995 through 2001 models) or tapered roller bearings (2002 and later models).

2   Remove the swingarm (see Section 16).

1995 through 2001 models
Refer to illustrations 17.3 and 17.4

3   Pry the seal from each side of the swingarm **(see illustration)**.

4   Rotate the center race of each ball bearing and check for roughness, looseness or play **(see illustration)**. If there's any doubt about bearing condition, replace the bearings as a set.

5   Bearing replacement requires a slide hammer and blind hole puller, which can be rented from tool rental dealers. Pull the old bearings out, using the special tools. Drive in the bearing grease holder, then drive in the bearing, using a bearing driver or socket.

6   Pack the grease retainer inside each bearing, and the space between the bearing balls, with molybdenum disulfide grease.

17.3 Pry the grease seals from the swingarm (1995 through 2001 models) . . .

17.4 . . . to expose the bearings for inspection

17.7 2002 and later models use tapered roller bearings with integral seals

18.2 Pull the driveshaft out of the swingarm

2002 and later models

Refer to illustration 17.7

7   Pull the bearing and integral seal out of each side of the swingarm **(see illustration)**. Pry the bearings if necessary, but take care not to damage the seals.

8   Check the rollers for pitting, flaking, scoring, rust, or the bluish tint that indicates overheating. Replace the bearings a s a set if these conditions are found.

9   If the bearings are replaced, the inner races must also be replaced. Inner race replacement requires a slide hammer and blind hole puller, which can be rented from tool rental dealers. Pull the old races out, using the special tools. Drive in the new races with a bearing driver or socket.

10   Pack the bearings and coat the seal lips with molybdenum disulfide grease.

18 Rear driveshaft - removal, inspection and installation

Removal

Refer to illustration 18.2

1   Refer to Section 16 and remove the swingarm.

2   Pull the driveshaft out of the swingarm, then pull the spring out of the driveshaft **(see illustration 14.2c and the accompanying illustration)**.

Inspection

Refer to illustration 18.4

3   Check the shaft for bending or other visible damage such as step wear of the splines. If the shaft is bent, replace it. If the splines at the rear end of the shaft are worn, replace the shaft. If the splines at the

18.4 If the universal joint is loose or clicks when it rotates, replace it

front end of the shaft (the universal joint) are worn, replace the universal joint.

4   Hold the driveshaft firmly in one hand and try to twist the universal joint **(see illustration)**. If there's play in the joint, replace it (but don't confuse play in the joint with its normal motion). Parts are not available to overhaul the U-joint, but it can be replaced separately from the driveshaft.

Installation

5   Installation is the reverse of the removal procedure. Lubricate the driveshaft splines with molybdenum disulfide grease. Don't forget to reinstall the spring.

Notes

Chapter 6
Brakes, wheels and tires

Contents

Specifications

Drum brakes

Brake fluid type	See Chapter 1
Brake lining minimum thickness	See Chapter 1
Brake pedal height	See Chapter 1
Front and rear drum diameter	
Standard	160 mm (6.299 inches)
Wear limit	161 mm (6.338 inches)*
Front waterproof seal lubricant	
Type	NLGI no. 3
Amount	14 to 16 grams (0.5 to 0.6 oz)

*Refer to marks cast into the drum (they supersede information printed here)

Disc brakes

Pad wear limit	See Chapter 1
Disc thickness*	
Standard	3.8 to 4.2 mm (0.15 to 0.17 inch)
Limit	3.0 mm (0.12 inch)

*Refer to marks cast into the drum (they supersede information printed here)

Wheels and tires

Tire pressures	See Chapter 1
Tire tread depth	See Chapter 1

Torque specifications

Drum to hub bolts	10 Nm (84 in-lbs)
Front driveaxle (hub) nuts	
400 models	78 to 100 Nm (58 to 72 ft-lbs)
450 and 500 models	78 Nm (58 ft-lbs)
Wheel cylinder bolts/nuts (drum brakes)	
6 mm	8 Nm (72 in-lbs)
8 mm	17 Nm (144 in-lbs)
Caliper mounting bolts (disc brakes)	44 Nm (33 ft-lbs)
Caliper slide pin bolts (disc brakes)	23 Nm (17 ft-lbs)
Splash guard bolts (disc brakes)	11 Nm (96 inch-lbs)
Front brake hose union bolts	35 Nm (25 ft-lbs)
Front brake pipe to wheel cylinder joint nuts (drum brakes)	16 Nm (144 in-lbs)
Master cylinder cover screws	2 Nm (17 in-lbs)
Master cylinder clamp bolts	12 Nm (108 in-lbs)
Brake panel bolts/nuts (drum brakes)*	
Front brake	30 Nm (22 ft-lbs)
Rear brake	
400 and 450 models	35 Nm (25 ft-lbs)
500 models	44 Nm (33 ft-lbs)

Torque specifications (continued)

Rear brake panel drain bolt
      400 and 450 models .... 35 Nm (25 ft-lbs)
      500 models .... Not specified
Rear wheel hub nuts
      400 models .... 137 to 160 Nm (101 to 116 ft-lbs)
      450 and 500 models .... 137 Nm (101 ft-lbs)

Discard the bolts or nuts and replace them with new ones each time they're removed.

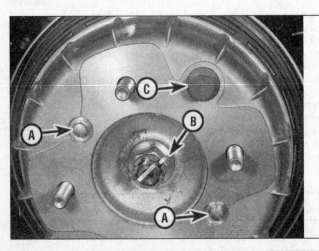

2.3 Loosen the drum-to-hub bolts (A) if you plan to separate the drum and hub; bend back the cotter pin (B) and remove the nut; the rubber plug (C) is for front brake adjustment

2.5 Replace the O-ring if the drum is separated from the hub

1   General information

The vehicles covered by this manual are equipped with hydraulic drum brakes on the front wheels (2004 and earlier models) or hydraulic disc brakes on the front wheels (2005 and later models). All models use a single mechanical drum brake mounted on the rear axle inboard of the rear wheels. All drum brakes are sealed to keep water out. The front brakes are actuated by a lever on the right handlebar. The rear brakes have two means of actuation: a lever on the left handlebar, which serves as a parking brake, and a pedal on the right side of the vehicle. The pedal and lever are connected to the rear brake assembly by cables.

All models are equipped with steel wheels, which require very little maintenance and allow tubeless tires to be used. **Caution:** *Brake components rarely require disassembly. Do not disassemble components unless absolutely necessary. If any hydraulic brake line connection in the system is loosened, the entire system should be disassembled, drained, cleaned and then properly filled and bled upon reassembly. Do not use solvents on internal hydraulic brake components. Solvents will cause seals to swell and distort. Use only clean brake fluid for cleaning. Use care when working with brake fluid as it can injure your eyes and it will damage painted surfaces and plastic parts.*

2   Front brake drums - removal and installation

Warning: *If a front wheel cylinder indicates the need for an overhaul (usually due to leaking fluid or sticky operation), ALL FOUR front wheel cylinders should be overhauled and all old brake fluid flushed from the system. Also, the dust created by the brake system may contain asbestos, which is harmful to your health (Honda hasn't used asbestos in brake parts for a number of years, but aftermarket parts may contain it). Never blow it out with compressed air and don't inhale any of it. An approved filtering mask should be worn when working on the brakes. Do not, under any circumstances, use petroleum-based solvents to clean brake parts. Use clean brake fluid, brake cleaner or denatured alcohol only!*

Removal

Refer to illustrations 2.3 and 2.5

1   Loosen the front wheel nuts. Securely block the rear wheels so the vehicle can't roll. Jack up the front end and support it securely on jackstands.

2   Refer to Section 14 and remove the front wheel.
3   If you're going to remove the front hub, remove the cotter pin from the front hub nut **(see illustration)**. Have an assistant hold the brake on and remove the nut with a socket and breaker bar. This is easier to do now, since you can use the front brakes to keep the hub from turning while you loosen the nut.
4   Remove the drum-to-hub bolts **(see illustration 2.3)**. Pull the brake drum off.
5   Inspect the hub O-ring **(see illustration)**. Since the O-ring's purpose is to keep water out of the brakes, replace it if its condition is in doubt.

Installation

Refer to illustration 2.6

6   Installation is the reverse of the removal steps, with the following additions:

a) *Pack the space between the drum seal lips with multipurpose grease **(see illustration)**. Be sure not to get any grease on the inside of the drum; if you do, clean it off with a non-residue solvent such as brake cleaner or lacquer thinner.*

b) *Tighten the drum-to-hub bolts to the torque listed in this Chapter's Specifications.*

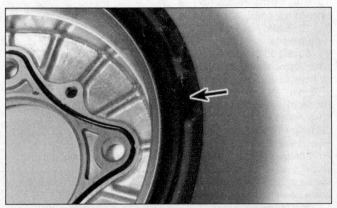

2.6 Pack grease into the space between the seal lips (the correct amount is listed in this Chapter's Specifications); be careful not to get any inside the drum

3.1 The maximum diameter (A) is cast inside the brake drum; measure the length of the seal from the lip (B) to the point where it contacts the shoulder on the outer circumference of the brake drum

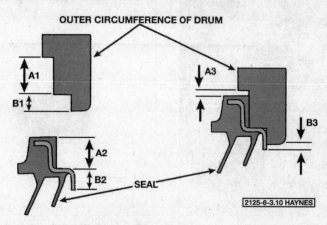

3.7 Calculate the seal's installed clearances - subtract measurement A2 from A1 to get clearance A3; subtract measurement B2 from B1 to get clearance B3

c) Tighten the hub nut (if it was removed) to the torque listed in this Chapter's Specifications and install a new cotter pin. If necessary, tighten the nut to align the hole in the spindle with the slots in the nut.

d) Once the nut is tightened properly, bend the cotter pin to secure it.

e) Refer to Chapter 1 and adjust the brakes.

3 Front brake drums - inspection and waterproof seal replacement

Inspection

Refer to illustration 3.1

1   Check the brake drum for wear or damage. Measure the diameter at several points with a drum micrometer (or have this done by a dealer service department or other qualified shop). If the measurements are uneven (indicating that the drum is out-of-round) or if there are scratches deep enough to snag a fingernail, replace the drum. The drum must also be replaced if the diameter is greater than that cast inside the drum **(see illustration)**. Honda recommends against turning brake drums.

2   Check the waterproof seal on the edge of the brake drum for wear (caused by rubbing against the brake panel). To do this, measure the length of the seal lip from the point where it contacts the brake drum to the point where it contacts the brake panel **(see illustration 3.1)**. Also check for damage such as cuts and tears. If the seal is worn or damaged, replace it as described below.

Waterproof seal replacement

Refer to illustration 3.7

3   This procedure is somewhat complicated and must be done correctly to ensure a watertight seal between the brake drum and panel. It requires a hydraulic press and a press plate bigger than the brake drum. An additional steel plate 140 mm (5.5 inches) in diameter and at least 10 mm (0.4 inch) thick is required to support the brake drum so it isn't warped during the press operation. If you don't have the necessary equipment, have this procedure done by a Honda dealer.

4   Carefully pry the waterproof seal off the edge of the brake drum.

5   It's important to press the new seal onto the drum just far enough, but not too far. To make sure this happens, you'll need to calculate the final clearance between the outer circumference of the drum and the seal, as well as between the inner circumference of the drum and the seal. These clearances will become smaller as the seal is pressed onto the drum, so calculating the clearances in advance will let you know when the seal has been pressed on far enough.

6   To determine what the final clearance should be, measure as follows.

7   Measure the depth of both recesses in the brake drum and the seal surfaces that will contact them **(see illustration)**. Calculate the

difference between these measurements to get the final clearances for the seal as follows:

a) Subtract measurement A2 from measurement A1 to get clearance A3.

b) Subtract measurement B2 from Measurement B1 to get clearance B3.

8   Write the clearances down for later use.

All models

9   Dip the new seal in water to lubricate it (don't use any other type of lubricant). Place the new seal on the edge of the brake drum, then set the drum seal side down on a press plate.

10   Place a steel plate about 5.5 mm (1.6 inch) in diameter and at least 10 mm (0.4 inch) thick on top of the brake drum so it won't collapse from the force of the press.

11   Slowly and carefully press the brake drum down into the seal, making sure not to press it too far. If the seal is damaged or is pressed on too far, remove it and start over with a new seal. Stop pressing when the measured clearances are equal to those written down in Step 17.

4 Front brake shoes - removal, inspection and installation

Removal

Refer to illustrations 4.2 and 4.3

1   Refer to Section 2 and remove the brake drum.

2   Rotate the retainer pins with pliers to align them with the slots in the pin holders, then remove the pin holders **(see illustration)**.

4.2 Rotate the ends of the retainer pins to align with the slot in the pin holder, then take the pin holders off

4.3 Pull the shoes apart and take them off the brake panel

4.8 Inspect the rubber grommets on the retainer pins and replace them if they're damaged or deteriorated

4.11a The assembled right brake should look like this . . .

3   Pull the shoes apart against the force of the spring(s) and take them off the brake panel **(see illustration)**.

Inspection

Refer to illustration 4.8

4   Check the linings for wear, damage and signs of contamination from road dirt or water. If the linings are visibly defective, replace them.

5   Measure the thickness of the lining material (just the lining material, not the metal backing) and compare with the value listed in the Chapter 1 Specifications. Replace the shoes if the material is worn to the minimum or less.

6   Check the ends of the shoes where they contact the wheel cylinders. Replace the shoes if there's visible wear.

7   Pull back the wheel cylinder cups and check for fluid leakage. Slight moisture inside the cups is normal, but if fluid runs out, refer to Section 5 and replace the wheel cylinder(s).

8   Inspect the rubber seals on the retaining pins **(see illustration)**. Replace them if they're worn, hardened or deteriorated. The seals are meant to keep out water, not just dust, so replace them if there's any doubt about their condition.

Installation

Refer to illustrations 4.11a, 4.11b and 4.12

9   Apply high temperature grease to the ends of the springs and shoes. Apply a thin smear of grease to each of the brake shoe contact points on the brake panel.

10   Hook the springs to the shoes, noting how they're installed (the hooked ends of the springs face outward).

11   Pull the shoes apart and position their ends in the wheel cylinders **(see illustrations)**. The flatter ends of the brake shoes fit into the wheel cylinder(s); the other ends fit into the adjuster(s).

12   Install the pin holders and pins. Compress the holders and turn the pins 90-degrees so the pins secure the holders **(see illustration)**.

13   The remainder of installation is the reverse of the removal steps.

---

5   Front wheel cylinders - removal, overhaul and installation

---

Removal

Refer to illustrations 5.2, 5.3a and 5.3b

1   Refer to Sections 2 and 4 and remove the brake drum and shoes.

2   From the back side of the brake panel, detach the brake hose from the wheel cylinder(s) **(see illustration)**.

3   Remove the wheel cylinder nut and bolt and disconnect the metal brake line from both wheel cylinders **(see illustrations)**. Work the wheel cylinder free of the sealant that secures it to the brake panel and take it off.

4.11b . . . and the assembled left brake should look like this

4.12 Compress the pin holders and turn the pins 90-degrees so they hold the pins securely

5.2 Unscrew the union bolt; use a new sealing washer on each side of the bolt on installation and position the neck of the hose between the stoppers (arrow)

5.3a Unscrew the brake pipe fitting (arrow) from the wheel cylinder with a flare nut wrench; remove the bolt and the nut (B)

5.3b Loosen the other end of the brake pipe and remove the nut and bolt

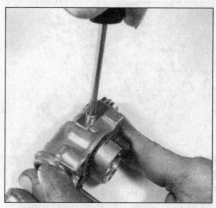

5.4a Wheel cylinder components

1   Boot
2   Piston
3   Piston cup seal
4   Wheel cylinder body
5   Lock spring
6   Screw
7   Adjuster wheel
8   Adjuster screw (left-hand threads)

5.4b Remove the screw and take off the lock spring

Overhaul

Refer to illustrations 5.4a and 5.4b

4   Remove the boot(s) from the cylinder(s) **(see illustration)**. Remove the adjuster lock spring and pull the adjuster out of the other end of the cylinder **(see illustration)**.

5   Push the piston(s) out of the cylinder.

6   Check the piston and cylinder bore for wear, scratches and corrosion. If there's any doubt about their condition, replace the cylinder as an assembly. Even barely visible flaws can reduce braking performance.

7   The piston cups and boots are available separately and should be replaced whenever the wheel cylinders are overhauled. Work the cup(s) off the piston(s). Dip new ones in clean brake fluid and carefully install them without stretching or damaging them. The wide side of the piston cup faces into the cylinder bore.

8   Remove the screw from the adjuster nut. Check the adjuster components for wear or damage and replace as necessary.

9   Assembly is the reverse of the disassembly steps, with the following additions:

a) *Coat the cylinder bore with clean brake fluid. Install the piston with the wide side of the piston cup entering the bore first. Be sure not to turn back the lip of the cup.*

b) *Lubricate the adjuster wheel(s) with silicone grease.*

Installation

Refer to illustration 5.10

10   Installation is the reverse of the removal steps, with the following additions:

a) *Apply a thin coat of sealant to the wheel cylinder contact area on the brake panel **(see illustration)**.*

b) *Be sure to install the wheel cylinders on the correct sides of the vehicle. Right wheel cylinders have the letter R cast into the cylinder body; left wheel cylinders are marked with an L.*

c) *Tighten the wheel cylinder bolts and nuts to the torque listed in this Chapter's Specifications.*

d) *Use new sealing washers on the brake hose union bolt. Position the neck of the brake hose between the stoppers on the brake panel. Tighten the union bolt and the metal brake line fittings to the torque listed in this Chapter's Specifications.*

e) *Refer to Section 8 and bleed the brakes.*

5.10 Apply sealant to the wheel cylinder contact areas

6.2 Disconnect the breather hose

6.3 Remove the brake panel mounting bolts (arrows)

6.4 Remove the O-ring (arrow) from the knuckle

7.4 Remove the union bolt (arrow); on installation, use a new sealing washer on each side of the bolt

7.5 Remove the mounting bolts (arrows); the UP mark on the clamp must be upright when the clamp is installed

6   Front brake panel - removal, inspection and installation

Refer to illustrations 6.2, 6.3 and 6.4

1   Refer to Section 2 and remove the brake drum. If you're planning to remove the brake shoes, refer to Section 4 (the brake panel can be removed with the shoes installed).

2   Disconnect the breather hose and remove the brake hose union bolt **(see illustration 5.2 and the accompanying illustration)**. If you're planning to remove the wheel cylinders, this is a good time to loosen the bolts and nuts, while the brake panel is securely bolted to the knuckle. The brake panel can be removed with the wheel cylinders installed.

3   Remove the brake panel mounting bolts **(see illustration)**. Lift the brake panel off the knuckle. **Note:** *Discard the bolts and use new ones on installation. The bolt threads have a special dry waterproof coating.*

4   Remove the O-ring from the knuckle and install a new one **(see illustration)**.

5   Installation is the reverse of the removal steps, with the following additions:

  a   *Use new brake panel bolts and tighten them to the torque listed in this Chapter's Specifications.*

  b) *Use new sealing washers on the brake hose union bolt (if equipped). Position the neck of the bolt between the stoppers on the brake panel and tighten the bolt to the torque listed in this Chapter's Specifications.*

7   Front brake master cylinder - removal, overhaul and installation

1   If the master cylinder is leaking fluid, or if the lever doesn't produce a firm feel when the brake is applied, and bleeding the brakes does not help, master cylinder overhaul is recommended. Before disassembling the master cylinder, read through the entire procedure and make sure that you have the correct rebuild kit. Also, you will need some new, clean brake fluid of the recommended type, some clean rags and internal snap-ring pliers. **Note:** *To prevent damage to the paint from spilled brake fluid, always cover the fuel tank when working on the master cylinder.*

2   **Caution:** *Disassembly, overhaul and reassembly of the brake master cylinder must be done in a spotlessly clean work area to avoid contamination and possible failure of the brake hydraulic system components.*

Removal

Refer to illustrations 7.4 and 7.5

3   Loosen, but do not remove, the screws holding the reservoir cover in place.

4   Place rags beneath the master cylinder to protect the paint in case of brake fluid spills. Remove the union bolt **(see illustration)** and separate the brake hose from the master cylinder. Wrap the end of the hose in a clean rag and suspend the hose in an upright position or bend it down carefully and place the open end in a clean container. The objective is to prevent excess loss of brake fluid, fluid spills and system contamination.

5   Remove the master cylinder mounting bolts **(see illustration)** and separate the master cylinder from the handlebar.

Overhaul

Refer to illustration 7.8

6   Remove the locknut from the underside of the lever pivot screw, then remove the screw.

7   Carefully remove the rubber dust boot from the end of the piston. Remove the separator from the bottom of the reservoir.

8   Using snap-ring pliers, remove the snap-ring **(see illustration)** and slide out the piston, the cup seals and the spring. Lay the parts out in the proper order to prevent confusion during reassembly.

9   Clean all of the parts with brake system cleaner (available at auto parts stores), isopropyl alcohol or clean brake fluid. **Caution:** *Do not, under any circumstances, use a petroleum-based solvent to clean brake parts.* If compressed air is available, use it to dry the parts thoroughly (make sure it's filtered and unlubricated). Check the master cylinder bore for corrosion, scratches, nicks and score marks. If damage is evident, the master cylinder must be replaced with a new one. If the master cylinder is in poor condition, then the wheel cylinders should be checked as well.

10   Remove the old cup seals and install the new ones. One cup seal is installed on the piston and the other cup seal is mounted on the end of the spring. Make sure the lips of the cup seals face away from the lever end of the piston. If a new piston is included in the rebuild kit, use it regardless of the condition of the old one.

11   Before reassembling the master cylinder, soak the piston and the rubber cup seals in clean brake fluid for ten or fifteen minutes. Lubricate the master cylinder bore with clean brake fluid, then carefully insert the piston and related parts in the reverse order of disassembly. Make sure the lips on the cup seals do not turn inside out when they are slipped into the bore.

12   Depress the piston, then install the snap-ring (make sure the snap-ring is properly seated in the groove with the sharp edge facing out). Install the rubber dust boot (make sure the lip is seated properly in the piston groove).

13   Install the brake lever and tighten the pivot bolt locknut.

Installation

14   Attach the master cylinder to the handlebar. Align the corner of the master cylinder's front mating surface with the punch mark on the handlebar.

15   Make sure the arrow and the word UP on the master cylinder clamp are pointing up, then tighten the bolts to the torque listed in this Chapter's Specifications. Tighten the top bolt fully, then tighten the lower bolt. **Caution:** *Don't try to close the gap at the lower bolt mating surface or the clamp may break.*

16   Connect the brake hose to the master cylinder, using new sealing washers. Tighten the union bolt to the torque listed in this Chapter's Specifications.

17   Refer to Section 8 and bleed the air from the system.

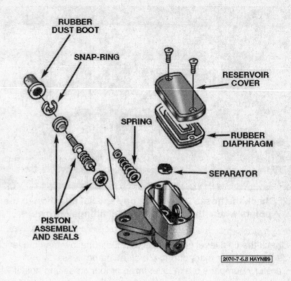

7.8 Master cylinder - exploded view

8   Brake system bleeding

Refer to illustrations 8.5a and 8.5b

1   Bleeding the brake is simply the process of removing all the air bubbles from the brake fluid reservoir, the lines and the wheel cylinders. Bleeding is necessary whenever a brake system hydraulic connection is loosened, when a component or hose is replaced, or when the master cylinder or wheel cylinders are overhauled. Leaks in the system may also allow air to enter, but leaking brake fluid will reveal their presence and warn you of the need for repair.

2   To bleed the brake, you will need some new, clean brake fluid of the recommended type (see Chapter 1), a length of clear vinyl or plastic tubing, a small container partially filled with clean brake fluid, some rags and a wrench to fit the brake caliper bleed valve.

3   Cover the fuel tank and other painted components to prevent damage in the event that brake fluid is spilled.

4   Remove the reservoir cap and slowly pump the brake lever a few times, until no air bubbles can be seen floating up from the holes at the bottom of the reservoir. Doing this bleeds the air from the master cylinder end of the line. Reinstall the reservoir cap.

5   Attach one end of the clear vinyl or plastic tubing to the brake caliper bleed valve and submerge the other end in the brake fluid in the container **(see illustrations)**.

8.5a Connect a plastic or rubber hose to the bleed valve; open and close the valve with a wrench

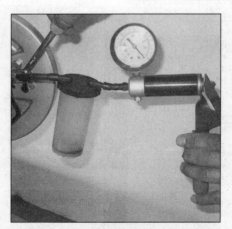

8.5b You can also use a vacuum pump like this one

8.5c Here's a disc brake caliper with a bleed hose attached to the valve

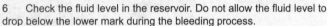

9.2 Check the hoses for cracks; pay special attention to the points where they meet the metal fittings (arrows)

9.4 Remove the retainers to release the hose

6   Check the fluid level in the reservoir. Do not allow the fluid level to drop below the lower mark during the bleeding process.

7   Carefully pump the brake lever three or four times and hold it while opening the caliper bleed valve. When the valve is opened, brake fluid will flow out of the wheel cylinder into the clear tubing and the lever will move toward the handlebar.

8   Retighten the bleed valve, then release the brake lever gradually. Repeat the process until no air bubbles are visible in the brake fluid leaving the wheel cylinder and the lever is firm when applied. Remember to add fluid to the reservoir as the level drops. Use only new, clean brake fluid of the recommended type. Never reuse the fluid lost during bleeding.

9   Repeat this procedure to the other wheel. Be sure to check the fluid level in the master cylinder reservoir frequently.

10   Replace the reservoir cap, wipe up any spilled brake fluid and check the entire system for leaks. **Note:** *If bleeding is difficult, it may be necessary to let the brake fluid in the system stabilize for a few hours (it may be aerated). Repeat the bleeding procedure when the tiny bubbles in the system have floated out.*

9   Brake hoses and lines - inspection and replacement

Inspection

Refer to illustration 9.2

1   Once a week, or if the vehicle is used less frequently, before every use, check the condition of the brake hoses.

2   Twist and flex the rubber hoses while looking for cracks, bulges and seeping fluid. Check extra carefully around the areas where the hoses connect with metal fittings, as these are common areas for hose failure **(see illustration)**.

Replacement

Refer to illustration 9.4

3   There are two brake hoses. One hose is attached to the master cylinder. The master cylinder hose runs to the metal joint. The metal joint is part of the lower hose assembly, consisting of the joint and two permanently attached lengths of hose which run to the wheel cylinders or calipers.

4   Cover the surrounding area with plenty of rags and unscrew the union bolts on either end of the hose. Detach the hose from any retainers that may be present and remove the hose **(see illustration)**.

5   Position the new hose, making sure it isn't twisted or otherwise strained, between the two components. Make sure the metal tube portion of the banjo fitting (if equipped) is located between the stoppers on the component it's connected to. Install the union bolts, using new sealing washers on both sides of the fittings, and tighten them to the torque listed in this Chapter's Specifications. If the hose is connected by a flare nut, hold it with one wrench and tighten the flare nut with another wrench.

6   Flush the old brake fluid from the system, refill the system with the recommended fluid (see Chapter 1) and bleed the air from the system (see Section 8). Check the operation of the brakes carefully before riding the vehicle.

10   Rear brake drum - removal, inspection and installation

Removal

Refer to illustrations 10.3 and 10.4

1   Refer to Section 15 and remove the right rear wheel.

2   Refer to Chapter 5 and remove the right rear wheel hub.

10.3 Remove the bolts (arrows) and take the cover off the brake drum

10.4 Inspect the O-ring (arrow) and replace it if there's any doubt about its condition

10.6 Replace the seal in the center of the drum cover if it shows signs of leakage

11.2 Straighten the cotter pins (arrows) and pull them out, then remove the washers

11.5 Check the brake cam and the pivot cups in the anchor pin (arrows) for wear and damage

3   Remove the drum cover bolts and take the cover off **(see illustration)**.
4   Remove the drum cover O-ring and pull the drum off **(see illustration)**.

Inspection
Refer to illustration 10.6
5   Check the drum cover O-ring for wear, deterioration or hardening **(see illustration 10.4)**. Since the O-ring is intended to waterproof the rear brake, replace it if there's any doubt about its condition.
6   Inspect the seal in the brake drum cover for wear or signs of leakage **(see illustration)**. If any defects are visible, pry the seal out and tap in a new one with a hammer and seal driver or a socket the same diameter as the seal.
7   Refer to Section 11 and look for leaks around the axle seal in the center of the brake panel. Replace the seal as described in Section 12 if there are any signs of leakage.
8   Refer to Section 3 for drum inspection details.

Installation
9   Installation is the reverse of the removal steps. Coat the lip of the drum cover seal with grease.

11 Rear brake shoes - removal, inspection and installation

Removal
Refer to illustration 11.2
1   Refer to Section 10 and remove the rear brake drum.
2   If you're planning to reinstall the brake shoes, mark them so they can go in their original locations. Straighten and pull out the cotter pins that secure the brake shoe washer and remove the washer **(see illustration)**.
3   Unhook and remove the brake springs **(see illustration 11.2)**. Slide the shoes off the pivot pins.

Inspection
Refer to illustration 11.5
4   Refer to Section 4 for shoe and lining inspection details.
5   Check the brake cam and pivot pins for wear or damage **(see illustration)**. If the brake cam shows wear or damage, refer to Section 12 and remove it from the brake panel. The anchor pins are permanent parts of the brake panel, so the panel will have to be replaced if they're worn.

Installation
6   Installation is the reverse of the removal steps, with the following additions:
a) Apply a thin film of high-temperature brake grease to the brake cam and pivot pins, as well as to the shoe contact areas on the brake panel. Be sure not to get any grease on the brake drum or linings.
b) Secure the brake shoe retaining washer with new cotter pins.

12 Rear brake panel - removal, inspection and installation

Removal
Refer to illustrations 12.3 and 12.5
1   Refer to Sections 10 and 11 and remove the brake drum and shoes.
2   Refer to Section 13 and disconnect the brake cables from the brake panel lever.
3   Disconnect the breather hose from the brake panel **(see illustration)**.
4   Remove and discard the brake panel nuts **(see illustration 12.3)**. Use new nuts on installation.

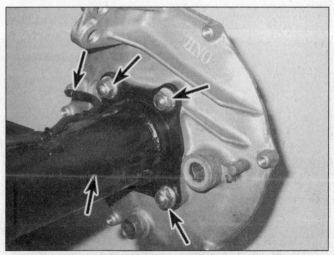

12.3 Disconnect the breather hose and remove the brake panel nuts (arrows) (one nut is hidden behind the axle housing); use new nuts on installation

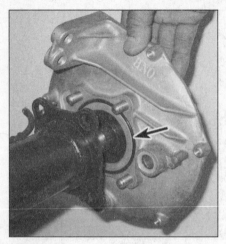

12.5   Pull off the brake panel; replace the O-ring (arrow) if there's any doubt about its condition

12.6   If the bearing in the center of the brake panel is rough, loose or noisy, replace it; pry out the seal if it shows signs of leakage

12.8a   Remove the snap-ring (arrow) . . .

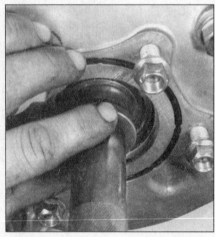

12.8b   . . . . and tap the bearing out with a bearing driver or socket; tap the new bearing in with a bearing driver or socket that bears against the bearing outer race

12.9a   Look for alignment marks on the cam and lever (arrows); make your own marks if necessary and unhook the spring (arrow)

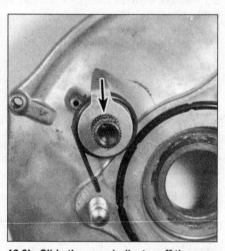

12.9b   Slide the wear indicator off the cam; the wide splines on cam and indicator (arrow) align with each other

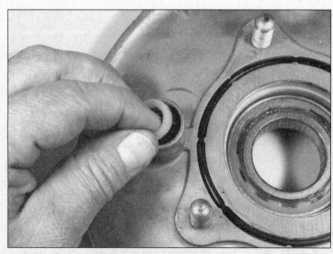

12.9c   Lift out the felt seal; soak the new one with oil on installation

5   Pull the brake panel away from the axle housing and take it off the axle shaft (**see illustration**).

Inspection

Refer to illustrations 12.6, 12.8a, 12.8b, 12.9a, 12.9b, 12.9c and 12.9d

6   Spin the bearing in the brake panel with a finger (**see illustration**). If it's rough, loose or noisy, replace it as described below. Also check the O-ring and seal for wear or damage and replace them if there's any doubt about their condition.

7   Pry out the seal with a removal tool or screwdriver (**see illustration 12.6**).

8   Remove the snap-ring and tap out the bearing from the brake shoe side with a bearing driver or socket (**see illustrations**). Tap in the new bearing with a bearing driver or socket that bears against the bearing outer race. Install the bearing from the axle housing side of the panel, with its sealed side facing the snap-ring. Drive the bearing just past the snap-ring groove, then install the snap-ring. Position the new seal with its lip facing the bearing and tap it in with the same tool used to install the bearing.

9   If the brake cam is loose in its bore or if the seals show any signs of leakage, remove the brake cam from the panel (**see illustrations**). Inspect the cam and its bore for wear and replace worn parts, then reverse the disassembly sequence to reinstall the brake cam.

10   Apply grease to the rubber seal and oil to the felt seal on assembly.

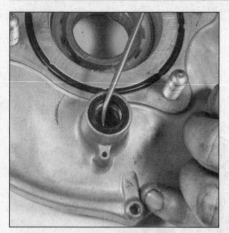

12.9d Pry out the rubber seal from behind the felt seal

12.13 If the brake panel drain bolt (arrow) is removed, install a new sealing washer

13.1 Remove the wing nuts and spacers, pull the cables rearward and slip them out of the slots (arrows)

13.3 Pull the cable housing back and slip it out of the slot (lower arrow); unhook the pedal spring (upper arrow)

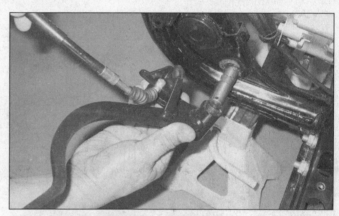

13.11   Slip the pedal off the shaft and disengage the cable end if you haven't already done so

Installation

Refer to illustration 12.13

11   Install a new O-ring in the brake panel groove **(see illustration 12.5)**.

12   Position the brake panel on the axle housing, making sure the O-ring isn't dislodged. Install new brake panel nuts (don't re-use the old ones) and tighten them to the torque listed in this Chapter's Specifications.

13   If the brake panel drain bolt was removed, install it with a new sealing washer **(see illustration)** and tighten it to the torque listed in this Chapter's Specifications.

14   The remainder of installation is the reverse of the removal steps.

13   Brake pedal, rear brake lever and cables - removal and installation

Brake cables

Removal

Refer to illustration 13.1

1   Unscrew the cable adjusting nuts all the way off the end of the cable, then remove the cables from their slots in the brake panel **(see illustration)**.

2   Thread the adjusting hardware and wing nuts back onto the cables so they won't be lost.

Pedal cable

Refer to illustration 13.3

3   Pull the pedal cable housing back from the bracket on the frame near the right swing arm pivot, then slip the cable out through the slot **(see illustration)**.

4   Turn the cable 180-degrees forward and slip it out of the slot in the top of the brake pedal.

Lever cable

5   Pull back the rubber boot from the left handlebar lever.

6   Refer to the brake cable adjustment procedure in Chapter 1 and back off the adjuster locknut at the handlebar lever and loosen the adjuster all the way.

7   Align the slots in the adjuster and its locknut with each other so they're facing directly away from the handlebar. Turn the cable out of the slots, then align it with the slot in the lever and slip it out.

Installation

8   Installation is the reverse of the removal steps, with the following additions:

a) *Lubricate the cable ends with multi-purpose grease.*

b) *Make sure the cables are secure in their slots and retainers.*

c) *Adjust brake pedal and lever play as described in Chapter 1.*

Brake pedal

Removal

Refer to illustrations 13.11 and 13.12

9   Disconnect the pedal from the cable as described above.

10   Lift the pedal as far as possible and unhook the pedal spring **(see illustration 13.3)**.

11   Straighten the cotter pin, pull it out and remove the washer. Slide the pedal off the shaft **(see illustration)**.

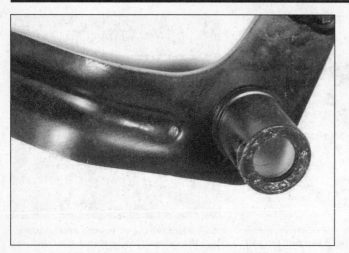

13.12 Inspect the seal on each side of the pedal

13.16 The punch mark on the handlebar (arrow) aligns with the seam in the lever bracket

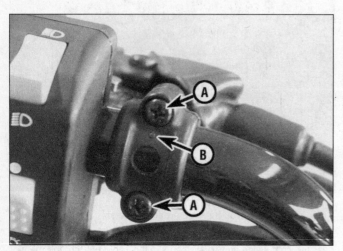

13.17 Remove the clamp screws (A); the dot on the clamp (B) is upward when installed

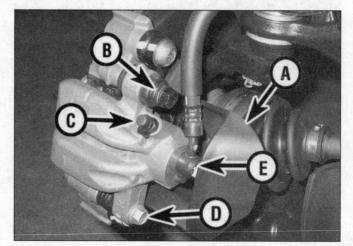

14.2a Disc brake caliper details

A	Splash shield	D	Lower mounting bolt
B	Upper mounting bolt	E	Brake hose
C	Bleed valve		

12   Check the seal on each side of the pedal for wear or damage **(see illustration)**. If any defects are visible, pry the seal out and push new ones in.

Installation
13   Installation is the reverse of the removal steps, with the following additions:
a) *Lubricate the pedal shaft and seal lips with multi-purpose grease.*
b) *Refer to Chapter 1 and adjust brake pedal height.*

Rear brake lever

Removal
Refer to illustrations 13.16 and 13.17
14   Disconnect the cable from the brake lever as described above.
15   Refer to Chapter 2 and disconnect the reverse lock cable.
16   Look for a dot on the handlebar next to the parting line of the lever and clamp **(see illustration)**. This mark is used to position the lever correctly on the handlebar.
17   Remove the lever mounting screws and take it off the handlebar **(see illustration)**.

Installation
18   Installation is the reverse of the removal steps, with the following additions:

a) *Make sure the handlebar and clamp parting line is aligned with the dot on the handlebar.*
b) *Install the handlebar clamp with its dot upward (see illustration 13.17). Tighten the upper screw securely, then tighten the lower screw. Don't try to close the gap between the bottom of the clamp and the lever.*

14   Front disc brake pads - replacement

Refer to illustrations 14.2a, 14.2b and 14.2c
Warning: *The dust created by the brake system is harmful to your health. Never blow it out with compressed air and don't inhale any of it. An approved filtering mask should be worn when working on the brakes. Do not, under any circumstances, use petroleum-based solvent to clean parts. Use brake cleaner only!*
Note: *Always replace all of the front brake pads (on both sides of the vehicle) at the same time.*
1   Refer to Section 17 and remove the front wheel.
2   Unscrew the caliper lower mounting bolt **(see illustration)**. Pivot the caliper up off the pads **(see illustrations)**.
3   Lift the pads out of the caliper and install new ones, making sure

14.2b Lift the caliper to expose the pads . . .

14.2c . . . then remove them from the bracket

the notches in the pads fit over the tabs on the caliper.

4   The remainder of installation is the reverse of the removal steps. Tighten the caliper bolt to the torque listed in this Chapter's Specifications.

15   Front brake caliper - removal, overhaul and installation

Removal

1   Refer to Section 17 and remove the front wheel.
2   Remove the splash guard from the caliper **(see illustration 14.2a)**.
3   Place a drain pan under the caliper, then disconnect the brake hose **(see illustration 14.2a)**. Secure a plastic bag over the end of the hose with a rubber band to prevent fluid loss and keep out dirt. **Note 1:** *If you're removing the caliper to service some other component, leave the hose connected. Support the caliper so it doesn't hang by the brake hose.* **Note 2:** *If you're going to overhaul the caliper, but don't have a compressor to remove the piston (and if the vehicle's hydraulic system is in reasonably good condition) you can remove the piston by pumping the brake lever in Step 5. If you decide to do this, leave the hose connected for now, then disconnect it after the piston has been removed.*
4   Remove the caliper mounting bolts **(see illustration 14.2a)**. Lift the caliper off.

Overhaul

Refer to illustration 15.5

5   Remove the caliper bracket bolts **(see illustration)**. Separate the bracket from the caliper.
6   If you don't have an air compressor, pump the brake lever to force the pistons out. To do this, block the piston of one caliper in place with a C-clamp. Pump the brake lever to force the other piston most of the way out, then secure it in that position with a C-clamp. Remove the C-clamp from the other piston and force it all the way out by pumping the brake lever. Grip the first piston with pliers (with the jaws wrapped with tape to protect the piston) and work it out of the caliper.
7   If you have a compressor, place some rags on a workbench to act as a cushion. Point the piston at the pile of rags, then carefully direct compressed air into the brake hose hole. **Caution:** *Use only small quick bursts of air to ease the piston out of the bore. If a piston is blown out with too much force, it could be damaged.* **Warning:** *Never place your fingers in the way of the piston. Doing so could result in serious injury.* Once the piston protrudes from the caliper, remove it.
8   Remove the pad spring from the bracket and remove the boots from the caliper and bracket **(see illustration 15.5)**.
9   Remove the old dust seal. Using a wood or plastic tool, remove the piston seal.

10   Remove the bleed valve and dust cap.
11   Clean the caliper parts with denatured alcohol, fresh brake fluid or brake system cleaner. Dry them off with filtered, unlubricated compressed air and inspect them carefully **(see illustration 15.5)**. Replace any obviously worn or damaged parts. Replace all rubber parts (caliper boots, piston and seals, etc.) whenever you disassemble the caliper. Inspect the surfaces of the piston and caliper bore for rust, corrosion, nicks, burrs and loss of plating. If you find defects on the surface of the piston or caliper bore, replace the caliper as an assembly. If the caliper is in bad shape, inspect the master cylinder too (see Section 7).
12   Lubricate the new piston seal with clean brake fluid and install it in the groove in the caliper bore. Make sure it's not twisted and is fully and correctly seated.
13   Install the new dust seal. Make sure that the inner lip of the seal is seated in its groove in the piston and the outer circumference of the seal is seated in its groove in the caliper bore.
14   Lubricate the piston with clean brake fluid and install it into its bore in the caliper. Using your thumbs, push the piston all the way in, making sure it doesn't become cocked in the bore.
15   Install the pad spring, boots and caliper bracket. Tighten the bracket bolts to the torque listed in this Chapter's Specifications.

Installation

16   Installation is the reverse of the removal steps, with the following additions:

a) *Use new sealing washers on the brake hose union if the hose was disconnected.*

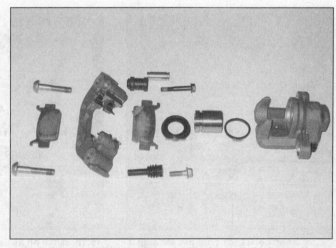

15.5 Disassemble the caliper and lay the parts for inspection

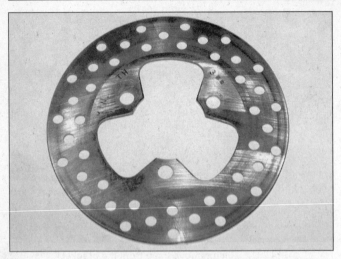

16.4a The minimum thickness of each front disc is stamped into the disc (disc removed for clarity)

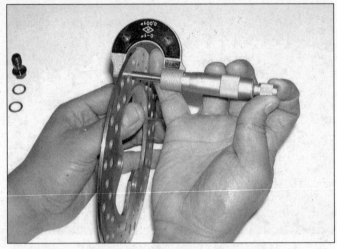

16.4b Check the thickness of the disc with a micrometer (disc removed for clarity)

b) *Tighten all fasteners to the torques listed in this Chapter's Specifications.*
c) *Bleed the brakes (see Section 8).*

16 Front brake disc and hub (2005 and later 500 models) - inspection, removal and installation

1   Remove the front wheels (see Section 17).

Inspection

Refer to illustrations 16.4a and 16.4b

2   Visually inspect the surface of the disc for score marks and other damage. Light scratches are normal after use and won't affect operation, but deep grooves and heavy score marks will reduce braking efficiency and accelerate pad wear. If the disc is badly grooved it must be machined or replaced.

3   To check disc runout, mount a dial indicator with its plunger touching the surface of the disc about 1/2-inch from the outer edge. Slowly turn the wheel hub and watch the indicator needle, comparing your reading with the disc runout limit listed in this Chapter's Specifications.

4   The disc must not be thinner than the minimum allowable thickness listed in this Chapter's Specifications (from wear or from machining). If the minimum thickness stamped into the disc differs from the value listed in this Chapter's Specifications, use the specifications on the disc

(see illustration). Check the thickness of the disc with a micrometer (see illustration). If the disc is thinner than the minimum, replace it.

Removal and installation

Refer to illustrations 16.6a, 16.6b and 16.6c

5   Remove the front wheels and brake caliper (see Sections 17 and 15).

6   Bend back the cotter pin and pull it out of the hub nut (see illustration). Have an assistant hold the front brakes on to lock the hub and unscrew the nut (see illustration). Pull the hub and brake disc off the spindle (see illustration). Discard the cotter pin.

7   Remove the disc retaining bolts and take the disc off the hub. Discard the bolts and use new ones on assembly.

8   Pry the dust seal out of the outer side of the hub. Drive in a new one, using as seal driver or socket the same diameter as the seal. Lubricate the seal lip with multipurpose grease.

9   Installation is the reverse of the removal steps, with the following additions:

a) *Use new disc retaining bolts and tighten them to the torque listed in this Chapter's Specifications.*
b) *Tighten the hub nut to the torque listed in this Chapter's Specifications, then install a new cotter pin. If necessary, tighten the nut further to align the cotter pin holes (don't loosen the nut to align the holes).*

16.6a Bend back the cotter pin and pull it out of the hub nut

16.6b While an assistant applies the front brake, loosen the hub nut

16.6c Pull the hub off the spindle (if the hub is stuck, remove it with a puller)

17.7 The directional arrow on each tire must point in the forward rotating direction of the wheel; if it doesn't, the tire is mounted backward or the wheel is on the wrong side of the vehicle

17.8 Install the wheel nuts with their curved sides toward the wheel

19.2 Bend back the cotter pin and pull it out, then unscrew the nut and remove the hub

17   Wheels - inspection, removal and installation

Inspection

1   Clean the wheels thoroughly to remove mud and dirt that may interfere with the inspection procedure or mask defects. Make a general check of the wheels and tires as described in Chapter 1.
2   The wheels should be visually inspected for cracks, flat spots on the rim and other damage. Since tubeless tires are involved, look very closely for dents in the area where the tire bead contacts the rim. Dents in this area may prevent complete sealing of the tire against the rim, which leads to deflation of the tire over a period of time.
3   If damage is evident, the wheel will have to be replaced with a new one. Never attempt to repair a damaged wheel.

Removal

4   Securely block the wheel at the opposite end of the vehicle from the wheel being removed, so it can't roll.
5   Loosen the lug nuts on the wheel being removed. Jack up one end of the vehicle and support it securely on jackstands.
6   Remove the lug nuts and pull the wheel off.

Installation

Refer to illustrations 17.7 and 17.8

7   Position the wheel on the studs. Make sure the directional arrow on the tire points in the forward rotating direction of the wheel **(see illustration)**.
8   Install the wheel nuts with their curved sides toward the wheel **(see illustration)**. This is necessary to locate the wheel accurately on the hub.
9   Snug the wheel nuts evenly in a criss-cross pattern.
10   Remove the jackstands, lower the vehicle and tighten the wheel nuts, again in a criss-cross pattern, to the torque listed in this Chapter's Specifications.

18   Tires - general information

1   Tubeless tires are used as standard equipment on this vehicle. Unlike motorcycle tires, they run at very low air pressures and are com-

pletely unsuited for use on pavement. Inflating ATV tires to excessive pressures will rupture them, making replacement of the tire necessary.
2   The force required to break the seal between the rim and the bead of the tire is substantial, much more than required for motorcycle tires, and is beyond the capabilities of an individual working with normal tire irons or even a normal bead breaker. A special bead breaker is required for ATV tires; it produces a great deal of force and concentrates it in a relatively small area.
3   Also, repair of the punctured tire and replacement on the wheel rim requires special tools, skills and experience that the average do-it-yourselfer lacks.
4   For these reasons, if a puncture or flat occurs with an ATV tire, the wheel should be removed from the vehicle and taken to a dealer service department or a repair shop for repair or replacement of the tire. The accompanying illustrations can be used as a guide to tire replacement in an emergency, provided the necessary bead breaker is available.

19   Rear wheel hubs - removal and installation

Refer to illustration 19.2

Removal

1   Refer to Section 14 and remove the rear wheel(s).
2   Bend back the cotter pin and pull it out of the hub nut **(see illustration)**.
3   Unscrew the hub nut and remove the washer.
4   Pull the hub off the axle shaft.

Installation

5   Installation is the reverse of the removal steps, with the following additions:
a) *Lubricate the axle shaft and hub splines with multi-purpose grease.*
b) *Tighten the hub nut to the torque listed in this Chapter's Specifications. If necessary, tighten it an additional amount to align the cotter pin slots.*
c) *Install a new cotter pin and bend it to secure the nut.*

Deflate the tire and remove the valve core. Release the bead on the side opposite the tire valve with an ATV bead breaker, following the manufacturer's instructions. Make sure you have the correct blades for the tire size (using the wrong size blade may damage the wheel, the tire or the blade). Lubricate the bead with water before removal (don't use soap or any type of lubricant).

Turn the tire over and release the other bead.

If one side of the wheel has a smaller flange, remove and install the tire from that side. Use two tire levers to work the bead over the edge of the rim.

Before installing, ensure that tire is suitable for wheel. Take note of any sidewall markings such as direction of rotation arrows, then work the first bead over the rim flange.

Use tire levers to start the second bead over the rim flange.

Hold the bead while you work the last section of it over the rim flange. Install the valve core and inflate the tire, making sure not to overinflate it.

Chapter 7
Bodywork and frame

Contents

Specifications

Torque specifications
Cargo rack bolts
    1995 through 2001 400 and 450 models ....   33 Nm (24 ft-lbs)
    All other models ....   37 Nm (27 ft-lbs)

1   General information

Refer to illustration 1.3

    This Chapter covers the procedures necessary to remove and install the fenders and other body parts. Since many service and repair operations on these vehicles require removal of the fenders and/or other body parts, the procedures are grouped here and referred to from other Chapters.

    In the case of damage to the fenders or other body parts, it is usually necessary to remove the broken component and replace it with a new (or used) one. The material that the fenders and other plastic body parts is composed of doesn't lend itself to conventional repair techniques. There are, however, some shops that specialize in "plastic welding", so it would be advantageous to check around first before throwing the damaged part away.

    A number of components are secured with reusable plastic retainers **(see illustration)**. To remove a retainer of this type, pry up the center button and pull the retainer out. To install, push the retainer into its hole (with the center button raised), then push the center button down to lock the retainer.

Note: *When attempting to remove any body panel, first study the panel closely, noting any fasteners and associated fittings, to be sure of returning everything to its correct place on installation. In most cases, the aid of an assistant will be required when removing panels,*

to help avoid damaging the paint. Once the visible fasteners have been removed, try to lift off the panel as described but DO NOT FORCE the panel - if it will not release, check that all fasteners have been removed and try again. Where a panel engages another by means of lugs and grommets, be careful not to break the lugs or to damage the bodywork. Remember that a few moments of patience at this stage will save you a lot of money in replacing broken panels!

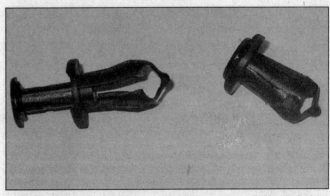

1.3 Pry up the center post to unlock the retainer (left); push the center post down to lock it in place (right)

2.1 Lift the seat latch (arrow) and disengage the seat hooks from the bracket

3.1 Remove the clips (arrows) from the front of the fuel tank cover

3.2 Carefully pull the posts free of the grommets and take the cover off

3.3 Remove two bolts and one retainer (arrows)

3.4 Remove two bolts and two retainers (arrows)

2   Seat - removal and installation

Refer to illustration 2.1

1   Lift the seat latch **(see illustration)** and lift the back end of the seat.

2   Disengage the hooks at the front end of the seat and lift the seat off the vehicle.

3   Installation is the reverse of removal.

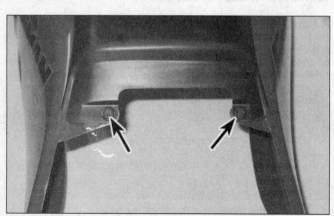

3.5 Remove the retainers (arrows) . . .

3   Side and fuel tank covers - removal and installation

400 and 450 models

Refer to illustrations 3.1, 3.2, 3.3, 3.4, 3.5 and 3.6

1   Unscrew the cap from the fuel tank and remove the clips from the front of the tank cover **(see illustration)**.

2   Carefully pull the two posts of the right side lower cover out of their grommets and take the cover off **(see illustration)**.

3   Remove two bolts from the front edge of the right side upper cover and one retainer from the rear **(see illustration)**. Don't take the cover off yet.

4   Remove two bolts from the front edge of the left side cover and two retainers from the rear **(see illustration)**. Lift both side covers and the fuel tank cover off as a unit.

5   Remove the two retainers that secure the rear edge of the tank cover to the side covers **(see illustration)**.

6   From the underside of the cover assembly, remove the two screws that secure the side cover to the tank cover **(see illustration)**. Slide each side cover forward to free the tabs on the tank cover, then separate the side covers from the tank cover.

7   Installation is the reverse of the removal steps.

2001 through 2004 500 models

8   Remove the seat (see Section 2). Pull the recoil starter cover off, disengaging its three posts from the grommets.

3.6 . . . and slide the covers to free the tabs from the slots

4.3 Remove the bolt and two screws at the top of each inner fender (arrows) . . .

4.4 . . . and remove the bolt and screw at the bottom, then remove the inner fender

4.7a Remove the upper mounting bolt on each side (arrow) . . .

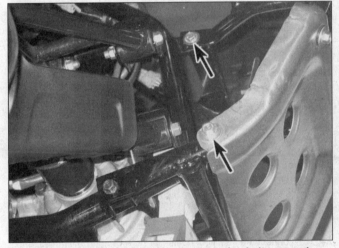

4.7b . . . and the lower and center mounting bolts on each side (arrows)

9   Remove the four trim clips that secure the right side cover. Pull the cover rearward to free its two front retaining tabs and lift it off.
10   On the left side, remove one screw at the upper rear corner of the cover and four trim clips around its edge. Pull the cover rearward to free its two front retaining tabs and lift it off.
11   Unscrew the cap from the fuel tank. Remove four trim clips, one at each corner of the tank. Pull the cover rearward to free its four retaining tabs and lift it off.

2005 and later models
12   The fuel tank and side covers are a single unit.
13   Remove the seat (see Section 2).
14   Remove the recoil starter cover and shift lever (see Chapter 2B).
15   Unscrew the cap from the fuel tank.
16   Remove the eight trim clips that secure the cover.
17   Pull the cover forward to free its two retaining tabs and lift it off.

4   Front cargo rack and fender - removal and installation

Refer to illustrations 4.3, 4.4, 4.7a and 4.7b

400 and 450 models
1   The front fender is a one-piece unit that spans the front of the vehicle and covers both front tires. A separate flap is attached to each side of the center unit.

2   Remove the side and fuel tank covers (see Section 3).
3   Working under the front fender, remove the bolt and two screws from each side of the vehicle (**see illustration**).
4   Remove one screw and one bolt on each side of the vehicle, then remove the inner fenders (**see illustration**).
5   Detach the mudguard from the lower rear edge of the front fender and detach the inner rear corner of the front fender from the frame.
6   Follow the wiring harness from the headlight to the connector and disconnect it.
7   Remove the upper, center and lower mounting bolts on each side of the vehicle (**see illustrations**).
8   With an assistant supporting one side of the front fender unit, lift it off the vehicle, taking care not to scratch the plastic.
9   Installation is the reverse of removal. Tighten the cargo rack bolts to the torque listed in this Chapter's Specifications.

2001 through 2004 500 models
10   From below, remove two 6 mm cargo rack bolts. From the sides, remove four 8 mm cargo rack bolts. Lift off the cargo rack.
11   Remove the two 6 mm bolts that secure the front bumper to the headlight housing.
12   Remove the four 8 mm bolts that secure the front bumper and lift it off.
13   Remove the fuel tank cover and side covers (see Section 3).
14   Remove the shift knob ((see Chapter 2A).
15   Disconnect the headlight connector (see Chapter 8 if necessary).

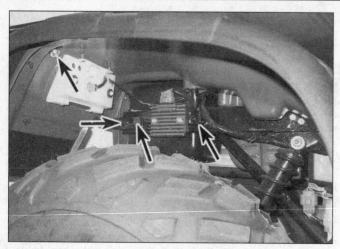

5.1 Remove the rear cargo rack mounting bolts (arrows) (right side shown)

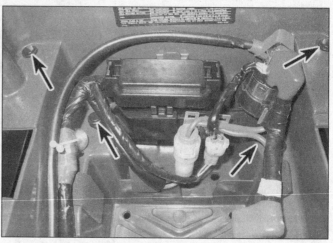

5.3 Release the wiring harness clips and remove the retainers that secure the harness bracket and rear fender (arrows)

16   Remove eight trim clips that secure the fenders (both front fenders are part of one unit).
17   Unscrew four self-tapping bolts.
18   Have an assistant help you lift the fender unit off, spreading the rear corners as necessary for clearance.

2005 and later 500 models
19   From below, remove two 6 mm cargo rack bolts. From the sides, remove four 8 mm cargo rack bolts. Lift off the cargo rack.
20   Remove the two bolts and four trim clips that secure the front bumper guard.
21   Remove the four 6 mm bolts and four 8 mm bolts that secure the skid plate and lower it away from the vehicle.
22   Remove the two 6 mm bolts and four 8 mm bolts that secure the front bumper and lift it off.
23   Remove the fuel tank cover and side covers (see Section 3).
24   Disconnect the headlight connector (see Chapter 8 if necessary).
25   Remove eight trim clips that secure the fenders (both front fenders are part of one unit).
26   Unscrew four self-tapping bolts.
27   Have an assistant help you lift the fender unit off, spreading the rear corners as necessary for clearance.

5   Rear cargo rack, fender and toolbox - removal and installation

400 and 450 models
Refer to illustrations 5.1, 5.3, 5.5 and 5.6
1   Remove the rear cargo rack's mounting bolts and lift the cargo rack off the vehicle **(see illustration)**.
2   Remove the battery (see Chapter 8).
3   Release the wiring harness retainers in the battery compartment and remove the retainers that secure the wiring harness bracket and the rear fender **(see illustration)**.
4   With an assistant supporting one side of the rear fender unit, lift it off the vehicle, taking care not to scratch the plastic.
5   If necessary, remove the fender flaps **(see illustration)**.
6   To remove the toolbox, remove its retainers and lift it out **(see illustration)**.
7   Installation is the reverse of removal.

2001 through 2004 500 models
8   Remove the battery, starter relay and fuse box (see Chapter 8).
9   Pull the recoil starter cover off, disengaging its three posts from the grommets.

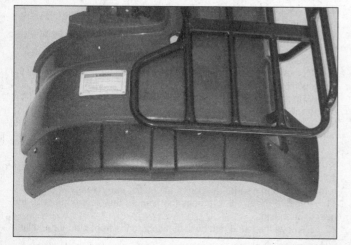

5.5 Remove the retainers along the edge to separate the flap from the fender

5.6 Remove the retainers (arrows) and lift out the toolbox

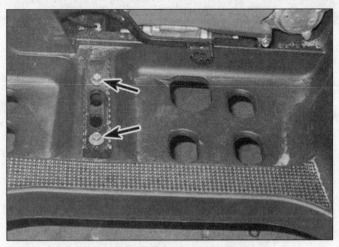

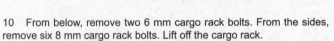

6.1 Remove the footpeg bolts (arrows) . . .

6.2a . . . the retainers and screws (hidden) at the front of the mudguard (make sure you remove all of the fasteners) . . .

10   From below, remove two 6 mm cargo rack bolts. From the sides, remove six 8 mm cargo rack bolts. Lift off the cargo rack.
11   Remove the left side cover (see Section 4).
12   Unscrew the radiator reserve tank cap (see Chapter 1 if necessary).
13   Remove one screw from the right side of the fender.
14   Remove four more trim clips form the top of the fender.
15   Remove four trim clips that connect each mudguard to the fender edge (eight clips total).
16   Locate the taillight connectors (two sets of two connectors each), and disconnect them.
17   Lift the fender off, guiding the starter cable and battery cables through the openings in the fender.
18   Installation is the reverse of the removal steps.

2005 and later 500 models

19   Remove the seat and fuel tank cover (see Sections 2 and 3).
20   Remove two trim clips and secure the cover to the rear fender forward of the cargo rack. Lift the cover off.
21   From below, remove four 6 mm cargo rack bolts and collars. From the sides, remove eight 8 mm cargo rack bolts. Lift off the cargo rack.
22   Remove one hex bolt, two Allen bolts and six trim clips that secure the rear fender. Lift the fender off, guiding the starter cable and battery cables through the openings in the fender.
23   To remove the taillight grilles from a 2005 or 2006 model, remove two screws and six trim clips that secure the taillight grille to each of the fender corners. Take the grille off.
24   To remove the corner trim pieces from a 2007 model, remove six trim clips that secure the corner trim to each of the fender corners. Take the trim off.
25   To remove the toolbox, remove one screw from each side and lift it out.
26   Installation is the reverse of the removal steps.

6   Mudguards and footpegs - removal and installation

Refer to illustrations 6.1, 6.2a and 6.2b
1   Remove the footpeg mounting bolts **(see illustration)**.
2   Remove the clips at front and rear edges of the mudguard, then lift it off the vehicle **(see illustrations)**.
3   Installation is the reverse of the removal steps.

6.2b . . . and the retainers at the rear of the mudguard (450 electric shift model shown)

7   Frame - general information, inspection and repair

1   All models use a double-cradle frame made of cylindrical steel tubing.
2   The frame shouldn't require attention unless accident damage has occurred. In most cases, frame replacement is the only satisfactory remedy for such damage. A few frame specialists have the jigs and other equipment necessary for straightening the frame to the required standard of accuracy, but even then there is no simple way of assessing to what extent the frame may have been overstressed.
3   After the machine has accumulated a lot of miles, the frame should be examined closely for signs of cracking or splitting at the welded joints. Corrosion can also cause weakness at these joints. Loose engine mount bolts can cause ovaling or fracturing to the engine mounting points. Minor damage can often be repaired by welding, depending on the nature and extent of the damage.
4   Remember that a frame that is out of alignment will cause handling problems. If misalignment is suspected as the result of an accident, it will be necessary to strip the machine completely so the frame can be thoroughly checked.

Notes

Chapter 8   Electrical system

Contents

Specifications

Battery
Type	Maintenance free
Capacity	12V, 12Ah
Current leakage limit	0.1 mA
Terminal voltage (fully charged)	13.0 to 13.2 volts

Bulbs
Headlights	
1995 through 2001	25/25 watts
2002 and later	30/30 watts
Spotlight	45 watts
Taillight (400 and 450)	5 watts
Brake light (400 and 450)	21cp
Tail/brake light (500 models)	
2005 and 2006	21/5 watts
2007	LED
Indicator lights	
400 models	1.7 watts
450 and 500 models	LED

Charging system
Charging output voltage	14.7 to 15.5 volts at 5000 rpm
Stator coil resistance	0.1 to 1.0 ohms at 20-degrees C (68-degrees F)

Starter motor
Brush length	
Standard	12.5 mm (0.49 inch)
Minimum	9.0 mm (0.35 inch)
Commutator diameter	Not specified

Fuse ratings

Main fuse	30 amps
Lighting fuse	15 amps
Cooling fan	15 amps
Ignition	10 amps
Accessory	10 amps
4wd (2002 and later 450 models)	10 amps
Electric shift motor (450ES and 500 models)	30 amps

Electric shift system

Angle sensor neutral resistance	4 to 6 ohms

Torque specifications

Alternator rotor bolt	108 Nm (80 ft-lbs)
Stator coil bolts	10 Nm (84 in-lbs)
Pulse generator bolts	6 Nm (52 in-lbs)
Reverse/neutral switch bolt (400 and 450)	12 Nm (108 in-lbs)*
Starter clutch Torx bolts	30 Nm (22 ft-lbs)*
Oil temperature sensor	18 Nm (13 ft-lbs)

*Apply non-permanent thread locking agent to the threads.

1   General information

The machines covered by this manual are equipped with a 12-volt electrical system. The components include a three-phase permanent magnet alternator and a regulator/rectifier unit. The regulator/rectifier unit maintains the charging system output within the specified range to prevent overcharging and converts the AC (alternating current) output of the alternator to DC (direct current) to power the lights and other components and to charge the battery.

An electric starter mounted to the engine case behind the cylinder is standard equipment. A recoil starter is also installed. The starting system includes the motor, the battery, the relay and the various wires and switches. If the engine kill switch and the main key switch are both in the On position, the circuit relay allows the starter motor to operate only if the transmission is in Neutral.

Foreman ES models replace the shift pedal with an electrical shifter, operated by a lever on the left handlebar. Rubicon models use a continuously variable transmission (Hondamatic) in place of the gear transmission used on Foreman models.

The front differential on 2002 and later 450 models can be engaged and disengaged electrically, shifting between four-wheel and two-wheel drive. **Note:** *Keep in mind that electrical parts, once purchased, can't be returned. To avoid unnecessary expense, make very sure the faulty component has been positively identified before buying a replacement part.*

2   Electrical troubleshooting

A typical electrical circuit consists of an electrical component, the switches, relays, etc. related to that component and the wiring and connectors that hook the component to both the battery and the frame. To aid in locating a problem in any electrical circuit, wiring diagrams are included at the end of this Chapter.

Before tackling any troublesome electrical circuit, first study the appropriate diagrams thoroughly to get a complete picture of what makes up that individual circuit. Trouble spots, for instance, can often be narrowed down by noting if other components related to that circuit are operating properly or not. If several components or circuits fail at one time, chances are the fault lies in the fuse or ground/earth connection, as several circuits often are routed through the same fuse and ground/earth connections.

Electrical problems often stem from simple causes, such as loose or corroded connections or a blown fuse. Prior to any electrical troubleshooting, always visually check the condition of the fuse, wires and connections in the problem circuit.

If testing instruments are going to be utilized, use the diagrams to plan where you will make the necessary connections in order to accurately pinpoint the trouble spot.

The basic tools needed for electrical troubleshooting include a test light or voltmeter, a continuity tester (which includes a bulb, battery and set of test leads) and a jumper wire, preferably with a circuit breaker incorporated, which can be used to bypass electrical components. Specific checks described later in this Chapter may also require an ohmmeter.

Voltage checks should be performed if a circuit is not functioning properly. Connect one lead of a test light or voltmeter to either the negative battery terminal or a known good ground/earth. Connect the other lead to a connector in the circuit being tested, preferably nearest to the battery or fuse. If the bulb lights, voltage is reaching that point, which means the part of the circuit between that connector and the battery is problem-free. Continue checking the remainder of the circuit in the same manner. When you reach a point where no voltage is present, the problem lies between there and the last good test point. Most of the time the problem is due to a loose connection. Since these vehicles are designed for off-road use, the problem may also be water or corrosion in a connector. Keep in mind that some circuits only receive voltage when the ignition key is in the On position.

One method of finding short circuits is to remove the fuse and connect a test light or voltmeter in its place to the fuse terminals. There should be no load in the circuit. Move the wiring harness from side-to-side while watching the test light. If the bulb lights, there is a short to ground/earth somewhere in that area, probably where insulation has rubbed off a wire. The same test can be performed on other components in the circuit, including the switch.

A ground/earth check should be done to see if a component is ground/earthed properly. Disconnect the battery and connect one lead of a self-powered test light (such as a continuity tester) to a known good ground/earth. Connect the other lead to the wire or ground/earth connection being tested. If the bulb lights, the ground/earth is good. If the bulb does not light, the ground/earth is not good.

A continuity check is performed to see if a circuit, section of circuit or individual component is capable of passing electricity through it. Disconnect the battery and connect one lead of a self-powered test light (such as a continuity tester) to one end of the circuit being tested and

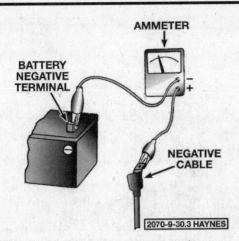

3.4 Checking for a battery drain with an ammeter

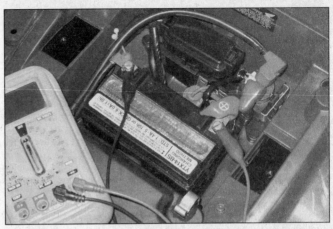

3.8 Measure open circuit voltage between the positive and negative terminals with the engine off

the other lead to the other end of the circuit. If the bulb lights, there is continuity, which means the circuit is passing electricity through it properly. Switches can be checked in the same way.

Remember that all electrical circuits are designed to conduct electricity from the battery, through the wires, switches, relays, etc. to the electrical component (light bulb, motor, etc.). From there it is directed to the frame (ground/earth) where it is passed back to the battery. Electrical problems are basically an interruption in the flow of electricity from the battery or back to it.

3 Battery - inspection and maintenance

Refer to illustrations 3.4 and 3.8

1   Most battery damage is caused by heat, vibration, and/or low electrolyte levels, so keep the battery securely mounted, and make sure the charging system is functioning properly. The battery used on these vehicles is a maintenance free (sealed) type and therefore doesn't require the addition of water. However, the following checks should still be regularly performed. **Warning:** *Always disconnect the negative cable first and connect it last to prevent sparks which could cause the battery to explode.*

2   Refer to Chapter 1 for battery removal procedures.

3   Check the battery terminals and cables for tightness and corrosion. If corrosion is evident, disconnect the cables from the battery, disconnecting the negative (-) terminal first, and clean the terminals and cable ends with a wire brush or knife and emery paper. Reconnect the cables, connecting the negative cable last, and apply a thin coat of petroleum jelly to the cables to slow further corrosion.

4   The battery case should be kept clean to prevent current leakage, which can discharge the battery over a period of time (especially when it sits unused). Wash the outside of the case with a solution of baking soda and water. Do not get any baking soda solution in the battery cells. Rinse the battery thoroughly, then dry it. If the battery continually runs down while the vehicle is not being used, there may be a short circuit that's draining the battery. To check, make sure the ignition switch is OFF, then disconnect the negative cable. Connect the positive terminal of an ammeter to the battery negative terminal and connect the ammeter negative terminal to the battery cable **(see illustration). Caution:** *Start with the ammeter at its highest range, then lower the setting until current flow registers. Otherwise, a high current flow may damage the ammeter.* If the current flow exceeds the current drain limit listed in this Chapter's Specifications, disconnect each of the vehicle's circuits in turn until you find the one with the short.

5   Look for cracks in the case and replace the battery if any are found. If acid has been spilled on the frame or battery box, neutralize it with a baking soda and water solution, then touch up any damaged paint. Make sure the battery vent tube (if equipped) is directed away

from the frame and is not kinked or pinched.

6   If acid has been spilled on the frame or battery box, neutralize it with the baking soda and water solution, dry it thoroughly, then touch up any damaged paint. Make sure the battery vent tube is directed away from the frame and is not kinked or pinched.

7   If the vehicle sits unused for long periods of time, disconnect the cables from the battery terminals. Refer to Section 4 and charge the battery approximately once every month.

8   The condition of the battery can be assessed by measuring the voltage present at the battery terminals (open circuit voltage); voltmeter positive probe to the battery positive terminal and the negative probe to the negative terminal **(see illustration)**. When fully charged there should be approximately 13 volts present. If the voltage falls below 12.3 volts the battery must be removed, disconnecting the negative cable first, and charged as described in Section 4.

9   Refer to Chapter 1 to install the battery.

4 Battery - charging

Refer to illustration 4.2

1   If the machine sits idle for extended periods or if the charging system malfunctions, the battery can be charged from an external source.

2   The battery should be charged at no more than the rate printed on the charging rate and time label fixed to the battery. Honda recommends a special battery tester and charger which are unlikely to be available to the vehicle owner. To measure the charging rate, connect an ammeter in series with a battery charger **(see illustration)**.

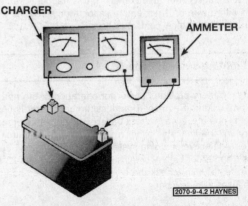

4.2 If the charger doesn't have an ammeter built in, connect one in series as shown; DO NOT connect the ammeter between the battery terminals or it will be ruined

3   When charging the battery, always remove it from the machine.

4   Disconnect the battery cables (negative cable first), then connect a voltmeter between the battery terminals and measure the voltage.

5   If terminal voltage is within the range listed in this Chapter's Specifications, the battery is fully charged. If it's lower, recharge the battery.

6   A quick charge can be used in an emergency, provided the maximum charge rate and time printed on the battery are not exceeded (exceeding the maximum rate or time may buckle the battery plates, rendering it useless). A quick charge should always be followed as soon as possible by a charge at the standard rate and time.

7   Hook up the battery charger leads (positive lead to battery positive terminal, negative lead to battery negative terminal), then, and only then, plug in the battery charger. **Warning:** *The hydrogen gas escaping from a charging battery is explosive, so keep open flames and sparks well away from the area. Also, the electrolyte is extremely corrosive and will damage anything it comes in contact with.*

8   Allow the battery to charge for the specified time. If the battery overheats or gases excessively, the charging rate is too high. Either disconnect the charger or lower the charging rate to prevent damage to the battery.

9   After the specified time, unplug the charger first, then disconnect the leads from the battery.

10   If the recharged battery discharges rapidly when left disconnected, it's likely that an internal short caused by physical damage or sulfation has occurred. A new battery will be required. A sound battery will tend to lose its charge at about 1% per day.

11   When the battery is fully charged, unplug the charger first, then disconnect the leads from the battery. Wipe off the outside of the battery case and install the battery in the vehicle.

5   Fuses - check and replacement

Refer to illustration 5.1

1   Most of the fuses are located in a fuse box next to the battery **(see illustration)**. There's also a 30-amp main fuse in the wire from the battery to the starter relay positive terminal. Electric shift models also have a fuse for the electric shift motor.

2   The fuses can be removed and checked visually. To check those in the fuse box, remove the seat (see Chapter 7) and open the cover. A blown fuse is easily identified by a break in the element.

3   If a fuse blows, be sure to check the wiring harnesses very carefully for evidence of a short circuit. Look for bare wires and chafed, melted or burned insulation. If a fuse is replaced before the cause is located, the new fuse will blow immediately.

4   Never, under any circumstances, use a higher rated fuse or bridge the fuse terminals, as damage to the electrical system could result.

5   Occasionally a fuse will blow or cause an open circuit for no obvious reason. Corrosion of the fuse ends and fuse holder terminals may occur and cause poor fuse contact. If this happens, remove the corrosion with a wire brush or emery paper, then spray the fuse end and terminals with electrical contact cleaner.

6   Lighting system - check

1   The battery provides power for operation of the headlights, taillight, brake light (if equipped) and instrument cluster lights. If none of the lights operate, always check battery voltage before proceeding. Low battery voltage indicates either a faulty battery, low battery electrolyte level or a defective charging system. Refer to Chapter 1 and Section 3 of this Chapter for battery checks and Sections 22 and 23 for charging system tests. Also, check the condition of the fuses and replace any blown fuses with new ones.

Headlights

2   If both of the headlight bulbs are out with the lighting switch in the On position, check the light fuse (see Section 5).

**5.1 The fuse box is located behind the battery (arrow)
(450 shown)**

3   If only one headlight is out, refer to Section 7 and disconnect the electrical connector for the headlight bulb. Use a jumper wire to connect the bulb directly to the battery terminals as follows:

a) Green wire (ground) terminal to battery negative terminal
b) White wire (low beam) terminal to battery positive terminal
c) Blue/black wire (high beam) terminal to battery positive terminal.

    If the light comes on, the problem lies in the wiring or one of the switches in the circuit. Refer to Sections 14 and 15 for the switch testing procedures, and also the wiring diagrams at the end of this manual. If either filament (high or low beam) of the bulb doesn't light, the bulb is burned out. Refer to Section 7 and replace it.

Taillight

4   If the taillight fails to work, check the bulb and the bulb terminals first, then check for battery voltage at the power wire in the taillight. If voltage is present, check the ground circuit for an open or poor connection.

5   If no voltage is indicated, check the wiring between the taillight and the lighting switch, then check the switch.

Brake light

6   See Section 10 for the brake light circuit checking procedure.

Neutral indicator light

7   If the neutral light fails to operate when the transmission is in Neutral, check the light fuse and the bulb (400 models only) (see Section 11 for bulb removal procedures). If the bulb and fuse are in good condition, check for battery voltage at the wire attached to the neutral switch on the right side of the engine. If battery voltage is present, refer to Section 16 for the neutral switch check and replacement procedures.

8   If no voltage is indicated, check the wiring to the bulb, to the switch and between the switch and the bulb for open circuits and poor connections.

7   Headlight and spotlight - bulb replacement

Headlight

Warning: *If the headlight has just burned out, give it time to cool before changing the bulb to avoid burning your fingers.*
Refer to illustrations 7.1a, 7.1b, 7.2, 7.3 and 7.5

1   Reach inside the front fender, remove the headlight cover screw (if equipped) and take off the cover **(see illustrations)**.

2   Pull the rubber dust cover off the headlight case **(see illustration)**.

3   Remove the bulb socket from the headlight case **(see illustration)**.

4   Pull the bulb out without touching the glass.

7.1a Remove the headlight cover (arrow)

7.1b Pull the tab on the rubber cover (arrow) . . .

7.2 . . . to pull back the rubber cover and expose the bulb socket . . .

7.3 . . . and remove the socket and bulb (don't touch the glass)

7.5 The Top mark on the rubber cover must be up when the rubber cover is installed

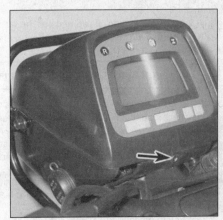

7.6 Remove the screw (arrow) and disengage the tabs

5   Installation is the reverse of the removal procedure, with the following additions:
a) *Be sure not to touch the bulb with your fingers - oil from your skin will cause the bulb to overheat and fail prematurely. If you do touch the bulb, wipe it off with a clean rag dampened with rubbing alcohol.*
b) *Align the tab on the metal bulb flange with the slot in the headlight case.*
c) *Make sure the Top mark on the rubber cover is upward* (see illustration).

Spotlight
Refer to illustrations 7.6, 7.7, 7.8, 7.9a and 7.9b

6   Remove the screw under the instrument cluster and disengage the tabs at the sides of the case, then lift the upper case off (see illustration).
7   Remove the bolt from each side of the spotlight and lift it off the vehicle (see illustration).
8   Remove the dust cover (if equipped) and detach the socket from the back of the spotlight (see illustration).

7.7 Remove the bolt from each side of the spotlight and lift it off

7.8 Remove the dust cover (if equipped) and detach the socket from the back of the spotlight

7.9a Disengage the socket clip . . .

7.9b . . . and pull the bulb socket out of
the spotlight

8.4 Loosen the headlight adjusting screw
(arrow), slide the headlight to change
adjustment and tighten the screw

9   Disengage the socket clip and pull the bulb socket out of the spot-light (see illustrations).

8   Headlight aim - check and adjustment

Refer to illustration 8.4

1   An improperly adjusted headlight may cause problems for oncoming traffic or provide poor, unsafe illumination of the terrain ahead. Before adjusting the headlight, be sure to consult with local traffic laws and regulations. Honda doesn't provide specifications for headlight adjustment.

2   The headlight beam can be adjusted vertically. Before performing the adjustment, make sure the fuel tank is at least half full, and have an assistant sit on the seat.

3   If you're working on a 1995 through 2001 model, insert a Phillips screwdriver into the vertical adjuster screw (the spring-loaded screw on the side of the headlight case), then turn the adjuster as necessary to raise or lower the beam.

4   If you're working on a 2002 or later model, loosen the vertical adjusting screw (see illustration). Slide the screw back and forth in the slot to change the adjustment, then tighten the screw.

9   Taillight and brake light bulbs - replacement

Taillight

Refer to illustrations 9.2a and 9.2b

1   The bulb socket is accessible beneath the fender.

2   Twist the bulb socket and pull it out of its housing, then pull the bulb out of the socket (see illustrations).

3   Check the socket terminals for corrosion and clean them if necessary.

4   Make sure the rubber gasket is in place and in good condition, then push the bulb into the socket.

Brake light

5   If the vehicle is equipped with a brake light, remove the lens securing screws and take off the lens.

6   Press the bulb into its socket and turn it counterclockwise to remove.

7   Installation is the reverse of removal.

10   Brake light switches - check and replacement

1   Brake lights are used on some models, as required by local area regulations.

2   Before checking any electrical circuit, check the fuses (see Section 5).

3   Using a test light connected to a good ground, check for voltage to the pink wire at the brake light switch. If there's no voltage present, check the pink wire between the switch and the ignition switch (see the wiring diagrams at the end of the book).

4   If voltage is available, touch the probe of the test light to the other terminal of the switch, then pull the brake lever or depress the brake pedal - if the test light doesn't light up, replace the switch.

5   If the test light does light, check the wiring between the switch and the brake lights (see the wiring diagrams at the end of the book).

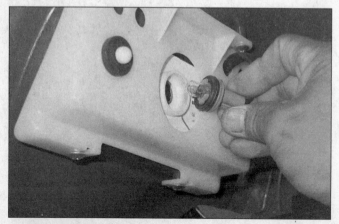

9.2a Pull the bulb socket out of the taillight housing . . .

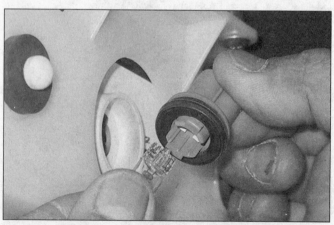

9.2b . . . and pull the bulb out of the socket

11.1 Pull the bulb socket out of the handlebar cover and pull the lens out of the socket . . .

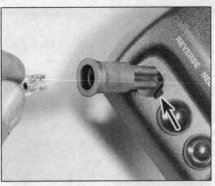

11.2. . . then pull the bulb out; if the bulb is hard to reach, slip a piece of rubber tubing over it and pull on the tubing to remove the bulb; align the socket lugs (if equipped) with the cover grooves (arrow) on installation

12.3 The fan control unit (arrow) is mounted at the front of the vehicle

Switch replacement

Brake lever switch

6   Disconnect the electrical connectors from the switch.

7   Remove the mounting screw and detach the switch from the brake lever bracket/front master cylinder.

8   Installation is the reverse of the removal procedure. The brake lever switch isn't adjustable.

Brake pedal switch

9   Disconnect the electrical connector in the switch harness.

10   Disconnect the spring from the brake pedal switch.

11   Hold the adjuster nut from turning and rotate the switch body all the way up until it clears the nut threads, then lift it out.

12   Install the switch by reversing the removal procedure. Position the switch so the brake light comes on when you operate the brake pedal.

11   Indicator bulbs (400 models) - replacement

Refer to illustrations 11.1 and 11.2

1   To replace a bulb, pull the appropriate rubber socket out of the handlebar cover, then pull off the lens **(see illustration)**.

2   Pull the bulb out of the socket **(see illustration)**. **Note:** *To reach the bulbs, which are deep within the sockets, push a piece of rubber or soft plastic tubing down over the bulb, then pull the tubing and bulb out. Use the same tubing to install the new bulb.*

3   If the socket contacts are dirty or corroded, they should be scraped

clean and sprayed with electrical contact cleaner before new bulbs are installed.

4   Carefully push the new bulb into position, using the same tubing that was used for removal, then push the socket into the handlebar cover.

12   Oil cooling fan - check and component replacement

1   These vehicles are equipped with an oil temperature warning system that turns on an indicator light on the handlebars or instrument cluster when the oil overheats. The system consists of an oil temperature sensor mounted on the underside of the engine, a control unit mounted at the front of the vehicle and the warning indicator light. The indicator light should come on for a few seconds when the engine is first started, then turn off. For operation in high temperatures, an electric fan comes on to cool the oil. **Note:** *Refer to Chapter 2D for cooling fan procedures on 500 models.*

Control system check

Refer to illustration 12.3

2   If the oil temperature warning light fails to operate properly, check the bulb (400 models) and replace it if it's burned out. The LED in the instrument cluster of 450 and 500 models can't be replaced separately.

3   If the fan doesn't operate properly, disconnect the electrical connectors from the control unit **(see illustration)**. If necessary, remove the front fender for access as described In Chapter 7.

4   Using an ohmmeter, make the following tests at the connector and note the results:

   a) *Light blue to body ground - 9.5 to 10.5 ohms.*
   b) *Blue to body ground - continuity.*
   c) *Green to body ground - continuity.*

5   If the ohmmeter readings aren't as specified, check the wiring for breaks or poor connections.

6   Turn the ignition switch to On. Using a voltmeter, check for battery voltage between the black/brown terminal and body ground, then between the pink terminal and body ground. If the voltmeter readings aren't as specified, check the wiring for breaks or poor connections.

Oil temperature sensor check

Refer to illustration 12.7

7   Disconnect the electrical connector from the sensor **(see illustration)**. With the engine cold, connect the ohmmeter between the switch terminal and ground. It should indicate the same reading as in Step 4a above. Now warm up the engine to normal operating temperature. The resistance reading should be considerably higher than in Step 4a.

8   If the sensor doesn't operate as described, replace it. If the sensor is good and the fan still doesn't operate, test it as described below.

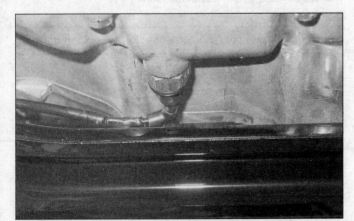

12.7 The oil temperature sensor is mounted in the underside of the engine (450 shown)

12.17 Unbolt the fan motor and shroud from the bracket

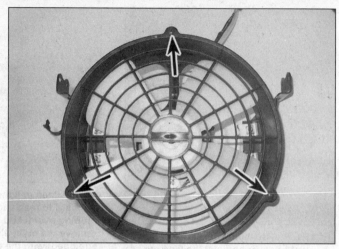

12.18 Remove the screws (arrows) to separate the grille
from the fan

12.19a Remove the nut (arrow)
and fan . . .

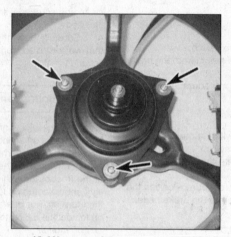

12.19b . . . and the mounting bolts
(arrows) to separate the motor from
the bracket

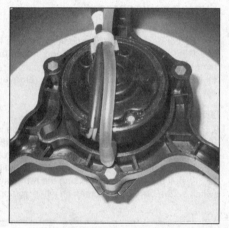

12.21 Route the wiring harness and
breather hose like this

Oil temperature sensor replacement

9   Drain the engine oil (see Chapter 1).
10   Unscrew the sensor from the engine.
11   Installation is the reverse of the removal steps. Use an electrically conductive sealer on the switch threads and tighten it to the torque listed in this Chapter's Specifications.
12   Fill the crankcase with the recommended type and amount of oil (see Chapter 1) and check for leaks.

Fan motor check

13   Start by removing the seat (see Chapter 7) and checking the fan fuse in the fuse box (see Section 5).
14   If the fuse is good, follow the wiring harness from the fan to the connector and disconnect it. Connect the fan motor directly to the battery with a pair of jumper wires. If the fan motor doesn't run, replace it.

Fan motor replacement

Refer to illustrations 12.17, 12.18, 12.19a, 12.19b and 12.21

15   Remove the oil cooler and fuel tank (see Chapters 2 and 3).
16   Disconnect the fan breather tube from the fan and free it from the retainer.
17   Unbolt the fan motor and shroud from the bracket and remove it from the left side of the vehicle **(see illustration)**.
18   Remove the screws and take the grille off the fan **(see illustration)**.

19   Unscrew the nut, pull the fan off the motor and remove the collar and cap **(see illustrations)**.
20   Remove the screws that secure the fan motor to the shroud, then lift off the motor and remove the collars and grommets.
21   Installation is the reverse of the removal steps. Route the harness and breather tube upward **(see illustration)**.

13   Ignition main (key) switch - check and replacement

Check

1   Follow the wiring harness from the ignition switch to the connector and disconnect the connector.
2   Using an ohmmeter, check the continuity of the terminal pairs indicated in the wiring diagrams at the end of the book. Continuity should exist between the terminals connected by a solid line when the switch is in the indicated position.
3   If the switch fails any of the tests, replace it.

Replacement

Refer to illustration 13.4

4   The ignition switch is secured to the handlebar cover by plastic prongs **(see illustration)**.
5   If you haven't already done so, unplug the switch electrical con-

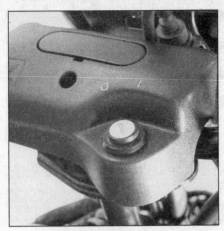

13.4 Squeeze the prongs to detach the switch from the handlebar cover

15.1 Remove the screws (arrows) to separate the switch housing halves

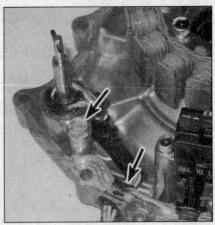

16.8 Pull out the grommet and unscrew the bolt (arrows), then remove the switch from the cover

nector. Squeeze the prongs and lift the switch out of the handlebar cover.

6   Installation is the reverse of the removal procedure.

14 Handlebar switches - check

1   Generally speaking, the switches are reliable and trouble-free. Most troubles, when they do occur, are caused by dirty or corroded contacts, but wear and breakage of internal parts is a possibility that should not be overlooked. If breakage does occur, the entire switch and related wiring harness will have to be replaced with a new one, since individual parts are not usually available.

2   The switches can be checked for continuity with an ohmmeter or a continuity test light. Always disconnect the battery negative cable, which will prevent the possibility of a short circuit, before making the checks.

3   Trace the wiring harness of the switch in question and unplug the electrical connectors.

4   Using the ohmmeter or test light, check for continuity between the terminals of the switch harness with the switch in the various positions. Refer to the continuity diagrams contained in the wiring diagrams at the end of the book. Continuity should exist between the terminals connected by a solid line when the switch is in the indicated position.

5   If the continuity check indicates a problem exists, refer to Section 15, disassemble the switch and spray the switch contacts with electrical contact cleaner. If they are accessible, the contacts can be scraped clean with a knife or polished with crocus cloth. If switch components are damaged or broken, it will be obvious when the switch is disassembled.

15 Handlebar switches - removal and installation

Refer to illustration 15.1

1   The handlebar switches are composed of two halves that clamp around the bars. They are easily removed for cleaning or inspection by taking out the clamp screws and pulling the switch halves away from the handlebars (**see illustration**).

2   To completely remove the switches, the electrical connectors in the wiring harness must be unplugged and the harness separated from the tie wraps and retainers.

3   When installing the switches, make sure the wiring harness is properly routed to avoid pinching or stretching the wires. If there's a locating pin inside the switch, make sure it fits into the hole in the handlebar.

16 Neutral/reverse switch - check and replacement

1   This procedure applies to the combined neutral/reverse switch mounted inside the alternator cover.

Check

2   Locate the wiring connector from the reverse and neutral switches under the rear fender (it can be identified by its wire colors).

3   Connect one lead of an ohmmeter to a good ground and the other lead to the terminal for the switch function being tested (light green wire for neutral; gray wire for reverse).

4   When the transmission is in neutral, the ohmmeter should read 0 ohms between the and ground - in any other gear, the meter should read infinite resistance.

5   When the transmission is in reverse, the ohmmeter should read 0 ohms between the reverse switch and ground/earth - in any other gear, the meter should read infinite resistance.

6   If the switch doesn't check out as described, replace it.

Replacement

Refer to illustration 16.8

7   Remove the alternator cover from the rear of the engine (see Section 24).

8   Free the wiring harness grommet from the cover (**see illustration**). Remove the switch lockbolt and take the switch out of the cover.

9   Install the switch in the case. Apply non-permanent thread locking agent to the threads of the lockbolt and tighten it securely, but don't overtighten it and strip the threads.

10   Reposition the harness grommet in the cover.

11   The remainder of installation is the reverse of the removal steps.

17 Starter switch - check and replacement

The starter is switch is part of the switch assembly on the left handlebar. Refer to Section 14 for checking and replacement procedures.

18 Starter relay - check and replacement

Refer to illustration 18.3

1   Refer to Chapter 7 and remove the battery seat.

2   Disconnect the negative cable from the battery.

3   Pull back the rubber covers from the terminal nuts, remove the

18.3 Remove the terminal nuts (arrows) and disconnect the cables, then disconnect the thin wires (450 shown)

19.3 Disconnect the cable and remove the mounting bolts (arrows), then lift the starter and pull it out (450 shown)

nuts and disconnect the starter relay cables **(see illustration)**. Disconnect the remaining electrical connector (thin wires) from the starter relay.

4   Connect an ohmmeter between the terminals from which the nuts were removed. It should indicate infinite resistance.

5   Connect a 12-volt battery to the terminals of the thin wires. The vehicle's battery can be used if it's fully charged. The ohmmeter should now indicate zero ohms.

6   If the relay doesn't perform as described, pull its rubber mount off the metal bracket and pull the relay out of the mount.

7   Installation is the reverse of removal. Reconnect the negative battery cable after all the other electrical connections are made.

19 Starter motor - removal and installation

Removal
Refer to illustrations 19.3 and 19.6

1   Disconnect the cable from the negative terminal of the battery.

2   Remove the right side engine cover.

3   Pull back the rubber boot and remove the nut retaining the starter cable to the starter **(see illustration)**.

4   Remove the starter mounting bolts.

5   Lift the outer end of the starter up a little bit and slide the starter out of the engine case. **Caution:** *Don't drop or strike the starter or its*

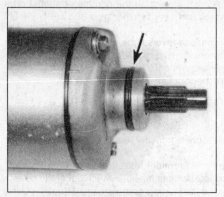

19.6 Pull the starter out and inspect the O-ring (arrow)

20.2 Make alignment marks between the housing and end covers before disassembly

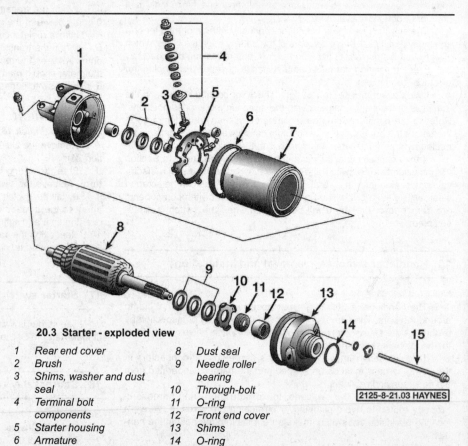

20.3 Starter - exploded view

1	Rear end cover	8	Dust seal
2	Brush	9	Needle roller
3	Shims, washer and dust		bearing
	seal	10	Through-bolt
4	Terminal bolt	11	O-ring
	components	12	Front end cover
5	Starter housing	13	Shims
6	Armature	14	O-ring
7	Lockwasher	15	Brush plate

2125-8-21.03 HAYNES

20.7 Unscrew the nut and remove the washers from the terminal bolt, noting their correct installed order

20.8 Lift the brush springs and slide the brushes out of their holders

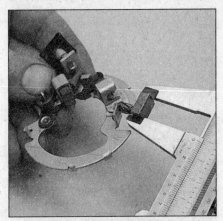

20.9 Measure the brush length and replace the brushes if they're worn

magnets may be demagnetized, which will ruin it.
6   Check the condition of the O-ring on the end of the starter and replace it if necessary **(see illustration)**.

Installation
7   Remove any corrosion or dirt from the mounting lugs on the starter and the mounting points on the crankcase.
8   Apply a little engine oil to the O-ring and install the starter by reversing the removal procedure.

20 Starter motor - disassembly, inspection and reassembly

1   Remove the starter motor (see Section 19).

Disassembly
Refer to illustrations 20.2 and 20.3
2   Make alignment marks between the housing and covers **(see illustration)**.
3   Unscrew the two long bolts, then remove the cover with its O-ring from the motor. Remove the shim(s) from the armature, noting their correct locations **(see illustration)**.
4   Remove the front cover with its O-ring from the motor. Remove the toothed washer from the cover and slide off the insulating washer and shim(s) from the front end of the armature, noting their locations.
5   Withdraw the armature from the housing.

Inspection
Note: *Check carefully which components are available as replacements before starting overhaul procedures.*
Refer to illustrations 20.7, 20.8, 20.9, 20.11a and 20.11b
6   Connect an ohmmeter between the terminal bolt and the insulated brush holder (or the indigo colored wire). There should be continuity (little or no resistance). When the ohmmeter is connected between the rear cover and the insulated brush holder (or the indigo colored wire), there should be no continuity (infinite resistance). Replace the brush holder if it doesn't test as described.
7   Unscrew the nut from the terminal bolt and remove the plain washer, insulating washers and rubber ring, noting carefully how they're installed **(see illustration)**. Withdraw the terminal bolt and brush assembly from the housing and recover the insulator.
8   Lift the brush springs and slide the brushes out of their holders **(see illustration)**.
9   The parts of the starter motor that most likely will require attention are the brushes. If one brush must be replaced, replace both of them. The brushes are replaced together with the terminal bolt and the brush plate. Brushes must be replaced if they are worn excessively, cracked, chipped, or otherwise damaged. Measure the length of the brushes and

compare the results to the brush length listed in this Chapter's Specifications **(see illustration)**. If either of the brushes is worn beyond the specified limits, replace them both.
10   Inspect the commutator for scoring, scratches and discoloration. The commutator can be cleaned and polished with fine emery paper, but do not use sandpaper and do not remove copper from the commutator. After cleaning, clean out the grooves and wipe away any residue with a cloth soaked in an electrical system cleaner or denatured alcohol.
11   Using an ohmmeter or a continuity test light, check for continuity between the commutator bars **(see illustration)**. Continuity should exist between each bar and all of the others. Also, check for continu-

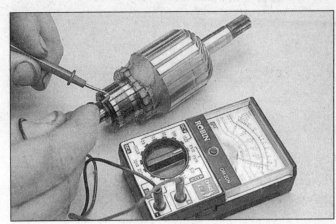

20.11a Check for continuity between the commutator bars . . .

20.11b . . . and for no continuity between each commutator bar and the armature shaft

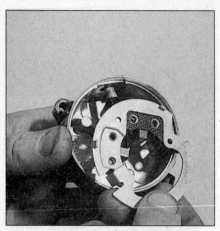

**20.16 Install the brush plate assembly
and terminal bolt**

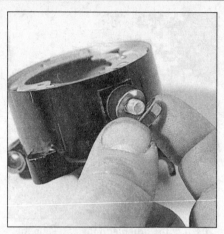

**20.17 Install the terminal bolt nut and
tighten it securely**

**20.19a Install the shims on the armature,
then insert the armature . . .**

ity between the commutator bars and the armature shaft **(see illustration)**. There should be no continuity between the commutator and the shaft. If the checks indicate otherwise, the armature is defective.

12   Check the dust seal in the front cover for wear or damage. Check the needle roller bearing in the front cover for roughness, looseness or loss of lubricant. Check with a motorcycle shop or Honda dealer to see

if the bearing can be replaced separately; if this isn't possible, replace the starter motor.

13   Inspect the bushing in the rear cover. Replace the starter motor if the bushing is worn or damaged.

14   Check the starter pinion for worn, chipped or broken teeth. If the gear is damaged or worn, replace the starter motor. Inspect the insulating washers for signs of damage and replace if necessary.

Reassembly

Refer to illustrations 20.16, 20.17, 20.19a, 20.19b, 20.20, 20.21, 20.22 and 20.23

15   Lift the brush springs and slide the brushes back into position in their holders.

16   Fit the insulator to the housing and install the brush plate. Insert the terminal bolt through the brush plate and housing **(see illustration)**.

17   Slide the rubber ring and small insulating washer onto the bolt, followed by the large insulating washers and the plain washer. Fit the nut to the terminal bolt and tighten it securely **(see illustration)**.

18   Locate the brush assembly in the housing, making sure its tab is correctly located in the housing slot.

19   Fit the shims to the armature shaft **(see illustration)** and insert the armature in the housing, locating the brushes to the commutator bars. Check that each brush is securely pressed against the commutator by its spring and is free to move easily in its holder **(see illustration)**.

20.19b . . . and locate the brushes on the commutator

**20.20 Fit the lockwasher to the front
cover so its teeth engage the cover ribs**

**20.21 Install the shims and washer on
the armature, making sure they're in the
correct order**

20.22 Fit the O-ring . . .

20.23 . . . and install the rear cover, aligning its groove with the brush plate outer tab

21.2 Hold the alternator rotor and try to turn the starter driven gear; it should turn smoothly clockwise, but not at all counterclockwise

21.3 Inspect the driven gear and its bearing

20   Fit the lockwasher to the front cover so that its teeth are correctly located with the cover ribs **(see illustration)**. Apply a smear of grease to the cover dust seal lip.

21   Slide the shim(s) onto the front end of the armature shaft, then fit the insulating washer **(see illustration)**. Fit the sealing ring to the housing and carefully slide the front cover into position, aligning the marks made on removal.

22   Ensure the brush plate inner tab is correctly located in the housing slot and fit the O-ring to the housing **(see illustration)**.

23   Align the rear cover groove with the brush plate outer tab and install the cover **(see illustration)**.

24   Check that the marks made on disassembly are correctly aligned, then fit the long bolts and tighten them securely **(see illustration 21.3)**.

25   Install the starter as described in Section 19.

21 Starter clutch and reduction gears - removal, inspection and installation

Starter clutch

Refer to illustrations 21.2, 21.3, 21.4a and 21.4b

1   Remove the alternator cover and rotor (Section 24). The starter clutch is mounted on the back of the alternator rotor.

2   Hold the alternator rotor with one hand and try to rotate the starter driven gear with the other hand **(see illustration)**. It should rotate clockwise smoothly, but not rotate counterclockwise at all.

3   If the gear rotates both ways or neither way, or if its movement is rough, remove it and its needle roller bearing from the alternator rotor **(see illustration)**.

4   Remove the Torx bolts and lift off the outer clutch **(see illustrations)**. Inspect the outer clutch and one-way clutch for wear and damage and replace them if any problems are found.

5   Installation is the reverse of the removal steps, with the following additions:

 a) *Place the flange side (wide side) of the outer clutch against the alternator rotor.*

 b) *Before you tighten the Torx bolts, turn the starter driven gear (see Step 2). It should rotate clockwise only; if it rotates counterclockwise, the one-way clutch is installed backwards.*

 c) *Apply non-permanent thread locking agent to the threads of the Torx bolts and tighten them to the torque listed in this Chapter's Specifications.*

Reduction gears

Refer to illustrations 21.6, 21.7, 21.8 and 21.10

6   Remove the alternator cover (Section 24). The reduction gears connect the starter motor shaft to the starter clutch on the back of the alternator rotor **(see illustration)**.

21.4a Remove the six Torx bolts . . .

21.4b . . . then remove the outer clutch and the roller assembly

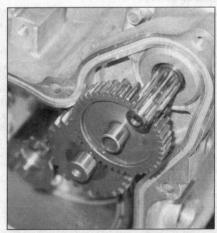

21.6 The reduction gears engage the starter shaft like this (450 shown)

21.7 Pull out reduction gear A and its shaft (upper arrow), then remove the thrust washer and reduction gear C (lower arrow)

21.8 The alternator rotor must be removed before the reduction gear shaft can be pulled out

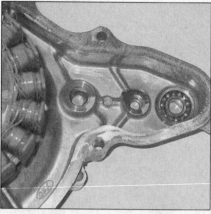

21.10 Check the starter shaft bearing in the cover for roughness, looseness and noise

7   Slide reduction gear A off the shaft and pull the shaft out of the crankcase (see illustration). Slide the thrust washer off of reduction gear C, then pull the gear off the reduction shaft.

8   To remove the reduction shaft from the crankcase, remove the alternator rotor (see Section 24). The reduction shaft can then be pulled out (see illustration).

9   Check the gears for chipped or worn teeth and replace them if necessary. Replace the thrust washer if it looks worn. If you need to remove the snap-ring from the reduction shaft, replace it with a new one.

10   Spin the inner race of the starter shaft bearing in the alternator cover (see illustration). If it's rough, loose or noisy, obtain a new bearing and put it in a freezer so it will shrink. Heat the case around the bearing with a hair dryer or similar tool and tap the bearing out, then tap the new bearing in with a bearing driver or socket the same diameter as the bearing. Caution: Don't heat the cover with a torch or it may warp, which will cause it to seal poorly against the rear crankcase cover.

11   Installation is the reverse of the removal steps. Be sure to install the reduction shaft (if it was removed) before installing the alternator rotor.

22   Charging system testing - general information and precautions

1   If the performance of the charging system is suspect, the system as a whole should be checked first, followed by testing of the individual components (the alternator and the regulator/rectifier). Note: Before beginning the checks, make sure the battery is fully charged and that all system connections are clean and tight.

2   Checking the output of the charging system and the performance of the various components within the charging system requires the use of a voltmeter, ammeter and ohmmeter or the equivalent multimeter.

3   When making the checks, follow the procedures carefully to prevent incorrect connections or short circuits, as irreparable damage to electrical system components may result if short circuits occur.

4   If the necessary test equipment is not available, it is recommended that charging system tests be left to a dealer service department or a reputable motorcycle repair shop.

23   Charging system - output test

Refer to illustration 23.3

1   If a charging system problem is suspected, perform the following checks. Start by removing the seat for access to the battery (see Chapter 7).

23.3 Connect a voltmeter between the battery terminals and measure voltage output with the engine running

2   Start the engine and let it warm up to normal operating temperature.

3   With the engine idling, attach the positive (red) voltmeter lead to the positive (+) battery terminal and the negative (black) lead to the battery negative (-) terminal (see illustration). The voltmeter selector switch (if equipped) must be in the 0-20 DC volt range.

4   Slowly increase the engine speed to 5000 rpm and compare the voltmeter reading to the value listed in this Chapter's Specifications.

5   If the output is as specified, the alternator is functioning properly.

6   Low voltage output may be the result of damaged windings in the alternator stator coils or wiring problems. Make sure all electrical connections are clean and tight, then refer to the following Sections to check the alternator stator coils and the regulator/rectifier.

7   High voltage output (above the specified range) indicates a defective voltage regulator/rectifier. Refer to Section 25 for regulator testing and replacement procedures.

24   Alternator stator coils, rotor and rear crankcase cover - check and replacement

Stator coil check

Refer to illustrations 24.1 and 24.2

1   Locate and disconnect the alternator coil connector from the regu-

24.1 Disconnect the alternator coil connector from the regulator/rectifier (arrow) (450 shown)

24.2 Connect an ohmmeter between the yellow wire terminals in the side of the connector that runs back to the stator coils

24.6 Hold the recoil starter pulley with a tool like this and unscrew the bolt

lator/rectifier on the right side of the vehicle frame above the rear tire **(see illustration)**.

2   Connect an ohmmeter between the yellow wire terminals in the side of the connector that runs back to the stator coils on the rear of the engine **(see illustration)**. If the readings are much outside the value listed in this Chapter's Specifications, repeat the test at the five-pin alternator connector, located on the right side of the vehicle slightly behind the recoil starter. If the readings are still outside the Specifications replace the stator coils as described below.

3   Connect the ohmmeter between a good ground on the vehicle and each of the connector terminals in turn. The meter should indicate infinite resistance (no continuity). If not, replace the stator coils.

Stator coil replacement

Refer to illustrations 24.6, 24.7a, 24.7b, 24.8 and 24.9

4   Remove the recoil starter (see Chapter 2).

5   Disconnect the oil temperature sensor wire and the reverse control cable (see Section 12 and Chapter 2). Follow the wiring harnesses from the alternator cover to the connectors and disconnect them.

6   Hold the recoil starter pulley with a special tool (Honda 07SMB-HM70100 or equivalent, such as a strap wrench) **(see illustration)**. Unscrew the pulley bolt and take off the O-ring.

7   Remove the alternator cover bolts **(see illustration)**. Take the cover off the engine and locate the dowels **(see illustration)**.

8   Disconnect the pulse generator connector and remove its Allen

bolts **(see illustration)**. Unscrew the three Allen bolts that secure the stator to the cover and remove it, together with the pulse generator and wiring harness.

24.7a Alternator cover bolts (arrows) (450 shown)

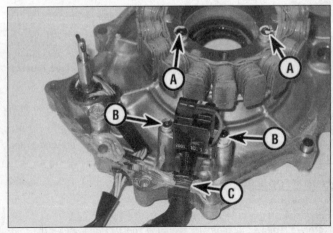

24.8 Pulse generator and stator coil details (450 shown)

A   Stator coil bolts (two of three bolts shown)
B   Pulse generator bolts
C   Harness grommet

24.7b Remove the cover and locate the dowels (arrows)

24.9　Replace the oil seal in the cover if it's been leaking or looks worn

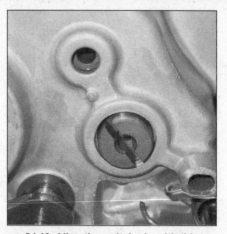

24.10　Align the switch pin with this shaft slot

24.12　Remove the rotor with a puller designed for the purpose

24.14　Remove the starter clutch needle roller bearing and washer (arrow)

24.20　Temporarily bolt the recoil starter pulley to the crankshaft to seat the rotor

24.21　Be sure there aren't any small metal objects stuck to the rotor magnets; an inconspicuous item like this Woodruff key (arrow) can ruin the rotor and stator if the engine is run

9　While the cover is off, check the oil seal for signs of leakage **(see illustration)**. If any problems are found, carefully pry the seal out of the cover, taking care not to damage the seal bore. Drive in a new seal with a seal driver or socket the same diameter as the seal.

10　Installation is the reverse of the removal steps, with the following additions:

　a) *Tighten the stator coil and pulse generator Allen bolts to the torques listed in this Chapter's Specifications.*

　b) *Remove all old gasket material from the alternator cover and crankcase. Use a new gasket on the alternator cover and smear a film of sealant across the wiring harness grommets* **(see illustration 24.8)**.

　c) *Make sure the cover dowels are in position.*

　d) *Align the pin on the neutral-reverse switch with the slot in the shaft* **(see illustration)**.

　e) *Tighten the cover bolts evenly, in a criss-cross pattern.*

　f) *Don't forget the O-ring on the rotor bolt. Tighten the bolt to the torque listed in this Chapter's Specifications.*

Rotor replacement

Removal

Refer to illustrations 24.12 and 24.14

Note: *To remove the alternator rotor, the special Honda puller (part no. 07733-0020001 or 07933-3950000) or an aftermarket equivalent will be required. Don't try to remove the rotor without the proper puller, as it's almost sure to be damaged. Pullers are readily available from motorcycle dealers and aftermarket tool suppliers.*

11　Remove the alternator cover (Steps 4 through 7 above).

12　Thread an alternator puller into the center of the rotor and use it to remove the rotor **(see illustration)**. If the rotor doesn't come off easily, tap sharply on the end of the puller to release the rotor's grip on the tapered crankshaft end.

13　Pull the rotor off, together with the starter clutch.

14　Remove the needle roller bearing and washer from the crankshaft **(see illustration)**.

15　Check the Woodruff key **(see illustration 24.14)**; if it's not secure in its slot, pull it out and set it aside for safekeeping. A convenient method is to stick the Woodruff key to the magnets inside the rotor, but be certain not to forget it's there, as serious damage to the rotor and stator coils will occur if the engine is run with anything stuck to the magnets.

Installation

Refer to illustration 24.20

16　Degrease the center of the rotor and the end of the crankshaft.

17　Make sure the Woodruff key is positioned securely in its slot. Lubricate the needle roller bearing with clean engine oil and install the washer and needle roller bearing on the crankshaft **(see illustration 26.14)**.

18　Check the make sure the starter reduction shaft is installed in the engine.

19　Align the rotor slot with the Woodruff key. Place the rotor, together with the starter clutch and starter driven gear, on the crankshaft.

20　**Note:** *Don't skip this step, or the rotor magnets may pull the rotor off the crankshaft when the alternator cover is installed.* Temporar-

24.26a Remove the rear crankcase cover bolts (arrows)
(2002 450ES model shown) . . .

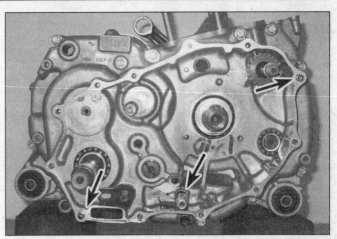

24.26b . . . take off the cover and locate the dowels
and washer (arrows)

24.27 Replace the rear driveshaft seal if it's been leaking
or looks worn

25.1 The regulator/rectifier unit is mounted on the frame under
the rear fender (arrow)

ily install the recoil starter pulley and tighten its bolt to seat the rotor securely on the crankshaft (see illustration). Remove the bolt and pulley once this is done.

21   Take a look to make sure there isn't anything stuck to the inside of the rotor (see illustration).

22   The remainder of installation is the reverse of the removal steps.

Rear crankcase cover

Removal

Refer to illustrations 24.26a, 24.26b and 24.27

23   Remove the alternator rotor as described above.

24   Remove the reverse lock lever and cable retainer (see Chapter 2).

25   If you're working on a 1998 through 2001 450 model, remove the speed sensor from the rear cover.

26   Remove the cover bolts (see illustration). Take the cover off, locate the dowels and remove the washer from the spindle at the bottom of the case (see illustration).

27   Check the rear driveshaft seal in the cover for wear or damage (see illustration). If any problems are found, carefully pry the seal out of the cover, taking care not to damage the seal bore. Drive in a new seal with a seal driver or socket the same diameter as the seal.

Installation

28   Installation is the reverse of the removal steps. Use a new gasket and make sure the dowels and washer are in position (see illustration 24.26b).

25 Regulator/rectifier - check and replacement

Check

Refer to illustration 25.1

1   The regulator/rectifier is mounted on the right side of the vehicle frame under the rear fender (see illustration).

2   Disconnect the wiring harness connector from the regulator/rectifier.

3   Connect a voltmeter between the red wire terminal in the harness side of the connector and a good body ground. It should indicate battery voltage (approximately 13 volts).

4   Connect an ohmmeter between the green wire terminals in the harness side of the connector and a good body ground. The ohmmeter should indicate continuity.

5   Connect the ohmmeter between the yellow wire terminals in the harness side of the connector. The ohmmeter should indicate 0.1 to 1.0 ohm.

5   If the voltage or ohmmeter readings aren't as described, check the wiring for breaks or poor connections. If there's a problem in Step 5, also check the alternator stator coils as described in Section 24.

6   If the wiring harness and stator coils are good, the regulator/rectifier may be defective (especially if the charging system output test in Section 23 indicates excessive output). It's a good idea to have it tested by a Honda dealer or substitute a known good unit before condemning it as trash.

26.10 Unbolt the cover from the shift motor and angle sensor

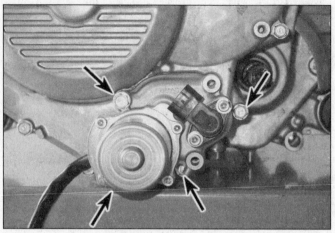

26.11 Angle sensor and shift control motor mounting bolts
(arrows) (lower left bolt hidden)

26 Electric shift system (450SE models) - check and component replacement

1   This system replaces the foot shift pedal on the external shift link-age with an electric motor, controlled by a switch on the left handlebar.

Troubleshooting

1   Switch the ignition Off and back to On. The system may reset and work properly, depending on the problem. If it does, operate the vehicle; if the problem occurs again, try to note the conditions that led up to the failure.
2   Check the main fuse, motor fuse, light fuse and ignition fuse and replace them if necessary (see Section 5). If you find a blown fuse, check its circuit for a short or bad connection.
3   Try to shift the transmission through the gear positions, using the removable hand lever supplied in the vehicle's tool kit. If you can't shift through the gears using the tool, there's a problem in the mechanical shift linkage (internal or external) (see Chapter 2).
4   Make sure the battery is in good condition and fully charged (see Chapter 1 and Section 4).
5   Check the system wiring for breaks or bad connections, referring to the wiring diagrams at the end of the manual.
6   Check the clutch adjustment (see Chapter 1).
7   If you're working on a 1998 through 2001 model, the electric shift system will stop working if the electronic control unit detects a com-ponent failure. If the problem is with second, third or fourth gear shift-ing (which is controlled by the ECU), the instrument cluster will display dashes, rather than indicating any of these gear positions.
8   2002 and later models can isolate the problem to a specific circuit or component by flashing trouble codes, using the neutral indicator in the instrument cluster.

Reading trouble codes (2002 and later models)

9   Turn the ignition On (if it isn't already), then Off and back to On. If there's a problem in the system, it will be indicated by the gear position indicator, which will flash a number of times to indicate a trouble code (one flash equals code 1, two flashes equal code 2, etc.). Trouble codes and their specific problem areas are:

Code 0 (no flashes) - The system is functioning normally.
Code 1 (one flash) - Electronic control unit
Code 2 (two flashes) - Shift switch or its circuit
Code 3 (three flashes) - Angle sensor or its circuit
Code 4 (four flashes) - Gear position switch or its circuit
Code 5 (five flashes) - ECU motor circuit (defective ECU)
Code 6 (six flashes) - ECU failsafe relay or its circuit
Code 7 (seven flashes) - ECU voltage converter circuit (defective ECU)
Code 8 (eight flashes) - Angle sensor, control motor or ECU
Code 9 (nine flashes) - Angle sensor, its circuit or ECU
Code 10 (10 flashes) - Pulse generator or its circuit
Code 11 (11 flashes) - Speed sensor, its circuit or ECU
Code 12 (12 flashes) - Gear position switch, its circuit or ECU

Angle sensor check and replacement

Check
Refer to illustrations 26.10 and 26.11
10   Unbolt the cover from the angle sensor **(see illustration)**.
11   With the ignition switch in the Off position and the transmission in Neutral, disconnect the electrical connector from the angle sensor **(see illustration)**.
12   Locate the terminal pins in the angle sensor that connect to the black/red and blue/green wires in the sensor wiring harness. Connect an ohmmeter between the terminals. The reading (angle sensor neutral resistance) should be within the values listed in this Chapter's Specifi-cations. Write the reading down for use in the next Steps.
13   Move the ohmmeter to the blue/green and yellow/red terminals. Using the manual shift handle supplied in the vehicle's tool kit, shift the transmission up through the gears. Note the ohmmeter reading and divide it by the reading written down in Step 12. The result should be less than 0.4 ohms.
14   With the ohmmeter still connected to the blue/green and yel-low/red terminals, use the manual shift handle to shift the transmission down through the gears. Note the ohmmeter reading and divide it by the reading written down in Step 12. The result should be greater than 0.6 ohms.
15   If the readings aren't within the specified range, replace the angle sensor.

Replacement
16   Remove the cover from the shift control motor and angle sensor **(see illustrations 26.10 and 26.11)**.
17   Disconnect the electrical connector from the angle sensor. Remove the Allen bolts and take the angle sensor off the engine.
18   Installation is the reverse of the removal steps. Be sure to align the flat in the angle sensor with the flat on the gearshift spindle.

Shift control motor check and replacement

Check
19   Remove the angle sensor as described above.
20   Follow the wiring harness from the shift control motor to the con-nector and disconnect it. Remove the motor's mounting bolts and take it off the engine **(see illustration 26.11)**.
21   Use a pair of jumper wires with probes on the end to connect the control motor directly to a 12-volt battery (the vehicle's battery will do if it's fully charged). The motor should turn. If it doesn't, replace it.
22   Installation is the reverse of the removal steps.

26.24 Remove the reduction gears and O-ring

26.26 Lubricate the reduction gear pivot bores and gears with special grease

27.4 The control unit is mounted at the front of the vehicle (arrow)

Reduction gear check and replacement
Refer to illustrations 26.24 and 26.26

23 Remove the motor as described above.

24 Pull out the lower gear, segment gear and upper gear (**see illustration**). Remove the O-ring from its groove.

25 Check all parts, especially gear teeth, for wear and damage. Replace the gears as a set if problems are found.

26 Installation is the reverse of the removal steps. Lubricate the gear's pivot holes with Esso Unirex N2 or N3 grease or equivalent (**see illustration**). Apply the same grease to the gear teeth.

Shift switch
27 The shift switch is located on the left handlebar. To remove and install the switch, refer to Section 14. To test switch continuity, refer to the continuity diagram, which is included in the wiring diagram at the end of this manual.

27   Selectable 4WD system (2002 and later models) - check and component replacement

1   This system uses a magnetic clutch to engage the front differential when 4wd is selected, providing power to the front wheels. When 2wd is selected, the magnetic clutch disengages, and the front driveshaft is disconnected from the differential. System components are the front final clutch (magnetic clutch), meter speed sensor, final clutch speed sensor, final clutch control unit and 2wd/4wd switch. The system has a built-in diagnostic capability which it allows it to flash trouble codes using the 4wd indicator in the instrument cluster.

Troubleshooting
Refer to illustration 27.4

2   Check the main fuse and 4wd fuse and replace them if necessary (see Section 5). If you find a blown fuse, check its circuit for a short or bad connection.

3   Make sure the battery is in good condition and fully charged (see Chapter 1 and Section 4).

4   Follow the system wiring from the control unit (see illustration) to the other system components. Check the wiring for breaks or bad connections, referring to the wiring diagrams at the end of the manual.

Reading trouble codes
5   Turn the ignition On (if it isn't already), then Off and back to On. If there's a problem in the system, it will be indicated by the 4wd indicator, which will flash a number of times to indicate a trouble code (two flashes equal code 2, three flashes equal code 3, etc. - there is no code 1). Trouble codes and their specific problem areas are:

Code 0 (no flashes) - The system is functioning normally.
Code 2 (two flashes) - Front final clutch speed sensor, its wiring harness or the control unit
Code 3 (three flashes) - Meter speed sensor (450), rear speed sensor (500), its wiring harness or the control unit
Code 4 (four flashes) - System voltage - the vehicle's charging system or the control unit
Code 5 (five flashes) - Control unit (450) or front final clutch system (500)
Code 6 (six flashes) - (450 only) Alternator, control unit wiring harness or the control unit

Meter speed sensor check and replacement (450)
Refer to illustrations 27.6, 27.7 and 27.9

6   Remove the cover from the sensor (**see illustration**).

7   Check for a loose sensor mounting bolt (**see illustration**). If it's loose, tighten it and see whether that solves the problem.

27.6 Remove the bolts (arrows) and take off the cover (450 shown)

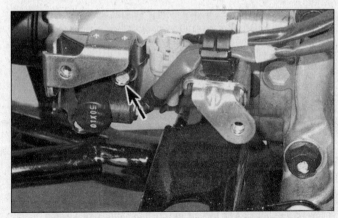
27.7 Check for a loose sensor mounting bolt (arrow)

27.9 The front final clutch speed sensor is mounted on the front differential

28.5 Remove the cluster mounting nuts (arrows) and take the cluster off

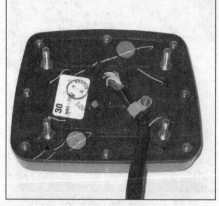

28.6a Remove the screws from the back side of the case (2002 450 model shown)

8   If the bolt isn't loose, unscrew it, remove the sensor and check it for physical damage. Replace the sensor with a new one if it's damaged. Also check the end of the sensor and the ring gear for debris and clean away any that you find. If the sensor looks good, reinstall it.
9   Disconnect the electrical connectors for the final clutch speed sensor **(see illustration)** and the meter speed sensor, then reconnect them. Drive the vehicle at a speed over 9 mph with 4wd engaged. If the 4wd indicator shows two flashes, replace the meter speed sensor. If it doesn't flash, the problem may be due to loose or dirty wiring connections or temporary electromagnetic interference.

Front final drive speed sensor check and replacement

10   Check for loose sensor mounting bolts **(see illustration 27.9)**. If they're loose, tighten them and see whether that solves the problem.
11   If the bolts aren't loose, unscrew them, remove the sensor and check it for physical damage. Replace the sensor with a new one if it's damaged. Also check the end of the sensor and the ring gear for debris and clean away any that you find. If the sensor looks good, reinstall it.

450 models
12   Disconnect the electrical connectors for the final clutch sensor and the meter speed sensor **(see illustration 27.7)**, then reconnect them. Drive the vehicle at a speed over 9 mph with 4wd engaged. If the 4wd indicator shows three flashes, replace the final drive speed sensor. If it doesn't flash, the problem may be due to loose or dirty wiring connections or temporary electromagnetic interference.

500 models
13   Swap the connectors for the front and rear speed sensors (three pins each, front connector black, rear connector yellow). Check the wire colors in the wiring diagram at the end of the manual to identify the connectors.
14   Switch the ignition off, then turn it on. With 4wd engaged, drive the vehicle above 4 mph for at least 30 seconds. If the 4wd indicator doesn't flash, check the wiring for breaks or bad connections. If it flashes twice, the problem is either a break or bad connection in the wiring or a bad control unit. If it flashes three times, the front speed sensor is bad.

Rear final drive speed sensor check and replacement (500)

15   Start by making sure the rear tires are the correct size and pressure (see Chapter 1).
16   Check the wiring for breaks or bad connections, referring to wiring diagrams at the end of the manual.
17   Unplug the rear speed sensor's wiring connector. Connect the positive terminal of a voltmeter to the black/orange wire terminal in the harness side of the connector and the negative terminal to the green/yellow wire terminal. With the ignition on, there should be voltage. If not, check the wires for breaks or bad connections.

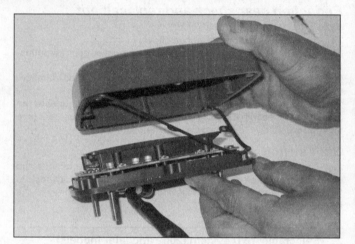

28.6b . . . lift the cover off and remove the gasket

18   Swap the connectors for the front and rear speed sensors as described in Step 13 above.
19   Switch the ignition off, then turn it on. With 4wd engaged, drive the vehicle above 4 mph for at least 30 seconds. If the 4wd indicator flashes three times, check the wiring for breaks or bad connections. If the wiring is good, the control unit may be bad. If it flashes twice, the rear speed sensor is bad.
20   Remove the speed sensor from the rear final drive unit **(see illustration)**. Check the speed sensor and ring gear for mechanical damage or foreign material. Replace damage parts and clean away any foreign material, then reinstall the sensor.

---

28 Instrument cluster - removal and installation

400 and 450 models
Refer to illustrations 28.5, 28.6a, 28.6b and 28.7
1   Remove the seat and front fender (see Chapter 7).
2   Disconnect the negative cable from the battery.
3   Remove the spotlight (see Section 7).
4   Follow the wiring harness from the cluster to the connector and disconnect it.
5   Remove the cluster mounting nuts and lift it out **(see illustration)**.
6   Remove the case screws and separate the case and gasket from the cluster **(see illustrations)**.
7   Remove the panel screws and separate the instrument panel from the case **(see illustration)**.
8   Installation is the reverse of the removal steps.

28.7 Remove the screws to separate the circuit board from the panel (2002 450 model shown)

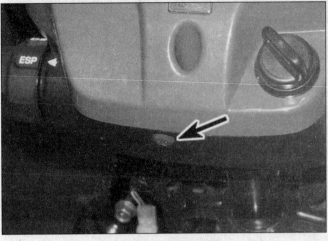

28.11a Remove the screw . . .

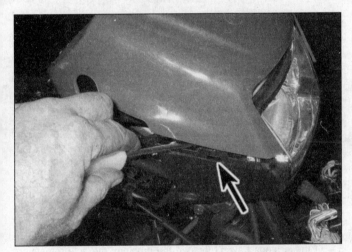

28.11b . . . and disengage the tabs to free the cover

28.11c Remove the handlebar front cover nuts (arrows) and take it off

500 models

Refer to illustrations 28.11a, 28.11b, 28.11c and 28.13

9   Remove the seat and front fender (see Chapter 7).

10   Locate the cluster wiring connector on the frame near the radiator cap (gray, 14 pins) and disconnect it. Free the wiring harness from any retainers.

11   Remove the screw that secures the handlebar upper cover, disengage the tabs and take it off **(see illustrations)**. Remove the nuts that secure the handlebar front cover and take it off **(see illustration)**.

12   If the vehicle is equipped with a global positioning system, disconnect the GPS wiring connector.

13   Remove the cluster mounting nuts and take it off **(see illustration)**.

14   Installation is the reverse of the removal steps.

29   Fuel gauge and level sensor (500 models) - check and replacement

Refer to illustration 29.6

1   If the fuel gauge doesn't work, see if the speedometer and indicators work. If they don't, check the instrument cluster wiring for breaks or bad connections. If the wiring is good, the cluster may be defective.

2   Remove the inner fender from the left side of the vehicle.

3   With the ignition OFF, disconnect the fuel level sensor connector.

28.13 Remove three nuts (arrows) that secure the cluster and remove it

Bridge the terminals in the gauge side of the connector with a piece of wire.

4   Switch the ignition ON. All of the fuel level indicator segments should be illuminated. If not, replace the instrument cluster.

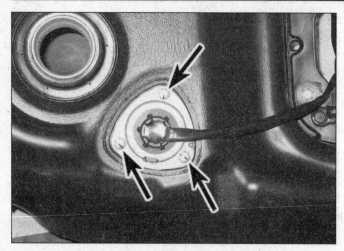

29.6 Unbolt the fuel level sensor from the tank

30.2 Remove the screw (arrow) to detach the reverse switch

5   Remove the fuel tank cover (see Chapter 7).
6   Unbolt the fuel level sensor and lift it out of the tank **(see illustration)**. Leave its wiring harness connected for now.
7   With the ignition ON, hold the sensor upright and lift the float. The fuel level indicator segments should illuminate.
8   Lower the float to the bottom. The RES indicator should blink. If all of the indicator segments blink, replace the instrument cluster.
9   If the gauge didn't perform properly during Steps 7 and 8, disconnect the sensor wiring connector. Connect an ohmmeter to the sensor terminals, then raise and lower the float. The ohmmeter should indicate 5 to 7 ohms with the float fully raised, and 204 to 210 ohms with it fully lowered. If not, replace the sensor.
10   Install the sensor in the tank, using a new rubber seal. Align the notch in the retaining ring with the tab on the sensor.
11   The remainder of installation is the reverse of the removal steps.

30 Reverse switch (500 models) - check and replacement

1   Remove the fuel tank cover and the inner front fender (see Chapter 7).

Check

Refer to illustration 30.2
2   Unplug the electrical connector from the reverse switch **(see illustration)**.
3   Connect an ohmmeter or test lamp between the switch terminals. There should be continuity (little or no resistance) with the shifter in the Reverse position. There should be no continuity in any other position.
4   If the switch doesn't perform as described, replace it.
5   Unplug the switch electrical connector if you haven't already done so. Remove the mounting screw and take the switch off **(see illustration 30.2)**.
6   Installation is the reverse of the removal steps. Align the pin on the switch with the hole in the base of the gearshift box.

31 GPS unit - check and replacement

1   The optional GPS receiver should take varying times to give a location, depending on how recently the engine has been run. If the engine is re-started within two hours, the location display should take about 25 seconds. If the engine is re-started after two hours, the location display should take about two minutes. If the vehicle has been moved over 60 miles with the ignition OFF, has been turned off for over a month, or if

the battery has been disconnected, the display may take as long as eight minutes.

Check

Indicator blinks continuously
2   If the indicator blinks continuously, remove the handlebar covers for access. Disconnect the GPS receiver's 6-pin connector and check for a bad connection.
3   If there isn't any visible problem with the connector, connect the positive probe of a voltmeter to the pink wire terminal in the side of the connector that runs back to the instrument cluster. Connect the negative terminal to ground. With the ignition switch ON, there should be about 5 volts. If not, the pink wire or instrument cluster is bad.
4   If there is voltage, switch the ignition off. Connect an ohmmeter between the green/orange wire's terminal in the side of the connector that runs back to the instrument cluster and ground. There should be continuity. If not, the green/orange wire or instrument cluster is bad.
5   If these steps haven't located the problem, the only remaining test is to substitute a known good GPS unit to isolate the problem to the GPS unit or instrument cluster. Since electrical components can't be returned once purchased, this should be done by a dealer service department or other qualified shop.

Display start-up time too long
6   Disconnect the negative cable from the battery, then reconnect it.
7   Turn the ignition switch to ON and wait until the GPS displays a position. Switch the ignition OFF, then back ON. The GPS should display a location again within 30 seconds. If it does, the system is working correctly.
8   If it doesn't, remove the handlebar covers for access. Disconnect the GPS receiver's 6-pin connector.
9   Connect the positive probe of a voltmeter to the pink/white wire terminal in the side of the connector that runs back to the instrument cluster. Connect the negative terminal to ground. With the ignition switch ON, there should be about 5 volts. If not, the pink/white wire or instrument cluster is bad. If there is 5 volts, the GPS unit is probably bad. Since electrical components can't be returned once purchased, this should be done by a dealer service department or other qualified shop.

Replacement
10   Remove the instrument cluster (see Section 28).
11   Unbolt the GPS unit, disconnect its wiring connector and take it out.
12   Installation is the reverse of the removal steps.

32.18 The gear position switch is secured by two screws (arrows)

32 Hondamatic transmission (500 models) - check and component replacement

1   The Hondamatic automatic transmission used in 500 Rubicon models has a sophisticated electronic control system, which is operated by the electronic control unit. A built-in self-diagnostic function stores codes when a problem is found, and indicates the problem by flashing the code numbers with the gear position indicator light in the instrument cluster.

Initial setting procedure

Note: *Read through this procedure before starting it. You'll need an assistant for some steps, and some require precise timing.*

2   This procedure must be done whenever the carburetor, throttle cable, angle sensor, throttle position sensor or electronic control module has been replaced. If it isn't done, the gear position indicator will flash steadily (half-second flash duration, followed by a half-second pause).

3   Place the sub-transmission shifter in the Neutral position.

4   Start the engine and let it idle. After 30 seconds, move the shifter to Drive and make sure the gear position indicator in the instrument cluster indicates D.

5   Ride the vehicle forward approximately 5 feet at a slow speed. Stop the vehicle, move the shifter to N and make sure the gear position indicator indicates N.

6   Switch off the ignition, then rotate the drive mode select switch to either the D1 or D2 position.

7   Hold down both of the shift select switches (the switches marked with up and down arrows on the left end of the handlebar). With the switches held down, have an assistant switch the ignition to ON while watching the gear position indicator. It should indicate N within a few seconds.

8   As soon as it does, let go of the switches, then quickly press and release the UP, DOWN and UP switches in that order. The gear position indicator should display a dashed line. As this happens, the control motor should operate (you should be able to hear it). Within 5 seconds, move the throttle from fully closed to fully open and back to fully closed.

9   If the procedure worked correctly, the display should change from a dashed line to N.

Troubleshooting

10   Check the main fuse, motor fuse, light fuse and ignition fuse and replace them if necessary (see Section 5). If you find a blown fuse, check its circuit for a short or bad connection.

11   Make sure the battery is in good condition and fully charged (see Chapter 1 and Section 4).

12   Check the system wiring for breaks or bad connections, referring to the wiring diagrams at the end of the manual.

Reading trouble codes

13   These vehicles can isolate the problem to a specific circuit or component by flashing trouble codes as described below. The system can store two codes at once, with the most recent problem displayed first. If there are two codes stored, the most recent one should be checked and repaired before the older one.

14   Switch the ignition to ON. Place the shifter in Neutral and make sure the instrument cluster displays N. Switch the ignition OFF.

15   Hold down both of the shift select switches (the switches marked with up and down arrows on the left end of the handlebar). With the switches held down, have an assistant switch the ignition to ON. Immediately release the switches, then push them both at once and hold them down for at least two seconds.

16   If there's a problem in the system, it will be indicated by the gear position indicator, which will flash a number of times to indicate a trouble code (one flash equals code 1, two flashes equal code 2, etc.). Trouble codes and their specific problem areas are:

Code 1 (one flash) - Ignition pulse generator
Code 2 (two flashes) - Rear vehicle speed sensor
Code 3 (three flashes) - Short in the gear position switch circuit
Code 4 (four flashes) - Throttle position sensor voltage out of specifications
Code 5 (five flashes) - Angle sensor (possible control motor lock-up)
Code 6 (six flashes) - Angle sensor voltage out of specifications
Code 7 (seven flashes) - Handlebar end shift switches (Up and Down) or circuit
Code 8 (eight flashes) - EEPROM failure (electronic control unit)
Code 9 (nine flashes) - Voltage converter circuit (electronic control unit)
Code 10 (10 flashes) - Fail-safe relay circuit (electronic control unit)
Code 11 (11 flashes) - Control motor driver circuit (electronic control unit)
Code 12 (12 flashes) - Electronic control unit
Code 13 (13 flashes) - Mode select or shift switches or their circuits

Gear position switch check

17   Locate the gear position switch connector on the connector bracket at the front of the vehicle.

18   Follow the wiring harness from the gear position switch **(see illustration)** to the connector.

19   Disconnect both connectors and check the wiring for breaks or bad connections. If it appears to be good, reconnect the connector at the gear position switch, but leave the ECM connector disconnected.

20   Using an ohmmeter, perform continuity tests between the switch wire for each gear position and ground. To do this, place the shift lever in each gear position in turn, then connect the ohmmeter's positive probe to the wires for each gear position in the side of the 21-pin ECM connector that runs to the switch (see the following steps for details).

21   With the shift lever in Low, there should be continuity (little or no resistance) between the white wire's terminal and ground (bare metal on the engine or frame). There should be infinite resistance between ground and the terminals for the light blue/white, light green/red, and green wires.

22   With the shift lever in Drive, there should be continuity between the light blue/white wire's terminal and ground (bare metal on the engine or frame). There should be infinite resistance between ground and the terminals for the white, light green/red, and green wires.

23   With the shift lever in Neutral, there should be continuity between the light green/red wire's terminal and ground (bare metal on the engine or frame). There should be infinite resistance between ground and the terminals for the white, light blue/white, and green wires.

24   With the shift lever in Neutral, there should be continuity between the green wire's terminal and ground (bare metal on the engine or frame). There should be infinite resistance between ground and the terminals for the white, light blue/white, and light green/red wires.

25   If the continuity tests were as described, disconnect the connector at the gear position switch. Repeat Steps 21 through 24, this time in the side of the switch connector that runs to the switch.

26   If the continuity tests still produce incorrect results, replace the gear position switch. If they now produce the correct results, the switch is good and the problem is in the wiring.

32.34 Note the installed position of the switch, then remove its mounting bolts and take it off

32.47 Unbolt the harness retainer (lower arrow) and remove the mounting bolts (upper arrow) - do not remove the bolts that hold the motor together

Gear position switch replacement

27   Locate the switch **(see illustration 32.18)**.
28   With the shift lever in Neutral, unbolt the switch, pull it out of the engine and remove its O-ring.
29   Lubricate a new O-ring with clean engine oil and install it on the switch.
30   Rotate the pin on the switch so its long end points to the N mark on the switch.
31   Slip the switch into the engine, engaging its pin with the slot. Note that the pin has long and short ends. The long side of the pin should point to the N mark on the switch. Be careful not to force it and damage the pin.
32   Install the mounting bolts and tighten them securely.

Throttle position sensor check

33   The throttle position sensor, mounted on the side of the carburetor, is precisely adjusted and secured by two shear-head screws to the carburetor. If a trouble code indicates a problem with the TPS or its circuit, check the wiring for breaks or bad connections. If the wiring is good, have the sensor adjusted (and replaced if necessary) by a dealer service department or other qualified shop.

Angle sensor system check and replacement

34   Locate the angle sensor on the crankcase **(see illustration)**.
35   With the ignition Off, disconnect the electrical connector from the sensor. Connect an ohmmeter to the sensor terminals (in the sensor, not the wiring harness) and measure the resistance. If it's not 1.6 to 2.4 k-ohms, remove the sensor and test it off the vehicle.
36   Clean all dirt away from the sensor so it doesn't fall into the crankcase when the sensor is removed. Remove the Allen bolts and take the sensor off.
37   Connect the ohmmeter to the terminals again (positive to blue/yellow and negative to green/yellow). Rotate the connection fitting inside the sensor with a screwdriver and note the reading. It should vary smoothly between zero and 1.6 to 2.4 k-ohms. If not, replace it with a new one.
38   Installation is the reverse of the removal steps, with the following additions:
   a) *Align the slot in the switch with the tab on the engine, then rotate the switch clockwise into its final installed position (bolt holes aligned).*
   b) *Tighten the Allen bolts securely, but don't overtighten them and strip the threads.*

Mode select switch check and replacement

39   The mode select switch is mounted inside the handlebar cover.
40   Remove the handlebar cover (see Chapter 7).
41   Disconnect the 21-pin connector from the engine control unit at the front of the vehicle.
42   Using an ohmmeter, test the mode switch continuity. There should be little or no resistance between the terminals in each gear position, as follows:
   a) *D1: Orange to blue/black to green*
   b) *D2: Blue/black to black/green and orange to green*
   c) *ESP: Orange to black/green and blue/black to green*
43   If continuity is incorrect at any of the switch positions, replace the switch.
44   Remove the retaining screw, push the two prongs inward and pull the switch out.
45   Installation is the reverse of the removal steps.

Control motor removal/installation

46   Remove the inner panel from the fender and the left side cover from the engine.
47   Follow the wiring harness from the control motor to the connector and disconnect it. Detach the wiring harness retainer from the engine **(see illustration)**.
48   Remove the two mounting bolts **(see illustration 32.47)**. **Note:** *Do not remove the three bolts that hold the motor together.*
49   Installation is the reverse of the removal steps.

---

33   Wiring diagrams

Prior to troubleshooting a circuit, check the fuses to make sure they're in good condition. Make sure the battery is fully charged and check the cable connections.

When checking a circuit, make sure all connectors are clean, with no broken or loose terminals or wires. When unplugging a connector, don't pull on the wires - pull only on the connector housings themselves.

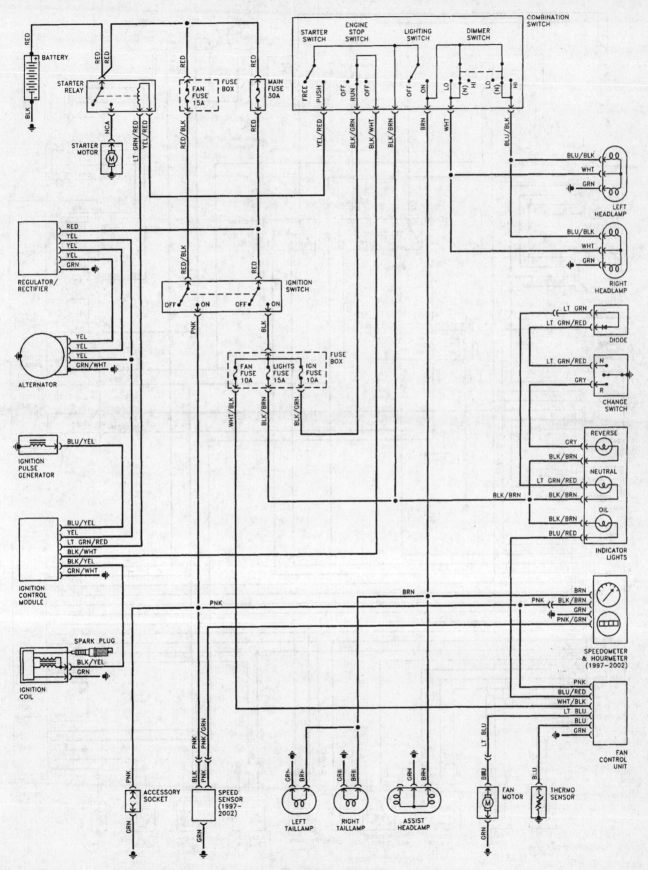

Typical TRX400 - all models

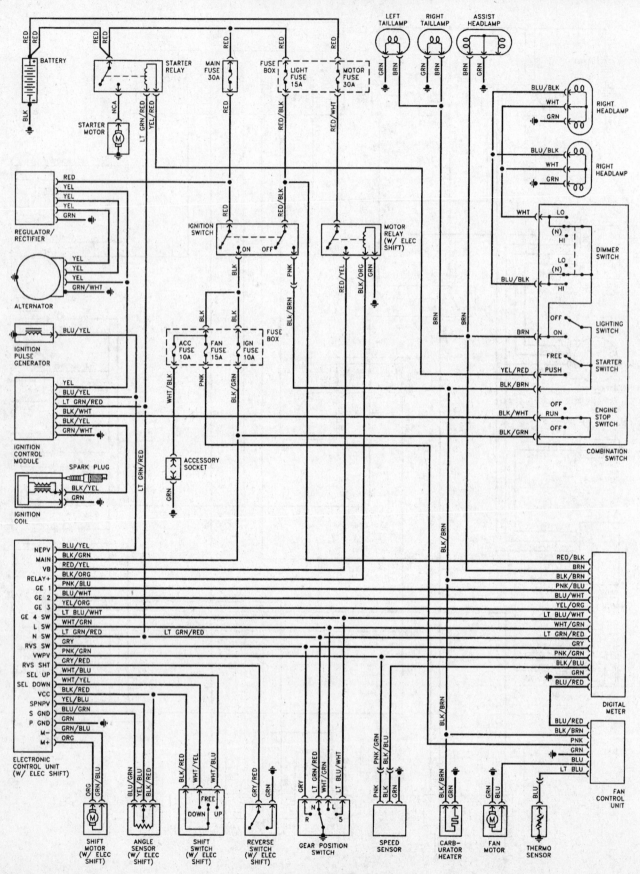

TRX450 - 1998 through 2001 models

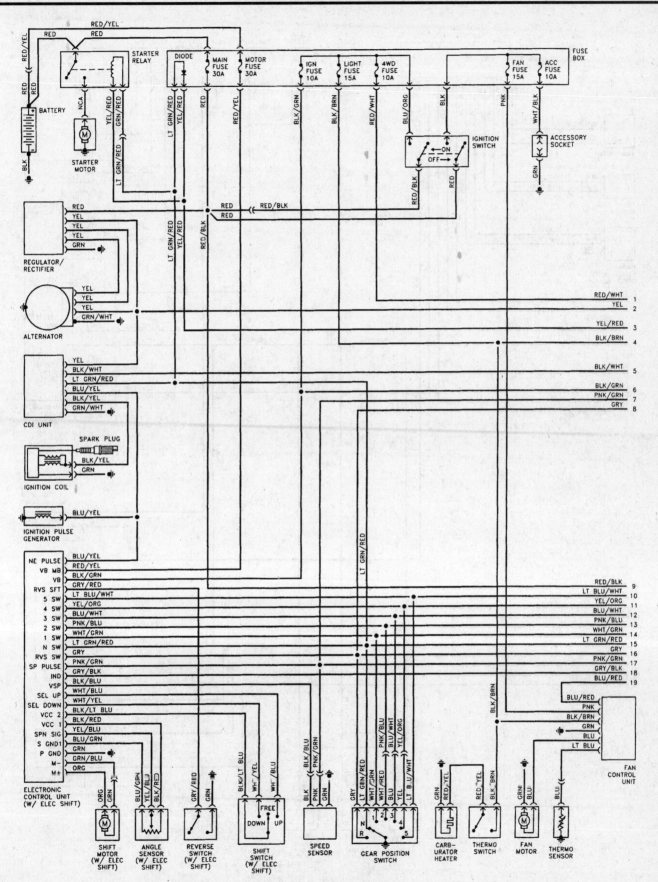

TRX450 - 2002 model (1 of 2)

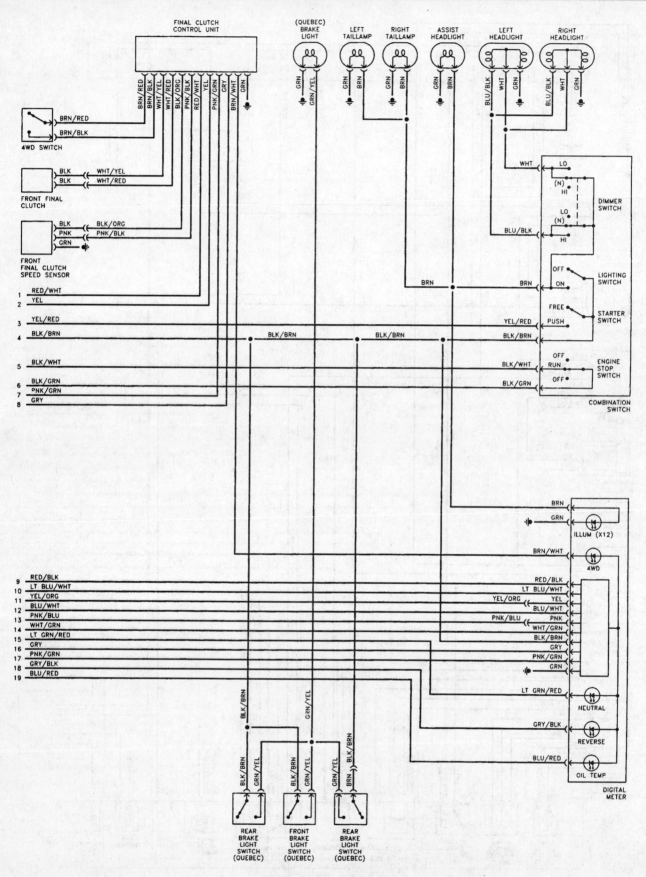

TRX450 - 2002 model (2 of 2)

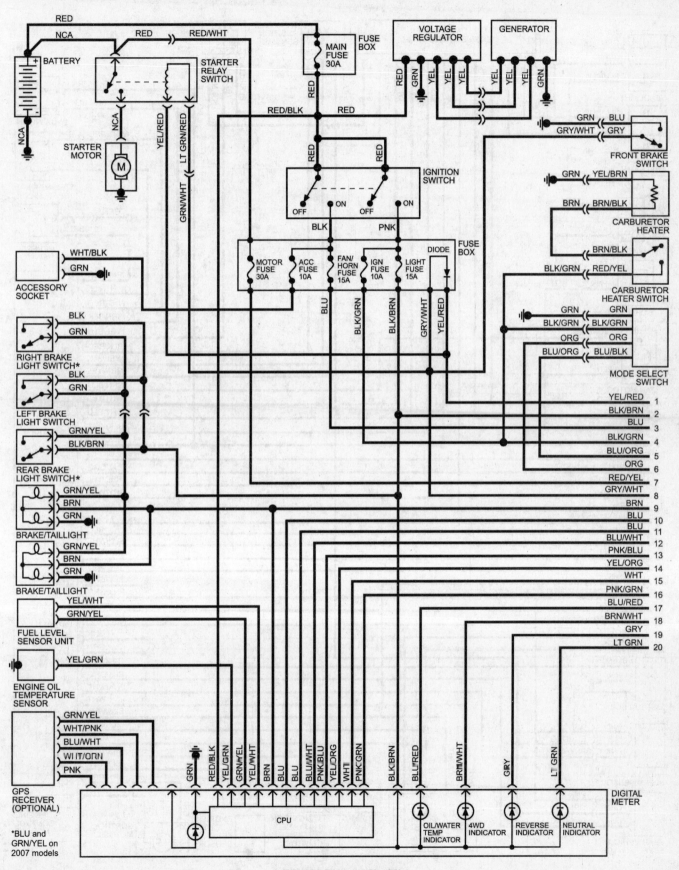

TRX500 Rubicon (1 of 2)

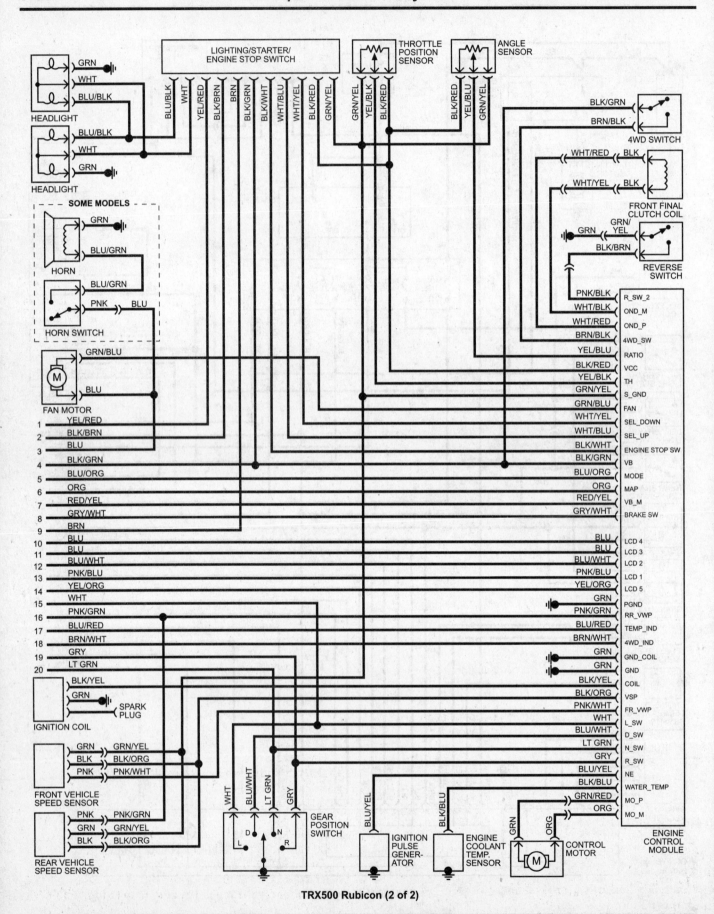

TRX500 Rubicon (2 of 2)

Index